A New World of Labor

THE EARLY MODERN AMERICAS

Peter C. Mancall, Series Editor

Volumes in the series explore neglected aspects
of early modern history in the western hemisphere.
Interdisciplinary in character, and with a special
emphasis on the Atlantic World from 1450 to 1850,
the series is published in partnership with the
USC-Huntington Early Modern Studies Institute.

A NEW WORLD OF LABOR

The Development of Plantation Slavery
in the British Atlantic

SIMON P. NEWMAN

PENN

UNIVERSITY OF PENNSYLVANIA PRESS

PHILADELPHIA

Published by
University of Pennsylvania Press
Philadelphia, Pennsylvania 19104-4112
www.upenn.edu/pennpress

Printed in the United States of America on acid-free paper
10 9 8 7 6 5 4 3 2 1

Library of Congress Cataloging-in-Publication Data

Newman, Simon P. (Simon Peter)
A new world of labor : the development of plantation slavery in the
British Atlantic / Simon P. Newman.—1st ed.
p.   cm.— (The early modern Americas)
Includes bibliographical references and index.
ISBN 978-0-8122-4519-6 (hardcover : alk. paper)
1. Slave labor—Barbados—History.   2. Contract labor—Barbados—
History.   3. Plantations—Barbados—History.   4. Slave labor—Ghana—
History.   5. Contract labor—Ghana—History.   6. Contract labor—Great
Britain—History.   7. Slave trade—Ghana—History.   8. Slave trade—Great
Britain—History.   9. British—Barbados—History.   10. British—Ghana—
History.   I. Title.   II. Series: Early modern Americas.
HD4865.B35N49   2013
331.11′734097298109032—dc23
2012046481

For Marina,
for everything and forever

Contents

Introduction

The small and remote island of Barbados appears an unlikely location for the epochal changes in labor that overwhelmed it and then much of British America in the seventeenth and eighteenth centuries. Lying some sixty miles farther out into the Atlantic than any other Caribbean island, and 166 square miles in size, Barbados is only twenty-four square miles larger than the city of Philadelphia and smaller than the combined boroughs of Brooklyn and Queens. Its location and small size meant that the Spanish and Portuguese had largely ignored Barbados, and it was uninhabited and densely forested when English settlers arrived in 1627. Yet within a quarter-century Barbados had become the greatest wealth-producing area in the English-speaking world, the center of a circum-Atlantic exchange of people and goods between the British Isles, West Africa, and the New World. Between 1627 and 1700 some 236,725 enslaved Africans disembarked onto the island, part of a mighty exodus, without equal in seventeenth-century England's New World colonies. By contrast, during those same years, as few as 16,152 enslaved Africans arrived in the Chesapeake colonies, while 119,208 traveled to the island of Jamaica. By 1808, a further 371,794 Africans had arrived in Barbados, meaning that during the era of the transatlantic slave trade well over 600,000 enslaved men, women, and children had been transported to the island.[1]

This exchange stimulated the creation of an entirely new system of bound labor, for on Barbados enslaved Africans were deployed in new ways in order to make it possible to grow, process, and manufacture sugar and its by-products on single, integrated plantations. The Barbadian system informed the development of racial slavery on Jamaica and other Caribbean islands, as well as in South Carolina and then the Deep South of mainland British North America. Drawing on British and West African people and precedents, and then radically reshaping them on Barbados, the island's planters had not so much discovered a New World as they had invented one.[2]

The movement of laborers between the British Isles, West Africa, and Barbados formed as fundamental a connection between these far-flung locations as did the flow of ideas, goods, and imperial power, the more familiar subjects of Atlantic World historiography. As they set out from the home islands, Britons took with them distinct ideas about bound labor and the control of this subaltern workforce. Eager to trade in West Africa, these Britons were required to accommodate radically different labor practices, while across the Atlantic in Barbados plantations developed that were dependent on a new bound labor system that overruled many of the fundamental precepts of unfree labor in both Britain and West Africa.[3]

During the seventeenth and eighteenth centuries, the need for skilled and unskilled labor in the expanding Atlantic World encouraged Britons to employ free and bound white workers, and free and enslaved African workers, in different ways in different locations and contexts. British understandings of bound labor thus existed on a continuum and encompassed white vagrants, convicts, and prisoners of war, bound Scots, Irishmen, and Englishmen, as well as African slaves and pawns in West Africa, and African slaves in Barbados. When given the opportunity the mid-seventeenth-century Englishmen who became Barbadian planters did not hesitate to use bound white laborers in brutal fashion, and many of these laborers died in service, while few of those who survived were able to rise out of abject poverty once nominally free. The transition to African slavery, beginning in the mid-seventeenth century, resulted in little improvement for white bound laborers and their descendants, and in terms of labor was not a radical shift from the English, Scottish, and Irish men and women who had worked the early Barbadian plantations. In stark contrast, British-owned slaves on the seventeenth- and eighteenth-century Gold Coast of West Africa worked in a more West African form of slavery, enjoying relatively high degrees of "freedom" while British bound workers often fared less well. Similarly, African-owned slaves, free mulattoes, local free Africans, and pawns (individuals held in temporary debt bondage, sometimes held as collateral for debt or as security for an agreement) were all part of the workforce that powered the British transatlantic slave trade. Free and bound laborers, including slaves, did not just produce commodities such as sugar and tobacco in New World colonies; their labor facilitated the trade in enslaved labor that made such plantation labor possible.[4]

Free labor, bound labor, and enslaved labor have often been regarded by historians as relatively static categories, with the result that slavery is cast at one end of a continuum as an absolute denial of freedom, which renders it a unique and "peculiar" form of labor. The representation of slavery as radically different from other forms of early modern labor has encouraged scholars to focus on slave resistance, searching for evidence of the ways in which the enslaved resisted total domination and struggled to obtain freedom from bondage. When seen in this light, slaves appear as political actors more than they do laboring people, and that has helped to shape and define historical research into the lives of the enslaved. This approach has had the unfortunate effect of—at least to a degree—simplifying slavery. Viewing the enslaved as would-be freedom fighters, always resisting and always seeking freedom, we have failed to fully contextualize the ways in which bondage, resistance, and freedom were both defined and experienced quite differently in particular places and at particular times. Even within the British Atlantic World, slavery was defined, enforced, and experienced in dramatically different ways.

In the seventeenth- and eighteenth-century British Atlantic World most workers were dependent, bound, or coerced in some way, and they were all denied various rights and liberties. True, slavery was a brutal and violent institution, and the chattel principle did indeed make it distinct from other forms of coerced labor such as impressment or indentured servitude. But the labor and violence of slavery must be understood as part of the spectrum of coercion of labor—some of it violent—in the early modern world. In terms of the daily experience of workers, slavery was not completely different from other systems of forced labor. Forced labor systems were more flexible and adaptable than scholars have recognized. The difference between slavery and other forced labor systems was more a matter of degree than of kind.[5]

Context was especially important in the early modern Atlantic World. Dramatic economic, social, and demographic changes occurred in the early modern British Isles, which profoundly influenced labor and laborers both there and in England's fledgling colonies. As England began to expand its empire, these changing practices came into contact with dramatically different labor regimes in West Africa, to which the English stationed on the Gold Coast were obliged to adapt if their outposts were to be viable. Meanwhile, Barbadian planters, all but free of the customary restraints of the eastern Atlantic, reinvented British and West African forms of bound labor.

From the British Isles to Barbados

English, Scottish, and Irish workers, most of them bound laborers, dominated the first generation of the Barbadian workforce, and they played the
largest role in the transformation of the island from an uninhabited and
forested idyll to a plantation economy. From the mid-1640s on, enslaved
Africans arrived on the island in ever increasing numbers, and the scale and
the success of what these white servants and enslaved Africans achieved is
made clear by Richard Ford's map of Barbados. Completed in 1675, it is
quite likely the first printed map of the economic development of an
English colony in the Americas, illustrating the extent of the changes that
sugar plantations had wrought in less than fifty years of settlement. The
map indicated every "Plantation, Watermill, Windmill & Cattlemill," and
the key furnished symbols for these three different types of sugar mills.
Only half a dozen small patches of woodland gave any indication of the
forests that had so recently covered the island, and an extensive network of
roads connected the parishes, towns, ports, and almost 850 plantations,
together with upward of 1,000 sugar mills. The map represented the colony
as a "fruitfull and pleasant" island, to which "resort yearly about 200 Vessels of all kinds." These ships carried "Sugar of all sorts viz. Muscovado,
clayed & refined." Yet most strikingly absent from the map were the people
carried to Barbados on these ships, the people who lived, worked, and died
on the island in such vast numbers, clearing its forests, erecting plantation
buildings and mills, and then planting and processing sugar.[6]

There are few surviving records of the experiences of the many white
bound servants who labored on the plantations of early and mid-
seventeenth-century Barbados. One exception is a plaintive letter written in
1676 in which the anonymous author revealed that he had been one of a
number of convicts sent to the island for a lengthy term of servitude. The
letter-writer referred to others in a similar situation, such as Samuel Stail,
the "man that stolle D. Duncans cloake"; "James Lying, the wright that was
in the coock stool with George," who had been punished on the "cucking"
or ducking stool; and "Margret Hamilton," who "cam out of the tolboth,"
the jail in the center of Edinburgh. Bound for as long as a decade, many of
the letter-writer's fellow Scots had fared poorly: "This is not a very whol-
some countrey," he wrote, and James Lying was one of the many to have
died as a bound laborer. The letter-writer asked his correspondent to pass

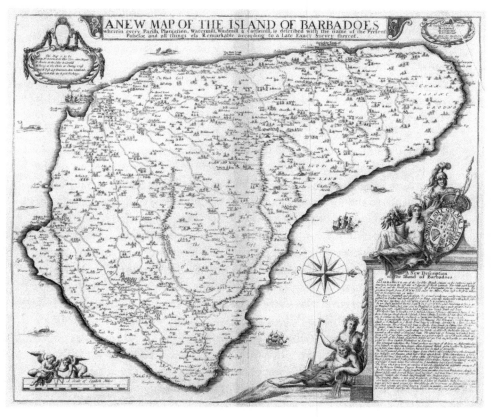

Figure 1. Richard Ford, *A New Map of the Island of Barbadoes* (London, 1685). Courtesy of the John Carter Brown Library at Brown University.

on the news of Lying's demise to "James Hamilton so much that he may acquaint James Baine of it."[7]

In comparison with many of his fellow Scottish bound laborers, this letter-writer had fared well. He had been purchased by Samuel Newton, one of the island's wealthiest planters, and then employed by Newton as a schoolteacher: the very existence of his letter bears witness to this man's literacy and relatively fortunate position. Yet the tone of this document makes clear that the writer still thought of himself as bound, and he knew that it was unlikely that he might "procure my liberty" in the foreseeable future. His letter was filled with loving salutations to the friends he expected never to see again, writing of "a speechless affectione in my breast," and he begged to "remember my love" to one friend, and "have my love remembered" to another. Although his living conditions were relatively good, this man was serving what he considered to be tantamount to a life sentence, and he wrote that he did not dare raise the possibility of achieving his freedom with his master, for "to follow this course ware to procure my masters displeasure," which might result in the worsening of his situation. The anonymous Scottish letter-writer was well aware of the brutal cost of bound labor on Barbadian plantations; were he to be sent to work in the sugar cane fields or in the sugar works, this man knew that he would be far more likely to die in service, like the unfortunate James Lying. "Wrytt for the love of God as often as ye can," the anonymous letter-writer had pleaded, desperate for contact with loved ones in Scotland.[8]

The hopelessness of life and death in servitude for the many thousands of seventeenth-century English, Irish, and Scottish bound laborers who were taken as convicts, prisoners, and vagrants and transported to Barbados challenges historians who have argued that bound white laborers in England's New World colonies could expect to outgrow their subordinate status and enjoy opportunities for advancement that would not have been available to them at home.[9] Richard O'Shea, almost certainly an Irishman taken prisoner by Cromwell's forces and transported to Barbados for a term of as long as ten years, died after years of servitude, bequeathing half of his meager belongings to his relatives and fellow Irish bound laborers Thomas and "young Richard Oshea," but reserving the remaining half for "my owne sonne . . . if he chance to come to this Island." O'Shea marked his will with a cross, and his illiteracy and the uncertainty of communications between Barbados and Ireland meant that he had probably labored during the brutal early years of sugar production without ever knowing the health and whereabouts of his immediate family members back in Ireland. The lengthy and harsh working regimen, the hazards of disease and malnutrition, and the power of planters and overseers who were willing and able to use violence to enforce discipline and extract labor all meant that for O'Shea and tens of thousands of other bound white laborers, servitude on Barbados lasted for life.[10]

Barbados is enormously significant in the labor history of the early modern British Atlantic, for it played a foundational role in defining how plantation labor developed throughout British America. Yet, in tracing the trajectory of labor in English America, recent historians have paid relatively little attention to the treatment of white bound laborers on Barbados, despite the fact that the island attracted more bound laborers, white and black, than any other seventeenth-century English colony. The significance of Barbadian regulation of bound labor in the development of slave codes is clear, yet what is needed is an understanding of how the treatment of bound whites on Barbados affected the evolution of ideas and practices of plantation slavery and the legal codes that defined it.

The Gold Coast and Barbados

The Portuguese and Spanish had discovered that the Atlantic currents and winds meant that it was far easier to sail across the Atlantic from West Africa than directly from Europe. As the British began establishing colonies in the Americas and then trading in West Africa, they began following a similar route, and throughout the seventeenth and eighteenth centuries many British ships sailed these two legs of what became known as the triangular trade. Because of its position west of the Caribbean and in the heart of the ocean currents from Africa, Barbados was very often the first New World land seen by crew and passengers of British ships. Moreover, as British trade in West Africa increased and the need for labor in Barbados and then other British colonies grew from the mid-seventeenth century on, the trade in people between West Africa and Barbados developed apace. The various British companies charged with the direction of West African operations placed operatives in Barbados, and a growing number of people spent time in both locations. In the second half of the seventeenth century, few locales in England's nascent empire were tied as closely as were West Africa and Barbados.

Dalby Thomas embodied these connections. Born in 1650, just outside of London, Thomas followed his father into trade and became a successful West India merchant. By the 1680s Thomas had emerged as an influential lobbyist for the West India interest, and in 1690 he published *An Historical Account of the Rise and Growth of the West-India Collonies, And of the Great Advantages they are to England, in respect to Trade*. His detailed knowledge of Caribbean agriculture and trade, and especially of sugar production, suggests that Thomas may well have spent some time in the islands. He knew that the sugar colonies produced enormous wealth for the mother country, boasting that "we at present exceed all Nations in the world in the true Improvement of that Noble Juice of the Cane," although he knew that such profits were possible only when "Industry is rightly apply'd by great Numbers of Laborious People." Writing more than a generation after the death of Richard O'Shea, Thomas was not referring to the "Laborious and Painfull" lives of British workers on New World plantations, but rather to the work extracted from enslaved Africans. "The Blacks are always Employ'd either in Hoeing, Dunging, and Planting in the wet [season]," he wrote, "or in Cutting, Carrying, Grinding, Boyling &c. in the Dry Season." Noting the difficulties involved in procuring sufficient numbers of white workers for labor in the Caribbean by the close of the seventeenth century, Thomas acknowledged that enslaved Africans had become "the main prop of a Plantation."[11]

Knighted in 1703, Thomas promptly set sail for the Gold Coast of West Africa, having been appointed governor of the Royal African Company (RAC).[12] He was charged with reviving the fortunes of a trading company whose main task was to guarantee a steady supply of cheap enslaved Africans for purchase and transportation across the Atlantic. But Thomas faced local labor problems that severely hampered his ability to maintain an effective and competitive trading presence on the Gold Coast and thus ensure the supply of enslaved labor on which British New World colonies depended. Such labor problems plagued British officials throughout the seventeenth and eighteenth centuries. At one point Thomas wrote to his superiors in London of his need for a white "Carpenter that understood ye making great Cannoe or small vessells," as well as for fifty Castle slaves to work in and for the British forts and trading posts: these "Negroes male & female . . . would be of great use & great profit."[13] The white laborers, artisans, soldiers, and sailors on the Gold Coast fared very poorly; at the end of the season in which Dalby Thomas himself died, Seth Grosvenor and James Phipps wrote from Cape Coast Castle, describing the debilitating and often deadly effect of the environment on all Britons who lived and worked there.[14]

A quarter-century later the governing council at Cape Coast Castle lamented that their white laborers and soldiers were so poorly paid that they could not afford sufficient fresh food, "for want of which many . . . sicken and die." Poorly paid, malnourished, and facing arduous labor in a hot and deadly disease environment, bound white laborers and soldiers on the Gold Coast died in large numbers; a list of all white RAC employees on

the coast in August 1674 revealed that 22 percent had died during the preceding eight months alone. The problem of white mortality was unrelenting, and in the mid-eighteenth century African Anglican chaplain Philip
Quaque could not spare time and paper to list all who had died, for "Deaths
are too striking an Instance to be relating [them] Annually." In another
letter he observed that "This country is very destructive to the Health of
many of the British Constitutions," and "the third part out of five" (three-
fifths) of soldiers and laborers had recently died, with "others very sick, &
infirm." In the face of such heavy mortality, maintaining British castles
and trading posts, and ensuring that British trade remained operative and
profitable, proved remarkably difficult. Perhaps not surprisingly, Quaque
reported that Cape Coast Castle was "in a very poor Condition, all falling
down over our Heads."[15]

Supplementing the uncertain and unhealthy supply of British laborers,
artisans, soldiers, and sailors, the labor of company-owned African slaves
and of local free and enslaved people proved essential to the British trading
presence on the Gold Coast. Over time, more and more of the skilled
artisanal work, the general unskilled labor, and the policing and care of
enslaved men and women bound for the Americas fell to British-owned
slaves, whose lives and work accorded with West African rather than British
traditions or Caribbean innovations regarding the status, conditions, and
treatment of bound laborers, much to the frustration of their British masters. Paid in trade goods, and generally living outside of the fortified British
trading settlements, these slaves lived semi-independent lives, negotiated to
improve their working conditions and to receive bounties and bonuses, and
on occasion even withheld their labor.

Britons on the Gold Coast could not survive and prosper without these
bound workers, and they constantly requested additional "Castle Working
Slaves." As he supervised the construction of the new British trading fort
on the Gold Coast at Anomabu, John Apperley reported that the four white
laborers at his disposal "are useless to me as no White men can work but 5
hours." In contrast, the company-owned slaves worked longer and were
more resistant to yellow fever and malaria, with the result that "the Black
bricklayers are the people I am to depend upon for building the Fort." Of
a newly received shipment of company slaves, Apperley had twelve working
as bricklayers, three as carpenters, three as blacksmiths, and five as general
laborers. Three years later Apperley had thirty-eight male and seven female
slaves working under him at Anomabu, including men and women such as

the "labouress" Aggubah, the laborers Glasgow and Jarrah, the bricklayers
Coffee and Yaow Bob, the canoeman Cudjoe, and the carpenter Bandoe.
All had been purchased in Gambia, and then taken by sea almost 1,500
miles to the Gold Coast, where they were set to work, often learning new,
British trades and crafts. Yet they worked as West African slaves, according
to local traditions and precepts, and free from the threat of transport to the
Americas.[16]

In stark contrast to these castle slaves were the hundreds of thousands
of enslaved Africans who arrived at and then passed through the British
castles, forts, and trading posts on the Gold Coast on their way to New
World plantations. A long-standing supporter of the West Indian planters,
Governor Dalby Thomas firmly believed that "those Hands Imploy'd in
our Collonies are for their Number the most profitable Subjects of these
Dominions." He supported the wealth-producing planters by aiding them
in procuring enslaved African laborers, and above all by negotiating an
important alliance with the Asante that helped guarantee a ready supply of
slaves. Thomas wrote angrily to his superiors in London of his need for the
manacles and chains necessary to secure enslaved Africans for transport to
British ships: "If you do not send the Pad Locks for Slaves necks & Chains
The Locks for their Leggs which we writ for so long since it will . . . only
be a means of Disappointing your Great Profitt." Thomas survived for eight
years on the Gold Coast, longer than most. During his administration, British ships transported approximately 61,289 enslaved Africans from the Gold
Coast to the New World, and perhaps as many as 20 percent of these disembarked in Barbados.[17]

From the Gold Coast to Barbados

We have no surviving memoirs of any of the enslaved Africans who
departed the Gold Coast during Dalby Thomas's administration. Remarkably, the narratives of a handful of the enslaved who departed over the
ensuing half-century do survive. These accounts generally include descriptions of life in rural Africa, the trauma of capture and enslavement, the
horrors of the Middle Passage and New World slavery, and finally, freedom.
William Sessarakoo described himself as the son of a wealthy Gold Coast
merchant known to the British as John Corrente, the "*Chief of Annamaboe.*" Sessarakoo grew up in the "*Fantin* Country," which was "as hap-
pily situated as any upon the *Gold Coast.*" Anomabu was, he declared, the

largest of the Fante towns, and the people were sufficiently numerous and powerful "so that the *English*, the *Dutch*, and the *French*, neither have, nor pretend to have had any coercive Power over them."African power ended at the water's edge, however, and Corrente's plan to send his son to England backfired when, upon arrival in Barbados in 1744, the ship's captain sold Sessarakoo into slavery. Like countless English, Scottish, and Irish bound laborers before him, and even larger numbers of fellow West Africans, Sessarakoo found himself "not only a Slave, but a Slave at such a Distance from his Country, Father, and Friends." Without external assistance, Sessarakoo acknowledged, he would have "lived and died in that deplorable Condition."[18]

Venture Smith also departed from Anomabu, less than a decade before Sessarakoo. His experiences were, however, rather more typical, for Smith was enslaved in Africa, and he left the Gold Coast in chains. Many years later he recalled in great detail his early years in rural West Africa, describing communities that cultivated the land and tended livestock. Captured by a large African army at the age of seven, he was forced to carry a heavy grinding stone and other supplies as he and his fellow captives were marched hundreds of miles to the Atlantic coast, where both captives and captors were in turn captured by the inhabitants of Anomabu. He recorded his experiences on the coast in a few sparse sentences:

> All of us were then put into the castle, and kept for market, and rowed away to a vessel belonging to Rhode Island, commanded by Capt. Collingwood, and the mate Thomas Mumford. While we were going to the vessel, our master told us all to appear to the best possible advantage for sale. I was bought on board by one Robertson Mumford, Steward of said vessel, for four gallons of rum and a piece of calico, and called Venture, on account of his having purchased me with his own private venture. Thus I came by my name.[19]

Transported to Barbados at the age of eight, Smith saw almost one-quarter of the ship's enslaved cargo perish during the Middle Passage. Virtually all of the survivors were sold to Barbadian planters, while Smith and three others were transported to Rhode Island. For many enslaved Africans, Barbados—the most easterly Caribbean island and the first port of call for many British slave ships—was their first and last sight of the New World.

Figure 2. "William Ansah Sessarakoo," by John Faber, Jr., after Gabriel
Mathias. Mezzotint. *Gentleman's Magazine* (London), vol. 20 (June 1750).
By permission of the University of Glasgow Library, Department of Special
Collections.

Especially during the seventeenth century, these ships sold a large proportion of their enslaved cargo to Barbadian planters.

Eventually Sessarakoo and Smith secured their freedom, making it possible for them to write and publish these accounts. Far more difficult to
uncover are the work experiences of the hundred of thousands of West
Africans who lived and died as slaves in Barbados. The narratives of two
elderly enslaved women were transcribed in 1799 by John Ford, rendered in

the dialect of the speakers. Like Sessarakoo, Ashy was a member of the Fante people, and she did not hesitate to proclaim "dis country here dat you call Barbados—um no good, um no good Massah." In contrast, she recalled that *"my Country is a boon country, a boon Country Massah, no like yours."* Sibell, despite her advanced age, could recall her African family members in great detail. As the memories flooded back, Sibell recalled how she had been moved from holding pens to a waiting ship. On board, alone and afraid, she had sought out "my country woman Mimbo, my country man Dublin, my Country woman Sally, and some more, but dey sell dem all about me." As Sibell relived the terrible isolation and fear that she had felt many decades earlier, "she burst into tears and could say no more." Reading these accounts more than two centuries later, the trauma of enslavement is all too apparent in the precious few words of these two women. What is far less apparent, however, is their experience of work in the gangs of Barbadian integrated plantations. These two women were unable or unwilling to speak of their present lives and conditions to their white interviewer, and very little survives in the words of the enslaved themselves describing plantation labor. To Britons, however, it was the labor of the enslaved that defined them: inspired by the juices of the sugar cane that was grown, harvested, and processed by enslaved Africans, one commentator described these workers as *"the very Spring and Sapp that nourished the Sugar Plantations."*[20]

This book's comparative approach builds from the premise that conceptualizing the enslaved as first and foremost coerced laborers allows us to reconstruct and understand more about their lives as defined by their status as bound workers. This approach enhances our understanding of the enslaved as human actors living within a coerced labor system that placed severe constraints upon their ability to mount any kind of opposition to slavery or gain any significant autonomy. Along with other historians, I locate slavery within a broad spectrum of other systems of labor, highlighting the shared working experiences of the enslaved and other workers. It is my contention that slavery and race may not have been so intrinsically interconnected as previous scholars have assumed.[21]

The scholar Joseph Roach has described the circum-Atlantic World as resembling "a vortex in which commodities and cultural practices changed hands many times." His observation most certainly applies to labor in the early modern British Atlantic World. The lives and work of laborers were

transformed in the British Isles, while Britons were required to accommodate local labor systems and local laborers in West Africa. During the late
seventeenth and eighteenth centuries, British operations—most notably the
trade in laborers themselves—grew ever more dependent on West Africans,
not as commodities but as laborers working according to local traditions
and practices. West African labor and the society in which it was rooted
were themselves changing, of course, but the British nonetheless always had
to adapt to, accept, and build upon quite distinct and unfamiliar West
African forms of free and bound labor.[22]

In Barbados, too, Britons proved able to adapt. A small and powerful
planter elite emerged with remarkable speed, and well before the advent of
sugar agriculture they were creating plantations powered by bound British
laborers. During the crucial period between the 1630s and the early 1660s,
Barbadian planters developed their new system all but completely free of
English oversight. They employed elements of traditional English forms of
labor and applied them to tens of thousands of vagrants, convicts, and
prisoners of war—men and women whose lives were forfeit and who were
sent beyond the legal and customary protections of the British Isles to a
small island on which the planter elite controlled government, justice, and
military power. By the time enslaved Africans began replacing bound Britons, the outlines of a new unfree labor system had already been drawn. Yet
their substitution by enslaved Africans did not improve the lives of many
bound white servants and their descendants: those who survived but did
not leave the island were marginal to Barbadian society and incredibly poor.
This book illuminates the experiences of hundreds of thousands of British
and African laborers whose lives were judged to be worth no more than the
sum of their productive labor. On the plantations of Barbados, and later
Jamaica, the Carolinas, and beyond, these bound laborers constituted an
entirely new kind of workforce, and the resulting system of plantation slavery came to dominate much of British America.

PART I

Settings

Chapter 1

England

In August 1562 a minor riot broke out in Upwell, a small fenland village on Norfolk's boundary with Cambridgeshire. Sixteen-year-old Nicholas Emneth was one of five young men who had failed to appear at the petty sessions, a court of summary jurisdiction at which justices of the peace enforced labor legislation. Servants and laborers were required to appear at the petty sessions in order to report their wages and the terms of their employment. Those who were discovered to be unemployed would be made to find work or have it forced upon them, and this was Emneth's fate. With a warrant in hand, local husbandman Adam Bellamye attempted to forcibly take Emneth into his service. But the village rose to the young man's defense: seven laborers, a tailor, a brewer, a husbandman, three married women, and "many others" freed Emneth. Given the local support enjoyed by the young man, it seems unlikely that Emneth was an unemployed and homeless vagrant, or that he was wilfully "idle." It is far more likely that he was a casual laborer, choosing when, where, and for whom he would work. Emneth's liberation was short-lived, for he was subsequently indicted at the Quarter Sessions, in part for resisting arrest, but mainly for being "vacant," for having been found to be unemployed and then refusing to enter Bellamye's service.[1]

The organization of labor and the compulsion to work were integral characteristics of early modern English society, and rulers and landowners sought to control a growing mass of under- or unemployed people. During the later sixteenth and early seventeenth centuries the number of jobless people, vagrants, criminals, and prisoners of war grew rapidly as a result of significant population growth, consolidation of land ownership, the disappearance of the traditional poor relief systems of the pre-Reformation Catholic church, and a series of rebellions and wars. Local and national authorities believed that these masterless men and women posed a threat to social order and good government. They passed laws and created new institutions to control the laboring poor and to force them to work, but such actions did little to reduce the ranks of the men and women who roamed the countryside in search of food, work, and shelter. At exactly the time that Barbadian planters developed an insatiable need for labor, England's social problems were exacerbated by a descent into religious and political conflict, civil war, and finally the Wars of the Three Kingdoms. During the early to mid-seventeenth century, English authorities were more than happy to ship tens of thousands of Britons to the island, most of them vagrants, criminals, and prisoners of war or rebellion. English principles and precedents informed the earliest use of bound labor in England's wealthiest colony. However, English attempts to control the labor of the rural workforce developed in new ways in Barbados, with little oversight by English authorities who were preoccupied with the domestic social and political situation.

The agricultural labor system that appeared to be in crisis in early modern England had taken shape in the wake of the catastrophic late fourteenth-century Black Death, following which the population of England had plummeted from some 3.5 million to approximately 2.1 million, where it remained until the early sixteenth century. Elsewhere in Europe the reduced population and the consequent scarcity of labor resulted in the institution of medieval forms of sharecropping, such as the mezzadria in Italy, binding rural workers to large landholders. In England, however, the demographic decline led to the development of the institution of service in husbandry, annual labor contracts between employee and employer that advanced new ideas about the nature and practice of bound labor. Service in husbandry was relatively attractive to householders and farmers who were anxious to ensure that they had sufficient labor for their needs, at affordable rates. Servants, the vast majority of them servants in husbandry, contracted to work for one year, for which they were provided room, board, and sometimes clothing, as well as a small wage paid quarterly or even at the end of the year. Food prices were relatively low during the period of reduced population, making it easier for employers to provide for their live-in servants. Facing a shortage of labor, masters were forced to compete in providing good food, working conditions, and decent payment in order to attract prospective laborers.[2]

The Ordinance of Laborers (1349) and the Statute of Laborers (1351) were intended, at least in part, to check the potential increase in the power and independence of servants in this land-rich and labor-poor environment by mandating and protecting the rights of masters. Government and the rural elite, as well as many lower and middling farmers, did not want the rural poor to enjoy the freedom exercised by Nicholas Emneth, working only intermittently for high wages as casual wage laborers. Consequently, annual terms of service were made compulsory for able-bodied men and women, and the premature departure of a servant was made punishable by imprisonment. Any persons without work were legally enjoined to labor for anyone who required workers, yearlong terms of service were established as the national standard, and wage rates were mandated, although these might differ locally. Together these provisions balanced out any advantages servants might have enjoyed, and also prevented them from abandoning one master in favor of another who offered better terms of employment. The Ordinance and the Statute of Laborers confirmed the deterioration of feudalism and its replacement by a wage-earning workforce. In place of the ancient rights of lords over tenants and serfs, these laws set out the rights of employers over employees. However, the very act of establishing national authority over employment and labor did confirm the contractual relationship between employers and laborers, and thus the means for popular assertions of rights as well as for imposition of obligations.[3]

For generations, service in husbandry benefited many in the rural population as a transitional stage between childhood and married adulthood and parenthood, providing preparation for an adult existence on the land as small farmers or, for those less fortunate, as cottagers and laborers. At its best, service in husbandry was beneficial to both employers and employees, and thus could foster relatively equitable labor relations. On the one hand, those whose landholdings were too large to be farmed by family members hired servants; on the other hand, the children of those who had little or no land hired themselves out as servants. Annual contracts, and the constant availability of those who served in this fashion, made service in husbandry more attractive to employers than casual labor. During periods of relatively low population growth and a scarcity of workers, a servant within the household for a year could be called upon when and where needed, and closely supervised by the master or mistress, whereas day laborers were not always on call or available when needed. Seasonal variations meant that live-in servants worked particularly long hours at certain times of year, but enjoyed a somewhat slower pace of work at other times.[4]

In theory rural servants were relatively well treated by their employers and were able to harness the power of the law to protect themselves in contractual relationships that covered their working conditions and remuneration. Service nonetheless constituted a category of unfreedom in which laborers signed away their independence for a year and were controlled by masters who enjoyed legally sanctioned power over their servants, just as they did over their wives and children. Servants were members of their master's household, not by virtue of blood or marriage but through annual contract. Most servants were young, between their mid-teens and mid-twenties, and for all intents and purposes these servants became dependent members of their master's family, a word used in early modern England to describe all members of the household. As late as the mid-eighteenth century, Samuel Johnson defined "family" as "Those who live in the same house; household."[5]

Servants in husbandry supplemented the membership of a great many households in late medieval and early modern England, providing farmers, householders, and some craftsmen with a significant proportion of their labor force. Their work and their pay were contingent upon age, experience, and gender. Henry Best, in his Farming Book of 1642, described his eight servants, the work they did, and the pay they received. At one end of the range of Best's six male servants was a relatively inexperienced young boy, perhaps in his first year as a servant in husbandry, paid twenty shillings per annum, in return for which he was required to be able to drive an ox plow and carry a three-bushel bag of corn. At the other end was the older, stronger, and more experienced foreman, who could be trusted with almost any job that Best would have undertaken himself, as well as supervision of the other servants, for which he received a wage of £3 6s 8d. Perhaps not surprisingly, Best provided less detail about the work of his two female servants, although he recorded that when interviewing candidates he sought expertise in washing, brewing, milking, baking, and general housewifery. Strong, hardworking, and experienced, his two female servants received wages of £1 4s and £1 8s, respectively. Male servants plowed, sowed, mowed, led and tended draft animals and sheep and cattle, harvested, loaded and unloaded and drove wagons, and worked with the larger animals. Female servants milked cows and took part in dairy production, tended chickens and smaller animals, weeded, made ale, cooked food, and assisted in various agricultural work. On smaller farms with fewer servants, female servants likely assisted in more of the farm work usually undertaken by men. Perhaps as many as 60 percent of early modern English men and women aged between fifteen and twenty-four worked as servants; in Coventry in 1523, two-fifths of households contained servants, who composed fully one-quarter of the population. The mean age of men and women when they first married confirms that a period of servitude was a precondition of marriage for many; throughout the seventeenth century the average age at marriage was over twenty-five for women and over twenty-seven for men.[6]

Henry Best's older, experienced, and well-paid foreman had quite likely started years earlier as an inexperienced and poorly paid boy. Negotiating a new contract each year, he had gained experience and ideally had been able to save money from his quarterly or annual payments. The same was true for female servants, and after a number of years of service in husbandry, having saved sufficient money for a "settlement," servants hoped to marry and set up their own households, perhaps with access to common land and grazing. From that point forward, the husband could supplement family income by hiring himself out by the day, by the week, or by the task. Thus laborers tended to be older than servants, and they lived not with their employers but in their own households, and they were significantly more independent than servants.[7]

The labor of servants was integral to the households of yeoman farmers and husbandmen. While it could function as a stepping stone to independence, allowing poor, landless young men and women to gain experience and money sufficient to establish their own households, there was a price to pay. During the long years of service these men and women sacrificed their freedom, and as dependent family members they were politically invisible. Unmarried and without property of their own, servants in husbandry were bound laborers, subject to the authority of their masters. While a day laborer with his own home was subject to an employer only for the time that he was hired, the servant in husbandry lived in the home of his master and was subject to his authority and required to obey him twenty-four hours a day for the entire year of service. The power of the master over his servants was not absolute, however, and was mediated by a number of factors. The servant in husbandry retained certain rights while in service, such as the right to testify in court or to bring proceedings against a master who had breached the terms of the contract that bound them together, and the right to marry. The usually oral contract between farmer and servant was binding and protected both parties. Law and order depended in part upon the respect of the governed for those with authority over them. Excessive and systematic abuse of power by masters over servants would have threatened a breakdown of the entire system, and tyrannical and abusive masters were liable to be regarded as a threat to the authority of all masters.[8]

Terms of service were carefully regulated, and in return for servants' labor, masters were bound to support servants during periods when there was little or no work to be done, when servants were injured or ill, and even when female servants fell pregnant; the servant could not use these or other events as an excuse to leave before the conclusion of the term of service. Under no circumstances could masters transfer a servant and his or her labor to another farmer. On smaller farms in particular, servants tended to share much the same standard of living as their master and his family, eating the same food and working alongside their master or mistress. Masters who treated servants well could expect them to work hard and perhaps to renew their contracts, and an employer's good reputation might well make it easier to recruit other suitable servants. Such an idealized vision of the master-servant relationship was often difficult to achieve, however; there were inevitable stresses and strains in the relationship. Servants were free to leave at the end of their year of service, and tens of thousands sought better terms and improved working conditions elsewhere. The relationship was a negotiation, and the annual term for servants in husbandry functioned best when it protected and benefited both master and servant. While not a full and formal apprenticeship, servitude trained the rural youth in the rural skills and crafts necessary for their own futures as farmers and laborers, as well as providing them with the financial means to begin independent adult lives.[9]

Masters might well seek advice from neighbors as to whether a prospective servant "be true and trusty, if he be a gentle and quiet fellow, [and] whether he be addicted to company-keeping or no." All of the activities of servants were to be carefully monitored, and their work overseen with particular care: one contemporary advised "trust them not more than need must . . . For almost all treacheries have been wrought by servants and the final end of their service is gain and advancement."[10] For all that they were dependent upon servants, masters saw these workers as posing a potential threat to the household, whether it was stealing food or farm and household goods, neglecting their duties, or performing so poorly as to risk damaging crops, livestock, and tools.[11]

The most independent of working men were wage laborers, many of them former servants who had saved enough to marry and establish their own households. Wage laborers were hired by employers by the day or for an agreed period or task, and this work provided additional income for men with smallholdings or common field rights that were insufficient for the needs of their families. Others did not own their own home and were unmarried; either they preferred or they had no choice but to travel in search of work and the best rates of pay. Recently, historians have argued that the dividing line between servants and laborers was blurred, given that some laborers contracted to work for quite long periods, and these contracts sometimes included food and even board as partial payment. Alexandra Shepard has demonstrated that the surviving testimony of both servants and laborers reveals that members of both groups often defined themselves as poor, possessed of little or nothing except their labor. A servant in Salisbury was typical in his lament that he "liveth onely by his hard labour not being otherwise any thing worth." While laborers may have felt more free and independent than bound laborers, their material circumstances were often markedly similar. Servants and laborers alike spoke of their labor as an asset and a mark of identity, yet evidence drawn from court proceedings illustrates that authorities took a rather different view. The testimony of both servants and wage laborers could be attacked as undependable, because such people were susceptible to bribery or coercion by their employers. Thus even wage laborers, with homes and families of their own, were in the eyes of the law far from fully independent.[12]

After two centuries of low population and plentiful food supplies, the situation changed dramatically in the sixteenth and early seventeenth centuries. English society and its labor system were challenged by rapidly increasing population levels, rising food prices, enclosure and engrossment of common lands, and increased rural unemployment and underemployment. Social and economic problems encouraged a hardening of attitudes toward laborers, and in the wake of the Protestant Reformation, Puritans were simply the most zealous exponents of a creed in which labor was regarded as godly and was required of all. Regarding the rapidly increasing ranks of homeless and jobless vagrants with fear and loathing, political and religious authorities condemned all who did not work and were not subject to the order imposed by a master as ungodly and criminal. Throughout the sixteenth and seventeenth centuries the authorities were preoccupied with ensuring that the poor worked and were properly supervised.[13]

This was a society in which only the wealthy were free from a legal obligation to work, and the ordeal of Nicholas Emneth reveals a great deal about the utilization of state power by early modern English authorities in their attempt to ensure that all able-bodied men, women, and youths worked. For generations a great many young English men and women had bound themselves out to husbandmen, farmers, gentlemen, and artisans as servants in husbandry, their annual contracts and rates of pay supervised by local authorities. Others, many with small homes and access to common land and pastures, labored by the day in order to make ends meet. Those who did not appear to fit into these categories of employment were, like Nicholas Emneth, bound out by the court to work for others, for anywhere from a year to a decade or more. Law, custom, and experience all showed that for many of the people who lived and worked in early modern England, their labor was neither completely free nor fully unfree, but rather featured elements of both conditions. The economic, demographic, and socio-political crises of the sixteenth and seventeenth centuries prompted English authorities to strengthen enforcement of existing laws and to create new ones, all in a desperate attempt to compel labor. Agricultural laborers and servants in early modern England lived and worked under conditions that in certain key ways prefigured free labor, bound labor, and even slavery as they would develop in England's New World colonies. Barbadian planters, many drawn from the middling ranks of English society, brought with them an understanding of how to compel and control labor, and in their hands bound labor and servitude would evolve into something entirely new.

In the later Middle Ages, and indeed as late as the early sixteenth century, both tradition and low population levels had meant that England's was a society in which most of the population, including impoverished rural laborers, had enjoyed access to at least some land, often through common rights of access. In Scotland, too, even the poorest "cottars" rented small subsistence plots, which together with grazing rights allowed their families to scrape a living. Those in England who labored as servants in husbandry could reasonably expect eventually to establish their own households, with at least some access to common fields and land. However, the dramatic increase in population levels helped destabilize this system, and played a significant role in changing the nature of labor and servitude. After a century of stagnation, English population levels began to grow rapidly in the early sixteenth century, from 2.4 million in the early 1520s to just over 3 million by 1551, and more than 3.6 million by 1581. The population growth rate rose from 0.6 percent in the 1540s to a remarkable 1.1 percent by the 1580s. Between 1500 and 1656 the population of England and Wales more than doubled, from 2.5 million to nearly 5.4 million. The social effects of this demographic trend were exacerbated by the early sixteenth-century disendowment of the medieval church and the dissolution of monasteries and chantries. In early sixteenth-century Essex, for example, between one-quarter and one-third of land had belonged to the Church, but by 1540 well over half of this land had been transferred to the Crown. Soon this land was sold, and by engrossing their land holdings the gentry enhanced their wealth and power both locally and nationally. In England, and also in Scotland and Wales, a growing rural population confronted an increasingly powerful land-owning class, who set about consolidating their estates by enclosing land and raising rents.[14]

As the population and economy expanded, the wasteland commons that had lain vacant for generations and shared common fields were equally vulnerable to enclosure and engrossment. While larger landowners were partially responsible, so too were smaller farmers and yeomen, who engrossed the common land. The neighbors of these entrepreneurial small farmers were rendered vulnerable by bad harvests, debts, and so forth, as a consequence of which many were forced to cede their access to common lands. Thus the yeoman farmer Thomas Dillamore was in 1636 farming the land that less than a century earlier had been owned and worked by fifteen men. As in this case, much of the engrossment of land was on a relatively small scale, a strip of land at a time, yet the overall effects were nonetheless devastating. Without access to common lands, small medieval landholdings proved less and less viable, and the rural poor in early modern England inhabited a society in which they had dwindling opportunities for work, and for the establishment of their own households.[15]

While engrossment by neighbors and fellow yeomen was as much of a factor as large-scale enclosure, throughout the sixteenth and into the seventeenth centuries many contemporaries identified wealthy landowners as the men who were responsible for the changes in the landscape and a whole raft of accompanying social and economic problems. Sir Thomas More famously complained of the sheep on enclosed, formerly arable land: "your sheep that were wont to be so meek and tame and so small eaters, now, as I hear say, be become so great devourers and so wild that they eat up and swallow down the very men themselves. They consume, destroy, and devour whole fields, houses, and cities."[16]

Authorities worried that enclosure of arable common fields and their conversion to pasture was destroying entire villages and communities and making it impossible for smaller yeoman farmers and husbandmen to survive. More castigated a typical engrossing landlord as "the very plague of his native country," responsible for throwing the rural poor out of their work and homes, who "must needs depart away poor, silly, wretched souls: men, women, husbands, wives, fatherless children, widows, woeful mothers with their young babes, and their whole household small in substance and much in number, as husbandry requireth many hands. Away they trudge, I say, out of their known and accustomed houses, finding no place to rest in."[17]

There existed a strong popular perception that by turning arable lands into pasture, enclosure and engrossment were throwing tens of thousands of smaller farmers off the land and denying many more the opportunities their forefathers and mothers had enjoyed to establish semi-independent households. Without homes or land, and unable to secure work, "what can they then else do but steal, and then justly pardy [by God!] be hanged, or else go about a-begging? And yet then also they be cast in prison as vagabonds, because they go about and work not, whom no man will set a-work."[18]

Reduced popular access to land, an increasing proportion of which was being put to pasture, as well as rapidly rising population levels, together contributed to a decline in wages and significant increases in the price of foodstuffs. Between 1500 and the 1650s food prices may have risen by as much as 550 percent, and periodic cycles of dearth and even famine compounded the problems faced by many. Poverty was nothing new, but during the sixteenth and early seventeenth centuries it was experienced by more people and on a larger scale than in several centuries. Structural under- and unemployment became endemic, towns and countryside alike seemed to be teeming with vagabonds, rootless and jobless men and women who were no longer employed on the land, and who had no prospect of ever achieving the "sufficiency" that would enable them to establish households of their own. Perhaps one-sixth of the English population spent some portion of their lives in London, trudging desperately from all corners of the country in search of work, telling evidence of a remarkably high degree of unemployment and mobility. Regarded as "masterless," the unemployed alarmed observers who expected all subjects of the realm to be within families and households, and subordinate to the legitimate authority of a masterful head of household.[19]

Continued population growth in the later sixteenth and the early seventeenth centuries worsened the situation. England expanded from just under 3 million inhabitants in 1561 to over 4 million by the dawn of the seventeenth century, and 5.23 million by 1651. Scotland's population of 700,000 in the mid-sixteenth century had risen to one million by the second quarter of the seventeenth century, while Wales grew from 250,000 in the mid-sixteenth century to 400,000 by 1650. As fast as the population grew, so too commodity and food prices rose, while real wages declined. During the reigns of Elizabeth and the first two Stuart monarchs the ranks of under- and unemployed wage laborers grew throughout the British Isles. Even those who worked were often desperately poor, mired in unavoidable structural poverty. At its worst this could result in famine, which haunted late sixteenth- and early seventeenth-century Scotland: in 1623, for example, perhaps one-quarter of the population of Dunfermline and as many as one-third of the people of Kelso died of hunger and disease.[20]

Historians can trace the contours of these dramatic changes, and they have attempted to explain both their causes and their effects. Contemporaries, however, had far less information about or understanding of what was happening around them, and many drew on religious and social beliefs to interpret their situation and society. This included assessing the condition and worth of the unemployed and homeless poor in terms of personal morality. Wealth, commercial success, and independence appeared to those who enjoyed it as evidence of personal merit and divine blessing, while they interpreted joblessness, poverty, and homelessness as proof of personal failings and immorality. One's economic condition, in short, appeared to be evidence of one's moral worth. "Man is borne to labour," proclaimed religious authorities, who were convinced that "poverty followeth idlenesse." All around, England clerics warned their congregations:

We have to muche experience thereof (the thyng is the more to bee lamented) in this realme. For a great part of the beggery that is among the poore, can be imputed to nothing so muche, as to

idlenes, and to the negligence of parentes, whiche do not bryng up
theyr chyldren, eyther in good learning, honest labour, or some
commendable occupation or trade, whereby when they come to age,
they myght get theyr living.[21]

Farmers and political authorities alike were deeply concerned by the unwillingness of potential servants and laborers to accept what these working people considered to be inadequate wages and inferior conditions. Moreover, the
elite were terrified that the increase in the number of vagrant "masterless"
men and women might inspire crime, disorder, and rebellion. However bad
the social and economic reality was, elite fears and perceptions perceived a
situation that was even worse: the specter of hosts of undisciplined and
mobile vagrants struck fear into the hearts of landowners and the authorities,
and this affected their attitudes toward the laboring poor.[22]

Apart from the mid-seventeenth-century New Model Army, England
had no standing army to soak up surplus manpower, and impressment for
Cromwell's wars in Ireland and the Caribbean appear to have informed
Thomas Venner's attempted uprising in 1657: a large and permanent army
was never really viable in early modern England. There were limitations on
the ways in which the existing legal system could be used to force men,
women, and children to labor, and the government responded by trying to
refresh and strengthen existing labor practices, while also seeking new solu-
tions to the problems they faced. The Ordinance and the Statute of Laborers were confirmed and updated in 1563 by the Statute of Artificers, which
was intended to ensure social stability in part through the preservation of
the large mass of rural people as a steady and quiescent labor force. Height-
ened labor mobility and large numbers of under- and unemployed people
concerned both governmental authorities and landowners, and this new
law sought to address such concerns. The Statute of Artificers redefined
servants who broke the terms of their contract as criminals; created mecha-
nisms to ensure standardized wages, eroding the power of some laborers to
negotiate more advantageous rates of pay; and laid out methods to require
and enforce vagrants to work. The new law accorded significant power to
local authorities, and justices of the peace were empowered to enforce various provisions within local contexts. The Elizabethan Statute of Artificers
articulated compulsion and control: all who were able were compelled to
work, and their labor was subject to the legally mandated authority of their
masters. Two decades later, Sir Thomas Smith went so far as to assert that

compelling vagrants and the under- and unemployed to work were among the "chief charges" of justices of the peace. This and related laws recognized the legal authority of heads of households, farmers, and landowners as agents of a larger society, enforcing social and religious discipline and ensuring peace and productivity within the realm. The head of each household ruled over a "little Commonwealth," a familial version of the state, and the government sought to confirm and strengthen this authority.[23]

The Ordinance and Statute of Laborers and the Statute of Artificers together illustrate the development of governmental attitude toward laborers, while enforcement of the laws shows the extent to which such attitudes were shared by the local elite. Jane Whittle's study of Norfolk reveals that these laws were regularly enforced by petty sessions and quarter sessions throughout the sixteenth century, which she suggests is quite likely to be indicative of broad and fairly effective enforcement of the labor legislation nationally, albeit with regional variations. Although enforcement in the fifteenth and early sixteenth centuries was rather more sporadic, as social problems grew between the mid-sixteenth and mid-seventeenth centuries these labor laws were being enforced across England in counties as diverse as Yorkshire, Devon, and Norfolk, in a systematic attempt to force young people and the unemployed into service. Whittle discovered numerous cases in Norfolk in which one master brought another to court for illegal procurement of a servant, which "implies an accusation of larceny, or theft of the servant." The Statute of Artificers thus encouraged masters and officials to regard not just the labor but the very body of a servant as a form of property. At the same time, the resistance of Nicholas Emneth and his friends reveal something of the ways in which the rural poor themselves reacted to this regulation of their labor, this control of their bodies, and this reduction in their freedom to work when, and for whom, they pleased.[24]

The number of laborers grew in the early seventeenth century, as an increasing population meant that not everyone who wanted to become a servant could secure such a position. High food prices and a labor surplus, particularly during the first half of the seventeenth century, meant that life was often extremely hard for those without regular or permanent work. Authorities worried by the rising number of jobless vagrants acted to ensure that the young and the unemployed were placed within a household, subject to the authority of a master, and made to labor. Nicholas Emneth was one of a great many English men and women who lost control over their own labor in this fashion.

Contemporaries were well used to the traditional distinction between the deserving and undeserving poor: the former composed of those who were worthy of charity because injury, illness, or old age meant that they were unable to provide for themselves, while the latter were judged to be poor because they refused to work. But in the early modern era religious and political authorities were forced to confront the existence of a new group, the laboring poor, whose condition was the result of their inability—through no fault of their own—to secure employment sufficient to provide for themselves and their families. Periodic harvest failures compounded the problem, and Elizabethan and Stuart governments were forced to change their understanding of the nature and causes of poverty, as well as develop new policies and practices to provide for the poor and ensure social stability. Virtually all of these policies centered upon work, and ensuring that all who were able would be put to work.[25]

Pauper apprenticeship was a particularly stark form of Elizabethan and Stuart labor discipline, and it appears to have been more common than historians once assumed. Orphans and the children of the laboring poor were bound out as apprentices, usually but not always in husbandry, and required to work for their masters for lengthy periods, perhaps as long as a decade or more. Such apprentices were required to "do all servile offices about the house, and be obedient to all his masters commandementes, and shall suffer such correction as his master shall thinke meete." Building on a range of Elizabethan poor laws and vagrancy statutes, authorities overrode reluctant parents and unwilling prospective masters, doing all they could to ensure that a new generation did not enter the growing ranks of unemployed and underemployed laborers. Enforcement was patchy: in 1617, for example, justices in Norfolk bound out over 500 children, while those in neighboring Suffolk bound out virtually none. In 1624 the Hertfordshire bench apprenticed over 1,500 impoverished children, and eighteen certificates completed by justices drawn from five different counties in 1633 described the binding out of almost 3,000 children. The impact on a single community might be enormous: in 1634 alone, some forty boys and girls were apprenticed in the Sussex village of Cuckfield, a community of no more than 1,200 people.[26]

Apprenticeship, often but not always in husbandry, could be forced upon orphans, the children of impoverished parents, and those judged unable or unwilling to secure annual contracts as servants in husbandry.

An apprentice in husbandry was bound to a single master for the length of his or her indenture, which ranged between three and eleven years. Designed to properly control idle or surplus youths, and to ensure a cheap and steady supply of labor for "the better advancement of Husbandrye and Tillage" by farmers and landowners, this was a far more prescriptive form of bound labor than service in husbandry, which significantly reduced the rights, the freedoms, and the long-term prospects of apprentices in husbandry. The surviving records suggest that two boys were bound out for every girl: on the one hand impoverished parents may have resisted the removal of young daughters, while on the other hand prospective employers may have been more willing to accept male farmhands. Either way, the tradition of forced service and labor was applied more readily to males than females. As a result, when people were bound for service outside of England, many more male than female bound laborers would be dispatched to the developing plantations of Barbados and other English colonies.[27]

Pauper apprenticeship and forced apprenticeship in husbandry were not the only ways in which the bodies and labor of men and women might be commandeered. Perhaps the most striking example of this was the Vagrancy Act of 1547, which instituted enslavement as a punishment for those who refused to work and subject themselves to the legitimate authority of a master. According to the law, any individual found "not applying them self to some honnest and allowed arte, Scyence, service or Labour" would be given three days to find work. Failure to do so, or entering service but then abandoning it before the end of the contracted term of labor, could result in the person being brought before two justices. If the charge was proved, the law mandated that the unfortunate man or woman be quite literally branded as a vagrant, and made the slave of the person bringing suit for a period of two years. The master did not have to treat his slave with the care demanded by the law in the case of servants, feeding the enslaved "breade and water or small drynke and such refuse of meate as he shall thincke mete." More tellingly, the master was free to "cawse the said Slave to worke by beating, cheyninge or otherwise in such worke and Labor how vyle so ever it be," and he was even empowered to place iron rings on the neck and the feet of the enslaved. Runaway slaves would be enslaved for life, and a second attempt to flee risked execution. Other provisions of the law extended existing practices. A vagabond child could be forced into apprenticeship without the permission of parents, and forced to serve until the age of twenty-four if male and twenty if female. Should this apprentice flee, he or she would be returned and reduced to the status of slave for the remainder of the term.[28]

While a form of serfdom if not slavery existed among coal miners and their families in seventeenth- and eighteenth-century Scotland, the institution did not exist elsewhere and it failed to take root in sixteenth-century England. The Vagrancy Act lasted only two years in England. In the wake of Ket's Rebellion in 1549 the law was repealed, and there is little evidence to suggest that it had ever been enforced. Nevertheless, the precedents for this law, its language and provisions, the survival of certain of its provisions long after its repeal, and the very fact of its passage in the first place all suggest that English authorities believed that in the right circumstances one individual could seize the body and labor of another, taking away liberty and independence and extracting work through violence. A poor law scheme in 1535 had proposed that vagrants be forced to work on various public works, and those who refused would be branded and even executed. Two different proclamations by Henry VIII had mandated that "ruffians, vagabonds, masterless men, common players and evil-disposed persons" could be sent to the galleys "there to row as a slave" at His Majesty's pleasure. Slavery existed, at least in theory, in English Common Law, but the Vagrancy Act of 1547 represented a new way of thinking after other measures had failed. For those who would not work, enslavement was proposed as a punishment, and as the most radical means of forcing work. While this official policy of enslavement was short-lived, the overriding principle of forcibly binding out children and the unemployed remained a vital part of both policy and practice throughout England.[29]

Such attitudes were clear in vagrancy legislation, the abiding principle of which was the obligation to labor. Parish officials and justices of the peace employed bridewells, forced service and apprenticeship, and other institutions to extract labor from all homeless and jobless vagrants who were fit and able to work. Before 1500 officials had sought to force people to work for strictly regulated wages in a society with more land than there were people to farm it. However, as the population grew to the point at which there were too many people for the work available, the laws were extended to require work at controlled wages or even for no wages. Authorities sought not only to ensure a steady and affordable labor supply, but also to keep the laboring population servile and compliant.[30]

In sixteenth- and seventeenth-century England there thus existed, both in theory and in practice, degrees of bound and even unfree labor. All who labored for others, whether laborers, servants in husbandry, apprentices in husbandry, or even apprentices, were bound by legal strictures that gave masters considerable power over them. Significant demographic and economic changes, together with the expansion of commercial activity throughout the British Isles, all encouraged the commodification of labor as a product to be sold and bought, and more significantly, to be owned. This enhanced the legal power of masters to ensure that they received compliance from those bound to serve them. The medieval right of a master to the good performance of a servant began developing into legal ownership of labor, and a right of control over the body of the laborer. The rural poor could be made to work, some for no recompense other than the most basic food, clothing, and lodging. Their masters were entitled to use violence and the officers and instruments of state power in order to force obedience and to extract labor.[31]

During the second half of the seventeenth century the social situation improved somewhat. The new commercial society and the development of overseas trade created new employment opportunities, and by the later seventeenth and throughout much of the eighteenth centuries food prices stabilized and real wages increased. Work, some of it in service in husbandry, was once again available, the standard of living and material prospects of the rural poor improved somewhat, and incentives to emigrate lessened. Thus, although their parents' and grandparents' generations had left the country in large numbers, during the early eighteenth century tens of thousands of Scots preferred to relocate from the countryside to Glasgow, which was being transformed by the tobacco, sugar, and textile industries from a small medieval city to a major manufacturing center. During the sixteenth and most of the seventeenth centuries rural society in the British Isles had endured one of its greatest crises, at least in terms of the lives and work of the rural population, and this had occurred at the very moment that new colonies and trading settlements were being established in Barbados, on the Gold Coast, and all around the North Atlantic.[32]

It was at precisely the right time, between 1627 and roughly 1660, that Barbadian planters seized their opportunity and drew tens of thousands of white laborers from the British Isles. Planters, farmers, and traders in the

Caribbean, the Chesapeake, New England, coastal West Africa, and at the end of the century the Middle Atlantic colonies all drew on the ranks of unemployed, vagrants, criminals, and prisoners of war from the British Isles as a source of labor. Voluntary and involuntary indentured servants from the British Isles crossed the Atlantic in large numbers, and they were of far greater significance in England's colonies than in those of any other European nation. Christopher Tomlins estimates that 60 to 65 percent of those traveling from the British Isles to England's mainland colonies during the seventeenth century were bound servants, declining to 40 to 42 percent in the eighteenth century.[33]

During the middle years of the seventeenth century, however, Barbados drew more bound laborers from the British Isles than any other English colony. Between 1650 and 1659, for example, as many as 69 percent of the bound white laborers arriving in the Americas from Britain landed in Barbados. Upon arrival these bound workers faced an exhausting work regime and dwindling prospects. While courts, local communities, and popular and political opinion had forced some restraint on the part of employers in England, conditions in Barbados proved very different. English authorities were desperate to free themselves of as many vagrants, criminals, and prisoners as possible. Thousands of miles away, a small group of Barbadian planters controlled government, the courts, and military power on their island, and they were effectively free of many of the legal and cultural restrictions that had limited British landowners in their treatment of laborers. With England and indeed the entire British Isles mired in political, religious, and military conflicts, the ruling elite in Barbados seized their opportunity, deploying labor free from many of England's customary restraints. They reconceptualized and reconstituted bound labor, both as a condition and as a mechanism for violently extracting work from men, women, and children who were bound to their master, and who had no choice but to serve.[34]

First white Britons—some of them voluntary indentured servants, but many more of them vagrants, convicts, and civil and military prisoners—were worked in new ways, under greater coercion, and for far longer than would have been true in the British Isles, and a great many of them died in this condition. While the earliest came voluntarily, they were followed by many more who were forced to travel. Some were "Barbadoz'd," kidnapped and sent to the island as captive laborers, while many more were imprisoned vagrants, convicts, and prisoners from war and rebellion who were sent abroad by the state. The result was a telling difference in volition: a great many of the white servants sent to Barbados had not voluntarily entered a contract, exchanging their labor for passage and food. Instead, they were more akin to pauper apprentices, vagrants, and even the slaves referred to in the notorious Elizabethan Vagrancy Act of 1547, men and women who did not control their labor or their bodies, people who were bound, not free. For many of those who were prisoners, and even those who were repeat-offender vagrants, their lives were forfeit in the British Isles. Labor in Barbados represented a reprieve from the gallows, and Barbadian planters did not hesitate to utilize and then expand the various forms of forced labor and labor discipline that had on occasion been implemented in early modern England, regarding their white servants as people who had lost the right to life and were consequently undeserving of traditional English rights and liberties. We have no idea how many people were sent from the British Isles to Barbados, but estimates of the number sent to the Americas from Ireland alone range between 30,000 and 100,000, and most of these went to Barbados.[35]

The settlement of Barbados thus took place in the context of dramatically shifting experiences and understandings of labor, servitude, and unemployment in the British Isles, and these very changes would help inform the ways in which Barbadian planters began adapting British practices in order to create new forms of bound labor suited to the particular needs of their new crops and the developing plantation system. The need for new forms of work inspired masters to draw on certain English laws and practices while ignoring others, creating new attitudes among masters toward the bound laborers whose work and bodies they owned, whether temporarily or permanently. A new mindset permeated the Barbadian elite, significantly different from the attitudes of farmers who commanded laborers in the British Isles, and planters thought of and treated bound white laborers and their descendants with disdain. Even when bound servants were freed and replaced by enslaved Africans, there was little place for these impoverished whites in the brave new world of Barbados. For many bound whites and for virtually all enslaved Africans, labor on Barbadian plantations would hold no promise of a brighter future.

Chapter 2

The Gold Coast

Britons who sought to trade on the Gold Coast during the seventeenth and eighteenth centuries were required to treat the West Africans they encountered with respect, and to engage with, understand, and utilize local free and bound labor in ways that differed quite dramatically from both the early modern British Isles and the developing plantation society of Barbados. West Africans enjoyed the upper hand in negotiating with Europeans eager to establish trading posts, and as a result Africans exercised considerable control over the terms of trade. Just as significantly, English companies and traders quickly found that in order to keep their forts and trading posts operative and successful they needed not only workers from the British Isles, but also increasingly large numbers of free and enslaved West Africans. By the later seventeenth century newly developed Barbadian sugar plantations had become dependent upon the slaves purchased, stored, and then shipped from English trading posts on the West African coast. As a result, the African trade quickly became essential to the English.

Familiar English categories of free and bound labor all but disappeared in and around the British castles, forts, and trading posts in West Africa. New labor categories and practices provided the foundation for commercial exchange between the British and West Africans, including the growing trade in enslaved Africans between West Africa and the Caribbean. Slavery in West Africa was a familiar and deeply rooted social system and mode of production, and "the institutionalization of enslavement, the formal structure of trade, and the codification of slavery in law and custom guaranteed that slavery was central to the production process." On the Gold Coast Britons had to engage with an African labor system on African terms, and dependence on enslaved and free Africans required all Europeans on the coast to comprehend and utilize entirely new ideologies and practices of labor.[1]

European trading operations and the transatlantic slave trade built upon a trade in bound labor that had existed in Africa for centuries. In Europe, land functioned as the main form of wealth-producing property, but along the Gold Coast "No man claimeth any Land to himself; the King keeping all the Woods, Fields, and Land in his hands; so that they neither Sow nor Plant therein, but by his content and licence." Consequently, throughout much of West Africa it was slaves rather than land that constituted the principal form of private property that could generate income; in Barbados and then other plantation societies in British America, these European and African systems would be combined. The holding, buying, and selling of slaves had traditionally allowed West Africans to profit from the assets inherent in the land, enabling individuals to enhance their wealth, power, and prestige. By the fifteenth century slaveholding had been institutionalized in the more densely populated interior of the Gold Coast, and slaves were employed in various ways, including agricultural labor, military service, and most especially gold mining.[2]

But until the arrival of European traders, coastal areas remained relatively marginal and less populated, with the result that slavery had been a rather less integral component of the small, peripheral, and relatively poor communities on the West African coastline. European observers of the sixteenth and early seventeenth centuries described these societies as being composed of people of authority (kings, nobles, and the gentry), merchants (who were often people of authority with the power to direct and benefit from trade), occupational or professional castes (men who had learned and inherited their occupation from their fathers or masters, including doctors, musicians, and priests), the common people, servants and slaves, women, and children. There was a notable malleability in these categories, and almost any "free" man or woman could be reduced to various forms of servitude or dependence, while conversely, slaves or their descendants could be assimilated into the households and other groups to which they belonged, essentially becoming free. Moreover, while the earliest Europeans on the Gold Coast saw people in coastal societies whom they regarded as slaves, and while people there were bought and sold, it does not necessarily follow that there was a clearly defined slave class within these sparsely populated coastal societies. If slavery and bound labor were familiar components of Gold Coast society, they were far from rigid and permanent in nature. It was only as trade and population increased in and after the seventeenth century that slavery became a more rigidly defined social and laboring category along the Gold Coast.[3]

Most slaves in Gold Coast societies served essentially domestic and agricultural functions, sharing these tasks with other household members. Slaves were not usually subject to sale outside of the community, unless found guilty of a crime. In the interior those slaves involved in gold mining and production had a rather different existence, and during the sixteenth and much of the seventeenth centuries gold merchants and producers were the main purchasers of slaves imported from outside of the region, at first from other Africans to the north and west and then later from the Portuguese and other Europeans. However, the importation of perhaps five hundred slaves per annum during this period did not create a slave society in the Gold Coast comparable with those that would evolve on the western side of the Atlantic, and until the late seventeenth and then the eighteenth centuries slavery in coastal communities remained relatively small-scale, and there was no large and distinct slave class or caste. The existence of pawns, or voluntary and at least in theory temporary slaves, further blurred the lines between free and enslaved people.[4]

Wealth and power on the Gold Coast were accrued by men who had multiple wives, servants, and slaves, with each wife inhabiting a separate household whose members created wealth by cultivating land allocated to their master. Poorer men had only one or perhaps no wife, and few if any servants or slaves, and thus were unable to increase their wealth. Thus, this was a society in which control of the labor of others (wives, servants, and slaves) created power and wealth. Free labor was in relatively short supply, and so marriage or the purchase of unfree labor by those who could afford it represented the primary means of social and economic advancement. Those unable to provide for themselves were likely to move from the ranks of free to those of servile laborers.[5]

However, the rapidly growing trade between Europeans and coastal West Africans had a significant effect on the place of slaves within these communities as well as their value outside of it. The arrival of increasing numbers of Europeans bearing a dizzying array of valuable trade goods encouraged the further commodification of this labor market, with bound laborers becoming valued as marketable commodities as much as wealth-producing household members. As European trade goods began flooding into West Africa, a growing number of enslaved porters were required to transport items to and from the coast, and over time more and more of the slaves of the Gold Coast were engaged in commercial rather than agricultural work. The array of goods penetrating African markets was remarkable, including a wide array of textiles, alcohol, manufactured pots, knives and metal goods, guns and gunpowder, tobacco, bar iron and copper, beads, and myriad other items. Coastal West Africans utilized their position as suppliers of these commodities and were very discriminating in their tastes in European goods, rejecting all but those goods that they most favored. Recalling a voyage to Cape Coast in the early 1690s, Thomas Phillips listed the "commodities that are most in demand upon the gold coast," going on to lament that he had taken "on account of the *African* company, muskets, niconees, tapseals, baysadoes, brass kettles, *English* carpets, *Welsh* plains, lead bars, firkins of tallow, powder, &c None of which did answer expectation."[6] Moreover, just as competing European nations sought to keep the terms of exchange as favorable to Europeans as possible, Africans did exactly the same, prompting annoyed complaints such as the following: "The Blacks at Annamoo lately made a law that no one shod sell a Slave for less than 8 Ounces to the Shipping & am sorry to acquaint you some of the Vessels have lately given it; this is setting a very bad Example, as no doubt they will often make such Laws when they find they have so good an Effect."[7]

West Africans coveted well-made guns and knives, high-quality fabrics, and the best possible manufactured items. Reporting on West African taste in fabrics, William Hickes reported that they were "Most taken with Colour . . . & lively to ye Eye, & what is white to be pure white and where Colours are to be mixed by Weaving or Staining They are most pleased with lively patterns."[8] Exasperated Britons complained about the damaged and inferior goods they were asked to sell and trade, as in the case of guns "with very bad locks & Screws, so short & so small that they often fall out," for "ye Natives are mighty Desirous of having every part . . . work & will refuse ye Gunns that hath not . . . Brass work on." Dalby Thomas, governor of Cape Coast Castle, observed to his superiors in London that "The blacks are very nice and curious in discerning and Distinguishing Colours," before complaining that his Dutch rivals were more adept at providing the fabrics and colors preferred by West African traders and consumers. Attempts to pass off inferior goods were rebuffed by West African traders and consumers, leading one British official to list these European-manufactured fabrics that he and his colleagues had failed to pass off as Asian-made as "not

Vendible." Reports from Britons on the Gold Coast regularly informed company officials in London that inferior or damaged goods could not be sold or traded, unless at a loss.[9]

This rapidly growing trade created wealth throughout West Africa, encouraging the development of larger and more powerful polities and kingdoms throughout the region. While slavery continued to function in traditional ways, these new states sought to consolidate their power with large numbers of slaves, both for internal use (sometimes as soldiers) and for sale to the Europeans. The increasing demand for labor in the New World led to not only the sale of ever more Africans to Europeans, but also a dramatic growth in the size and significance of West African coastal communities, and the significance of slave labor to and within these societies. Over the course of the seventeenth century the Gold Coast changed from a gold mine for Europeans into a "slave mine." At first many of the slaves taken across the Atlantic had come from Angola and Kongo, as well as from Senegambia and Benin. With the rapid expansion of the slave trade after 1650, an increasing number of slaves came from the Slave Coast (the Bight of Benin), and then in the late seventeenth century and throughout the eighteenth century from the Gold Coast and the Bight of Biafra. At the outset the Gold Coast purchased most of these slaves for export from the interior, but a succession of wars for control of parts and then all of the Gold Coast region produced a steady flow of more local slaves. During the late seventeenth century anywhere between a few hundred and 2,000 slaves left the Gold Coast each year, rising to an annual average of approximately 7,000 during the early eighteenth century, peaking at 10,000 or more during the third quarter of the eighteenth century, and then falling back to about 9,000 annually in the 1790s. As many as one million slaves from the Akan-speaking area of the Gold Coast crossed the Atlantic during the eighteenth century, almost one-quarter of total West African exports, and it was the Dutch and most especially the British who dominated the European side of this trade. Although large-scale warfare made possible the capture, sale, and export of hundreds of thousands of West African slaves, the trade conducted on the coast—of which slaves were but one of a large number of valuable commodities—depended upon a containment of political violence that enabled trade to continue and expand. Thus at the same time that societies and polities in the interior were fragmented by warfare and large-scale enslavement, relatively stable commercial networks were developed and consolidated on the Gold Coast itself.[10]

During the height of this transatlantic slave trade, the largest single group of slaves in the rapidly developing Gold Coast communities in which European trading castles and forts were established were the "castle" slaves, the large groups of European-owned bound Africans who populated, maintained, and defended the trading posts. While local rulers and wealthy merchants often commanded large bodies of dependents, including slaves and pawns, few could match the hundreds of slaves owned by the British at Cape Coast Castle, Anomabu, Accra, and other Gold Coast castles, forts, and trading posts. Castle slavery developed and existed as a hybrid form of bound labor, rooted in West African traditions and operating according to West African precepts, yet owned and directed by alien Britons who trained these bound Africans in British artisanal crafts. Yet despite the existence of bound white British laborers in these forts, and the simultaneous development of plantation racial slavery in the Americas, each of which provided different models of bound labor, castle slavery continued to exist as a predominantly West African form of labor throughout the period of the transatlantic slave trade. Castle slaves not only lived and labored in West African traditions, they were also regarded by their European masters in local terms, as men and women who were not members of a rigid and fixed caste but rather were simply one category of a complicated and fluid array of working people on the Gold Coast.

Stretching approximately two hundred miles from Cape Three Points in the west to the mouth of the Volta River in the east, the rocky shores of the Gold Coast proved more suitable for permanent and defensible European trading forts than the sandy lagoons of the Ivory Coast to the west, or the swampy deltas of the Slave Coast to the east. Before the arrival of the Europeans, the residents of Gold Coast communities had lived on the periphery of the West African world, and the Atlantic Ocean at their backs had been less a means of travel and communication than a mighty barrier. Coastal West Africa had not been densely populated: fishing, salt-making, and agriculture had occupied the small communities on the coast, with gold mining, agriculture, and associated urban crafts dominating the more densely populated interior. Local markets and inland and river trade routes facilitated the movement of salt and fish inland from coastal producers who were otherwise relatively isolated. In the interior, artisans included skilled metal workers who worked iron and gold, as well as textile workers, although apart from gold virtually all metals and fabrics had often come along internal trade networks from the African interior and beyond. By the middle of the sixteenth century, Portuguese, Dutch, Danish, English, French, and other European ships were finding their way to the Gold Coast, although for much of the seventeenth and eighteenth centuries the English and Dutch were the dominant European presence along the Gold Coast. From a West African perspective the period up to the middle of the seventeenth century was characterized by European trade for gold (as well as for ivory and various other commodities). Thereafter, New World demand, as well as various wars within West Africa, triggered both a growing European need for and an increasing West African supply of enslaved people, and the Atlantic slave trade came to dwarf the gold trade.[11]

Many of the Africans encountered by sixteenth- and seventeenth-century European traders on the Gold Coast were Akan, a people whose area of settlement spanned the entire Gold Coast between the eastern edge of the Ivory Coast and the western limits of the Slave Coast, and stretched some two hundred miles into the interior. When the English began trading in the second half of the seventeenth century, Denkyria dominated the western part of the Gold Coast, exercising significant control over trade routes, gold production, and commerce with the Europeans. A powerful military state, Denkyria expanded, taking control of smaller polities. In the center of the Gold Coast were the Akyem, a major rival of Denkyria and a polity that used gold to purchase slaves from outside the region who were then deployed as agricultural laborers, porters, and gold miners. On the eastern edge of the Gold Coast Akwamu was a smaller and less militaristic polity, weaker than both Denkyria and Akyem, in which fishing, salt production, farming, and pottery making dominated. Over the course of the eighteenth century, despite the continued independence of small city-states such as Elmina, Cape Coast, and Anomabu, conquest of smaller coastal territories by the Barbor Fante and other groups led to increased political consolidation on the Gold Coast, and Europeans began referring to the region as "Fantyn" or "Fanteland." Later in the eighteenth century virtually all of the Gold Coast region was conquered by the Asante Kingdom. Throughout the era of the Atlantic slave trade Europeans were required to deal with all of these polities and their varying trade requirements. The coastal communities alongside the major European forts and trading posts were the nexus of African-European relations and trade, but it was the larger Akan and later the Asante polities, based further inland, that controlled many of the goods and enslaved people drawn from the interior that were coveted by European traders.[12]

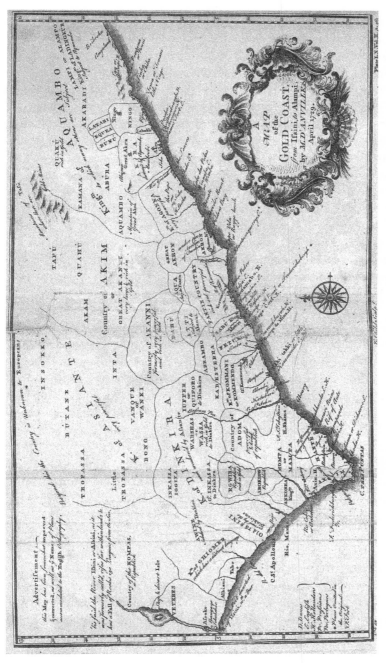

Figure 3. "A Map of the Gold Coast from Isini to Alampi, by M. D'Anville. April 1729," in Thomas Astley (ed.), *A New General Collection of Voyages and Travels* (London, 1745–47). Courtesy of the Library Company of Philadelphia. The map shows the various communities of the Gold Coast, including "Fantin country, rich and powerful" (directly above the compass rose), a clear statement of the relative power of Gold Coast inhabitants who allowed the British and other Europeans to trade.

Because of its importance in this trade and its suitability for the construction of trading castles and forts, the Gold Coast functioned as the operational center for European trade along the entire West African coast. São Jorge da Mina (Elmina) was the first of the major European forts on the Gold Coast, built in the early 1580s by the Portuguese and then captured in 1637 by the Dutch, who subsequently held the castle for more than two centuries. Some six miles to the east of Elmina was Cape Coast Castle, which was controlled first by Sweden and then by Denmark before finally falling to the English in 1664. Cape Coast Castle would continue to serve as the British headquarters in this region until Ghanaian independence in 1957. These two mighty castles were the headquarters for a network of smaller West African castles, forts, and trading posts, many of them positioned along the Gold Coast. Each European outpost developed a symbiotic relationship with the local villages and towns, and these communities expanded in size and commercial significance to meet the needs of the Europeans and to facilitate the profitable trade between Africans and Europeans. With their strongest defensive aspects facing the sea, the forts and castles were designed to protect valuable trading bases and exclusive trading relationships against the depredations of rival European nations: wars between European nations far outnumbered military confrontations between the Europeans and their African hosts. However large and imposing the European forts and their cannon may have appeared, the small number of Europeans within them, their distance from military support and reinforcement, and their absolute dependence upon numerically superior and well-armed local Africans for supplies and trading goods all meant that Europeans enjoyed significantly less power in West Africa than they did in their established colonies in the Americas. Europeans along the coast seeking to reinforce their position were required to establish strong links with local rulers, which involved paying rents for the lands on which their buildings stood, as well as periodic "dashees," or payments and gifts. The European sites on the Gold Coast were neither colonies nor bases for penetration into the African interior, but rather "sites of joint enterprises" between West Africans and Europeans.[13]

The rapid accumulation of wealth made possible by the expansion of trade triggered significant urbanization and population growth along the Gold Coast, moving small costal communities from the periphery to the commercial center of West African society. In the mid-sixteenth century Cape Coast had been a small village of no more than twenty homes, but by

1680 this number had grown to more than five hundred; during roughly the same period the population rose from approximately one hundred to between 3,000 and 4,000. By 1669 the population of Elmina, the town adjacent to the Dutch castle of the same name, was home to some 8,000 people, compared with fewer than 1,500 who were at that time inhabiting New Amsterdam in the Americas. A generation later Elmina's population had risen to between 12,000 and 16,000, making it at as large as or even larger than Boston, New York, Philadelphia, or Charleston, the major urban settlements of mainland British North America.[14]

As the trade in slaves between West Africans and Europeans grew, the Gold Coast emerged as a major supplier of these human commodities, and the region enjoyed the lion's share of the massively expanded eighteenth-century transatlantic slave trade. The British and the Dutch were able to largely exclude other European nations from the rich Gold Coast trade, and these two nations maintained their West African headquarters almost within sight of one another, the British at Cape Coast Castle and the Dutch at Elmina. Many of the European forts, castles, and trading posts along the Gold Coast had originally been constructed for the gold trade, and facilities for slave trading were initially limited at best. However, during the eighteenth century older castles and trading posts were remodeled, and new ones like the purpose-built British castle at Anomabu were constructed, with the Atlantic slave trade as their primary purpose. The British headquarters at Cape Coast Castle were rebuilt in order to incorporate very large holding cells for enslaved male and female Africans, awaiting delivery to British slave ships.[15]

By the end of the seventeenth century the slave trade dominated the West African and European trading relationship. Between 1500 and 1600 the approximately 328,000 slaves transported from Africa to the New World represented about 30.4 percent of the total number of slaves exported from Africa during the century (most of the remainder traveled north across the Sahara to the Ottoman Empire and beyond). The seventeenth century saw a dramatic expansion in both the number and proportion of exported African slaves crossing the Atlantic: some 1,348,000 Africans crossed the Atlantic in chains, representing 60 percent of all slaves exported from Africa during these years. However, the greatest expansion occurred during the eighteenth century, when the more than six million slaves transported to the Americas accounted for 82.4 percent of African slave exports. British slavers alone transported 3.1 million Africans between 1700 and 1808, taking the large majority to the sugar islands of the Caribbean.[16]

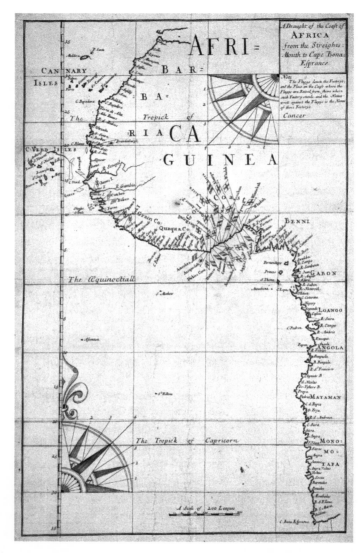

Figure 4. "A Draught of the Coast of AFRICA from the Streights Mouth to Cape Bona Esprance," Royal African Company map, 1663–1681. The National Archives, MPG1/221. European forts and trading posts on the Gold Coast and the Slave Coast (Bight of Benin) are shown by national flags, and the concentrated European presence in this area is evident. The map also reveals limited European knowledge of the West African interior.

Therefore, throughout its history, the transatlantic slave trade was wholly dependent upon West Africans who provided trading venues, trade goods (including enslaved people), and free and bound labor. The trading acumen and the political power of African hosts were readily apparent to Europeans who visited the Gold Coast. Erick Tilleman commended West African merchants and traders who "are well versed in *negotien*," Nicolas Villault observed that "They have a great deal of wit, [and] are solid in their judgements," and John Atkins applauded the "superiour Genius of these Gold-Coast *Negroes*." Jean Barbot recorded that the "Blacks of the gold coast are for the most part very rich, through the great trade they drive with the Europeans, both aboard their ships and ashore, bartering their gold, for several sorts of European commodities, of which they make a vast profit up the inland." The English officials charged with facilitating trade knew this best of all, and many echoed Samuel Eyles's assessments "that Civil treatment & a kind behaviour is best," for they understood that this and the importations of those goods that West Africans most desired "is ye only way to bring them to trade with us." One British governor of Cape Coast Castle frankly acknowledged the power of local Africans, going so far as to conclude that "we have no Power over them" and that "we are their Servants."[17]

The large majority of the European castles, forts, and trading posts along the Gold Coast were built alongside existing coastal communities, and the two expanded in a symbiotic and dependent relationship. Occupying a liminal space between the European-dominated Atlantic World and the African polities within the interior, the coastal settlements were usually led by traditional local hereditary rulers and new caboceers, middlemen who facilitated trade and who were key figures in a new and powerful commercial class. Gold Coast communities were transformed from isolated and marginal fishing and salt-making villages into major economic centers. Although in one sense the residents of these coastal communities were little more than middlemen between the European powers and the Akan and later the Asante polities of the interior, it was their labor and proficiency that made all trade possible. Residents of Gold Coast and other coastal communities quickly developed an ability to meet the needs of Europeans, not simply for goods but for the labor, materials, and services necessary to maintain trading posts, facilitate trade, and transport goods and people between ship and shore. Specialized production fed and clothed slaves on their way to the coast, as well as both slaves and Europeans in coastal forts and factories, and furnished food for Europeans and slaves during the Middle Passage. The trading and slave ships that arrived on the coast were as dependent on coastal communities as were the Europeans in coastal forts, as the lack of harbors and large-scale "bulking" facilities meant that ships often spent months on the coast, trading and acquiring slaves, all the time needing local food and supplies. Between 1751 and 1775, for example, British ships spent an average of 173 days each year on the West African coast.[18]

Perhaps it was on the Gold Coast, more than any of the other coastal areas of West Africa, that stable communities were best able to develop and provide such "ancillary services" as food production, skilled and unskilled labor, transportation services, as well as mediation and translation. British trade and operations on the Gold Coast depended upon a mixed workforce, composed of British clerks, officials, and bound and free workers and craftsmen; free mulatto officials and workers; British-owned African slaves, many of them skilled craftsmen; and an array of local free African workers, as well as African-owned slaves and pawns. While the burgeoning Atlantic slave trade meant that slavery as an institution was transformed from its sixteenth-century status as a relatively marginal feature of coastal society into a major economic institution, it nonetheless remained rooted in local ideas and practices. In the north, Islamic ideas had permeated local cultures and the ideas and practices of slavery, yet on the Gold Coast European and New World attitudes toward and practices of slavery had little direct influence on West Africa, and the great changes in slavery occurred across the ocean, out of African sight.[19]

In order to secure peaceful relations with local African communities, the Royal African Company (RAC) and other European companies were required to pay annual rents and to make a series of presents to local leaders and communities. In 1776, for example, ten such monthly payments were made to "the Principal Kings, Caboceers and others" at Cape Coast. These included monthly payments of £4.10.0 to Ando, the Dey of Fetu, for "the General rent" of the land on which stood Cape Coast Castle; £1.10.0 to the "Caboceers of Cape Coast" for the right to load and unload goods along the shore; £3 to Arnooney Coomah, king of Anomabu and "the most powerful Man we have to deal with"; and fifteen shillings to Geyshie, a local militia commander, for "his particular attachment to the English." Britons on the Gold Coast forwarded precise orders for luxury goods that were required as gifts for the local and more distant leaders who facilitated trade. When the Asante ruler proposed inaugurating a coastal market that would

Figure 5. Henry Greenhill, "Cabo Corso Castle on the Gold Coast" (1682). Courtesy of the British Library Board. This British slave ship is anchored far closer to the castle than was in fact possible (most ships were anchored in "the roads," approximately one mile offshore); British soldiers mustered inside the castle; and the growing Fante community outside of the castle (again, this is pictured far closer to the walls of the castle than was actually the case).

have been of material benefit to British traders, the governor of Cape Coast
Castle sent a detailed list of expensive presents for both the Asante and
the Fante rulers, including large damask umbrellas, lined white satin cloth,
engraved silver swords, and gold-headed canes bearing the company's
crest.[20]

In addition to these payments to local rulers and caboceers were more
irregular "Presents and Dashees" to local people and workers, the latter
being "the Blacks word for present," which represented a significant
expense for the British. The payment of both *"customary* presents and
extraordinary presents" cost the RAC over £10,000 worth of goods on the
Gold Coast for the years 1770–1776 alone. A list of forty-nine separate payments to the leaders and people of the town of Cape Coast in 1776 totaled
£247 in customary and £153 in extraordinary disbursements, including such
items as a customary payment of £3 "To the Towns people paying their
respects on New Years Day"; a payment of over £55 to "the King of Ashantee endeavouring to adjust the differences between him and the Fantees,
and thereby prevent a war between the two Nations"; a payment of over £2
to "an inland Caboceer for liberty to cut timber on his grounds"; a payment
of 12 shillings to "the Towns people assisting to hawl on shore one of the
Company's Boats"; a customary payment of nearly £9 to "the Towns people
celebrating their Harvest feast"; and a payment of just over £1 made to "a
Messenger from the Dey of Fetu." Such was the power of local Africans
that every action by the British, every British or African anniversary or
celebration, and every British request came at a price.[21]

Similarly, every disagreement between Europeans and Africans had to
be settled by a negotiation or "palaver," many of which resulted in gifts
and payments by the Europeans. Reporting that disputes and palavers had
cost the RAC almost £1,885 between 1770 and 1776, a statement of RAC
accounts justified the expense as follows:

> When it is considered what a litigious, troublesome set of people
> the Fantees are, among whom the principal of our Forts are situated
> . . . [and] that the grand Object we are placed here for is to encour-
> age a free and open trade, and that there is no possible means of
> doing so effectually as by cultivating so far as lays in our power a
> good means of doing so that so effectually as by cultivating so far as
> lays in our power a good understanding with the Natives around us

. . . when it is considered that the charge under this head is bur-
thened with the Expence of every piratical act of every Black or
White whose conduct comes under the cognizance of the Governor
of the Castle; that it is also charged with every expence attending
any attack made by the Natives and Company's Slaves, which are
often very serious, as well as with many other charges nearly of a
similar nature, the whole sum expended under this head will appear
trifling indeed.[22]

Relations between local leaders and communities and the Europeans who
sought permission to erect fortified trading posts on their territory and then
enjoy exclusive trading rights varied according to such factors as the relative
size and power of the community, their relations with other, often larger
neighboring communities, and their need for European goods. One visiting
Briton believed that the largely autonomous community at Anomabu was
"the strongest on the whole Coast," with the result that the British were so
"horribly plagued" by their hosts "that they are sometimes even confined
to their Fort, not being permitted to stir out." Desperate to construct a
defensible fort at what would become a key location in the eighteenth-
century transatlantic slave trade, Britons faced Anomabu residents who
declared every possible site or source of materials to be sacred ground,
knowing that they could then exact heavy payments. Their small numbers
constantly depleted by disease, Britons were heavily outnumbered by their
hosts, who not only exercised significant control over the terms of trade,
but also were able to exert pressure on the Europeans in other ways.
Coastal Africans frequently stole goods, and occasionally they kidnapped
European-owned slaves and pawns or enticed bound laborers to escape.
Nowhere was this more true than at Anomabu. Writing from Cape Coast
Castle in 1754, Governor Thomas Melvil complained that at Anomabu British "Slaves are either stolen or decoyed in order to plunder us for their
redemption." Making construction even more difficult, surveyor John
Apperley reported "our Storehouses & sheds broke open, our Deal
boards & working Tools stole[n]" by local people.[23]

At the center of British trading operations on the Gold Coast were a
small core of British free and bound laborers, soldiers, sailors, clerks, merchants, and officials. However, confronted by a deadly disease environment,
difficult working conditions, and local people eager to exploit any advantage over European traders, it was impossible for the Britons on the Gold

Coast to maintain and protect their trading castles and posts without the labor and the assistance of local people. Dependent as they were upon this workforce of local Africans and of company-owned slaves, British agents on the Gold Coast recognized the need to keep workers happy, and at times it appeared that more time, money, and effort were devoted to West African workers than to those from the British Isles. Accounts of expenditure illustrate this, as when in 1776 at Cape Coast Castle, four pounds and ten shillings worth of goods were disbursed "To the Town's people and Company's Slaves" who had gathered to greet the governor upon his return from Sekondi. On another occasion, the "Company's slave Gardener" was compensated after he was injured. When the heirs of Birempon Cudjoe, upon whom the British had relied as an intermediary, visited the governor, they were given gifts. Almost £9 worth of goods was given to the townspeople of Cape Coast "celebrating their Harvest feast," and a further £48 "on account of Christmas." Successful operation of the fort, and the trade it was intended to foster, depended upon smooth relations between the British and those whose work they needed, and thus cooperation was not without cost.[24]

Such expenditure clearly concerned officials in Britain, for the reports from the Gold Coast contained full and frank justifications of all such costs. Clearly irked by penny-pinching complaints from London, one official on the Gold Coast responded that such costs were "unavoidable, and cannot be lessened," while those West Africans in receipt of British presents and dashees "by no means conceive them as presents, but as customary dues."[25] Bomboys, local Africans who were employed as foremen, personified British attempts to protect their goods and their interests, and to preserve good relations with local people. As people "of weight & consequence in Town," some bomboys organized workers such as canoe men who were employed by the British to transport people and goods between ship and shore, and ensured that theft was minimized. More significantly, these men were paid stipends in order "to secure peace and Quietness."[26]

For British officials on the Gold Coast, it was all too clear that trade was completely dependent upon good relations with local free and enslaved Africans, with company-owned slaves, and with company-employed white workers and soldiers. In the eighteenth century, as Barbadian plantations became less dependent upon white bound labor and ever more dependent on enslaved African labor, so too the Gold Coast castles from whence so many of those slaves departed became increasingly reliant on castle slaves, mulattoes, and local African workers. But if bound black labor was vital to the British on both sides of the Atlantic, it operated in dramatically different ways in these two different societies. In Barbados, traditional West African forms of slavery evaporated, and the enslaved were subjected to a labor system rooted in English precedents that had been comprehensively redrawn by an elite planter class with few restrictions on how they controlled and deployed bound labor. There were precedents for the masters and overseers of workers in Barbados and throughout the Americas to consider their legal control over those who labored as jurisdiction over the very bodies of these workers, and for masters to consider themselves as holding the labor of their servants as a kind of property. While the former was related to the twinned polities of household and state, the latter reflected an economic relationship. The way was clear for masters to treat labor as an economic resource that they had paid for and thus could control, and for not just the labor but the bodies of laborers to be treated as property. What would develop in Barbados, however, would be rather more than the sum of its parts, more than a modified version of British and West African practices. Barbadian planters created not simply a new form of plantation organization, but also new ideas about and practices of bound labor to service it—ideas and practices that were a world apart from Britain and the Gold Coast.[27]

Chapter 3

Barbados

The island of Barbados appeared an unlikely location for the transformation of British and West African labor systems, and for the creation of new forms and organization of work to support the agriculture and manufacturing that took place on integrated plantations. When the first Englishmen set foot on the island in 1625 it was all but completely covered by a forbiddingly dense and almost impenetrable forest. In addition to scattered evidence of earlier Arawak inhabitants who had abandoned the island almost a century earlier, the English found a great many wild hogs, fresh water, and plentiful supplies of fish in the surrounding waters. The English returned in 1627, this time intent on establishing a permanent settlement. Within a quarter-century Barbados had become the richest of England's American colonies. During this epochal first generation it was white Britons who dominated the bound workforce, carving out plantations from the forest and soil of the island, and powering a radical new system of labor, informed by and yet dramatically different from British precedents.[1]

Lois Carr and Lorena Walsh have observed that in the Chesapeake the "customs of the mother country might be modified in the light of New World conditions, usually to the detriment of the laborer, but they could not be entirely eradicated." On Barbados, however, a society quickly developed in which some of the most oppressive forms of English labor were taken up and strengthened by an increasingly powerful planter elite, whose members operated with relatively little interference from England and with even less regard for customary restraint in the deployment and treatment of a servile workforce. Although a handful of slaves were present on Barbados from the time of its first settlement, made up of some Africans and a few indigenous peoples from elsewhere in the Americas, the island was prepared for agriculture and the first plantations cleared and worked by a predominantly white workforce from the British Isles. Tens of thousands of bound workers from the British Isles lived and worked, and many died, under an unprecedentedly harsh regime that paved the way for their replacement by enslaved Africans a generation later. Living beyond English law, society, and culture, elite planters on Barbados created integrated plantations that would, with the introduction of sugar cultivation, make them fabulously wealthy. Largely free of English oversight, tradition, and law, they perfected a violent and oppressive system of bound labor to power the plantations that generated such wealth for them and for the mother country.[2]

The first English settlement was established at Holetown, near the center of the western coast of the island. It had been sponsored by the merchant house of the brothers Sir William and Sir Peter Courteen, but they failed to secure a charter or any official sanction for their activities, and in July 1627 Charles I made a proprietary grant of the island to Scotsman James Hay, Earl of Carlisle. A subsequent battle between the Courteens and Carlisle ended with victory for the latter. Preoccupied with religion and politics at home, Charles I granted Carlisle enormous power over the infant colony. Carlisle then allowed a group of London merchants to outfit and organize their own expedition to the island. In the spring of 1628 they established a base on Carlisle Bay on the southwestern edge of the island, about seven miles south of the original Holetown settlement. The first task facing settlers was the backbreaking work of clearing heavily forested areas and converting the land to productive agriculture, all of which would require a substantial amount of labor. Although many Caribbean islands and the nearby South American mainland had significant indigenous populations who might constitute such workforces, the English had to bring laborers to Barbados. As yet the English were only marginally involved in the trade for slaves on the West African coast, although privateers and pirates occasionally captured ships laden with enslaved Africans and then sold this human cargo at low prices to English colonists. By and large it was men and women from the British Isles, and English forms and precedents, that gave shape to the workforce that cleared the island and created and worked its plantations.[3]

The land adjacent to the coast was the first to be partially cleared, and crops were planted between the roots and stumps of recently felled trees. Sir Henry Colt, visiting the island in 1631, was far from impressed: "Your

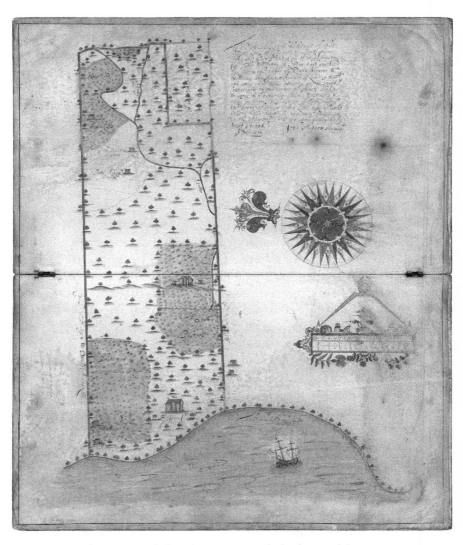

Figure 6. John Hapcott, "This plott representeth the forme of three
hundred acres of Land part of a Plantation called the Fort Plantation of
which 300 acres Cap. Thos. Middleton of London hath purchased . . ."
(1646). Courtesy of the John Carter Brown Library at Brown University.
This shows the early development of Barbadian plantations, with the
clearing of some but by no means all of the trees and woodland.

ground & plantations shewes whatt you are, they lye like ye ruines of some village lately burned,—here a great timber tree half burned,—in an other a rafter singed all black. Ther stands a stubb of a tree above two yards high, all ye earth covered black with cenders nothing is cleer . . . all things carringe ye face of a desolate & disorderly shew to ye beholder." Yet the work of clearing the heavily forested island was monumental. The map of the Fort plantation, created two decades or more after the plantation had been laid out, showed that although many trees and stumps remained, a great many more had been cleared. Even Sir Henry Colt was impressed, remarking that "Ye ground is heer moor cleerer than any of ye rest." The forests were neither quickly nor easily cleared, however, and John Oldmixon recorded that for years the branches of felled trees "were so thick and unmanageable as requir'd more Help than could be procur'd, to lop and remove them off the Ground."[4]

After clearing the land adjacent to the coast, the formidable work of clearing the Barbadian interior was soon under way, and it proceeded at a brisk pace. When Richard Ligon arrived in Carlisle Bay in September 1647, a mere two decades after the arrival of the first settlers in Holetown, he found twenty-two ships at anchor, with smaller boats ferrying goods, crops, and people between ship and shore. The bustle of the port, with staple crops being loaded onto ships as fast as laborers, slaves, foodstuffs, and other goods were unloaded, impressed Ligon as being as "quick stirring and numerous, as I have seen it below the bridge at London." The evidence of the rapid transformation of the landscape was everywhere to be seen, and Ligon related "what had been told me by the most ancient Planters, that we found there, and what they had by tradition from their Predecessors. For, few or none of them that first set foot there, were now living." These men told Ligon that over the past two decades numerous ships had arrived from England filled "with men, provisions, and working tooles, to cut down the Woods, and clear the ground, so as they might plant provisions to keep them alive."[5]

Ligon indirectly acknowledged the scale of the work involved in making Barbadian land ready for commercial agriculture when he noted that even though some cheap land was still available, it was preferable to rent or purchase a cleared "plantation that was already furnisht, and stockt with Servants, Slaves . . . a sugar worke, and an Ingenio": the latter, spelled in different ways in seventeenth-century English texts, is a rough translation of *ingenio*, the Spanish term for a sugar mill in particular, and the apparatus of sugar processing and manufacture in general. Between 1623 and 1625 the price of Virginia tobacco had doubled, allowing Chesapeake colonists to generate profits by shipping tens of thousands of pounds of tobacco to England. The new arrivals in Barbados were eager to follow suit and make their fortunes from what was at that time the British New World's most valuable staple crop. Inhabiting a frontier society reminiscent of the Chesapeake two decades earlier, the early settlers shipped their first tobacco crop to London within a year of their arrival, but it was "earthy and worthlesse"; this poor quality and a developing glut in the European tobacco markets doomed Barbados tobacco. By the early 1630s islanders were cultivating cotton, and as the price of this commodity fell at the end of the decade, many shifted to indigo. Once again, however, a saturated market depressed prices.[6]

Historians traditionally assumed that the success of sugar proceeded from the failure of these earlier crops. According to this interpretation, by the late 1630s Barbados was struggling from the failures of tobacco, cotton, and indigo, and an externally funded "sugar revolution" transformed the island's fortunes, paving the way for the development of large-scale plantation slavery. It appears likely, however, that limited successes during the 1630s and early 1640s had in fact allowed some planters to amass larger estates and generate profits, and these nascent planter elite were able to reinvest in larger plantations with larger and increasingly diversified labor forces. Moreover, Russell Menard has recently shown that during the 1640s planters continued to grow cotton, tobacco, and indigo, and that servants and then slaves were imported to work all of these crops. Both servant and slave populations continued to increase, and it was only in the later 1640s that sugar began to dominate on increasingly large plantations with rapidly growing bound workforces. Sugar was first used as currency on the island in 1644, and by 1648 some 60 percent of commercial transactions involved payments in sugar. As early as 1645 some 40 percent of the island was planted in sugar, growing to 80 percent (and thus virtually all commercially viable land) by 1767.[7]

With competing proprietors, land claims in the first few years were unclear and often contested. Some extremely large grants of land had been made to a handful of individuals, while many more enjoyed relatively small pieces of land. With remarkable speed all of the land fit for cultivation was taken up, however, and as they began making money from tobacco, cotton, indigo, and finally sugar, the more powerful planters began consolidating their holdings in optimally sized large plantations. By the middle of the seventeenth century, little over two decades after first settlement, a planter class had already taken shape, with a small and powerful group of great planters at its heart. In 1680 the 175 great planters on Barbados, drawn from no more than 159 families, controlled over 54 percent of the island's property, both real and human. Approximately 20,000 whites and nearly 39,000 enslaved Africans were on Barbados in 1680, and thus the great planters who owned half the island composed less than 1 percent of the island's white population and only one-third of 1 percent of the island's population as a whole. Many were second- or third-generation settlers, and sixty-two of these families—including the Allyn, Codrington, Drax, Frere, Guy, Hothersall, Pears, and Yeamans families—had owned plantations on the island since the 1630s. The families of the great planters dominated the Governor's Council or sat in the Assembly, forming a cohesive and commanding ruling elite. By 1680 the highest political, military, and judicial offices were controlled by these elite planters: seventy-seven held at least one such post, and a good many held two, three, or even four simultaneously. As many as 109 of the 175 great planters held office: twenty-five of the remainder were women and Quakers who were ineligible, while virtually all others were absent from the island. The great planters enjoyed nearly unrestrained political and judicial power on Barbados, and they shaped the island to suit their interests.[8]

Within a half-century of first settlement Barbados moved from the margins of the Caribbean to the center of the Atlantic World, generating huge wealth by means of a new crop and the transformation of work and production that it required. Sugar produced this change, making the fortunes and enhancing the power of a select few planters. During the 1630s some planters began experimenting with sugar cane, primarily as a source of animal feed and of fuel. When Brazilian sugar production dropped during the early 1640s, and English investors provided capital and labor, plantation-scale cultivation of sugar rapidly developed in Barbados, securing the colony's future. Technical knowledge and skilled agriculture came from northeastern Brazil, where sugar agriculture and manufacturing were already dependent upon slavery, of both indigenous people and imported West Africans. The Portuguese had long been familiar with West African slavery, and generations before the English arrived in Barbados the Portuguese and the Spanish had adapted African slavery for use in sugar plantations on the eastern Atlantic islands of São Tomé, Madeira, the Canary Islands, then in the western Atlantic islands of Santo Domingo, Puerto Rico, and Cuba, and also on the mainland in Brazil. In the sugar fields, enslaved West Africans were organized into gangs, while free and enslaved foremen supervised the highly skilled slaves who processed the crop and made sugar, many of them mulatto or second- or third-generation creolized Afro-Brazilians. Long familiar with and trusting of the abilities of West Africans, the Portuguese had no hesitation in building their entire sugar-making enterprises on the labor and skills of these men and women.[9]

Yet while the English on Barbados learned about growing and processing sugar from the Brazilians, planters on the island did not replicate the social organization of labor, or (at least initially) the complete dependence on an entirely enslaved workforce. The requirements of sugar farming and production and the potential profits to be realized by integrating these on single plantations encouraged Barbadian planters to deviate from both Portuguese and English precedents. Often combining the roles of cane grower, mill owner, sugar manufacturer, and rum distiller, the owners of English integrated plantations deployed bound laborers, machines, and the land itself in radically new ways, on a dramatically larger scale, and with far higher financial returns than had ever before been known in the English-speaking world. The Portuguese had been using enslaved African labor for two centuries, and in the middle of the seventeenth century the English were only just beginning to trade on the coast of West Africa, primarily for gold rather than slaves. Instead, the English on Barbados continued developing a plantation labor system created over the preceding two decades, built upon English precedents and beliefs, and dependent upon bound English labor. New crops, new conditions, and the absence of customary English restraints upon the power of employers over servants and bound laborers all meant that Barbadian planters had to learn and develop agricultural techniques radically different from anything known in the British Isles, and with sugar they confronted a crop that required as long as eighteen months to mature. Unlike farms in the British Isles, virtually all agricultural work was done by humans. Draft animals played little role, and all digging, planting, weeding, harvesting, and so forth was done by men and women using the simplest of farm tools, mainly hoes, bill hooks, and axes. By developing such an intensive labor system, planters were able to justify the cost of imported bound laborers, keeping them fully occupied throughout the year.[10]

The transition to sugar massively increased the need for labor. In 1645 one planter wrote to his uncle in Scotland, excitedly explaining that those who switched from other crops to sugar "prosper well," and that he had planted his first canes. However:

> want of servants is my greatest bane and will hinder my designe. The bilding of my house and setting Upp of my Ingenue will cost above 50000 of Tobacco because I have not work men of my owen. In January next god willing I shall begin to make sugar. So pray if you come near to any port where shipping comes hither . . . procure and send me [servants]. . . . Lett them be of any sort men women or boys of 14 years of age, what I make not use off and are not serviceable for mee I can exchange with others.

Bound white men, women, and children were needed to plant, tend, and harvest the sugar cane, and then to build and work the sugar mills, the sugar works, and the distilleries.[11]

Circumstances on Barbados and the needs of planters meant that the work and conditions of white laborers changed rapidly, and soon bore little resemblance to familiar patterns of agricultural labor and service in the British Isles. Hilary Beckles concludes that white bound labor in Barbados was "a new and different institution," one that replaced the "traditional values and ideologies of paternalistic master-servant relations" with "the systematic application of legally sanctioned force and violence." In mid-seventeenth-century England, agricultural servants may have represented as much as 10 percent of the wage-earning population, composing approximately half of all hired, full-time rural workers. Such workers were between free and bound, for although this work was strictly regulated by law, the servants were also somewhat protected by the annual, legally enforceable contracts they had entered with farmers. However, the servants who worked the land in Barbados were more bound property than free individuals. The relatively high cost of travel to Barbados meant that longer periods of service were necessary to cover costs, and planters were reluctant to commit themselves to indentures that were as long as ten years. Thus indentures—and servants themselves—became transferable, allowing planters to treat laborers as commodities, and as a significant form of wealth in a society in which manual labor was so vitally important. Local conditions, the new kinds of agriculture and their needs, and the significant political and judicial power of planters all served to limit the rights of indentured servants, and the dwindling supply of land to reward those who survived their indentures encouraged planters to increase their control over a potentially rebellious servant population, including servants who survived their terms of service and remained on the island.[12]

While some servants had voluntarily entered into a contractual agreement, particularly during the earliest years of the colony, indentured servitude in Barbados did little to protect the rights of servants. Long terms of service, the local disease environment, and a brutal work regimen all contributed to high mortality rates among servants: a 1687 list of twelve white servants who had worked on the Newton plantation recorded that five had died in service during the preceding year. The power of planters to define the terms of bound laborers' service was reflected in their ability to mold legislation and government policy in Barbados. The preprinted indenture forms of the later seventeenth century required that prospective indentured servants appear before and be examined by a justice of the peace, so as to ensure that all who signed indentures were "voluntary, free and willing at their own Liberties," rather than those whose labor and bodies had been stolen by "Sinistery means." Nonetheless, these forms remained a record of young Englishmen who "Voluntarily Covenanteth, Promiseth and Granteth" their labor for—in the case of these particular forms—a period of four years, in return for passage, "Meat, Drink, Apparel, Lodging and Washing," but with the terms and nature of labor defined not by English custom or law but rather by "the Custom of the Country" in Barbados. Moreover, at "the end of the said Term" the planter would again be bound by local practice, "to give, pay and allow unto" the bound laborer no more than what was allowed to him or her "according to the Custom of the Country." Barbadian practices, not British traditions, determined the conditions of servitude and the treatment of servants.[13]

Indentured servants in Barbados served for far longer periods than English annual laborers, from between three and ten years, and they were bought, sold, and traded in a manner unknown in Britain. Servants in Barbados enjoyed virtually no rights that were enforceable in planter-dominated local courts, and they were controlled by a brutal planter class whose members did not hesitate to use violence to control and punish members of their workforce. Planters' control of the courts, Council, and Assembly meant that servants could expect little relief or redress from the legal system. Disputes between planters and their bound servants were heard before one of the island's courts of common pleas, presided over by "One Judge, and Four Assistants" appointed by the governor. Although Barbados had been settled for barely a generation, this "ancient Custom and practice within this Island" was enshrined as the cardinal principle of law and enforcement, and custom and practice indicated that planters exercised enormous power over their bound servants. Any servant "judged to bring any suit frivolously" against his or her master could expect to receive thirteen lashes: alternatively, a bound servant who shall "unjustly trouble his Master or Mistress with Suits in Law" could have his term of bound labor increased by the planter-dominated court. Few clauses of Barbadian laws referred to the rights of bound servants, while many referred to the power and authority of planters over their laborers. It is little surprise that the surviving records are so silent on successful cases brought by servants against masters.[14]

Throughout the seventeenth and early eighteenth centuries, the large majority of bound white servants arriving in Barbados were male. Even among the earliest voluntary migrants, young men predominated. Of the forty-nine passengers aboard the *Virgin*, which sailed to Barbados in 1639, only eight were "servant maids." The number of voluntary migrants declined rapidly in the years after the island's first settlement, but the preponderance of males continued: not one of the twenty-six laborers traveling to Barbados in 1683 whose indenture forms survive in a collection in the Folger Library was female. But as early as the 1640s, planters who faced an uncertain supply of voluntary laborers were increasingly dependent upon involuntary unfree workers drawn from English and Scottish prisons, or from the ranks of captives from wars and rebellions. Mixed in with these were an unknown number of boys and youths, kidnapped, spirited, and "Barbadosed" for work on the island. The result was a largely male servile class, composed of people from a surprisingly wide array of occupations. Men leaving London included not just husbandmen and laborers, but also weavers, shoemakers, blacksmiths, clothiers, bricklayers, tailors, butchers, carpenters, coopers, gardeners, gunners, soldiers, woolmakers, and even occasional buttonmakers, glaziers, drapers, pipemakers, scriveners, silversmiths, tallow chandlers, vintners, and wigmakers. Few would continue in their previous occupations; most would labor in the sugar fields.[15]

Servants who survived their often lengthy terms and were subsequently freed faced few opportunities and many legal restrictions intended to keep them subservient. In December 1652 the Barbados Assembly passed an act to deal with the problem of "loose, idle, vagrant persons in and about this Island, who are of no certain employment, and have no constant residence, or place of abode." Amplifying contemporary English attitudes and laws, this act empowered the planter justices of the peace to record the names of these former servants and send this information to the governor, who might act to ensure "that all such persons may be employed in some necessary work." With all of the island's usable land taken up, even the fortunate servants who survived could seldom hope to secure the land and independence that service in husbandry might have earned them in England. Consequently, they found themselves permanently at the mercy of a developing plantocracy that required them to work in support of the sugar economy.[16]

During the 1640s Barbados began developing the large-scale integrated sugar plantations that were so completely dependent upon ruthlessly exploited bound labor, at the same time that England, Ireland, and Scotland were being torn apart by the Wars of the Three Kingdoms. The tremendous political and social dislocation at home provided the backdrop for the creation of a new society and labor system in Barbados. Over the course of the decade, many smaller farmers who had worked owner-operated plantations with at most two or three servants gave way to larger plantations dependent upon large bound workforces. During these years a shift from bound white to enslaved African laborers began in earnest, but throughout the decade white laborers remained integral. By the middle of the 1640s there were approximately 8,300 planters on the island, and probably more than 20,000 other whites, most of them bound laborers. In 1641 the average plantation was thirty-seven acres with 1.5 bound workers, most of whom were indentured servants: a decade later the average plantation had grown to eighty-three acres and depended upon the labor of six indentured servants and eleven African slaves.[17]

The transition from bound white to enslaved African labor was built upon the hope that sugar could succeed where previous crops had failed. Ligon, who arrived just as sugar was taking a firm hold on the island, recorded that "when the Canes had been planted three or four years, they found that to be the main Plant to improve the value of the whole Island: And so bent all their endeavours to advance their knowledge in the planting, and making Sugar: Which knowledge, though they studied hard, was long a learning."[18] The skill, technology, and capital that were necessary for successful sugar production were made worthwhile by enormous potential profits. Despite the fact that "the great work of Sugar-making, was but newly practised by the inhabitants" of Barbados, Ligon and his associates were able to negotiate the lease of a well-equipped and fully functioning plantation. It consisted of:

> 500 Acres of Land, with a faire dwelling house, an Ingenio [sugar works] plac't in a roome of 400 foot square; a boyling house, filling room, Cisterns, and Still-house; with a Carding house, of 100 foot long, and 40 foot broad; with stables, Smiths forge, and rooms to lay provisions of Corne and Bonavist [beans]; Houses for *Negroes* and *Indian* slaves, with 96 *Negroes*, and three *Indian* women, with their Children; 28 Christians, 45 Cattle for worke, 8 Milch Cowes, a dozen Horses and Mares.[19]

During these early sugar years many planters remained "ignorant in three main points"—namely, the "manner of Planting, the time of Gathering, and the right placing of their Coppers in their Furnaces"—so although Ligon "found many Sugar-works set up, and at work . . . the sugars they made . . . were hardly worth the bringing home for *England*." When he left the island just over two years later, the planters "were much better'd; for then they had the skill to know when the Canes were ripe. . . . Besides they were grown greater proficients, both in boyling and curing them, and had learnt the knowledge of making them white. . . ." As a result sugar "is now grown the soul of trade in this Iland." When Ligon departed in 1650, the island had the largest population of any English settlement in the New World. A year later Barbados exported approximately 3,750 tons of sugar to England, rising to over 9,500 tons by 1669.[20]

Sugar was the most valuable of all the staple crops grown by English colonists in the New World, earning tremendous profits for planters and completely transforming the island, which soon boasted "buildings very fair and beautiful, and . . . houses like castles. By 1700 English planters in Barbados, Jamaica, and the Leeward Islands supplied almost half of all of the sugar consumed in Europe. Bridgetown had become "the finest and largest" city "in all the Islands, if not in all the English colonies abroad," serving as focal point for one of the richest trades in agricultural output in the world. Sugar and consequent commercial success, together with political and social stability, made Barbados an attractive venue for investment. Land prices rose rapidly throughout the seventeenth century, with the remarkably cohesive planter elite controlling most of the richest land in the English empire. Many of the great sugar magnates of the late seventeenth and eighteenth centuries had been present since early on, originally surrounded by numerous small yeoman farmers and planters. Up until the advent of large-scale sugar agriculture, labor had been more valuable than land, because of the cost of clearing it. Thereafter the profits to be made from sugar increased the value of land, encouraging the displacement of smaller landholders and the subdivision of the largest landholdings into more manageable plantations, in turn creating optimally sized plantations of between three and five hundred acres. The process of consolidation was rapid: in 1673 more than two-thirds of the colony's arable land had been composed of a great many plots and plantations of fewer than three hundred acres, but the 1680 census revealed that the 175 largest planters held over half of all landed property. Contemporary observer John Scott concluded that between 1645 and 1667 the number of landowners had declined from 11,200 to 745, an exaggeration, to be sure, but an accurate reflection of a significant trend. Richard Ligon's mid-seventeenth-century map indicates the extent of plantation agriculture on Barbados, and already the names of many of the elite planters and their great plantations can be found on his map. By the late seventeenth century these Barbadian planters were the wealthiest men, by far, in British America, and the sugar they shipped to the British Isles was more valuable than all of the tobacco and other crops and products shipped from all of the mainland North American colonies combined. The rise of this cohesive and integrated class of elite planters was, in Richard Dunn's words, "the chief distinguishing feature of island society," first in Barbados, and later throughout the English Caribbean.[21]

The systems of sugar agriculture and processing that developed in Barbados, and then spread out around the Caribbean and eventually into mainland North America, were impressive accomplishments. Barbados moved from the margins of the English empire to the commercial center, as its trade in people, sugar, and goods with West Africa, the British Isles, and other British colonies increased. Integrating and then redefining New World and traditional English farming methods in the development of an unfamiliar crop; learning intricate and highly specialized harvesting, sugar production, and distilling techniques; and utilizing bound labor in a manner and on a scale unknown in their homeland, planters created a singularly efficient integrated plantation system. Their combination of specialized

Figure 7. Richard Ligon, "A topographicall Description and Admeasurement of the Yland of Barbadoes in the West Indyaes," in Ligon, *A True & Exact History of the Island of Barbados* (London, 1657). By permission of the University of Glasgow Library, Department of Special Collections. Ligon's map shows the development of plantations in the midst of the transition to sugar, with most plantations still hugging the coastline. The map indicates that some of the interior remained wooded and relatively unpopulated, with hogs running wild, and slaves running away toward the highlands of the "Scotland" district. The camels and the solitary indigenous person are somewhat more fanciful, and are likely a reflection of the artistic license of Ligon's map maker.

agriculture and semi-industrial processing and manufacturing created sites of production more akin to a modern factory than to an early modern farm. All aspects of sugar agriculture and manufacture occurred on the plantation and were undertaken by bound laborers, revolutionary developments that transformed first Barbados and then other Caribbean colonies. Commercial success was achieved by the appropriated labor of tens of thousands of British servants and hundreds of thousands of African slaves. While bound labor had played a significant role in the early development of Barbados, including the clearing of the forests and the early production of tobacco and indigo, it was the growing of sugar cane and the production of sugar cane, rum, and other products that revolutionized the labor of large numbers of white Britons and countless enslaved Africans.[22]

The traditions of service in husbandry that provided, at least in theory, a relatively equitable arrangement between farmer and servant were superseded in Barbados by the development of radically different power relations between masters and white servants. The more extreme forms of pauper and vagrant apprenticeships, and the binding out of people as long-term servants, were the English precedents that in Barbados developed into the defining features of the plantation labor system. Indeed, in the mid-seventeenth century many of those sent from the British Isles were already unfree, including convicts, vagrants, and prisoners of war. The nature of this labor force helped to justify the deployment of these unfortunates as bound laborers with little freedom and few prospects. The law passed by the Barbados Assembly in 1661 for "the good Governing of Servants" began with the observation that the "Interest and Substance of this Island consists in the Servants brought to and disposed of in the same, and in their Labour during the Term they have to serve." Some of the most oppressive and least free forms of English labor would be reworked in Barbados into the "custom of the country," a new unfree labor system for a new crop in a new world.[23]

PART II

British Bound Labor

Chapter 4

"White Slaves"

British Labor in Early Barbados

The social, economic, and political situation of the British Isles aligned neatly with the needs of the developing Barbadian sugar economy, for conditions in the British Isles encouraged the migration of laborers to Barbados. Enclosure and engrossment, rising population and prices, and declining wages combined to leave many young Britons with limited or no employment, while vagrancy laws, rebellions, and wars created a surplus population of men who were a burden to the state. Yet conditions on the island soon made migration unattractive even for impoverished and unemployed English agricultural workers. Opportunities for the voluntary servants declined rapidly, and as conditions of labor deteriorated the supply of voluntary servants diminished dramatically. By the mid-1650s many in the British Isles would travel to labor on the island only if they were "Barbadosed," meaning that they had been kidnapped or "spirited" away, illegal practices that may have helped secure a few more bound workers but rendered Barbados an increasingly unattractive option for voluntary laborers. Desperate for the workers on whom they depended, planters and their English agents worked hard to secure state support for regular shipment of large numbers of unfree, bound laborers, and by the mid-1640s Barbados had the largest market in bound white laborers in English America. Plantations on Barbados, including early sugar agriculture and manufacture, were fashioned by English, Scottish, and Irish bound laborers. Many died, but by the mid-1650s some 12,000 bound white men, women, and children labored on Barbadian plantations.[1]

With England preoccupied by the Civil War and the ensuing Wars of the Three Kingdoms, a Barbadian workforce composed of vagrants, criminals, and prisoners had few rights and protections. Thus, although it was grounded in the traditions of early modern English service and labor, indentured servitude in Barbados quickly developed into a radically different labor system. As historian Trevor Burnard has observed, "It took little time for the English coming to the islands to be caught up in a system that seemed internally logical and perfectly natural." Freed from the restrictions of English courts and customs, planters deployed and controlled bound laborers whom they judged to be vagrants, criminals, and prisoners rather than free-born English agricultural workers. Planters treated their bound laborers as chattel, "gathered upp . . . transported . . . [and then] Exchang'd for Commodities . . . at different rates & according to their condition or Trade by which they are rendered more usefull and beneficiall to their Masters." Initially, English officials had believed that at the conclusion of their terms of service, indentured servants would become "free to plant for themselves," and the Earl of Carlisle had intended that once they had completed their terms of service, all indentured servants would receive ten acres of land as part of their "freedom dues." However, the small size of the island, the growing power of large landholders, and the latter's absolute dependence on subservient cheap labor in order to make a profit from staple crops all meant that very few servants were able to achieve the dream of land ownership and a decent life. The names of only fifty-nine of the approximately two thousand servants who left Bristol for Barbados between 1654 and 1675 appear on the list of landholding freemen in the island's census of 1679, and even these most likely owned small, marginal plots.[2]

In 1639 English aristocrat Thomas Verney wrote to his father requesting twenty able men, including several with specific skills, and he later returned to England and persuaded a number of men from his family's estate in Buckinghamshire to travel back with him to Barbados as indentured servants. Verney, however, like other Barbados planters, did not treat his servants well. After some died and others fell ill through overwork in the hot climate, he found that he could not afford to support nonworking servants and so sold their indentures, and then wrote to his father requesting a new cohort of healthy servants. He made sure to request that his father conceal the truth about what had happened to the members of the original group. Verney was all too aware that it would be difficult to persuade more of the family's servants and retainers in England to travel voluntarily to Barbados, and he suggested that his father might secure a ready supply of bound workers "with the great help of Bridewell and the prisons."[3]

Thus, as early as the late 1630s, barely a decade after the colonization of Barbados, this planter recognized that the supply of voluntary white servants was drying up, and that vagrants, convicts, and other bound men might supply the deficit. Verney's treatment of servants, even men from his family's estate, as little more than chattel was typical of Barbados planters who bought, traded, sold, and even gambled servants whom the law regarded as taxable property rather than as individuals. Such treatment, to say nothing of hunger, poor clothing, and insufficient shelter, meant that even during the earliest years of the colony, voluntary indentured servants did everything possible to escape from Barbados. Writing of his visit to the island in 1631, Sir Henry Colt recalled that white laborers "continually pestred our shipp," and that forty "of ye planters servants when I was ther, stoll away in a Dutch pinnace." It is scarcely surprising that the number of men and women who voluntarily signed indentures to serve on the island's plantations declined rapidly.[4]

Contemporaries were all too aware of the significance of the island's bound workforce, and in 1664 a committee of the Council of Foreign Plantations began a list of recommendations for the improvement of English colonies with the observation: "It being universally agreed that people art the foundation and Improvement of all Plantations and that peopl. art increased principally by Sending of Servants thither, It is necessary that a Settled course be taken for the furnishing them with servants."[5] The authors of these recommendations made no distinction along racial lines, simply noting that "Servants are either Blacks or Whites," and it was labor rather than race that initially defined workers on the early Barbadian plantations. The committee went on to note that while merchants had traditionally depended upon white servants, this had become a worryingly uncertain and insufficient source of labor as fewer and fewer Britons were willing to travel to Barbados. Suggesting that an act of Parliament might be necessary, the committee recommended various measures "for a more . . . orderly Supply," including the transportation of "all felons and such as are condemned to death" for a period of seven years' service, "all Sturdy beggars . . . and other incorrigible Rogues and Wanderers" for a period of five years, as well as the "poore and Idle" of English villages and parishes for an unspecified time. With magistrates and the Crown sharing the price paid for each of these felons and vagabonds, the task of ridding British society of undesirables was potentially a profitable one for the authorities. The committee relied upon experience and common practice when drawing up these

recommendations, for from the late 1640s on a majority of the white servants shipped to Barbados were convicts, rebels, or prisoners of war. Usually barred from returning to the British Isles on pain of death, and quite
likely to die before completing their lengthy terms of service, many must
justifiably have felt that they were bound laborers for life. If the earliest,
voluntary indentured servants had been free men and women looking to
improve their lives, these people were swiftly replaced by unfree bound
laborers, who had not come to Barbados by choice. Oldmixon recorded
that white servants were classed in two categories: "such as sell themselves
in *England*, *Scotland*, and *Ireland*, for 4 Years, or more; and such as are
transported by the Government from those three Kingdoms, for Capital
Crimes."[6]

As a result of the increasing number of involuntary bound white laborers in Barbados, visitors and planters alike were inclined to view the labor
force of Scottish, Irish, and even English vagrants, criminals, and prisoners
as being of low social and moral worth, as dangerous, expendable, and in
need of forceful control. Writing in 1654, Henry Whistler articulated this
outlook perfectly: "This Island is the Dunghill wharone England doth cast
forth its rubidg[.] Rodges and hors and such like peopell are thos which
are generally Broght hear: A rodge in England will hardly make a cheater
heare: a Baud brought ouer puts one a demuor comportment, a whor if
hansume makes a wife for some rich planter."[7]

As plantation agriculture took hold of Barbados, the rights and the
prospects of the laborers on whom the system depended dwindled, and
there existed an unwillingness among planters to acknowledge the rights of
current or even former bound servants who were nominally free men. What
was perhaps of the greatest significance was planters' fast-developing sense
of bound laborers as a new kind of workforce, inferior and contemptible,
composed of commodities to be utilized rather than free-born individuals
with rights. Richard Ligon acknowledged this commodification of labor in
the most explicit terms when he alluded to laborers as property, writing
that among the "Commodities these Ships bring to the Island; are, *Servants*
and *Slaves*, both men and women," before going on to list less valuable
imports such as livestock, tools, and so forth.[8]

Merchants, civic authorities, and colonial proprietors in the British Isles
all encouraged the shipment of laborers to Barbados, but few ventured to
the island themselves, and they little comprehended how quickly and how
completely servitude on a Barbadian sugar plantation differed from English

apprenticeship and service in husbandry. Many of the moral imperatives that underlay traditional agrarian labor relationships in early modern England were abandoned, and new attitudes and codes of practices sanctioned the brutal exploitation of bound workers. Servants were the largest expense for planters, and apart from sugar itself, servants constituted the most easily transferable embodiment of capital. Planters were free to buy and sell indentured servants, to bequeath them in wills or to win or lose them in games of chance, and these servants could be used as collateral for loans and were taxed as property. In theory it was the labor of indentured servants that could be treated in this fashion, but in practice and most certainly in the experience of the servants themselves, they were commodified, body and soul. English servants in husbandry had annual contractual agreements with specific individuals, and the contract died along with either party. In Barbados the contract did not die along with the planter, and indentured servants were disposed of as part of his estate. The "custom of the country" overrode the English common law in defining relations between planters and indentured servants, illuminating both planters' attitudes to their servants and these men and women's declining options and increasing hopelessness. Institutionalized, and given the full force of law by a servant and slave code in 1661, the promise of indentured servitude envisioned by the Earl of Carlisle evaporated. Planters succeeded in fashioning a system in which servants were not free people contracted to work for others, but were instead a capital investment with many of the characteristics of property. While in England many workers enjoyed a relatively high degree of freedom outside of the time they labored for employers and masters, in Barbados all of their time was owned and controlled by masters who proved eager to exploit this advantage to the full.[9]

During the 1640s an average of two thousand white laborers traveled each year to the island, a fourfold increase in the number of servants brought annually to the island during the preceding decade. The number continued to rise, reaching 3,000 per annum by the early 1650s, at which point there were about 13,000 indentured servants alive on Barbados, a telling indicator of high mortality rates and the desperate attempts by bound laborers to leave either before or after their terms of service ended. Richard Dunn records that in 1683 a total of 712 white servants and freemen were recorded as arriving in Barbados, while 446 people departed from the island. It is unclear what proportion of these were servants or former servants, and some were planters, merchants, and others returning home from the island or leaving it for only a short time. What is clear, however, is that the mortality rates for white servants were high throughout the seventeenth and early eighteenth centuries, particularly for those convicts and prisoners condemned to serve for a decade. Many, quite possibly a large majority of such servants, did not survive their terms of service, and when this is taken into account, the departure of 446 and the arrival of 712 whites would be far from sufficient to maintain white population figures. Facing dire poverty and near starvation, those former servants who did survive and were unable to secure work in the militia or as overseers abandoned the island if they could. As early as 1667 one Barbadian lamented that as many as 12,000 white men had already left Barbados, "wormed out" of their small settlements by greedy neighbors: the island was weakened, he claimed, because land was monopolized into so few hands.[10]

The ranks of bound whites on Barbados were soon dominated by homeless and jobless vagrants, by those who had been incarcerated in English and Scottish jails for a variety of offenses, and by the civilian and military prisoners of war, captured in wars and rebellions between 1639 and 1746. By and large this was a predominantly male involuntary workforce, many of whose lives were forfeit to the state. Planters treated such men as expendable bound workers who could be worked long, hard, and even to death, poorly fed and housed, and few in this situation could hope for a better life in the future. They were exactly what planters sought, cheap and expendable labor, and they powered the first Barbadian plantations and the early development of the island's sugar economy. While the flow of prisoners of war, convicts, and vagrants may have been irregular, they were nonetheless ubiquitous in the workforce as the shift from tobacco, cotton, and indigo to sugar took place. All were men (and sometimes women) who had lost even more of the rights stripped away from voluntary indentured servants, and they were often bound for as long as a decade, more than a life sentence for many of them. In Barbados planters found it easy to treat bound white laborers in new ways, as workers with virtually no rights, as commodities to be used with little if any restraint.

Whether correctly or not, contemporaries believed that white servants were more susceptible to tropical diseases, including yellow fever, edema (dropsy), and yaws, than were the African slaves who eventually replaced them. Rather than concluding that white servants should be protected, however, masters generally sought to extract as much labor as quickly as possible, for the smallest outlay of expenses, in order to maximize profits.

Visitors to the island were awed by the sight of white servants, many without shoes and shirts, laboring in the fields alongside slaves. Writing in the mid-seventeenth century, Richard Ligon observed that slaves "are kept and preserv'd with greater care than the servants . . . [who] have the worser lives, for they are put to very hard labor, ill lodging, and their dyet very sleight." Without doubt, the systematic and brutal exploitation of white bound laborers eased the transition to slavery on Barbados, for planters had become accustomed to treating their plantation workers as unfree, lacking in virtually all human rights, and expendable.[11]

The deteriorating socio-economic situation in the late sixteenth-and early seventeenth-century British Isles meant that an easily available supply of involuntary laborers could be found wandering the streets and in the jails of both England and Scotland. The 1664 report of the Council of Foreign Plantations acknowledged that middlemen in England had made "it their profession to . . . gaine poor or idle persons" who were "gathered upp" and sent to New World colonies, where they were purchased "at different rates & according to their condition or Trade by which they are rendered more usefull and beneficiall to their Masters." The committee proposed that Parliament should enhance this previously voluntary system, consigning the "poor and Idle" of towns and countryside alike, "all Sturdy beggars . . . and other incorrigible Rogues and Wanderers," as well as "all felons and such as art condemned to death" to terms of five, seven, or more years of service in England's New World colonies.[12]

Vagrants and convicts formed a substantial part of the bound white workforce in seventeenth-century Barbados. English magistrates shared with the Crown the fees paid by merchants for the indentures of vagrant children, giving officials added incentive to round up homeless and jobless young boys. Typical were Francis Cherry, who had "neither family not mother living," and George Fawre, who was "very poore and not able to maintain himself." Both were sent to Barbados by London magistrates in 1681. These boys were only eleven years old, bound to labor on sugar plantations for as long as a decade, although there was a very good chance that neither would survive the term of service. Vagrants and convicts were also sent to Barbados from Scotland. Early in the seventeenth century Edinburgh magistrates petitioned the Privy Council of Scotland, complaining that the city was "filled and pestred with a number of theives and whores," who ignored regular punishments and banishment and "remaine in the toune committing the greatest of villanies." The magistrates requested and subsequently received permission "to send all such men and women who shall be legallie found guiltie of whoredom or theift aff this kingdome with the first conveniency to Barbados," thus beginning the process of sending Scots prisoners to labor and die in the Caribbean. This involuntary migration did not lessen until the Navigation Acts of the 1660s excluded Scotland from England's colonial trade. Encouraged by various loopholes, however, Scottish merchants continued to present themselves as men who were working "to promote the Scottish and Inglish plantation . . . for the honour of their countrey," and who were striving "to frie the kingdom of the burden of many strong and idle beggars, Egiptians, common and notorious whore and theives and other disolute and louse persons banished or stigmatized for gross crymes." While the process started as a way of ridding Scottish cities of more obdurate criminals, it was not long before young men and women who had done little wrong found themselves sent to Barbados in chains, most likely to an early death and with little hope of ever again seeing their homes. Thus when Edinburgh apprentices and "trades youthes" began carousing and upsetting the peace, an apprentice mason and an apprentice painter were seized as the ringleaders of "the said tumult" and were banished to Barbados: in all probability, both were in their mid-teens.[13]

Authorities regarded the crimes of homelessness and joblessness as justification for imprisonment and banishment to Barbados. In an effort "to disburden the kingdome of strong and idle beggars, vagabonds" and the like, the merchants and master of the ship *Glasgow* requested and received authorization to require "all sheriffes, stewarts, justices of peace and magistratts of burghes . . . to apprehend and delyver to the petitioners all such persons as shall be condemned by their sentence as idle vagabonds, haveing no means or way of subsistence but by stealing and begging, to the effect they may be caryed to the plantations in the foresaid ship."[14] It seems likely that the *Glasgow* left Scotland with many prisoners on board, to be traded and sold to planters and then replaced with sugar for the journey back. As late as 1685, Christopher Jeaffreson reported that as many as five hundred Scottish convicts were ready for transportation from Edinburgh. Ordinary Scots men and women had thus been first criminalized and then commodified, and during the 1650s and 1660s a great many were transported as bound laborers, deprived of rights and liberty, to be bought and sold and left forever on an island thousands of miles from their homeland. To the merchants who sent servants to Barbados, these men and women were recorded in their ships' inventories as "freight," or as "half-freight" in the case of juveniles.[15]

Not all of the Scots transported from jails were vagrants and common criminals. Prisoners of conscience were sent to labor in Barbados throughout the seventeenth century, and especially in the wake of the rebellions in 1666 and 1679 in which Presbyterian Covenanters rose up against the restoration of the episcopacy in Scotland. For example, in 1655 four young men were transported to Barbados for ten years after they had been found guilty of interrupting the sermon of a minister: all were quite likely Covenanters. Following the rebellion in 1666 the Scottish Privy Council appointed a committee to examine imprisoned religious rebels, in order to establish the creed of those imprisoned and their willingness to renounce their beliefs and pledge allegiance to Charles II and the new religious order. Those deemed the most incorrigible, who had "risen in armes and are by their oune confession clearly guilty of rebellion and refuse the alledgeance and Declaration," were, on the order of the King and his privy Council, deemed to be "guilty of rebellion [and] to be sent to Barbadoes with the first opportunity."[16]

In addition to vagrants and criminals, the frequent wars and rebellions of the seventeenth and early eighteenth centuries provided the English and then the British state with large numbers of prisoners. European laws of war sanctioned extreme measures against soldiers and civilians alike: "With Pyrates, Rebels, Robbers, Traytors, and Revoltes," observed William Fulbecke in 1602, "the Law of Armes is not to be observed and kept."[17] Expensive to maintain, imprisoned rebels and prisoners of war could usually expect to be executed or, if they were very fortunate, pardoned and then released. The labor needs of England's New World colonies, especially Barbados and then later Jamaica, provided a convenient and indeed profitable alternative for officials who wanted neither to execute tens of thousands nor to release them without penalty. Instead, capital sentences were commuted to banishment to the plantations with a fixed term of service, usually of ten years. The single largest group of prisoners of war and rebellion to be sent to Barbados was dispatched during the period of the island's greatest need for laborers. During the 1640s and 1650s the Wars of the Three Kingdoms resulted in Cromwell's army capturing soldiers and civilians in England, Wales, Scotland, and Ireland. Following the Battle of Worcester in 1651, for example, Oliver Cromwell's army captured some 10,000 prisoners. While many English prisoners were conscripted into the New Model Army and sent to fight in Ireland, some were joined with many thousands of Scottish prisoners who were sent to English colonies as bound laborers, with the greatest number going to Barbados. One survivor of this exodus recorded that he was among a group of 1,300 sent to Barbados, where each was sold for about eight hundred pounds of sugar. No seasoning period to adjust to the climate and conditions was allowed these new servants, and this prisoner recalled, "I had to sweep the plantation yard the first day; on another day I fed the pigs and thereafter I had to do the kind of work usually performed by the slaves. Our food was very bad and consisted only of roots."[18]

Repeat offender vagrants, criminals, and especially prisoners from wars and rebellions had, in the eyes of the law, forfeited their freedom and per-haps even their lives, which provided Barbadian planters with justification for regarding them as so very much less than free-born men with rights and liberties. For all intents and purposes many of these bound white labor-ers became virtual slaves in Barbados. In the coming years, more expensive enslaved Africans were commonly afforded a seasoning period. White ser-vants were not valuable enough to warrant such treatment, yet they had cost enough to make planters eager to extract as much labor as rapidly as possible, before the new arrivals died. Housed in inferior dwellings "almost like dog-houses," and denied virtually any meat as part of a decent diet, a great many did not survive the disease environment, the work regimen, and their decade-long indentures. Of the 1,300 prisoners who had accompanied one prisoner to Barbados, "As far as I know no one returned except myself." Only a fortunate few of the prisoners from the Wars of the Three Kingdoms returned home from Barbados. Among these were Walter Lyon and Thomas Smith, who had been captured during Cromwell's subjection of Scotland, and then "exyled to Barbadoes, where they continued in great slavery and bondag untill his Majestys happy restauration," after which they "returned to Scotland, their native countrey."[19]

A remarkable petition provides an indication of how victims of this proc-ess experienced transport, sale, and labor in Barbados. Having been taken prisoner in 1654, the two authors arrived in Barbados in May 1656 and were promptly sold to planters "according to their working faculties." Suffering the "most insupportable Captivity, they now generally grinding at the Mills, attending the Fornaces, or digging in this scorching island, having nothing to feed on (notwithstanding their hard labour,) but Potatoe Roots, nor to drink but water."[20] These men found themselves being "bought and sold still from one Planter to another," and any infraction led to their being "whipt at their whipping-posts, as Rogues, for their masters pleasure." Condemning those who "deal in slaves and souls of men," the authors complained bitterly at the "sale and slavery of your poor Petitioners." Their published petition to Parliament contained letters and pleas from others in a similar situation, virtually all of whom referred to themselves as slaves, and who wrote not just on their own account but also on behalf of "fellow sufferers left behind" on Barbados. Yet despite such pleas by the fortunate few who returned to Britain, the practice of sending convicts, vagrants, and prisoners to Barbados would continue for almost a century.[21]

A great many prisoners came to Barbados from Ireland. Following the Irish uprising against oppressive English and Scottish planters in 1641, the Irish had recaptured all but Dublin and Derry. A decade later, many Irish volunteers traveled to England to join the Royalist cause, and when captured these Irish Catholics were treated with singular brutality by the Protestant Parliamentarians: Sir William Bereton, for example, hanged every Irish prisoner he took. This set the scene for the English reconquest of Ireland, and for actions against all who resisted. Oliver Cromwell and his armies regarded the Irish not simply as Catholic, but as almost savage, barbarous papists worthy of few, if any, of the rights accorded English and Scottish convicts and prisoners. In September 1649 the defenders of Drogheda refused to surrender, and Cromwell instructed his conquering army to give no quarter. Thousands of men, women, and children were massacred, and Cromwell wrote with enthusiasm that this was "a righteous judgement of God upon these barbarous wretches." He considered it a mercy that many of the survivors were to be "shipped for the Barbadoes." With savage and bloody efficiency, the English armies set about the reconquest of Ireland, and many of those not killed were dispatched to Barbados, Jamaica, and other colonies. One contemporary estimated that some 34,000 men were sent to the Americas, close to one-sixth of Ireland's adult male population, and more of these went to Barbados than to any other colony. In the Clonmacnoise Decrees in December of 1649, Ireland's Catholic hierarchy condemned the English attempt to destroy Catholicism, uproot "the common people" and dispatch them to "the Tobacco Island" (Barbados), and then replace them in Ireland with English soldiers and settlers. English merchants seized their opportunity, petitioning Cromwell for permission to transport Irish prisoners "out of Ireland for planting in the Caribbee Islands," before returning with cargoes of tobacco, sugar, and other crops.[22]

The number of Irish prisoners sent to England's New World colonies is unknown, although it was quite likely in the tens of thousands, the majority of whom would have been transported to Barbados. What is clear, however, is that in addition to being regarded as savage, uncivilized, and without rights, these Irish prisoners arrived in Barbados at what was, for them, a particularly inopportune time. The rapid development of sugar during these years led to a trebling of land value between 1645 and 1655, effectively excluding virtually all who might survive their lengthy term of bound labor from any prospect of eventual land ownership. Imprisoned in Ireland by English invaders, forced to labor in Barbados for planters who did not want them to ever enjoy meaningful freedom and economic sufficiency, despised for their Catholicism, and with their condition countenanced by English authorities, Irish bound laborers had little hope and nothing to lose.[23]

Hilary Beckles has estimated that during the pivotal years between 1650 and 1690 at least 40 and as much as 50 percent of the island's servant population was Irish. It was common for Irish servants to be worked alongside early African slaves. The Irish prisoners were treated with singular brutality by Barbadian planters, who disdained them as illiterate Catholic savages who they feared were likely to join with African slaves in bloody rebellion. Given the nature of their treatment, such fears may have been well founded, and it seems likely that one of the first maroon groups on the island was a multiracial group of about thirty Irish and African slaves and servants who took shelter in the remaining forested land in St. Philip Parish during the mid-1650s.[24]

Rebellion by these bound servants was a constant threat. Richard Ligon observed that "cruell Masters will provoke their Servants so, by extream ill usage, and often and cruell beating, as they grow desperate, and so joyne together to revenge themselves upon them. In 1649 Ligon witnessed the results. The bound laborers' "sufferings being grown to a great height . . . some amongst them, whose spirits were not able to endure such slavery, resolved to break through it, or die in the act." Convinced that a majority of the island's bound white workforce were sympathetic to the planned rebellion, Ligon recorded with relief that it had been betrayed, and that eighteen of their leaders had been executed. As the number of enslaved African laborers grew, the fear of servant rebellion expanded and planters dreaded the forging of an alliance between the Irish and Africans. Militia groups during the latter decades of the seventeenth century appear to have been composed primarily of English and Scotsmen, differentiating them not just from runaway enslaved Africans but also from the Irish. Planters were so terrified of potential alliances between Irish Catholics and black slaves that in March 1689 the island's council ordered free blacks believed to be Catholic to be "sold or transported and sent of[f] this Island to be sold accordingly." For Barbados planters in the mid- to late seventeenth century, the years when the plantation system and racial slavery solidified, a rebellious combination of slaves, Irishmen, and Catholics was the stuff of nightmares, and a rebellion in 1692 featuring Irish Catholics and African slaves saw the nightmare taking a horrifyingly real form, with Irishmen alleged to have prepared to get soldiers on the island drunk and incapacitated.[25]

French Jesuits such as Father Anthony Biet, who arrived in Barbados in 1654, helped keep Catholicism alive, albeit hidden, on the island. As Jennifer Shaw has argued, Irish Catholics maintained religious rituals, especially those surrounding birth and death. Father Biet recorded seeing the cabins of white servants alongside those of slaves, meaning that day-to-day interactions and experiences were shared between servants and slaves. By the late 1660s Barbados was home to substantial Scottish and Irish populations, and Highland Scots likely included Catholics among their number. At the same time, the rising slave population included an undetermined number who had been exposed to and perhaps even converted to Catholicism as slaves of the Portuguese. In the face of this polyglot population, and at a time of a deep-seated and pervasive fear of Catholicism, the efforts of the English government and the island's Assembly to enforce religious conformity on bound and free alike is very understandable. As early as 1667, the Lords of Trade and Plantations in London ordered "all Negro slaves & serv[ants] remaining in the said colonies be instructed in the principles of the same religion," building on previous religious requirements for residents and expanding them to cover African slaves and white servants.[26]

Even after the supply of Irish prisoners had dried up, more prisoners were found in England and Scotland to replace them. Following the Monmouth Rebellion against James II in 1685, over six hundred rebels were sent to labor in New World colonies, and over half of these went to Barbados. They journeyed in terrible conditions, with mortality rates on board the five ships of between 5 and 7 percent, and the survivors were eagerly purchased by planters anxious to replace whites who had lived out their indentures and either fled the island or retreated to small marginal communities, refusing to labor voluntarily for large planters. By this point enslaved

Africans dominated the agricultural workforce. Few of the prisoners had skills that were of direct utility in sugar production—thirty-three of sixty-seven men aboard the *Jamaica Merchant*, for example, were textile workers—yet all were purchased with alacrity. With an average age of 23.6 years they were young, and the ten-year indentures offered planters the opportunity to invest in training these men and to obtain a decent return on their investment through years of increasingly skilled labor. Bound for a long period, these men would differ from their predecessors in that they were less likely to work in the sugar fields, and they enjoyed relatively privileged positions in comparison with the enslaved Africans who now dominated the plantation workforce. Others were employed as militia tenants, white men that large planters were legally bound to employ as a militia force to police the growing population of enslaved Africans and to defend the island against foreign attack. When the new monarchs William and Mary began considering pardoning all of the Monmouth rebels, Governor James Kendall and the Barbados Council protested that this would unfairly harm planters who had "taught them to be boilers, distillers, and refiners, and neglected to teach any others as they would have otherwise have done." An unwillingness to hamper the lucrative sugar trade may have had an effect, for the former rebels were not freed until March 1691, by which time many had already died. The political allegiance of these white men was clearly of less significance to Barbados planters than was their status as bound laborers, albeit skilled artisans rather than the common field workers of earlier generations.[27]

Henry Pitman provided a firsthand account of the experiences of the Monmouth rebels sent to Barbados, recording that he and his brother were among a group of nearly one hundred prisoners "given to JEREMIAH NEPHO; and by him sold to GEORGE PENNE." Pitman was under no illusions about his status, lamenting, "thus we may see the buying and selling of free men into slavery." Pitman's family had paid to ensure better working conditions for him and his brother, but once in Barbados they were both sold to a planter and denied any rights or liberties. Their master was angered by their unhappiness at their situation, and "he grew more and more unkind unto us, and would not give us any clothes. . . . Our diet was very mean." Planters were at liberty to deny convicts and prisoners the most basic rights supposedly guaranteed to white bound laborers, in this case denying adequate food and clothing, and not hesitating to use violence.

When Pitman complained, "My angry Master, at this was greatly enraged . . . he could not content himself with the bare execution of his cane upon my head, arms and back, although he played so long thereon, like a furious fencer, until he had split it in pieces; but he also confined me close prisoner in the Stocks (which stood in an open place), exposed to the scorching heat of the sun; where I remained about twelve hours."[28]

The brothers remained with this master for fifteen months, until debt forced him to sell them to a merchant, after which they "remained in the merchants' hands as goods unsold": Pitman recognized that even with his skill as a surgeon he was a commodity, a piece of property, rather than an individual. Like a great many of the vagrants, convicts, and prisoners of war bound for such lengthy terms, Pitman's brother died in service. Recognizing that he was likely to suffer a similar fate, Henry Pitman contrived to escape Barbados on a small boat, and of the escapees on board, six were prisoners from the Monmouth Rebellion. As one of the few bound whites to escape from the island, Pitman was able to return to the British Isles and publish an angry account of his sufferings. Of the Monmouth rebels who remained, many died before their release, and only five of them are recorded as having managed to survive and go on to secure small and marginal plots of land. A few appear to have become overseers, some continued as wage laborers or militia men on plantations, and others wandered the island dependent upon vestry poor relief. Others presumably left the island.[29]

In the mid-seventeenth century planters began shifting from white servants to black slaves as the latter became a more cost-effective investment, for as white bound laborers became more scarce and thus more expensive, the number of West African slaves increased and their price fell. Richard Dunn posits a rapid change, while Hilary Beckles describes a more gradual transition. The supply of voluntary indentured servants diminished at the very time that expanding sugar agriculture and production required large numbers of laborers, and it is clear that demand for labor far exceeded the supply of bound workers from the British Isles. The criminals, vagrants, and prisoners of war, who from the early 1640s on constituted the bulk of bound white laborers arriving in Barbados, were by definition an occasional and irregular source of bound workers, and planters depended upon the government and merchants for a supply of these unfree laborers. England, and then Britain, would continue to transport political and civil prisoners out of the British Isles for another two centuries, and the rising number of unemployed and homeless vagrants appeared to promise a seemingly limitless supply of workers who could be used and regulated with singular brutality in Barbados. However, the very success of the integrated plantation system developed on Barbados signaled the end of white servitude. By 1680 white servants in Barbados had been all but completely displaced by slaves on most plantations and in related activities: only fishing, dock work, boating, and plantation management remained largely white activities. The process was uneven, and demand for white servants remained strong throughout the seventeenth century, perhaps in part because many of these servants were prisoners of war and rebels with few rights, and planters could expect to benefit from their labor for as long as a decade, placing them in skilled and supervisory positions over the growing enslaved workforce, all at little cost. In 1686 the Barbados Assembly passed a law detailing the conditions of service of political and military prisoners: their decade-long indentures could not be sold off the island, they were prohibited from marrying white servants, they could not be freed before their terms had expired, and those who attempted to escape would be whipped and branded "FT" to mark them as fugitive traitors. The transition from white servitude to black slavery was eased by the existence of thousands of such servants, who could be worked longer and harder than voluntary white servants elsewhere in the British Americas. Thus, as late as the 1680s at least 107 planters purchased the indentures of Monmouth rebels, even though the transition from white servitude to black slavery was well under way. However, for all of the hardships faced by the Monmouth rebels, few were worked as harshly as the Irish prisoners of a generation earlier, and instead of working alongside slaves in the sugar cane fields, most were employed in managerial and more skilled occupations.[30]

The final group of prisoners of war to be shipped to Barbados were Scottish Highlanders, who were banished in the wake of the Jacobite Rebellion of 1745. Over half of nearly three hundred prisoners were sent to Barbados, and most appear to have been spared execution on condition that they bound themselves to London merchant Samuel Smith for transport to the plantations. A handful were young men, such as sixteen-year-old herd boy Francis Reynold from Aberdeenshire, but the large majority were older men: prisoners of war from rebellions were often older than voluntary indentured servants or the vagrants and criminals selected by merchants for transport to the colonies. Angus Balon, miller to the Laird of Ardgloch in Caithness, was forty-nine years old; Thomas Gordon, a farmer on the lands of the Duke of Gordon near Aberdeen, was fifty-eight years old; and Alexander Morrison was a fifty-year-old distiller from the Isle of Mull. The Highlanders sent to Barbados were on average more than thirty-four years old, and nearly 60 percent of them were over thirty years of age. This contrasts sharply with the servants who had voluntarily signed indentures and come to Barbados on board the *Virgin* more than a century earlier, with an average age of under twenty-one. While the prisoners in 1746 may have been popular with Barbadian planters because they were Scots, their age meant that they were close to twice as old as the young male servants and slaves favored by planters. By this point slaves were already responsible for virtually all of the unskilled and the skilled labor on and off plantations, and one of the few remaining jobs for white laborers was policing the enslaved population as overseers or as members of the militia.[31]

Thus, even the infusion of these new Scottish prisoners into the Barbadian workforce did little to revitalize white servitude. By the mid-eighteenth century there were probably fewer than one thousand bound white laborers left on the island, down from some 13,000 in 1652. In 1789 William Dickson referred to the Jacobite prisoners as men "whose lives were justly forfeited to their country," neatly encapsulating their status as far less than voluntary indentured servants, but rather as virtual slaves who owned neither their labor nor their bodies. Dickson reported that over forty years later only one of their number "still survives . . . lodged in the poor-house in Bridgetown, totally blind and superannuated." Each year the Scots and their descendants on the island would treat this man, perhaps their oldest compatriot, to a dinner on St. Andrew's day, the feast day of the patron saint of Scotland.[32]

The ethnicity of white bound laborers was clearly a significant consideration for Barbadian planters. English servants were generally accepted without comment, whereas Irish servants were loathed and feared, and Scots were the most favored and prized of all. Between the mid-sixteenth and mid-seventeenth centuries Barbadian planters regarded Scots as the most able, reliable, and hardworking of white bound laborers, while the Irish were regarded by planters in diametrically opposed terms and were treated very poorly as a result. In 1667 one observer worried that the Irish composed "a very great part" of the population of bound laborers, noting that these most lowly of white servants were "derided by the negroes as white slaves." In the same year Lord William Willoughby, governor of Barbados, wrote that the island had "2000 Irish, I wish I had soe many Scotts for them," and many Barbadian planters would have agreed.[33] When changes in the Navigation Acts had restricted the supply of Scottish servants, the Barbados Assembly petitioned the English government.[34] Governor Willoughby echoed this plea in a letter to the Privy Council, lamenting the "greate want of Servants in this Island."[35]

A decade later Barbadian planters continued to complain about the lack of good servants from the British Isles. A document entitled "Grievances of the Inhabitants of Barbados" recalled, "In former tymes Wee were plentifully furnished wth. Christian servants from England & Scotland, but now Wee can get few English. . . . Nor have Wee many Scotch servants in regard our entercourse wth. that Kingdome is almost wholy cutt off by the Act of Navigacion. . . . And for Irish servants Wee finde them of small value, our whole dependence therefore is upon Negroes.[36] Competing with other British colonies in the Caribbean and on the North American mainland, and with perhaps the worst reputation as a destination for white bound laborers, it is perhaps no surprise that Barbados struggled to secure a sufficient and regular supply of white servants. The dwindling supply of long-term bound white laborers was a vital factor in their shift to enslaved African plantation workers.

While the vast majority of bound white Britons between the late 1620s and the 1660s labored in the fields attending to staple crops, there was always demand for artisans whose skills could be profitably employed on plantations, including carpenters, smiths, and potters. As plantations became integrated units of production, the more work that could be performed on site by the bound workforce, the greater the planter's profits. Skilled workers like joiners, potters, and coopers most likely spent at least some of their time practicing their crafts: in contrast, many of the unskilled laborers who had traveled the four thousand miles to the island spent virtually all of their time in the fields. The erection of new plantation buildings and sugar factories, as well as the creation of the tools and storage facilities for crops and products, and the materials necessary for their safe transportation across and beyond the island, all depended upon skilled workers. Such men were highly desirable, and the indentures of suitably qualified "Mechanicks" usually sold "for much more" than those of unskilled laborers. Twenty-six-year-old blacksmith James Hooper and twenty-two-year-old tailor Humphrey Golding signed indentures and sailed to Barbados in the spring of 1683. Part of the minority of skilled voluntary migrants, and possessing skills that were of value on Barbadian plantations, they could expect to enjoy better conditions during their four-year terms than would have been enjoyed by unskilled bound laborers, especially the many vagrants, convicts, and prisoners who were involuntary migrants. In addition to practicing their crafts, these skilled men could expect to be employed in training Africans, whose learned craftsmanship would by the late seventeenth century render white skilled labor all but unnecessary.[37]

The need for skilled craftsmen on Barbados was such that some felt they could set their own terms: thus, one journeyman carpenter felt able to propose the terms of his own employment, requesting "meat Drink washing and Lodging and all Tools fitting for a Carpenter and threescore pound a year": however, the owners of the plantation balked at his proposals and rejected them. Nonetheless, when men such as the highly skilled joiners Joseph Boroden from Wednam in Buckinghamshire and John Ford of Westbury in Wiltshire arrived in Barbados from Bristol in the second half of the seventeenth century, their ability to fashion not just plantation items but also furniture and other items beyond the ability of less skilled bound laborers rendered them among the most useful and highly valued servants.[38]

Also important were the potters who were able to use local clay and the kilns that appeared all over seventeenth-century Barbados to manufacture the large pots required for the processing of Muscovado sugar. The skills of potters like Ambrose Bissickie, a servant who hailed from Bristol, were invaluable to planters. In fact, by the latter decades of the seventeenth century, planters who owned clay, kilns, and the labor of skilled potters were enhancing their profits by selling sugar pots to neighboring plantations. By 1775 there were at least nineteen pot kilns spread around the island, but the skilled workforce operating them had changed completely, as slaves usurped the position of white craftsmen. Beginning in the later seventeenth century slaves were trained as potters, or were encouraged to use the West African skills in pottery manufacture that some brought with them, and they in turn became an important skilled workforce on the larger plantations.[39]

Dale W. Tomich has observed that sugar works such as the ones that developed on Barbadian integrated plantations bore a "greater resemblance to modern factory production than to the characteristic organization of handicrafts and manufactures in Europe from the sixteenth to the eighteenth centuries." Commercial production of sugar required, above all else, a large labor force, planting, tending, harvesting, hauling, grinding, boiling, and so forth, with much of the work occurring at the same time, requiring division of labor and a high degree of skill and specialization. The seamless integration of these different processes and separate workforces created a successful plantation. Sugar manufacturing was extremely skilled and diffi-cult work. The first skilled sugar makers on Barbados were most likely enslaved Africans from Brazil, but these were soon supplanted by white men, many of them current or former bound laborers, who dominated the highly skilled processes of cane processing and sugar production for the next quarter-century.[40]

Sugar boilers and distillers ranked highly among the servants whose indentures commanded the highest prices, but there was skill and physical strength in virtually all of the work of the sugar plantation. In the fields, laborers leaned over to cut the thick canes, stripping off the leaves and bundling the canes for transportation to the sugar works. The cane was then fed into the mills, and as it passed back and forth a dark cane juice flowed out and then on through pipes and cisterns to the boiling house. There the juice was boiled again and again in a series of copper kettles, with the boiler skimming off impurities. At precisely the right moment, when the sugar had been cleared of all imperfections, the boiler tempered the mix with lime juice to promote crystallization, then rapidly transferred the boiled sugar to cooling pots. The sugar was then packed into clay pots for a semi-refining process, and the molasses allowed to drain off: some would be used as animal and human food, but much would be distilled into rum. Timing and speed were crucial, for once ripe the cane had to be cut before wind, weather, or its own weight toppled and ruined the valuable crop. If the cane were not milled and boiled within a few hours, the juice would ferment, and so during harvest season sugar works operated around the clock: Ligon describes sugar production happening continuously from Monday to Saturday night. Moreover, if boiling sugar was quickened and tempered (by the addition of lime juice, to end the boiling and clean the fluid), or extracted from pots at the wrong time, it could be ruined. One planter informed his plantation manager that it would be in the processing and especially the boiling of sugar that "your cheife skille will be required," warning him to take the "greatest Care Imaginable." Milling and boiling were dangerous at all times, but when undertaken for long periods of time in exceptionally hot conditions, with servants and slaves working well beyond the point of exhaustion, terrible accidents were far from uncommon.[41]

As slaves began to dominate the plantation workforce, planters had white servants train certain slaves in the key skills and processes of sugar production, and by the end of the seventeenth century most of this highly skilled work was no longer performed by white men, whether bound or free. During the early stages of this transition, bound and freed white men might hope to work as artisanal craftsmen or skilled sugar-makers on plantations, the most highly skilled posts, which thus attracted the best conditions. But soon even these jobs were performed by enslaved Africans. The only significant plantation task that remained available to white men was that of overseer.

In contrast with skilled white servants were the far more numerous unskilled white bound laborers. Generally aged between sixteen and thirty, they were sold for a fairly standard price as general laborers, from about £7 each in the later 1630s to as much as £14 by the mid-1650s. In the early to mid-seventeenth century this bound white labor force powered the Barbadian plantation system, transforming agricultural labor and society in the Caribbean and beyond. Their work had begun with the clearance of the heavily forested landscape: by 1650 more than half of the forests had been removed, and by 1667 contemporaries were complaining of a shortage of timber. Then came the early experiments with various staple crops, including tobacco, cotton, and indigo, all of which required hard physical labor for the planting, the maintenance, the harvesting, and the processing of the crops. The relatively rapid transition to sugar in the 1640s and 1650s began with a relatively simple planting system, wherein holes were dug by stick or hoe about three feet apart, with a single cane cutting placed in each hole before being covered by soil. Simplicity did not, however, equate to ease: this was backbreaking work, requiring laborers to lean over constantly. When mid-seventeenth-century observers described white servants and black slaves working alongside one another in plantation fields, these workers were quite likely planting or maintaining these early sugar crops, constantly weeding to prevent young canes from being strangled by oppressive and fast-growing creepers, and then finally harvesting them. Canes could grow to between eight and ten feet in height, and were to be cut cleanly about five inches from the ground, again requiring laborers to bend over to cut through thick, fibrous material before carrying it for transportation to the plantation's sugar works.[42]

Beginning in the middle of the seventeenth century, as sugar replaced tobacco, indigo, and cotton, white female bound laborers were spared from field work on sugar plantations. It is important to remember, however, that in earlier decades, bound white women had labored alongside men in the plantation fields. Thereafter the declining number and proportion of bound white women were assigned to various forms of plantation work associated with housework, the tending of food crops and animals, nursing, cooking, and clothes production and repair. These areas of work were soon taken over by enslaved women, leaving bound and even free white women with extremely limited options. As the seventeenth century wore on, female white servants were of less and less utility to planters, as illustrated by the complete replacement of female seamstresses by enslaved textile workers on the Codrington plantations by 1700. As the proportion of enslaved African women arriving on the island increased, the proportion and the number of bound white women steadily diminished. Tellingly, Ligon's analysis of life, work, and society in mid-seventeenth-century Barbados, the most full and complete account that we have, makes no mention of bound white women, although he did discuss enslaved African women.[43]

Bound white laborers arriving in Barbados and other Caribbean islands were far more likely to die within a few years of their arrival than would have been true had they remained at home. Those with the longest terms of service, the vagrants, criminals, and prisoners of war, were the least likely to survive. Ligon recorded that servants of all kinds were rarely allowed a seasoning period and rest. Having been brought from ship to plantation, servants were often required to construct their own improvised cabins out of branches and leaves. "The next day they are rung out with a Bell to work, at six a clock in the morning, with a severe Overseer to command them," Ligon wrote. Should it rain, he went on, these newly arrived servants would have to wear their wet clothes to sleep in, or shiver without them. With no change of clothes, and the most basic of lodgings and diet, "if they be not strong men, this . . . will put them into a sicknesse." Given that numerous servants died before the expiration of their terms, many must have seen little difference between themselves and the growing number of enslaved African laborers.[44]

While skilled laborers might expect to receive somewhat better treatment, working and living conditions, and food, all servants were subject to a harsh disciplinary regime, and they knew that they could be whipped by masters and overseers for any faults. Ligon knew that if servants dared to complain about their conditions, "they are beaten by the Overseer; if they resist, their time is doubled." This former planter recalled that he had "seen an Overseer beat a Servant with a cane about the head, till the blood has followed, for a fault that is not worthy the speaking of." Perhaps knowing how shocking his account might be to readers in the British Isles, Ligon recorded his own distress at witnessing such scenes: "Truly, I have seen such cruelty there done to Servants, as I did not think one Christian could have done to another."[45]

The dramatic expansion of sugar production meant that relatively little of the island's arable land was devoted to food production. The importation of food and of clothing became a major expense for planters, and they attempted to keep such costs to a minimum. At the start of the eighteenth century John Oldmixon compared the diet of white servants in Barbados unfavorably with the food enjoyed by English servants in husbandry, concluding that "Their Diet is not so good, as those who have been us'd to Rich Farmers Tables in *England*."[46] Twenty years earlier Sir Thomas Montgomery, shocked by what he saw in Barbados, had gone much further in his appeal to the Lords of Trade and Plantations: "I beg . . . care for the poor white servants here, who are used with more barbarous cruelty than in Algiers. Their bodies and souls are used as if hell commenced here and only continued in the world to come. They want the merest necessities of food and raiment, and many die daily in consequence."[47] In the late 1660s an observer recorded that he had "inspected many [of] their plantations and have seen 30, sometimes 40, Christians—English, Scotch, and Irish—at work in the parching sun without shirt, shoe, or stocking . . . [while] their Negroes have been at work at their respective trades in a good condition." Not only were most if not all white servants convicts or prisoners, working alongside slaves in plantation fields, but their shoes and clothing were inferior to those allowed the more valuable enslaved Africans.[48]

An act passed by the Assembly in 1702 acknowledged that "many Masters" had followed "their wills and pleasures" in determining what allowances to grant their servants. The act specified that masters should provide "six pounds of good wholesome and sound flesh, or fish *per* Week, with sufficient ground provisions, or other bread kind." Adequate clothing should be provided each quarter, but there is no evidence that this law was strictly enforced, and a clause that threatened a whipping for servants who unjustly accused masters of failing to provide adequate food and clothing well illustrated the continuing power of the masters.[49] Five years later Oldmixon recorded that the clothing of servants usually consisted of "Ozinbrig Jackets and Drawers, and sometimes of coarse Cloth. The Male Servants have thick Drawers, Shoes, Stockings, Caps, and Canvas Waistcoats allow'd them. And the Females have Shifts, Petticoats, Waistcoats, Shoes, and Stockings, made neat and serviceable."[50] This is more a description of the ideal than the norm, however, although it may have been closer to the truth by the early eighteenth century, when servitude was on the wane and the few remaining servants were in skilled or supervisory positions and had risen in status above enslaved Africans. For much of the seventeenth century, however, servants were often denied adequate clothing. The mother of one prospective servant wrote to planters "that she is fearfull her son should worke for the Negroes nor with other slaves bundled up," and rather than have him labor as and with slaves, she "resolved to keep him at home."[51]

The "Act for the good Governing of Servants" was passed by the Barbados Assembly in September 1661, and it says as much about the "custom of the country" over the preceding three decades as it does about plantation owners' desire to retain mastery over their remaining white servants. Consolidating several previous laws, this new act moved beyond previous legislation in order to "prevent the bold extravagancy and wandering of servants" through "the good regulating and governing of Servants in all things concerning their Masters and themselves." Any servant jailed for a criminal offense would have his or her service extended for double the length of time served in jail. Not just servants but any ships' captains or others who might harbor runaways were targeted by this law, which detailed fines and punishments for any who dared to deprive masters of their property, as well as fines for constables who neglected their duty in pursuing and apprehending runaways. The would-be runaway servant could expect to serve an additional term of three years for the offense. Similarly, any free man who made a planter's female servant pregnant would be liable to serve that planter for three years, while the unfortunate female servant would have her term extended by two years. The sheer brutal, violent power exercised by masters became clear in a provision of this new law designed to protect servants against murder by their masters. Admitting that some masters "have exercised great violence and great oppression, to, and upon their Servants, through which some of them have been murdered and destroyed," the law specified that no servant who died during his or her term of service could be buried before the body was examined by a justice of the peace or a constable "and two Neighbours of the Parish." Failure to comply would result in a penalty of "twenty thousand pounds of *Muscovado* Sugar": in short, a fine was all that would be imposed on a planter who killed a servant and buried the body before it could be examined by outsiders. Moreover, there is little evidence to suggest that this law was invoked and used against murderous planters.[52]

Planters enjoyed enormous control over white servants, and Ligon admitted that "if the Master be Cruell, the Servants have very wearisome and miserable lives." Verbal and physical resistance was brutally punished, and even the most minor offenses could result in physical punishment and an extension of the already long period of servitude. Thus Edmond Hollingsteade complained in September 1657 that his servants George Dumohan and Walter Welsh had "rebelliously and mutinously behaved themselves towards him their said master and mistress," and the two Irish servants— prisoners of war sent by Cromwell—received thirty-one lashes apiece. Masters could deal with "impudent, saucy and provoking" servants by reporting them to a local justice of the peace, who was required by law "to inflict such corporal punishment as he shall judge the crime to deserve."[53]

Perhaps of more general significance was the almost total control planters enjoyed over servants and their lives. Like farmers whose households included servants in husbandry, Barbados planters enjoyed ownership of all of a servant's time, not just the hours of labor, or the work that was contracted for. This enabled the planter to restrict and control all aspects of the life of a servant. It was white men and women from the British Isles who first experienced such a dramatic reduction of personal freedom, not African slaves. Laborers were the most expensive commodities purchased by planters, and local laws and the "custom of the country" allowed planters to fully exploit their investments. Consequently, and because of the lengthy terms that many served, these servants more fully resembled pauper or vagrant apprentices, bound to serve a master for as long as a decade.

The ethnic and religious differences between white servants, along with the brutal control exercised by the planter class, meant that white servants were unable to unite and organize in any significant manner. Planters hated the Irish servants who dominated the flood of prisoners reaching the island during the crucial 1650s, while Scottish servants and former servants received somewhat better treatment. This, to say nothing of religious and cultural differences, effectively divided the white servant class. The discrimination persisted against those who survived their period of bound labor, and planters were more likely to give work to any whites other than the Irish. As a consequence, Irish servants and former servants were far more likely to engage in petty crime, as well as consort with African slaves in illegal trading, prompting a new code for Irish servants that resembled black slave codes more than the usual legal restrictions on white servants. Irish servants who left their masters' plantations without permission would be whipped, and even free Irishmen could be challenged and physically punished for wandering the island for no apparent reason. Moreover, even though Irish men and women were effectively disbarred from labor and property ownership, any found without a fixed residence could be forced into a further year of service. Such was the fear of the Irish that even free white Englishmen were to be whipped and jailed if they sold arms to Irish servants and freemen. Former servants remained dependent upon the planter elite for work and opportunities, and the few who secured the most desirable posts as overseers or members of the island's militia were effectively co-opted into the island's brutal systems for control of bound labor.[54]

However, the horrific conditions faced by servants led to at least one attempted rebellion. Shortly before Ligon's arrival in Barbados in 1647, a major servant rebellion had been narrowly averted: "Their sufferings being grown to a great height, & their daily complainings to one another (of the intolerable burdens they labour'd under) being spread throughout the Iland; at the last, some amongst them, whose spirits were not able to endure such slavery, resolved to break through it, or die in the act."[55] At this point white bound laborers constituted a majority of the plantation workforce, and thus were a major threat. Ligon believed that "the greatest number of servants in the Iland" had been sympathetic to the rebels, who determined "to fall upon their Masters and cut all their throats, and by that means, to make themselves not only freemen, but Masters of the Iland." The plot was discovered only a day before the planned rebellion, and eighteen of the ringleaders were executed. As if to excuse the execution of such a large number of men for a rebellion than had not in fact occurred, Ligon argued that these leaders were "so haughty in their resolutions, and so incorrigible, as they were like enough to become actors in a second plot." The fact that this planned rebellion more closely resembles a slave uprising than a traditional English or North American servant uprising illustrates the radically different working conditions and lives experienced by white servants in mid-seventeenth-century Barbados.[56]

As the number of enslaved Africans increased in the second half of the seventeenth century, however, the objectives of bound and freed white servants inevitably changed. William Dickson perceived that a growing racial divide and fear inevitably bound white planters and servants together. He described "an impassable boundary line between black and white servants." On the one hand, planters increasingly used their black slaves to undertake much of the skilled and unskilled labor required on the island, leaving few options for bound and freed white servants and their descendants. On the other hand, fear of violent slave rebellion, and a developing sense of racial difference and of white superiority, meant that there was little hope of any form of shared class identity and action by bound blacks and the rapidly declining population of bound whites. If white men who survived their period of bound labor were fortunate enough to secure employment on plantations, it was usually as overseers and members of the militia. The white people were charged with using violence, both real and threatened, to keep order among the fast-growing enslaved population. Some former white servants were unable to secure such work, and having survived the full term of their service, men like Robert Frument and Othoniell Higges found in the 1670s that they had no option but to continue working for the planter to whom they had previously been bound. Now serving as wage rather than bound laborers, a few were even reduced to working in the cane fields alongside African slaves.[57]

During the 1630s servants had cost planters an average of approximately £7 each, but increasing demand and a dwindling supply meant that by the mid-1650s the cost had risen to between £10 and £14, and the cost continued to rise during the 1660s. In contrast, the price of slaves steadily declined, from about £40 in 1630 to £20 in 1645. Moreover, throughout the second half of the seventeenth century the price of sugar in Europe declined steadily. The increasing affordability of slaves, planters' dislike of the numerous Irish servants who came to the island during the 1650s, and the need to cut labor costs to a minimum all made the transition from white servitude to black slavery both economically feasible and socially desirable. This did not, however, inevitably lead to improvements in the lot of servants. A new law in 1703 governing relations between masters and white servants noted that "many times Servants are very impudent, saucy and provoking to Masters, and Mistresses of families, or their Overseers, and committing many irregular crimes, abuses and misbehaviours." The law proceeded to lay out the

rights and powers of masters over servants, and specified the legally sanctioned punishments for obdurate servants.[58]

Life remained very hard for former servants who stayed on in Barbados.
As early as the 1660s the only white former servants who could afford to eat
meat on a regular basis were those who had secured regular employment as
craftsmen.[59] By the end of the seventeenth century, Governor Russell
reported to the colonial authorities in London on the deplorable state of
former bound white servants:

> There is no encouragement given to white servants when their time
> is expired, for they have only about forty shillings given to them for
> all their services, and no other inducement to stay in the Island.
> The other Colonies offer so much encouragement that servants leave
> Barbados as soon as their term is ended. I dare say that there are
> hundreds of white servants in the Island who have been out of their
> time for many years, and who have never a bit of fresh meat
> bestowed on them nor a dram of rum. They are domineered over
> and used like dogs, and this in time will undoubtedly drive away all
> the commonalty of the white people and leave the Island in a
> deplorable condition, to be murdered by negroes or vanquished by
> an enemy, unless some means be taken to prevent it. Nor can we
> depend upon these people to fight for defence of the Island when,
> let who will be master, they cannot be more miserable than their
> countrymen and fellow-subjects make them here.[60]

Russell suggested that an act of Parliament might force Barbados planters
to provide a properly equipped and paid militia force, into which freed
white male servants might be integrated. In addition, Russell believed that
small grants of marginal land would give former servants a degree of self-
sufficiency, a vote in Assembly elections, and a stake in the system, thereby
making these "poor miserable creatures" a little "more comfortable." He
sought British action on this suggestion, for, as he wrote, "I am sure that
the people [of Barbados] will never do it for themselves."[61]

Parliament did not act on Russell's suggestions, and as he predicted, the
Barbados Assembly was unwilling to improve the lot of impoverished white
former servants. The transition from servitude to freedom brought little
improvement on an island where planters controlled virtually all of the
good arable land and restricted access to skilled and well-paid work. In fact,

in the five years following Russell's letter, Barbados planters recruited more than two thousand former soldiers to serve as militia tenants on the island, clearly believing that these new recruits would be more dependable as defenders of the plantocracy than disaffected former white servants. With this massive deployment of an armed force dedicated to the preservation of the plantation system and the wealth of the great planters, maltreatment of white servants could continue unabated: African slaves, white bound laborers, and freed whites were powerless against such a military force. During the late seventeenth and the early eighteenth centuries, prisoners of war made up a significant proportion of the dwindling population of white servants, and they continued to serve for long terms, suffer harsh treatment, and face few options should they survive their term of service.[62]

In an attempt to increase the flow of servants, the Barbados Assembly reduced the term of service significantly, to as little as three years. This had the effect, however, of doubling the price of white servants, at exactly the time that various factors in Britain and West Africa both increased the trade in slaves and brought down the overall cost. By the late seventeenth century, Barbadian planters had replaced almost all of their white servants with African slaves, keeping only the minimal number of whites required by law. In 1679 Henry Drax drafted instructions for Richard Harwood in the management of his plantations, noting, "I shall Not leave you many white servants[,] the ffewer the better werve itt No Incumbantt duty on all to keepe the Number the act of Malitia reqwirs for the Countreys service, which Number [I] shall endevor to Send you Imediatly after my Ariwall In England." Barbadian planters were legally obligated to maintain one white militia man for every ten African slaves in order to protect the island against foreign attack and domestic insurrections. However, the fact that one of the wealthiest planters on the island was not leaving a sufficient number of servants illustrates planters' reluctance to allocate land and resources to what they regarded as an unnecessarily high number of white militia tenants.[63]

During the transitional years of the final decades of the seventeenth century, bound white laborers occupied a liminal space between slavery and freedom, and they were recorded in terms that associated them and their labor with slaves. Thus, for example, a 1687 list of "Christi[a]n Servants" on the Newton plantation placed the names of these servants adjacent to a list of enslaved children "borne to the Estate," the names of twenty-nine slaves, and a list of livestock. Twelve white servants were

named, all male, but five of these had already died in service. The list ends
with a notation that seven "season'd Servts. [had been] bought to supply
the places of the Season[ed] dead ones." As slaves began to replace bound
whites, there was little appreciable improvement in the status and identification of white servants. They were listed and identified as property, to be
bought and replaced, and soon to be supplanted by an almost entirely
enslaved workforce. Almost two decades later the proportion of white servants had declined at the Rendezvous plantation, where an "Inventory of
the Negroes, horses, Cattle and All other Appurtenances" taken on 17 February 1705 began with a detailed listing of 240 male and female slaves of all
ages and conditions, and then noted "White Servants Three" before moving on to list real estate, livestock, and other chattel goods. Even as bound
white servants all but disappeared from the plantation workforce, and
although their working conditions had improved somewhat, they nonetheless remained akin to chattel, to be listed and associated with enslaved
laborers and livestock.[64]

Richard Dunn has suggested that a significant number of former servants became planters, but Hilary Beckles has convincingly argued that
from very early on the island's more powerful planters had made it difficult
for former servants to receive the ten acres to which they were supposedly
entitled. According to Beckles, planters used every conceivable method to
postpone or reduce the value of any kind of payment to former servants,
and to keep them dependent and with no choice but to labor. More
recently, Christopher Tomlins has suggested that throughout British
America the ubiquity of indentured servitude has been overemphasized,
and that this was "a temporary not a permanent condition." Tomlins questions historians' belief that servitude had such a "distinctive influence on
early American labor systems." In Barbados, however, the proportion of
bound white servants who were convicts and prisoners was unusually high.
The lives of these men and women were forfeit; they served such long terms
that many died in service. Few of the survivors or their descendants who
remained on Barbados enjoyed anything other than dire poverty, and the
colonial norm of familial labor outlined by Tomlins simply did not exist in
Barbados. While his observations hold true for the Chesapeake and other
British colonies, they do not apply to Barbados.[65]

A fortunate few servants, or their descendants, did succeed in creating
lives for themselves, but they were far from typical. Richard Harwood, the
man who ran Henry Drax's Drax Hall and Hope plantations, was the son

of John Harwood, a Royalist soldier captured in 1643 and sentenced to Barbadian servitude. By 1680 Richard Harwood owned five acres of land, and after working for Drax he became the agent of a London merchant. In 1685 he purchased the time of some of the Monmouth rebels, profiting from the same kind of bound labor that his father had been forced to perform, and a year later Harwood was appointed to the island's governing council. Elite planters on the council were appalled by the appointment of a man of "servile condition" who was no more than a "mere overseer," however, and after the Glorious Revolution, Harwood's name was struck off a list of council members sent to London, with the words "suspected papist" written beside his name. Even the few servants and their descendants who improved their lot could not easily lose the stigma of their earlier status. But with land and opportunities concentrated in so few hands, Harwood's success was exceptional, and the majority of servants and their descendants did not prosper. Edmund Burke, who was likely a former Irish prisoner who had been condemned to bound labor in Barbados, made his mark on a will on 7 March 1661. Desperately poor, Burke had little to bequeath: he left his hammock and clothes to Dennis MacSwaine and his wife in gratitude for their care of him during his final sickness, and a chest to his wife Margaret. In 1670 another of the Irish bound laborers, Desmond Dehollerine, left a set of buttons to Breyand Haugh, a hammock to Richard Kelly, another hammock to Elizabeth Cammar, a hat to Edward Cammar, and miscellaneous clothes to Teague Kelly and John Copper. Having only just outlived his decade of forced labor, Dehollerine had precious little to show for his years of work, and he bequeathed his paltry possessions to fellow Irishmen and -women and their children.[66]

There was little love lost between the planter elite and former white servants and their descendants. Planters regarded poor whites as being of criminal and Celtic ancestry, and from the seventeenth century on they were regarded as problematic at best. The descendants of those who survived came to be known by the derogatory label of "redlegs," a derogatory Scots term for Scottish highlanders and Irishmen. In 1798 John Williamson found a group in the hills of a portion of the island that is known to this day as Scotland. He described them as "descendants of a race of people, transported in the time of Cromwell . . . called Redlegs . . . [and] as degenerate and useless a race as can be imagined." A generation later the planter elite continued to complain about impoverished whites who begged or who depended on the charity of slaves and yet who were "as proud as Lucifer

himself." Sir Andrew Halliday regarded them as "the most indolent, ignorant, and impudent race of beggars that were ever tolerated in any community." At the dawn of the nineteenth century, John Poyer observed that
there were no opportunities for the descendants of bound white servants:
"Few plantations have a sufficient number of [enslaved] labourers to culti-
vate their fields, yet many slaves are employed as tradesmen, who would be
equally as profitably engaged in agricultural occupations, while the industrious [white] mechanick is destitute of employment." Despite having had
their freedom stripped away, and having worked as the first major labor
force that powered the early integrated sugar plantations of Barbados, the
few who survived the experience found themselves not simply in dire poverty, but maligned in precisely the same terms as their forefathers and
mothers, who had been banished from England, Scotland, and Ireland as
lowly, worthless, and without rights.[67]

By the late eighteenth century white servants no longer figured on many
plantation inventories. The lengthy and detailed inventory of the Codrington and associated plantations taken on 2 May 1783 recorded 280 acres of
land on the upper (home) plantation and 478 acres on the lower plantation,
as well as listing windmills, boiling and distilling houses and other buildings, and myriad tools. The names of 273 slaves were listed, but the only
reference to whites was implicit, in the record of "30 Militia Coats, 20
Musketts, 19 Bayonets." These large plantations no longer used white
bound labor, although a handful of former white servants and their descendants lived on poor plantation land as militia men and their families. From
previously being treated as virtual slaves and listed as chattel property, former white servants and their descendants were now marginalized. Many
were no longer listed on plantation inventories, and their presence on the
land was implicit in the records, their significance clearly limited in the
eyes of the planters and those who documented the plantations and their
worth.[68]

The increasing number of slaves resulted in a corresponding decline in
the opportunities for free whites to work or acquire land. Planters made
money by having slaves perform virtually all work, with the result that wage
levels and opportunities for whites diminished. By the late 1660s, "The
planters, grown now full of Negroes, design to have all other tradesmen,
sugar boilers, refiners (or at least many of them) of their blacks; for to effect
which, they place with all their tradesmen Negroes." Training slaves in
skilled plantation work and a variety of crafts, bound white artisans and

skilled workers were effectively eliminating their own work, both as bound laborers and as freemen. At first, certain kinds of work were reserved for whites: for example, in the mid- to late seventeenth century, forts and roads had been built by free and bound white laborers. But by the end of the seventeenth century this work was done by gangs of slaves, hired out by their owners at lower rates than the whites. Visitors to the island found that virtually all work was done by enslaved people, or even occasional free blacks. In 1750 George Washington, perhaps thinking of his native Virginia where many white indentured servants had completed their terms and then risen in society, was struck by the fact that "There are few who may be call'd midling people they are either very rich or very poor." The latter group was largely composed, Washington went on, of the militia tenants and their families. Mandated by law but barely supported and living on the worst land, these impoverished whites, Washington recognized, "can't [help] but [be] very poor."[69]

John Poyer was confident in his belief in white racial superiority and the need to maintain racial unity in the face of a large population of enslaved Africans. In 1801 he wrote to Lord Seaforth, the newly arrived governor of Barbados, that "every possible encouragement should be afforded to the poor" white population of the island, at the expense of the free black population of Barbados and of the enslaved craftsmen who performed so much of the island's skilled work. Poyer bemoaned the fact that "many Slaves are employed as Tradesmen . . . while the industrious white mechanic, is destitute of employment; or if he work, is ill-treated." But the island's planter elite were unsympathetic: the profits they earned from the varied work undertaken by their slaves gave them no incentive to improve the conditions of poor whites who they and their forefathers had grown used to regarding as something resembling a lower caste. In the absence of any real slave rebellions in eighteenth-century Barbados, a race-first mentality had not assumed as much importance as elsewhere. David Lambert concludes that Poyer's attempt to unify the white population of Barbados was "utterly rejected" by the planter elite.[70]

When George Pinckard arrived on the island in 1795, he found impoverished whites relegated to scraps of isolated and unproductive land:

> remote from the great class of merchants and planters, and who obtain a scanty livelihood by cultivating a small patch of earth, and breeding up poultry. . . . They are descended from European settlers,

but . . . are reduced to a state not much superior to the condition of free negroes. This numerous class of inhabitants, between the great planters and the people of colour, forms a striking feature, distinguishing Barbadoes from the more recently settled colonies.[71]

Pinckard visited one such "large family of Barbadian cottagers" living in a small cabin in a remote mountainous spot, "seldom exposed to the intrusion of visitors." Another such family, "of long standing in the island," grew ginger and raised poultry. "They were poor, like the others, and compelled to labour much in full exposure to the sun. Like the negroes, too, their diet consisted chiefly of vegetables." Even as slaves assumed virtually all of the plantation labor originally undertaken by white bound laborers, the descendants of the latter group remained poor and marginal. Their race and nominally free status kept them from plantation work, yet disallowed them from almost any other means of making a living. The only work guaranteed to free white men in eighteenth-century Barbados was fishing, and dock work and other activities related to shipping, and then only because slave owners were reluctant to give enslaved Africans access to boats and ships. By 1833 Edward Eliot deplored the fact that "not one in twenty of the working shoemakers in Barbados is a white man. The working carpenters, masons, tailors, smiths, &c. are for the most part men of colour."[72]

Bound labor, both white and black, had built Barbados, generating tremendous wealth. However, as enslaved African labor came to dominate the workforce, the integrated plantations and the larger plantation economy left virtually no space for free white workers. By the early eighteenth century, Barbados's declining white population was concentrated in the urban areas of Bridgetown and Speightstown, in the parishes of St. Philip and Christ Church in the southern portion of the island, and in the highlands of the northern and eastern parishes. These areas featured some of the most arid land on the island, which was least suitable for sugar plantations, and consequently was home to the highest concentration of poor whites. In 1715 there were almost 17,000 whites on Barbados, and with over 40 percent under the age of twenty and an almost equal sex distribution, natural increase alone should have been resulting in a fairly rapidly increasing white population. Some were still bound laborers, but even among those who had secured freedom, poverty, poor nutrition, and greater susceptibility to disease all kept average family sizes quite low, and only just over 7 percent of this white population was fifty or older. For white bound laborers and their descendants, escape from the island was almost always their best option.[73]

From the late seventeenth century on, visitors to the island described a large class of poor whites, almost completely excluded from the labor market and reduced to scratching out a living on the most marginal land. In the eighteenth and well into the nineteenth centuries observers saw that "a large white population are in the lowest state of poverty and wretchedness."[74] Even those in Bridgetown were seldom able to secure sufficient work, and one early nineteenth-century observer noted that of all races and sorts of people in the town,

> the poor whites are the lowest, and the most degraded: residing in the meanest hovels, they pay no attention either to neatness in their dwellings or cleanliness in their persons; and they subsist too often, to their shame be it spoken, on the kindness and charity of slaves. I have never seen a more sallow, dirty, ill looking, and unhappy race; the men lazy, the women disgusting, and the children neglected: all without any notion of principle, morality, or religion.[75]

Rather than eliciting sympathy, these poor whites drew the wrath of planters who despised the descendants of the men and women whose labor had built their plantations, describing them as worthless beggars who depended upon the charity of slaves to survive, and as "the most indolent, ignorant, and impudent race of beggars that were ever tolerated in any community." In part this was because these whites were seen as potentially dangerous, trading goods, food, and alcohol with slaves, some of it appropriated from planters, which white men and women could take to towns and markets. But such attitudes were also based on traditional attitudes toward the vagrants, the criminal poor, and the Irish, who had together composed a significant portion of the bound white labor force. These people were imprisoned and forced to work against their will, and then held responsible for their own impoverished condition. Such attitudes persisted and were applied to the descendants of these bound laborers, the "redlegs."[76]

The rise of integrated plantations on Barbados created a unique white underclass, the descendants of bound white workers who could no longer work, and in Coleridge's words "a class of people which I did not meet with in any of the other islands."[77] Even the militia tenants were, Coleridge suggested, excluded from society as a whole:

> They owe no fealty to the landlord, make him no acknowledgment, and entertain no kind of gratitude towards him . . . the greatest part of them live in a state of complete idleness, and are usually ignorant and debauched to the last degree. They will often walk half over the island to demand alms . . . and it is notorious that in many cases whole families of these free whites depend for their subsistence on the charity of slaves. Yet they are as proud as Lucifer himself, and in virtue of their freckled ditchwater faces consider themselves on a level with every gentleman in the island.[78]

By the end of the eighteenth century roughly 16,000 white people lived in Barbados: planters and the merchant elite made up about one-quarter of these, while smaller planters, plantation managers, professionals, small merchants, and the "ten-acre" men who owned very small landholdings together accounted for an additional quarter. The remaining half of the white population were the impoverished descendants of the island's original bound laborers. Half of these were militia tenants, small holders with less then ten acres of land, fishermen, and a few craftsmen, while the remaining quarter of the island's white population were destitute.[79]

The condition of bound white laborers in Barbados in the early to mid-seventeenth century, and of their descendants in the years that followed, differed starkly from those on other Caribbean islands. Voluntary migrant laborers from England, Scotland, and Ireland generally populated the English Leeward Islands, and many of these became planters, bookkeepers, merchants, plantation managers, and attorneys. In late eighteenth and early nineteenth-century Jamaica, even poorer whites, many of them former bound laborers, were able to improve their situation. Many secured relatively good work as plantation supervisors, slave drivers, managers, bookkeepers, and overseers, and they aspired to become planters and slave owners themselves.[80]

The experience of white bound laborers and their descendants in Barbados thus differed dramatically in comparison with similar groups elsewhere in the Caribbean. Barbados was settled and developed plantation agriculture earlier, at a time when social problems and political dislocation in

England combined to produce a huge number of bound whites with few rights. These laborers were brutally exploited by planters who operated plantation workforces with little oversight by English authorities. During these foundational years, slavery and bound white labor were utilized in similar fashion, and differentiation between the two had yet to harden. A generation later, as Jamaica and the other English Caribbean colonies took shape, the flow of bound white workers had dwindled, while the influx of enslaved Africans had increased, and a new attitude toward slave laborers had taken shape.

It was on this small island that an integrated plantation system and an accompanying labor system were created, to say nothing of the attitudes toward labor fostered by this new system. These were then exported to the rest of the British Caribbean and the deep south of the American mainland. Many of the "white slaves" of Barbados, along with their descendants, were placed outside of English traditions of servitude and North American adaptations of this model, as described by Christopher Tomlins. The result was that in this one island, the absolute differences between white servitude and African slavery posited by Tomlins were far less apparent: the laws that he describes regulating African slaves and their labor were on Barbados initially applied to white servants.[81]

What is perhaps most remarkable about Barbados is that the small planter elite maintained their disdain for the descendants of the bound white laborers who had created the plantation economy. Poor and unable to improve their lot, they inhabited small patches of marginal land, and they traded food and stolen commodities with slaves, earning the hostility of planters. The descendants of the maligned and marginalized poor of Scotland, Ireland, and England were held in the same disregard as their ancestors. By the end of the eighteenth century racial slavery had completely supplanted white servitude, and few of the original white servants survived. However, some of the descendants of indentured servants, including the prisoners from British jails and the captives from wars and rebellions, can be found on Barbados to this day, many with the Irish and Scottish surnames of their ancestors.

Chapter 5

"A Company of White Negroes"

The Lives and Labor of British Workers on the Gold Coast

Labor in British trading operations on the West African coast differed dramatically from the organization of work in mid-seventeenth-century Barbados. While bound British laborers dominated the workforce that cleared the Caribbean island and established the plantation system, Britain's Guinea Coast operations throughout the later seventeenth and the eighteenth centuries were manned by a surprisingly small number of bound and free British laborers, artisans, and officials. Even by the turn of the eighteenth century, no more than a few thousand Europeans were stationed on the entire West African coast between the Senegal and the Calabar Rivers, in trading posts and forts stretched over some three thousand miles of coastline between the southern extremes of the western Sahara and the eastern section of modern Nigeria. The greatest concentration of these outposts was along the Gold Coast, which had originally been constructed to facilitate and defend the trade in gold, ivory, and spices, and then expanded to support the transatlantic slave trade. Close to the center of the Gold Coast was Cape Coast Castle, which quickly developed into the leading British trading post and the command center for their entire West African trading operation. Located some three thousand miles from Africa House, the RAC headquarters in Leadenhall Street, London, Cape Coast Castle developed into the largest and best-maintained British structure on the entire West African coast, a mighty white-walled castle, with dozens of heavy cannon upon its walls; underground holding cells for male and female slaves awaiting transportation to the Americas; storerooms for food, drink, building, and other supplies, as well as the vast amount of trade goods; and lodgings for the company's governor, clerks and officials, artifi-cers, laborers, soldiers, sailors, some free blacks and mulattoes, and some of the company-owned slaves.[1]

Europeans rarely ventured beyond the tree line of the mighty African forests that lay within sight of their forts and castles, spending their time within a stone's throw of the ocean that had carried them to West Africa. A potentially lethal disease environment meant that many Britons were incapacitated for much of their time on the Gold Coast, and few survived for long. Throughout the seventeenth and eighteenth centuries the size of the white workforce at Cape Coast Castle and the other forts along the Gold Coast fluctuated dramatically, dependent as it was upon mortality rates, and upon regular supply and reinforcement from Britain to replace those who had died or were too ill to work. Guinea worm, sleeping sickness, dysentery, yaws, and bilharzia all had an effect, but yellow fever and malaria were the greatest killers, and it appears to have been all but impossible—as is true today—for an individual to spend a year on the Gold Coast without being bitten by a mosquito carrying the malarial infection.[2]

Simply keeping British forts standing and secure proved a difficult and endless task, and poor pay and high mortality rates made it difficult to recruit sufficient skilled craftsmen, laborers, and soldiers. The small num-ber of Britons were soon required to work alongside free and enslaved Afri-cans, often teaching them the skills required by British officials, and the lines between white and black, free and bound, and skilled and unskilled workers all blurred. Furthermore, a growing number of free mulattoes occupied a liminal space between Britons and West Africans, working in various unskilled, skilled, and even professional positions for the British, and also developing families and trading businesses in the local community. Britons alone were incapable of maintaining their Gold Coast trading oper-ations, and they came to depend heavily upon the labor of free and bound Africans and free mulattoes.

Early modern European states seldom had the resources to maintain trading operations in Africa as exclusively governmental operations, and so most nations would adopt one or several strategies: they might grant a company of investors privileged access to the trade; erect, maintain, and defend trading posts for use by authorized merchants; or allow unfettered access by all who flew under their nation's flag. The British dominated the eighteenth-century transatlantic slave trade, but this success was not the work of a single and successful company. Between the late sixteenth and the late eighteenth centuries, British interests along the West African coast were represented by a succession of fragile and struggling commercial operations, as well as by numerous private ships and merchants. However, although the various incarnations of British companies failed to make large profits for shareholders, they nonetheless provided sufficiently secure state-sanctioned and state-protected West African bases to enhance Britain's share of the lucrative transatlantic slave trade, and by the late seventeenth century English vessels carried almost two-thirds more slaves to the Americas than their leading rivals—the Dutch and the Portuguese—combined. British domination of the trade increased over the course of the eighteenth century, and approximately three million Africans crossed the Atlantic in mainly privately owned British ships from London, Liverpool, and Bristol.[3]

Cape Coast Castle had begun as a small trading settlement built by Swedish traders and local laborers in the early 1650s on the site of a minor fish market. It was captured by the Danish in 1657, who lost the fort to the Dutch two years later. The English took control of Cape Coast in 1664, and retained the castle until Ghanaian independence in 1957. With the Dutch developing Elmina, an equally imposing fortress less than ten miles west along the Gold Coast, it was the English who transformed Cape Coast into a mighty fortified warehouse. Elmina and Cape Coast Castle were quite possibly the largest buildings in eighteenth-century sub-Saharan Africa.[4]

By the end of the seventeenth century there were approximately sixty European forts, castles, and factories along the Gold Coast, and a much larger number of African towns and villages whose inhabitants facilitated trade between Europeans and West Africans. The communities on the Gold Coast expanded and diversified as they consolidated their position as trade nexuses: writing in the 1680s, Jean Barbot described the town beside Cape Coast Castle as containing "fully 500 huts arranged in streets and alleys, all forming a large village," and he believed the market there "to be the largest in all Gold Coast, and even the largest in all Guinea."[5] Yet few Britons were resident on the Gold Coast, in large part because extraordinarily high mortality rates meant that a great many served and died in post. Of those Britons who did live and work on the Guinea Coast, the greatest number were based in Cape Coast Castle, with others spread around the secondary forts and trading posts such as Anomabu, Accra, Winneba, Tantamkweri, Appollonia, Dixcove, Sekondi, and Commenda, as well as Whydah on the

Figure 8. "East Prospect of Cape Corse, or Coast Castle and North-West Prospect of the Same," in John Green (compiler), *A New General Collection of Voyages and Travels* (London, 1745–47). Courtesy of the British Library Board.

Slave Coast to the east of the Gold Coast. Recalling his time on the Gold Coast during the 1680s, trader Erick Tilleman listed the personnel at Cape Coast as including "a *Director-Governor* in charge of the entire trade, a chief merchant, a priest, two assistant merchants, a vice-bookkeeper, a chief officer, a *Magasin-Mester*, four assistants, two barbers, two sergeants, three constables, three corporals, six *Adels-Burser*, two drummers, eighty common soldiers, and two *Professor*, as well as the *Mulattoes*, slaves, and the Natureller [who are] servants of the Christians."[6] The governor or agent general might be assisted by two or more merchants, two to four "factors," and a similar number of "writers" or clerks. A chaplain, a surveyor, a bookkeeper, a steward, and a surgeon rounded out the complement of officers. These were the senior officials employed by the RAC to facilitate trade. The success of their work depended, however, on the craftsmen, laborers, and soldiers whose work maintained and protected the buildings in which they lived and worked, including carpenters, smiths, bricklayers, masons, coopers, armorers, and gardeners. During the eighteenth century the full complement at the expanded Cape Coast Castle might include the governor, a chaplain, a secretary, an accountant, a surveyor (charged with maintaining the company's buildings on the old Coast), a register (responsible for pay and personnel), a deputy accountant, a deputy surveyor, two officers of the guard who commanded the company's soldiers, a warehouse keeper and deputy warehouse keeper, several "factors" who supervised and recorded trade, as many as ten or more "writers" who copied documents and learned the business of West African trade, and a fluctuating number of European artisans and craftsmen, soldiers, sailors, and laborers. However, the British complement was rarely, if ever, anywhere close to full strength.[7]

At the height of the transatlantic slave trade there were quite possibly more Africans in Britain than there were Britons on the Gold Coast, yet the relatively small British cohort in West Africa were responsible for coordinating a large and lucrative trade, upon which both New World planters and British manufacturers were dependent. Simply maintaining the skeletal British presence on the Gold Coast was an expensive and arduous endeavor, and the buildings that housed and protected Britons, their trade goods, and the slaves awaiting transport required constant maintenance. Some materials such as bricks and lime were eventually manufactured locally, but a great many necessary supplies such as timber, tools, nails, and tar had to be shipped from Britain, along with the skilled craftsmen to use them. While it was possible for those who survived local diseases and then ascended through the ranks on the Gold Coast to do very well for themselves, for most of the Britons on the Gold Coast life was short and brutal. RAC employees on the Gold Coast inevitably struggled to make ends meet and often ended up indebted to the Company and thus obliged to extend their terms of service. A constant supply of British laborers was integral to the very existence of these castles and forts, which were the bedrock of British trade on the Gold Coast, and thus to the transatlantic slave trade itself.[8]

The geography and the weather conditions of the Gold Coast contributed to the burden of work facing Europeans. Great rolling waves swept onto the sandy beaches and rocks, and in the absence of natural harbors European ships had to anchor well offshore: all goods and people ferried between ships and shore were carried on smaller vessels, usually Gold Coast canoes built and crewed by West Africans. This environment had a corrosive effect on every structure that the Europeans erected along the Gold Coast and on all of the supplies and trade goods they brought ashore. The "great swell that constantly rolls upon this whole coast from the vast *Atlantick* ocean" created a constant crashing surf, which filled the coastal air with a salty spray and mist that rapidly eroded stone, iron, wood, and fabric. The Gold Coast experienced two wet seasons, the first beginning in early May and the second in early October, and these rainy seasons exacerbated the harm done to buildings and supplies by the sea. Year after year, governors and officials regularly reported to their superiors in London on all of the problems caused by the environment. In 1681 Cape Coast Castle officials were "forced to support our Tottering Tower, some of which lately Fell in and would infallibly have tumbled, the next Raines and endangered the lives of many, besides the spoyling of the great warehouse." In a refrain that became almost constant, this letter ended with a long list of materials needed to repair and restore the company's buildings, including, for example, "a considerable store of all sorts" of nails, carpenters' tools, timber, and canvas. Almost a century later another governor reported from Cape Coast Castle, in strikingly similar terms, that his surveyor believed that "the Rains which are near setting in, would greatly hurt if not bring down some of the Arches," and the governor himself agreed that "The Rains as usual will retard us a great deal."[9]

Without constant and extensive maintenance all of the British establishments on the Gold Coast deteriorated rapidly. Early in the eighteenth century, for example, Andrew Thompson reported that the fort at Anomabu "is in a ruinous Condition, has wanted repairing this 8 or 10 years and they are afraid of being Murdered by it's Fall." Three years later officials at Cape Coast reported that "this Castle in particular being very much out of Repairs," and begged for necessary building supplies, even going so far as to suggest that a supply of bricks might serve as ballast in the supply ships coming from England: a month later the "Necessity for the speedy repairs wanting at your sev.al Forts, to preserve them from ruin obliges us to Repeat our Request" for supplies and craftsmen.[10]

Throughout the entire era of the transatlantic slave trade the Gold Coast climate and conditions harmed Britons as much as damaged the buildings they inhabited. Recalling ten slave-trading voyages that he had taken from Africa to the Americas between 1786 and 1800, John Adams suggested that when "selecting a crew for a voyage to Africa, preference should invariably be given to those officers and men who have been inured to that climate. . . . Neither officers or seamen should be employed in any duty on shore . . . where natives can be procured capable of performing these duties." The west coast of Africa was a notoriously dangerous environment for Europeans, and especially for those who lived and worked in the castles and forts. Writing a century before Adams and describing a slaving voyage that stretched from 1693 to 1695, Thomas Phillips recorded that his ship had carried thirty men to serve as soldiers and laborers at Cape Coast Castle, all in rude health, but during the two months the ship spent on the coast "they were near half dead, and scarcely enough of the survivors able to carry their fellows to the grave."[11]

An inventory of sixty-six English "Factors Artificers and Soldiers" living on the Gold Coast in August 1674 ended with a list of sixteen who had died during the preceding seven months, including a cooper, a blacksmith, two armorers, a surgeon, and several soldiers. During the six months between November 1684 and April 1685 thirty-six Englishmen died on the Gold Coast, approximately one-quarter of the total white workforce. By the early eighteenth century the life expectancy for officers of the Royal African Company on the Gold Coast was between four and five years, while among rank-and-file soldiers, laborers, and artisans the death rates were even higher: of forty-eight soldiers who arrived at Cape Coast Castle in February 1769, only eight were still alive at the end of May. Even in the late eighteenth century, after more than two centuries of trade on the West African coast, mortality rates for Europeans enduring their first year on the Gold Coast ranged between 30 and 70 percent, and among those who survived, between

8 and 12 percent would then die annually thereafter. By way of comparison, mortality rates in early seventeenth-century England averaged between 2.5 and 3 percent, while after the initially high death toll the annual mortality rates in the Chesapeake and Carolina colonies during the seventeenth century averaged 5 to 7 percent.[12]

Even among the Britons who survived, illness and debility were common, and it was not unusual for a majority of RAC employees on the Gold Coast to be laid up, while others appeared pale and unhealthy. Survivors of malaria suffered chills and fever when they were reinfected, which was a common occurrence. Many suffered from dracunculiasis or the Guinea worm, a parasite contracted by drinking standing water, which resulted in the growth of a worm (often more than one or even two feet in length) in muscle tissue. Eventually the worm emerged through a painful blister on the skin, and if not extracted correctly, the decaying body of the worm could cause infection, great pain, and incapacity. Until late in the eighteenth century, unaware of germ theory, most Britons at home or in West Africa associated the high death rates with the climate of the Gold Coast. By the end of the seventeenth century, and indeed throughout the eighteenth century, the reputation of the West African coast as the "White Man's Grave" was increasingly well established.[13]

The records of the Royal African Company contain numerous letters from officials on the Gold Coast reporting on the debility or death of personnel, and they regularly alluded to the climate, conditions, and change in diet as causal factors. In 1705 Dalby Thomas lamented: "Many of yor white people dyes for want of Victualls & cloaths, it being hard with them to change Dyett at their first Comeing, besides ye alteration of ye Climate, & is ye bane of your shouldiers to be without warme Cloathe, shoes stockings, those that lyes warmest in ye Night most healthfull."[14] Work on the Gold Coast was constantly interrupted by ill health or death. In 1680, officials at Cape Coast Castle reported that "Wee have recvd. your Sheet Lead butt both the Plummers are dead." A generation later Dalby Thomas wrote that the carpenter at Cape Coast Castle had completed "a great Cannoe" but that he had "died before it was caulked," rendering the incomplete vessel useless. A decade later officials at Cape Coast Castle noted, "The Armourer died ye 30th Ult & we have not One Person on the Coast that knows how to preserve & clean Arms & trading Guns, wch is a great Misfortune" both for trade and for defence. A list of personnel serving at Cape Coast Castle and Anomabu between October 1752 and March 1754 included an "Ingineer, Secretary Writer Mason Bricklayer Carpenter Smith Brickmaker Sawyer & Carpenter Smith Cooper," but each of these had died by the end of 1758.[15]

Official reports to London from Cape Coast Castle regularly mixed lists of trade goods, supplies, and building materials received and traded with accounts of the condition of buildings, curt statements of the death or ill health of company employees, and pleas for both fresh supplies and more men.

> The goods in Generous Jenny arrived in good Condition. Dutch Knives in great demand—Small perpetts and Niconees of no use. . . . Mr. Witherd the Writer. Mr. Spencer dead. . . . Balance now Sent of all Dead persons Estates which have been Sold & Settled. . . . Want Writers. . . . The Mary Brig.ne: Capt. Rayner dispatched with 150 Slaves. . . . The Surgeon and the Lieutenant dead. Are destitute of Medicines. . . . Desire a Supply of Artificers, Soldiers &c.—Bricks, Farri[er]s, Stone [masons] . . . have 50 Choice Slaves in the Castle after compleating Captain Austins Complement. . . . List of Living & Dead from Ulto Sept 1719 to Ulto March 1720—Since which dead Mr. Fitzgerald, Saml. Freeman, John Brusher, Christphr Fisher, John Thompson . . . have but 20 Soldiers remaining.[16]

After reporting the death of another surgeon, the Governor's Council at Cape Coast Castle pleaded "we pray that your Honours will take into Consideration th[e] present Misfortune of your servants on this Coast for want of a Gent. Experienced in Physick wee are also destitute of Medicines."[17] Medical care and treatment of the sick were expensive: in 1772, for example, the annual cost exceeded £347, rising to £409 during the following year. "The principal part of this charge is the cost of the Medicines sent out by the Committee," to which was added: "Wine, Spirits and Sugar, or other comforts for the use of the Sick. Wood for the use of the Hospital. lights for Do. and the Surgery. Medicines occasionally bought from the Shipping or others on the Coast. Sileasias for Bandages, Sheets and other articles wanted in the Surgeons Shop."[18]

Even the most hardworking and successful of the Britons on the Gold Coast were frequently stymied by the ill health and deaths of their colleagues and workers. Such was the experience of John Apperley, the skilled surveyor who planned and supervised the construction of the new British fort at Anomabu in the mid-eighteenth century, which would become a major outlet for Gold Coast slaves during the last half-century of the transatlantic slave trade. Apperley reported in March 1755: "The Country agrees but indifferently with the Artificers that were sent out, I've 7 of 'em now in the hospital at Cape Coast." His lament was echoed by officials at Cape Coast Castle, who reported that "All the Artificers who came out with Mr. Apperley have been sick," and that "our great want of tradesmen to build the fort at Annamaboe" had slowed progress considerably. Having masterminded a more successful construction program than many of his predecessors, Apperley himself died on 18 August 1756, shortly before the completion of the fort.[19]

Correspondence from Britons on the Gold Coast back to RAC officials in London was often dominated by appeals, many of them quite desperate, for personnel to replace Britons who had died, and for the materials needed to maintain the castles and forts and their operations. The RAC archives contain many thousands of these almost timeless appeals, dating from the mid-seventeenth century until the end of the slave trade in the early nineteenth century. In 1678 Nathaniel Bradley and his colleagues at Cape Coast Castle wrote describing "a great need" of materials ranging from tools to paper, pens, and ink. As was often the case in such pleas, materials and workers were listed together, and skilled labor appeared to be as much a commodity as the tools and materials employed by such craftsmen: thus, Bradley appealed for "two hand hammers a standing vice, files of all sorts & sizes, two stock-makers 2 Smiths 2 Armourers." A year later Bradley and his colleagues repeated their appeal, stating that the "following is of absolute necessity for Finishing the Castle without wch: all will be at a stand," and then included a long list of materials such as "40 Casks of nails of all sorts [and] 100 Sheets of Lead." The relentless appeals to London by Gold Coast officials for appropriately qualified artisans underlines the vital import of these men's labor.[20]

Constantly suffering from an insufficient supply of the British labor necessary for the maintenance of the forts and trade, officials became increasingly dependent upon a polyglot workforce, including not just a small and fluctuating number of Britons, but also free mulattoes, RAC-owned slaves, and both free and bound local West African workers. White Britons and their mulatto offspring remained at the heart of trading operations, but throughout the era of the transatlantic slave trade they were massively outnumbered by enslaved and free African workers, without whom

Britain's transatlantic slave trade could not have operated. The wages paid to white men far outweighed the payments made to company-owned slaves or to free African employees. In 1770, for example, "White Men's Salaries" amounted to just over £8,680, "Black Men's Pay" cost just over £958, "Free Canoemen & Labourers Hire" totaled almost £789, and the cost of goods given to "Castle Slaves" for their upkeep was £2,640. However, while the wages paid to white men far exceeded those paid to local free blacks or the living costs disbursed to company slaves, these wages were not enjoyed equally. Senior officials accounted for a large proportion of the white men's salaries, and the fact that employees were paid in trade goods and local currency or crackra (an adulterated gold dust) did little to benefit the lower ranks of English workers in West Africa. The constantly shifting nature of European trade on the Gold Coast meant that as certain commodities became more common, their value fell, and over the course of the eighteenth century the market for certain textiles and other European goods became saturated. At the same time, African consumer tastes shifted, resulting in a lessening in the value of those goods deemed less desirable. For all of these reasons, the trade goods that constituted the bulk of the wages paid to RAC employees were often worth considerably less than their nominal value. Unable to raise sufficient funds to buy food, clothing, and other necessities, many of the lower-ranked RAC employees sank into debt and obligation, often forcing those who survived to extend their terms of service. Furthermore, company officials determined which goods were used as wages, and it appears that less valuable goods were sometimes passed off to white employees. While free black employees and even company-owned slaves could violently protest or withhold their labor if paid with substandard or lower-value goods, British laborers, soldiers, and sailors, bound by their indentures and outnumbered in an alien and often deadly environment, enjoyed little leverage.[21]

Service on the Gold Coast was arduous for all Britons, but most especially for craftsmen, laborers, and soldiers. John Atkins observed that Cape Coast "consists of Merchants, Factors, Writers, Miners, Artificers and Soldiers," but that

> excepting the first rank . . . [they] are all of them together a Company of white Negroes, who are entirely resigned to the Governor's commands, according to the strictest Rules of Discipline and Subjection; are punished (Garison fashion) on several Defaults, with

Mulcts, Confinement, the Dungeon, Drubbing, or the Wooden Horse; and for enduring this, they have each of them a Salary sufficient to buy *Canky*, *Palm Oil*, and a little Fish to keep them from starving: for tho' the salaries sound toleraby in *Leadenhall-Street* . . . the General (for the Company's good) pays them in *Crackra* . . . and diables them from taking any advantage of buying Necessaries from Ships coasting down.[22]

Atkins painted a bleak picture of men forced to "sign over their Liberty; none being admitted to depart "till he has adjusted all Accounts." It was difficult for even a shrewd and sober laborer to avoid debt, and all of the company's white employees were "liable to be mulcted for Drunkenness, Swearing, Neglects, and lying out of the Castle, even for not going to Church, (such is their Piety:) and thus by various arbitrary Methods, their Service is secured *durante bene placito*."[23] Each year the RAC sent tens of thousands of pounds worth of goods to the Gold Coast, but these consisted primarily of items to be traded with Africans, and materials necessary for the maintenance of the trading posts and the conduct of trade. Only a relatively small portion of the items shipped out were for the immediate use and benefit of company employees, such as medicines, clothing, preserved food, and some alcohol, although even this latter commodity was generally reserved for trade and for use as wages for local Africans and maintenance costs for company slaves. White laborers and soldiers tended to drink local palm wine.[24]

The Englishmen hired by the RAC to work on the Gold Coast as agents, writers, factors, surveyors, and surgeons were often educated professionals. Many must have calculated that their wages, higher than those paid to white laborers and soldiers or to free Africans and mulattoes, would have improved their living conditions and chances of survival, and that they could make their fortunes not from their official income but by trading on their own account, and by rising through the ranks to more senior posts. In contrast, the relatively low salaries, poor food and conditions, few opportunities for advancement, and the high risk of fatal illness and disease combined to make the lot of laborers, soldiers, and craftsmen far less appealing. Consequently, from the mid-seventeenth century on it proved very difficult for the RAC to recruit a sufficient number of appropriately skilled craftsmen, and unskilled laborers and soldiers. The RAC was forced to rely upon the crimps in London, the middlemen who were charged with securing workers for their Gold Coast forts and trading posts. It was not until 1757 that the RAC matched the bounties paid by the East India Company, and the lower rates on offer for work in Africa had made it extremely difficult to secure a sufficient number of workers willing to sign three-year indentures. Company officials in London were responsible for procuring and dispatching skilled craftsmen and artisans sufficient for the needs of their trading posts on the West African coast, who were to be paid in trade "goods and merchandise at a fair and market price according to the custom of the said coast for maintenance and support."[25]

But of those who did travel to the Gold Coast, only a fortunate few survived their full terms and were able to petition the governor to arrange their return to England: records of the deaths of white employees far outnumbered reports of company officials having "discharged those, whose time is expired, and desire it—Samuel Skerington, John Maxwell. . . ." The records of the RAC tell us little of the lives and work of these craftsmen, laborers, soldiers, and sailors. Almost all of their own words are lost to us, and they tend to appear only indirectly in the official company records, when they first arrive on the Gold Coast, in the records of their payment, and on those occasions when they got into trouble either within the British community or in their dealings with local people. But most common of all was the appearance of the names of these British workers in the lists of those too ill to work, or in the records of their deaths and the disbursement of the few goods that they left behind them.[26]

Governors and officials constantly complained that many supposed craftsmen and artisans sent to the Gold Coast were in fact unskilled, and had misrepresented their qualifications in order to secure better indentures. Desperate for any recruits, the RAC in London often signed up men and boys who were of little use to officials on the Gold Coast. In 1712, for example, a correspondent at Cape Coast Castle reported:

Wee have Received aShore the Passengers sent by Her Majesty's Shipps the Falmouth and Mary Gally a List of them your Honours has inclosed. As also of what Dyed in the Passage; We find many of them to be Boys and not above twelve or thirteen Years of Age & others very helpless Creatures which are only a Charge without any Service to your Honours. And Severall that was Entertained for tradesmen knows nothing of their Business, the which We thought

Convenient to Acquaint Your Honours of, that you might please to direct better Care to be taken in what is sent for the future.[27]

Back in London, company officials were all too well aware of the value and utility of skilled craftsmen and able laborers and soldiers, and they were eager for such men to stay in service on the Gold Coast, while ridding themselves of the expense of supporting inadequate workers. In 1689 an official in London had written to officials at Cape Coast Castle that "Those persons whom you found not Capable of business you have done well in sending them home to Ease us of their Charge but able men for our service you must give them Encouragemt. to stay willingly for we find it very hard to gett men to go into yor. Parts to stay." The surveyor John Apperley complained that "white men as artificers and labourers are quite useless to me here therefore look upon their wages as money thrown away." However, Apperley's mid-eighteenth-century preference for free and enslaved African craftsmen and laborers trained in British crafts obscured the significant achievements of generations of English artisans and laborers who had constructed and maintained Britain's Gold Coast forts in the later seventeenth century, and trained enslaved Africans in the European crafts. For all the hard work and skilful craftsmanship of Africans, British men played a vital role in building and maintaining the forts that made possible the trade in gold and slaves, and in training the British-owned slaves who continued this work throughout the eighteenth century.[28]

While the seventeenth- and eighteenth-century Britons who arrived on the Gold Coast may have been attracted by the romance of gold and the hope of making their fortune in the gold and slave trades, the harsh conditions and the low salaries of all but a few meant that most Britons struggled to do anything more than survive. The harsh and potentially deadly environment encouraged many to abandon caution and to eat, drink, and be merry until they died. Especially during the months of heavy rain, when relatively little work could be completed, a culture of heavy drinking, occasional violence, and sexual relations with local women was common, especially among soldiers and laborers.[29]

The most fortunate of Britons serving on the Gold Coast were the senior officials, who were better paid, better housed, and better fed. These officers were able to participate in the lucrative trade in gold, slaves, ivory, and other commodities on their own accounts. Consequently, although it was difficult to recruit laborers, soldiers, and artisans, there was a waiting list for official posts on the Gold Coast, and senior positions were often secured only by recommendation. By 1751 even lowly writers (clerks) enjoyed annual salaries of £60, troop commanders £80, surgeons £200, and accountants £500. It was not uncommon for men who had started on the bottom professional tier as writers to end up as governors of smaller castles and forts, and even of Cape Coast Castle itself, a level of advancement unlikely in Britain. A good example was James Phipps, whose family connections with Cape Coast governor Dalby Thomas led to his appointment as a writer, and he arrived at Cape Coast Castle as a teenager in 1703.[30] Phipps's father hoped that James would not "go to Africa merely to see the country and take the air, but to raise yourself in the world that you may come home and enjoy your friends in much better air in your own country."[31] That is precisely what Phipps did. Less than a year after his arrival Phipps was promoted to the post of second factor at Accra, and in 1709 he was again promoted and returned to Cape Coast Castle as one of the chief agents. Thereafter Phipps became chief agent and warehouse keeper at Cape Coast Castle. When Dalby Thomas died in 1711, Phipps and Seth Grosvenor assumed joint control of operations on the Gold Coast until 1719, when Phipps was appointed captain-general, with complete authority over British trading operations on the West African coast.[32]

Just like artisans and soldiers, some of the professionals who worked on the Gold Coast had signed indentures committing them to three years of service. Thus the surgeon and apothecary John Lyle signed an indenture in September 1721 in which he "contracted and agreed to serve the said Royal African Compa. of England at their Severall Settlements on the Coast of Africa." All too aware of the short life expectancy of their servants on the coast, and of the constant need for expertise in the concoction and administering of medicines, the indenture included in his responsibilities the stipulation that "the said John Lyle during the time he resides at & before he leaves each Settlement shall make it his business & endeavour to teach qualify & instruct some of the Compa. Servants either Whites or Blacks whose capacity & inclinations he shall find proper." During the era of the slave trade there were seldom more than about fifty RAC officers along the entire west coast of Africa, together with a larger number of merchants and factors. The governor of Cape Coast Castle was in overall command of British operations, and was president of the Council, which was composed of the governors of the main forts and trading posts, including Anomabu, Accra, Winneba, and Tantamkweri on the

Gold Coast and Whydah on the Slave Coast. The greatest concentration of officers was at Cape Coast Castle, but staff were spread out among all of the British castles and forts. These staff usually included a chaplain, a secretary, an accountant, a surveyor (and deputy surveyor) charged with maintenance of the company's buildings, a register who dealt with pay and personnel, a deputy accountant, two officers of the guard in overall command of the company's soldiers, about five assistant surveyors, roughly seven factors who recorded all trading transactions, and as many as ten writers who copied all documents while learning the business of trade on the Gold Coast. The governor and senior officers of the RAC enjoyed the best conditions of Britons on the Gold Coast. Writing of Cape Coast Castle in the period immediately after the transatlantic slave trade had ended, Sarah Lee remarked, "Wherever there are Englishmen there are luxuries." She described the officers' apartments at Cape Coast Castle as "well furnished, and even decorated, and generally faced with verandahs, or galleries, running along the first floor."[33]

The importance of the various officers to the entire trading operation was underscored by the reports to London of sick and dying officers and the pleas for replacements. To use the example of surgeons, in early 1704 Governor Dalby Thomas reported that "Dor. Williams has been very ill, [and] if he should dye, [we] should loose a very usefull man." Two decades later the Council reported the loss "of Our surgeon and Lieutenant whome it has pleased God to remove out of this world, and we pray that your Honours will take into Consideration the present Misfortune of your servants on this Coast for want of a Gent. Experience in Physick." A generation later it was the same story, with Charles Bell writing from Cape Coast Castle to report that the company's "Surgeon Died of the yellow fever at Annamaboe." In this case a replacement had arrived in timely fashion, and "Mr. John Kilvingston lately taken into the service by Mr. Melvil succeeds Mr. Innes as Surgeon."[34]

Commercial activity was central to the work of RAC officers on the Gold Coast, especially the factors. Perhaps because their work took them out into the neighboring communities and onto the visiting ships, the factors suffered the highest rates of illness, debility, and death among RAC officers. John Atkins observed that "most of our Factors to have dwindled much from the genteel Air they brought; wear no Cane nor Snuff-box, *idle in Men of Business*, have lank bodies, a pale Visage, their Pockets sown up, or of no use."[35]

Despite the company's absolute dependence upon traditional British crafts and skills, craftsmen were regularly required to work in very nontraditional ways on the Gold Coast, and both artisans and the work that they undertook changed radically between the late seventeenth and the turn of the nineteenth centuries. The men employed to build and maintain British forts were initially drawn from the ranks of British craftsmen, journeymen, and apprentices, yet all were contracted under three-year indentures as wage laborers, undermining the independence that skilled craftsmen in Britain aspired to achieve. Consequently, few fully qualified artisans were willing to sign such indentures, and many who traveled to the Gold Coast appear to have been journeymen or even apprentices or others with only limited skill and training. Moreover, the fiercely protected apprenticeship system that defined skilled labor throughout the British Atlantic World was undermined by the RAC's desperate need for skilled labor, which led to their requiring artisans to train white laborers, company-owned enslaved Africans, and mulattoes in the basic skills of their crafts. These practices would have been all but impossible back in Britain.

On rare occasions craftsmen brought their wives with them to the Gold Coast, as in the case of bricklayer Robert Swallow, who traveled to the Gold Coast in 1695 with his wife, whose passage was provided by the RAC with the promise of further "Acky money for her Diet,—provided she is usefull to her husband in making bricks &c." Most craftsmen came to the Gold Coast alone, but sometimes making provision for disbursement by the RAC of part of their income to wives. Correspondence occasionally passed between London and Cape Coast Castle regarding such arrangements, as when bricklayer John Maine, "a good servant to yor Honrs," discovered that his wife Dorothy "is married to another Husband so he humbly desires your Honours would be pleased to Order noe more money to be paid her upon any pretence whatsoever but that your Honours would order it to be paid him here." The British mainland and the Gold Coast were a long way apart, and separation must have meant real hardship both for those who served in West Africa and for those they left behind.[36]

Hampered by relatively low salaries, unattractive contracts, poor prospects for advancement, and the deadly climate, the RAC struggled to recruit a sufficient number of skilled craftsmen. Often men were hired for skilled work, only for officials on the Gold Coast to discover that they were in fact unskilled: RAC directives to redeploy and pay such men as unskilled laborers and soldiers did little to relieve the desperate need for artisans. The frustration of officials on the Gold Coast was apparent in complaints such as the one sent to the RAC in 1712, reporting that of the new arrivals on the *Falmouth* and the *Mary*, "Severall that was Entertained for tradesmen knows nothing of their Business." Four decades later John Apperley echoed this complaint when he reported that "Out of the 5 suppos'd Bricklayers that were sent out I have but one that is a profess'd bricklayer the other 4 know nothing of Bricklayer's work." Only very rarely did the reverse happen, when a laborer or soldier was discovered to have useful professional skills. John Roberts was delighted to learn that "a White Soldier in this Castle . . . was bred a Brickmaker." The soldier was immediately reassigned and given supervision of several slaves in order to make bricks.[37]

Disorderly and troublesome laborers and artisans caused the RAC further problems. Governor Thomas Melvil complained that one group of tradesmen sent by the RAC were "a dissolute set" and that it was "impossible to keep 'em always Sober." Melvil worried that the RAC, desperate to recruit skilled craftsmen, had negotiated indentures that gave officials on the Gold Coast little authority over their skilled employees, who had "lately quarrell'd wth. the blacks, wounded some, & some of them [the white artisans] were likewise wounded." He concluded that the craftsmen "should be under such covenants that we may lawfully punish 'em when they deserve it, otherwise we had better be without 'em."[38]

Officials on the Gold Coast complained constantly of the problems they faced because of the ill health and premature deaths of skilled craftsmen. In December 1705, for example, James Phipps and Walter Charles lamented: "We are also at the Last Extremity for want of skillfull Tradesmen haveing neither Armourer Smith Bricklayer nor even a Carpenter that's good for any thing the two under y: denomination being soldiers taken off the Guard and understand very Litle of the matter."[39] Later in the month they reiterated the problems that they faced by demanding:

> There is an Absolute necessity for Armourers Coopers & other Tradesmen . . . all of ye Forts being out of Repair we have Employed wt Tradesmen could be Spared at this place at Accra all this last Summer & they are Still there, the Repairs being not yet Compleated for want of a sufficient Number of Tradesmen. . . .
>
> We begg yr. Hons. will Consider the usefullness of such tradesmen & humbly hope you will allow some good Encouragement for

inducing a well qualified Person to come out of England as mastr.
Armourer together with two or three Others of ye same Employ.[40]

Two years later these officials reported that the fort at Anomabu was all but
in ruins for "want of quality Tradesmen wth other Necessarys, several times
mention'd to you."[41]

While the number of British artisans on the Gold Coast declined over
the course of the eighteenth century, the RAC still strove to maintain a
corps of white laborers and soldiers. In 1764 Erasmus Carver was commissioned by RAC officials in London to recruit "sober, good working men"
as craftsmen, laborers, and soldiers. With the promise of an annual salary
of £25 in trade goods, Carver succeeded in recruiting six soldiers, who
received new uniforms and two guineas apiece when they signed three-year
indentures. In addition to recruiting such men, the RAC reassigned those
who proved ill qualified for skilled work as laborers or soldiers to more
lowly and poorly paid positions. When necessary, laborers might serve as
soldiers and sailors, but especially in the seventeenth century they often
worked at similar tasks to and alongside the company's unskilled or semiskilled African slaves and the free laborers hired from local communities.
On the Gold Coast, race did not separate and define either skilled or
unskilled labor.[42]

The men employed as laborers, soldiers, and sailors in the British forts
on the Gold Coast were only rarely required to take up arms against neighboring European posts, and even more rarely called upon to fight local
Africans. Company soldiers were more like policemen who guarded the
forts and their weapons, stocks of trade goods, and slaves; ensured that
company-owned slaves and white employees were kept in line and did not
fight with local people; and protected the persons and goods of British
officials and traders. As earlier, a few arrived with their wives, who were
paid a half-salary in exchange for unspecified work for the Company. Thus,
in 1751 the register of soldiers at Cape Coast Castle recorded that Catherine
Frazier had arrived with her husband William, and that Elizabeth Jones had
accompanied her husband William. Catherine died eighteen months later.[43]

With no need for a full military force, the number of soldiers employed
by the company rarely exceeded the number of officers, and in time of war
it was the ships and crewmen of the Royal Navy who conducted much of
the fighting undertaken by Britons, which is not surprising given that most
conflict involved naval battles or assaults on other nations' coastal forts. In

the late seventeenth century the total number of soldiers stationed in about ten often lightly fortified trading posts along the entire Gold Coast rarely exceeded one hundred, a number that had not increased a century later, despite the fact that Britain had by then become the major European force in the transatlantic slave trade. The Company employed large numbers of local Africans as soldiers only during local or international wars, although over time the mulatto population furnished a growing number of RAC soldiers and junior officials.[44] The soldiers were not paid particularly well, and their lives were hard and often short. Barbot recorded that "the common sort," especially

> labourers and soldiers, are expos'd to all sorts of fatigues and hardships upon every command, without those comforts and supports which officers have. Besides all this, they are generally men of no education or principles, void of foresight, careless, prodigal, addicted to strong liquors, as palm-wine, brandy and punch, which they will drink to excess . . . some, and perhaps no small number, are over fond of the black women, whose natural hot and leud temper soon wastes their bodies, and consumes that little substance they have: tho' such prostitutes are to be had at a very inconsiderable rate, yet having thus spent their poor allowance, these wretched men cannot afford to buy themselves convenient subsistence, but are forced to feed on bread, oil, and salt, or, at best, to feast upon a little fish. Thus . . . they fall into several distempers, daily exposing their lives to danger, very many being carry'd off thro' these excesses, in a very deplorable condition, by fevers, fluxes, cholicks, consumptions, asthma's, small pox, coughs, and sometimes worms and dropsies.[45]

In 1751 senior soldiers received adequate pay, such as "Serjeant" Hugh Irvin, who received an annual salary of £50, and Corporal Peter Falkingree, who received £36, but common soldiers such as Samuel Porter, John Harris, John Baylis, and William Christian were paid only £27 per annum, and soldiers who were incapacitated were reduced to half-pay. While this was more than the £18 paid annually to soldiers in the British army in 1800, wages on the Gold Coast were paid in trade goods and thus were subject to local exchange rates, and the standard of living of company soldiers on the Gold Coast was even lower than that of most soldiers in the army.[46]

The letters and records sent from the Gold Coast to London recorded and commented on the deaths of soldiers as frequently as the deaths of craftsmen. In 1712, for example, officials at Cape Coast Castle complained that they had endured "a very sickly season, and lost many of our New Soldiers, and many are still sick, and daily dying. Insomuch that we fear, before the Departure of the Men of War, few of the Soldiers we Received by them will be Living, and here at Cape Coast we have not now above ten upon the Guard."[47] Of forty-eight soldiers who arrived at Cape Coast Castle in February 1769, all but eight died within three months. On occasion company officials sought to alleviate the conditions endured by the soldiers, as in the Act of Council passed at Cape Coast Castle in 1737 raising soldiers' salaries (paid in adulterated gold dust and trade goods) by 50 percent because "fresh provisions of all kinds are at a high price in and about Cape Coast Town for want of which many of the soldiers sicken and die."[48]

A handful of British sailors based in Britain's Gold Coast forts and trading posts were nominally responsible for the smaller craft that transported people and correspondence between Cape Coast Castle and the outlying forts. The line between soldiers and sailors was fluid, with sailors performing the duties of soldiers when they were based in the forts. When "Richard Dick a European Sailor of a very good Character" was given responsibility for the RAC boat based at Cape Coast Castle, it was recorded that he would "be kept on the books at Cape Coast Castle as a soldier." On occasion such men, whether by choice or on the orders of the governor, were transferred to visiting ships that were shorthanded. Slave ships often spent months on the coast, trading goods and negotiating the purchase of gold and slaves, during which time West African diseases spread to the ship's crew and killed many of them. Thus in 1713 the slave ship *Catherine* "was very badly manned having but eight on Board, So that for the Security of the Voyage Wee spared two of our Soldiers out of the Castle that was Sailors."[49] On other occasions RAC officials sought to rid themselves of sickly soldiers who were a drain on resources. In 1774 Governor David Mill complained that he would be glad to discharge

the Ulcered and Sickly Soldiers; but though I have of late, offered several Masters of Ships £5– Sterling a head, for carrying them off, I cannot get any one to take them: I should therefore, beg leave to propose, that an agreement be made with the Masters of the Store Ships, to carry off annually such of these poor unfortunate Men, as

can be of no service to us here; otherwise they must remain a bur-
then on your Establishment.[50]

The governor ended his letter by reporting that he had "inlisted 12 young
Mulattoes as Soldiers, who are by far the fittest for this Climate." He
intended to try to phase out British soldiers, replacing them with mulattoes,
hoping to thus "be better Garrisoned, and save Money that Soldiers from
England cost us, which is no trifle."[51]

The difficulty in recruiting a sufficient number of suitably qualified artisans, together with the high mortality rates among those who came to the
Gold Coast, prompted the RAC to encourage the training of free and
enslaved Africans and mulattoes, and from the late seventeenth century on
British craftsmen schooled Africans in the European practices of such skills
as carpentry, brickmaking and bricklaying, masonry, and ironwork. The
result was that RAC officials, both in London and on the West African
coast, began associating enslaved Africans with traditional white artisanal
crafts. In 1695 John Morice wrote from London to the governor and Council at Cape Coast Castle with the news that a carpenter and joiner named
William Gabb and a bricklayer named Philip Young had been hired and
that each had been promised additional bounties should they "instruct any
Negro to be an Artificer Joyner Carpenter Bricklayer or any other needful
Artist."[52] A little under a decade later Dalby Thomas wrote from Cape
Coast Castle: "We are in want of a Good Armourer or two that understands
how to make every part of a lock. . . . If you are pleased to send an Armourer or two Pray let them be Masters of their Trade and that know how
to mend and braze and let them bring all manner of Tools & instruments
with them for those purposes and if they bring three or four setts they will
be ye better able to instruct your Black people here."[53]

The result was that white craftsmen at Cape Coast Castle and the other
British forts, many of them young and relatively inexperienced, acted as
master craftsmen who trained apprentices drawn from the ranks of the
company-owned slaves. With the white craftsmen themselves often working under conditions and terms that would have been unacceptable in
England, traditions of craft labor and apprenticeship were undermined, and
a new skilled workforce emerged within the ranks of the RAC's own slaves.
Thus in the mid-1770s the skilled workforce at Cape Coast Castle was largely
composed of bound Africans: the enslaved bricklayers were building a new

bastion at Cape Coast Castle and repairing a ruined parapet; the laborers were filling the new bastion with rubbish; the carpenters were building a new roof above the castle's gallery; the sawyers were providing planks for all of these operations; the smiths were creating the ironwork for the gun carriages to be used at Anomabu; the coopers were constructing barrels for carrying mortar or rubble; the armorers were cleaning muskets and making keys.[54]

John Apperley carried this practice to its logical conclusion, and for the construction of the new fort at Anomabu he relied almost completely upon enslaved and free black skilled labor.

> As I find the Black bricklayers are the people I am to depend upon for building the Fort, out of the 23 Men Slaves Capn. Bruce brought [from] Gambia, I've made 12 of 'em Bricklayers, 3 Carpenters & 3 Smiths and I believe they'll answer our expectations being the only method I could fall upon to get Artificers. I have consulted with Mr. Melvil & can find no speedier method for haveing of this Fort built than by having a good supply of slaves from Gambia from 15 to 22 Years of Age, that they may be put to trades as soon as they arrive . . . the support of yr Forts upon the Coast this in particular depends very much upon it as you have no Artificers worth mentioning on the Coast.[55]

Governor Melvil approved of the plan to employ "4 or 5 compleat tradesmen with good salaries, not to work themselves but to oversee the Gambians & teach 'em how to work," hoping that Apperley's skill and the extensive building project at Anomabu would make it into "a school to breed tradesmen, who will afterwards put all ye Forts into repair & keep 'em so wth very little charge to you."[56]

In 1758 a list of Britons bound for Cape Coast Castle included a twenty-three-year-old carpenter, a twenty-five-year-old mason, and an eighteen-year-old gunsmith, men whose ages indicate that these tradesmen were at best journeymen and perhaps even apprentices. Their role was to supervise and train Africans, but by this point it was the company's slaves who undertook most of the work: indeed, with few sufficiently qualified and healthy white craftsmen available, it was increasingly the more highly skilled slaves who undertook training and supervision of their fellow Africans.[57] The regular letters to the RAC lamenting the deaths of British craftsmen and the desperate need for replacements began to diminish in tone and quantity over the course of the eighteenth century, and a typical entry in the "Diary of Employment of Labourers at Cape Coast Castle" showed how Africans were now responsible for the work of maintaining existing buildings and creating new ones.

11 August 1777.

11 Bricklayers, 7 Carpenters, 4 Sawyers, 5 Smiths, 3 Armourers, 4 Coopers, 9 Artificers' Boys, 16 Labourers, 31 Labouresses, 6 Stoneblowers . . .

Bricklayers Employ'd in Paveing Mr. Grossle's Bastion[;] Carpenters still Makeing shutters [for the windows of the white officials' apartments] and New Gates for the Garden[;] sawyers [illegible] for Canoes [;] Smiths makeing New Iron work for 4 New Gun Carriages at Annomaboe[;] Armourers cleaning the Soldiers Arms[;] Coopers Makeing Tubs for the Labouresses to carry shells in[;] Labourers in the Garden clearing the Walks & Labouresses still picking Shells[;] Stone Blowers blowing stone for Paving Mr Grossle's Bastion.[58]

The only clearly identified Briton on the list of workers and their tasks at Cape Coast Castle was the governor himself, John Grossle, for all of the listed manual workers, both skilled and unskilled, were enslaved Africans belonging to the RAC. Subsequent entries noted changes in the work assignments and, when there were no changes, recorded "The Rest of the Slaves Employ'd as yesterday." The work changed according to need, as smiths made garden hoes or nails, or carpenters trimmed boards for the coopers' use in constructing barrels, but whatever the task it was skilled slaves rather than British artisans that maintained the forts and trading posts and thus made the British slave trade possible.[59]

Toward the end of the transatlantic slave trade the British government deposited large numbers of convicts on the Gold Coast, providing an infusion of men and women to work as soldiers and laborers in British forts. Although the number of Britons on the Gold Coast increased dramatically, the scheme was an unmitigated disaster. Freed from jails and with British officials powerless to control them, the prisoners ran riot and "became the Terror of all your Servants, as well as the Natives." The former convicts set out "to plunder and rob the Natives of every thing they could lay their hands on," while in Cape Coast Castle "they broke open our stores, stole thereout our property, and put us in Fear of our Lives." The RAC had intended to distribute the 170 new arrivals among all of the British forts along the Gold Coast, but the criminals resisted the idea and insisted that "they *would not be dispersed* in small parties, but would remain altogether in one Body." Eventually the situation improved, as the climate and local diseases had their inevitable effect, and within six months only sixty of the contingent were fit for duty. Not all died: some appear to have joined the crews of passing slave ships, while others who were placed on board a captured ship were reputed to have killed their officers and become pirates. Subsequent shipments of smaller groups of prisoners throughout the 1780s were no more successful, although these were more readily integrated into the British workforce, and officials in Cape Coast requested that the British authorities "endeavour to pick out such as have been brought up to useful Trades: among those now received, there is not even a Bricklayer, Carpenter, or any Tradesman that can be useful to us."[60]

In addition to free and enslaved Africans, mulattoes became a vital part of the British workforce on the Gold Coast. The mulatto populations in and around the forts grew steadily over the course of the seventeenth and eighteenth centuries. By the end of the seventeenth century Barbot reported, "The natives of Mina are all either black or mulattoes. Of the latter there are about two hundred families." The relationships between British men and African women, whether enslaved or free, had little if any legal standing in Britain, but enjoyed a degree of respect and status in West Africa. While the fluid social situations occasioned by the huge international trade made rape of enslaved women or casual sexual encounters with both free and enslaved women possible, there were also relatively formal and longer-term arrangements that were regarded as marriages in accordance with local customs. Some involved contractual arrangements between the white man and the family of his African partner, whose mother might expect to receive a gift in goods, followed by a monthly stipend. One historian has estimated that the cost might equal approximately one-third of the salary of a newly arrived writer or factor, making marriage an expensive proposition, albeit one that might bring savings and even income through the labor of a wife. Moreover, marriage to a local woman brought entree into the local community, improved language skills, and familial and trading connections. The close relationships between these men and women, and the families they formed, can be seen in the substantial legacies left to wives and children. The limited life expectancies of white men on the Gold Coast meant that many mulatto children knew little or nothing of their fathers. As the mulatto community increased in size, the daughters of interracial unions themselves entered into relationships with white men, intensifying the connections between the mulatto community and the Europeans.[61]

Mulatto boys were often employed in the castles, and some were sent to Britain for education and training. Often literate, fluent in English and perhaps other European languages as well as local African languages, these men sometimes trained in commerce or crafts: many, such as mulatto William Norman, a skilled carpenter, were employed by the RAC. Male members of the mulatto communities formed a semiprofessional middling sort in and around the British forts and castles, and their labor eased relations between Africans and Europeans and facilitated the trade between them. Thus, in the middle of the eighteenth century, RAC employees included the writer Frederick Adoy, the "Mulatto Bomboy" Quow Reveer, the gunner Quomino, the cook Quaroo, and the soldiers Howe, William Ogle, Cudjoe, Quamino Apracoe, Peter Brown, Benjamin Lewis, Frederick Stackmore, and Joseph Gordon, all of them mulatto.[62]

In late 1788 several leading men in Cape Coast Castle "founded a School for the Education of Twelve Mulattoe Children," which the governor and his Council regarded as "a very meritorious Action, and [one] from which Posterity may reap great Pleasure and Advantage." RAC officials in London commended "the laudable Design of the Governor, his Council, and the other Gentlemen," and the company furnished the new school with "an Assortment of Books, consisting of Primers, Spelling Books, Testaments and Bibles, of a common Edition." While self-serving in the sense that this school was intended for the sons of the men who created it, the founders pledged that its object was "not merely the Welfare of Children, belonging to the Servants of the Committee." This school appears to have been the successor to one established by Philip Quaque, a son of Birempon Cudjoe, the caboceer at Cape Coast, who was educated in England, ordained as the first African priest in the Church of England, and then appointed by the Society for the Propagation of the Gospel and the RAC as the missionary to the Africans and mulattoes of the Gold Coast. His school was for mulattoes, and several of its graduates entered the service of the RAC as clerks and writers. To this day Quaque's grave may still be seen below the guns inside the westerly wall of Cape Coast Castle; comparatively few British graves are as well marked.[63]

It appears likely that Britons actively sought out mulattoes for privileged positions, believing them better suited to the climate and more resistant to local diseases than whites, and more closely connected to the British interest than local Africans. As the European presence on the Gold Coast increased, the larger European forts created their own militia units, matching the hereditary *asafo* military companies within the local African communities. RAC-owned slaves created their own company, while eventually the growing body of mulatto offspring of European men and African women created more military companies.[64] The ill health of many Europeans on the coast encouraged the governors of the forts and castles to rely upon these black and mulatto soldiers; thus one governor of Cape Coast Castle concluded a report on "the Ulcerated and Sickly" white soldiers by reporting, "I have within these six Months inlisted 12 young Mulattoes as Soldiers, who are by far the fittest for this Climate; and in order to avoid having occasion to Indent for Soldiers from Europe, I shall get more Mulattoes, and if I can get a sufficiency, we shall be both better Garrisoned, and save the Money that Soldiers from England cost us."[65] As a consequence the accounts for European castles and forts routinely included the wages of black and mulatto soldiers. In 1750, for example, the authorities at Cape Coast Castle employed Chasee, Triton, Apponherry, Quashee Adadoe, Bonetta, and Yeon as "Black Soldiers." Free black and mulatto soldiers served alongside white soldiers at most of the British forts and trading posts along the Gold Coast, as in the case of Quomino and Howe at Dixcove, or William Ogle, Quamino Apracoe, Peter Brown, and Cudjoe at Tantumquerry.[66]

The soldiers of the local communities and those associated with the European forts were proud of their militia companies, and on one occasion the governor of Cape Coast Castle requested "Coullers or flaggs" for "ye Black Souldiers one Red another blew, another Yellow," for being able to parade such colors on ceremonial occasions "would please ye Slaves & other black men of ye Town." The imposition of European ideas of military service and discipline did not always sit well with West Africans, however. On one occasion fifteen white, black, and mulatto soldiers abandoned their posts at Cape Coast Castle because "three of them were severely punished for repeated Neglect of Duty," and all fifteen reacted negatively to this and to "the White Serjeant's and Corporals teaching them the real Duty of Soldiers, which they have been totally unacquainted with." Although closely identified with the Europeans, members of the mulatto community none-theless pursued their own priorities. This process was embodied in Edward

Barter, a mulatto educated in England between 1690 and 1693 at the expense of the Royal African Company. Upon his return to the Gold Coast, Barter at first served the RAC before setting up as an independent and increasingly powerful merchant. Whether independent men such as Barter, or RAC employees such as clerks, craftsmen, and soldiers, mulattoes were none too willing to submit to British regulation and discipline.[67]

The development of a successful trade in slaves, gold, and other commodities over the course of the seventeenth and eighteenth centuries required well-maintained castles and trading forts along the Gold Coast, well stocked with trade goods and staffed by British officials, merchants, craftsmen, soldiers, mulatto employees, and company-owned slaves. However, the harsh conditions and the deadly disease environment meant that mortality rates for Britons worse than those of the early seventeenth-century Chesapeake persisted throughout the era of the transatlantic slave trade. The continued British presence and eventual domination of the transatlantic slave trade was no small achievement, but it was heavily reliant upon a constant flow of new British laborers, soldiers, craftsmen, and officials, men who died in astonishingly high numbers. Just as significantly, the British increasingly depended upon the work of large numbers of company-owned slaves, the local mulatto population, and the good offices of an elite professional class of local African caboceers, linguists, and bomboys, who made possible the successful employment of local Africans, and the conduct of trade with Africans from near and far. As such British trade on the Gold Coast constituted a complex multiracial and multiskilled operation.

Labor for the British, the mulattoes, the pawns, and the British-owned slaves in the castles and forts along the Gold Coast developed in ways that would have been quite alien to Britons in the Americas or back in Britain itself. Racial and professional barriers blurred as white craftsmen in Britain and West Africa trained enslaved and free blacks and mulattoes as craftsmen and professionals, and the races worked together in manual, skilled, clerical, and trading work on the African coast. For white craftsmen, soldiers, and laborers, conditions on the Gold Coast were atrocious. The lucky few who survived were sometimes able to rise through the ranks and make a good living, but few prospered. In contrast, free and bound Africans and mulattoes enjoyed longer lives and were sometimes able to exercise significantly more control over the terms of their labor than were their British co-workers. To slave owners in the Americas, and to employers in Britain, the apparent inversions of race, labor, and status that occurred on the Gold Coast would have appeared very strange. They were made possible and even necessary, however, because of the precarious position of the British and the other Europeans in West Africa, dependent as they were upon the work and good will of their African hosts.

PART III

African Bound Labor

Chapter 6

"A Spirit of Liberty"

Slave Labor in Gold Coast Castles and Forts

The ill health and high mortality rates endured by Britons on the Gold
Coast often meant that "no other than Blackworkmen [*sic*] of any signi-
fication" were available to RAC officials. As a consequence, British forts
and their trading operations necessarily depended more heavily upon the
labor of Africans and mulattoes than on the work of British craftsmen,
laborers, soldiers, and sailors. Some of these West Africans were enslaved
or free wage laborers from the local community, others were the mulatto
offspring of white RAC employees and local women, and a few were
"pawns" whose labor belonged temporarily to the British. But by far the
most significant category of British workers included the large contingent
of "company," "castle," or "factory" slaves, who came to dominate the
ranks of the British workforce between the mid-seventeenth and the late
eighteenth centuries. The British slave trade could not have existed, let
alone prospered, without this enslaved workforce in and around British
forts and trading posts.[1]

In the late seventeenth century the RAC began a regular practice of
buying slaves in Gambia and shipping them south to the Gold Coast, in
order to maintain and reinforce a permanent bound workforce of skilled
and unskilled company-owned Africans. For almost a century and a half,
these men and women formed a constant and vital workforce within a
larger Atlantic World, at the nexus of a trade that linked the British Isles,
southern Asia, and the Americas. At a time when bound labor was undergo-
ing radical changes in Barbados and elsewhere in British America, the
situation of these company slaves remained relatively fixed, for their
enslavement was defined primarily by West African norms.

Familiar British ideas about the nature and practice of free and bound labor, as well as developing ideas about race and labor, confronted a radically different modus operandi on the coast of West Africa. In theory at least, Britons who in the later seventeenth and the eighteenth centuries signed indentures to serve three years on the Gold Coast were working in a British tradition that had already been adapted to colonial contexts in the Caribbean and North American colonies. However, any resemblance to life and work in Britain or in North America quickly evaporated in the face of horrific conditions, extremely high mortality rates, and relatively little chance of survival and an improvement in one's situation. As a consequence, the lives of surviving British craftsmen, laborers, and soldiers and sailors on the Gold Coast were dramatically different from those of the majority of indentured servants in Britain's North American colonies, although there were similarities with the bound laborers in mid-seventeenth-century Barbados.[2]

In contrast, company-owned enslaved Africans enjoyed comparatively good lives, far better than the enslaved men and women bound for New World plantations, and often apparently better than the lives of British laborers, artisans, and workers who were nominally bound only by indenture or contract. Throughout the late seventeenth and for most of the eighteenth centuries, these company slaves were protected against transportation to the Americas, and were thus guaranteed lives and working conditions molded more by West African traditions than British expectations. As such, these men, women, and children enjoyed a fair degree of agency, often living outside the British forts and trading posts. They received what was for all intents and purposes a wage with which they purchased food, clothing, and supplies, and they formed a remarkably independent and powerful group of workers. In West African society many slaves lived and functioned within family units, while others served in larger blocks as gold miners, soldiers, or attendants of rulers. All were regarded as occupying a station in life, one defined largely by labor and status, and castle slaves occupied a similar position. RAC officials found they had little choice but to regard their enslaved workforce as being composed of individuals who expected to be treated with respect. Thus, for example, British officials allowed castle slaves a great degree of freedom in family formation, and recognized the families that their enslaved workers formed. When, for example, the slave gardener was moved from Anomabu to Cape Coast Castle in 1778, "he with his Wife and 2 Children came up: it would have been cruel to have parted the Family." Such concern for enslaved families was seldom a consideration for white planters in the British Americas, who were able to modify the institution thousands of miles away from West African norms and practices.[3]

On the Gold Coast traditional African forms of slavery and bondage coexisted with European variations, as well as the bound labor of white Europeans, and in the communities in and around the forts and castles of the Gold Coast all of the variations of bound and free labor found throughout the northern Atlantic coexisted. Given the relative lack of power of white Europeans on the West African coast, the forms of slavery that developed in the Americas where white masters enjoyed such enormous power were never able to dominate patterns of labor. Skilled and unskilled castle slaves enjoyed a remarkable degree of agency, and fashioned communities and families over which their British masters had relatively little authority. They enjoyed as much and on occasion even more control over the terms of their labor than did many white men in Britain or British North America and the Caribbean, for the latter could be bound to labor with far less control over their lives. The greatest contrast, however, was between castle slaves and the tens of thousands of slaves who passed through the forts and trading posts that castle slaves helped maintain: the latter were bound for the Americas and forms of plantation slavery in which they would enjoy little power or liberty.

As a consequence of their dependence upon the labor of company-owned slaves, Britons on the Gold Coast were required to develop policies and practices for the management of a group of workers who operated within a labor system unlike anything that existed in the British Isles. In 1702 the RAC codified the treatment of company slaves, collating past and present policies and practices. Officials in London mandated that castle slaves were to be converted to Christianity, allowed to marry freely (usually other castle slaves, but over time to local free West Africans, too), taught skills to enhance their value and utility, and cared and provided for in ill health or when they were no longer able to work. The RAC purchased slaves from Gambia, some fifteen hundred miles distant from the Gold Coast, so that they would have no cultural or familial connection with Africans on the Gold Coast, and thus could not run away for fear that they would be captured by local Africans and sold as slaves to be shipped to the Americas. By the early eighteenth century the RAC in London required their officials in Gambia and on the Gold Coast "to look upon as a Standing Order" the injunction to buy choice young male and female slaves for transfer between the two locations and then service as castle slaves. In 1708, for example, officials at Cape Coast Castle determined that the British forts along the Gold Coast "Wants Four Hundred Slaves from Gambia & Whydaw for Coast use also Workmen &c from England are wanted"; this kind of equation of the labor of company-owned slaves with that of skilled British craftsmen bound to the company was very common. The policy of purchasing slaves from afar worked in the sense that few company slaves are recorded as having eloped; their lives as castle slaves were far better than would likely have been the case had they risked escape into an alien society in which strangers were likely to be captured and sold for export. Only a handful of the castle slaves actually lived within the British posts, however. The majority made their homes in their own community outside the forts, which placed them in close proximity to local Africans. Their British owners hoped that castle slaves would constitute an alien community rather than integrate fully into local West African communities, and to a degree this proved to be the case. On numerous occasions British officials were forced to arbitrate between local people and their own castle slaves. Over time there was a degree of integration of castle slaves into local West African society and culture, however, mainly through trade and marriage.[4]

Having survived West African diseases such as yellow fever during childhood, castle slaves had developed immunities that afforded them greater protection than was enjoyed by Britons. However, they suffered as much from injury and other illnesses as did white workers. In 1753, for example, a report from Cape Coast Castle barely differentiated between castle slaves and Britons, reporting, "We are at present in a very distress'd situation here with Sickness & Guinea worms. . . . Every body is recovering. The Company's Slaves are likewise afflicted with Worms." John Apperley sent a detailed report listing all of the castle slaves under his supervision at Anomabu in the mid-1750s, recording both their skills and their condition. Out of forty-four castle slaves, eleven were listed as "sick" or "old," and those incapable of any work were returned to Cape Coast Castle with its better medical facilities. Lists of castle slaves invariably included some older men and women, and many more men, women, and children who were too unwell to work.[5]

Although cheaper over the long term than the weak and ailing British laborers and craftsmen, castle slaves were nonetheless expensive to maintain, costing the RAC £20,622 for the years 1770–1776, one-third of the

£59,243 paid to white employees, and over three times as much as the £6,741 paid to free African canoemen and laborers. The cost of this workforce was increased by the ill health, injury, and old age of many of the castle slaves. Explaining the expenditure of more than £20,000, the Cape Coast Castle accounts noted that castle slaves were divided into six categories: those who were healthy and fit to work; "Those laid up with worms and other disorders . . . these worms often lay them up six and even twelve months"; "Women pregnant, and others suckling young Children"; "The Old and Infirm"; "The Superannuated"; and children "too young for Labour." At any one time, only a minority of castle slaves might be fully fit and able to work, and a muster of the 174 slaves at Cape Coast Castle in May 1780 established that only 59 were fit for work. However, although castle slaves may have suffered the same ailments and injuries as their white fellow-laborers, they enjoyed lifetime security, retiring in their mid-fifties with small pensions. At times British officials on the Gold Coast complained of the cost of maintaining such people, as when Governor John Roberts requested permission to discharge the "old, idle, supernumerated and insolent" slaves who consumed valuable resources. Recognizing the disquiet this would cause among the company's most significant body of workers, however, officials in London refused this and virtually every similar request.[6]

All who lived and worked on the Gold Coast knew that illness and debility were part and parcel of daily life. RAC officials acknowledged that the total number of castle slaves "appear indeed a large number, and are naturally supposed equal to the labour of repairing and rebuilding" British castles and forts. Because those who were "healthy and fit for Duty" were generally outnumbered by the many rendered unfit for full work by disease, injury, age, or pregnancy and nursing, however, RAC officials on the Gold Coast often found themselves shorthanded. A listing of castle slaves at Winnebah in 1799, for example, illustrated the ill health that plagued the older slaves: all three of the enslaved who were older than fifty were unfit: "Tom, 62, bricklayer, nearly blind . . . Branja, 64, labourer, very infirm . . . Eccoah, 58, washerwoman, infirm."[7]

Because they were so integral to British trading operations, castle slaves were provided with some of the best medical treatments and medicines available to their owners. For example, worried that a particularly virulent smallpox epidemic might wipe out most of the contingent of castle slaves, in 1789 the Governor's Council at Cape Coast Castle took the unusual step of deciding to inoculate the slaves in order "to prevent calamitous Consequences . . . [and] the Loss of so useful a Body of black people." Temporary shelters were erected for the castle slaves some distance from Cape Coast, in order to isolate them from local Africans and the castle's residents, where they were "inoculated by Mr. Dawson our Assistant Surgeon."[8]

Despite the ill health of castle slaves, these slaves nonetheless provided the greater part of the skilled and unskilled labor required for the day-to-day British trading operations on the Gold Coast. In 1749, for example, the RAC owned some 367 slaves on the Gold Coast, including 10 carpenters, 3 brickmakers, 3 goldsmiths, 2 doctor's servants, 2 gold takers, 7 blacksmiths, 9 bricklayers, 5 cooks, 3 coopers, 3 armorers, 1 gunner, 7 chapel servants, 20 canoemen, as well as 79 women, 137 men, and 76 children who constituted more general laborers. At Cape Coast Castle and at all of the smaller forts and trading posts on the Gold Coast, castle slaves vastly outnumbered all other workers and officials. At Dixcove in 1737, for example, there were two RAC "Chiefs, a Writer, a Serjeant, four Soldiers, a Master Sawyer, two Cabboceers . . . one Linguist . . . and three Canoe men" on the company payroll, but these fifteen Britons and free Africans were outnumbered by the "41 Castle working Slaves." By the mid-eighteenth century, listings of skilled castle slaves at the various British forts on the Gold Coast often identified them as "artificers," acknowledging their craft and professional skill with a title traditionally reserved for white craftsmen. Cape Coast Castle had carpenters, bricklayers, sawyers, brickmakers, blacksmiths, and coopers; Dixcove had a blacksmith; Commenda had a carpenter and seven sawyers; Winnebah had a bricklayer and a carpenter; Accra had one blacksmith; and Whydah had two carpenters, three sawyers, and two blacksmiths. The records contained no mention of any white craftsmen who were fit for work.[9]

When there was no pressing work, castle slaves would undertake secondary tasks such as making nails and bricks, whitewashing walls, and so forth, but there were usually more urgent needs. In July 1777, for example, the enslaved bricklayers were building a new bastion for Cape Coast Castle and repairing a collapsed parapet. Unskilled laborers and "laboresses" hauled rocks and rubbish to fill the new bastion, while coopers were busy making barrels for the transport of mortar and rubble. Sawyers felled trees and cut three-inch-thick planks, while carpenters laid a new roof above the castle's gallery. The blacksmiths were employed on the ironwork for gun carriages to be used at the newly rebuilt fortress at Anomabu. The armorers were cleaning and repairing muskets, and making new keys, while girls and women were working in the castle gardens. Younger girls and women in ill health were often employed in the company's gardens, adjoining the forts, in order to help guarantee a supply of fresh fruits and vegetables for the castle's inhabitants, and for the crew and cargo of slave ships. One month later the work had moved on, and the bricklayers were paving the top of the new bastion, while carpenters were making wooden shutters for the windows of the private apartments of senior company officials and new wooden gates for the gardens. The blacksmiths were still working on the gun carriages, and "laboresses" were collecting and carrying stone to be used in paving the bastion.[10]

Three years later the fifty-nine slaves fit for work at Cape Coast Castle were employed in a similarly wide variety of activities:

> 5 Men and a Boy Bricklayers covering the Arches of the new Gallery; 13 Men and one Woman attending the Bricklayers. 3 Men and a Boy Carpenters making a Door for a Warehouse or fitting up a new seven hand Canoe. 3 Men blowing Stone. 3 Armourers cleaning Arms and other necessary work about the Castle. 6 Men and one Woman gone to the Country to bring Wood for the Lime Kiln, One Man and Two Women gone to the Country to bring Wood for the Cook Room. 6 Women to sweep the Castle and officer's Rooms. Two to sweep the Governor's Apartments, the Bastions near it and Secretary's Office. Two to sweep the Accountant's Rooms. Two to sweep the Pantry and Cook Room. Two to attend the sick and sweep the Hospital. The above Women carry Water from the Tank to the different Apartments and other necessary Work. Two to wash the Governor's and other Officer's Linnen. 6 Men with 12 Women and Girls in the Garden. 7 Canoemen gone wth the Doctor's Assistant to Commenda. Two waterside Bomboys, One Bomboy of the Slaves, One Gunner and Mate.[11]

Facing arduous working conditions, "the Sun being so extreamly hot here," British workers and craftsmen labored for five hours per day, but castle slaves generally worked for seven hours, and at Cape Coast Castle the start and end of their shifts were marked by the castle bell.[12]

From the late seventeenth century on, company slaves were trained by and worked alongside skilled white craftsmen, learning British trades and skills, leading to a community of skilled slaves. African craftsmen soon began playing key roles in construction and maintenance of British operations on the Gold Coast. As early as 1682 James Nightingale at Commenda wrote to the governor at Cape Coast Castle: "I desire you would be pleased to send up one of the blacke bricklayers to oversee the building for whome wee now only waite, delaying the foundation for one fitt person to direct the same."[13] Twelve days later Nightingale wrote to acknowledge that he had received "Yankey with his materials." Yankey, a skilled bricklayer, was one of many castle slaves who performed such work for the British throughout the era of British involvement in the transatlantic slave trade. Over time, fewer and fewer white workers were involved in the training process, and African slaves dominated the skilled and unskilled workforce of the British forts, including the training of new enslaved workers, in a reflection of the artisanal apprenticeship system of British America within the ranks of the enslaved.[14]

Company officials, both in London and on the Gold Coast, agreed on the utility of "putting out Children of Castle working Slaves to Trades" as apprentices, thus ensuring a regular supply of skilled craftsmen. At times specific trades and skills were mentioned, as when Governor Dalby Thomas suggested that with a new supply of castle slaves he could employ white sailors to "breed Blacks to be Seamen good Enough." This became a common refrain, as when William Mutter wrote from Cape Coast Castle in 1764 requesting "50 or 60 young Gambian Slaves," promising that he "would sett 30 or 40 of these to learn the Bricklayer, Carpenter & Smith's trades." A decade earlier officials at Cape Coast Castle reported that they had received "20 Gambia Slaves by his Majesty's Ship Hind, & 19 by yor Sloop Africa." Clearly delighted with the new arrivals, who "promise very well," the author reported that "twelve men are put to be Bricklayers, the others to other trades." The next paragraph of this letter reported "our great want of tradesmen" from Britain, revealing the full extent of the need to rely upon African slaves for skilled labor. The author could see only "one effectual way" of accomplishing the major construction project at Anomabu, perhaps the largest undertaken by the British on the Gold Coast during the eighteenth century. He proposed that "4 or 5 compleat tradesmen" from England might be employed to supervise a large number of castle slaves, who would be responsible for the great majority of the skilled and unskilled labor required for the construction of the new Anomabu fort. "In constantly supplying us with Gambia Slaves," the letter continued, "Annamboe will prove a school to breed tradesmen, who will afterwards put all ye Forts into repair & keep 'em wth very little charge to you."[15]

Writing in 1756, John Apperley listed the castle slaves working at Anomabu, with the "old slaves distinguished from the Gambia Slaves that arrived here since I came on the Coast." There were twenty-six Gambia slaves, most of them as yet untrained, which was reflected in the descriptive appellations of unskilled "laborers" and "laboresses." In contrast, all of the seventeen men listed as "old slaves" had been working for the British long enough to acquire skills: nine were, like Coffee, Yaow Bob, Quaw, and Cudjoe, listed as bricklayers; four, including Quacow, Bandoe, Coffee Bob, and Jamboe, were carpenters; Qashee was a brickmaker, Samboe a goldsmith, Annamansah a blacksmith, and Cudjoe a canoeman. However, none of the six females included in the list of "old slaves" were recorded as having a skill or occupation, and all were recorded as laboresses. Thus, just as apprentices and journeymen learned skills and became recognized as craftsmen in Britain and British North America, company-owned male slaves developed similar skills over time, and their status and conditions of work changed as they became sufficiently skilled. The situation was rather different for female castle slaves. William Cross's description of stones and bricks "being brought up with a great deal of ease by the women" at Commenda in 1686 speaks volumes about the arduous unskilled or semiskilled labor that was the lot of female company slaves.[16]

Female castle slaves, called "laboresses," were rarely associated with specific occupations such as gardening and cleaning. Cooking, rarely listed as a female skill, was more generally the domain of male slaves, and at least some of the enslaved Africans identified as cooks were male. Women's work was arduous and physical, and women were often tasked with carrying the raw materials needed for construction, such as stone, clay, and shells. Yet just like male company slaves, these women enjoyed a degree of agency and relative freedom that was unknown to many of the female slaves on American plantations. Like enslaved African women in the Caribbean, however, female castle slaves did face sexual predation, especially if they worked and resided within the castle as domestic servants. The growing population of mulattoes bore witness to the prevalence of sexual relationships between white men and both castle slaves and local, free African women. It is clear that some Britons formed relationships with African women from the local community, as a result of which they enjoyed trading benefits and access to food and other goods that might come from such a relationship.

However, the surviving records are generally silent on the status of the mothers of the mulatto children who lived in and around the forts. Mulattoes were almost always listed separately from castle slaves in RAC accounts and inventories, which suggests that in accord with West African practices children inherited the status and condition of their fathers, and thus only the children of castle slave couples were born slaves, while all of the children of white fathers were free. Despite the relatively high degree of agency enjoyed by castle slaves, it does seem likely that at least some of the women among them faced the double burden of labor faced by many women in the Americas, whose owners demanded both forced labor in the fields, and forced labor in the production and rearing of more slaves.[17]

On occasion British officials suggested sending castle slaves to Britain in order that they might be properly apprenticed to master craftsmen and receive a complete professional training. Having concluded that the poor quality, ill health, and premature deaths of British artisans on the Gold Coast made it extremely difficult for such craftsmen to fully and properly train castle slaves, professionally trained RAC slaves who could then properly train more slaves upon their return to the Gold Coast, appeared a sensible proposition. William Mutter, for example, thought "It wou'd be a very good scheme if it cou'd be done at a moderate expence if you were to have 12 stout young Gambian Slaves brought up to the following trades at any country town in England, Vizt. 2 Blacksmiths, 2 Coopers, 4 Masons, & 4 House Carpenters."[18] Similarly, Nathaniel Senior proposed "to have 5 or 6 young Negro Lads sent home yearly for 5 or 6 years successively, to be made Bricklayers, Carpenters, Smiths & Coopers." He complained that because white "tradesmen seldom stand it for any time in this Country" the slave craftsmen upon whom the company depended were often insufficiently qualified, "& the Black Fellows on the Coast know so little of their Business 'tis extremely difficult to bring up others under 'em."[19]

The training of castle slaves in Britain would have constituted something approximating a full apprenticeship, but with the crucial difference that the apprentices would have no chance of becoming journeymen or master craftsmen who might enjoy the liberty of self-employment. Instead, they and their skilled labor would have remained the property of the RAC, although their skills would have earned them privileged status and living and working conditions. The apprenticeship of slaves was not unknown in Britain. However, only a very small number of castle slaves were dispatched to Britain, including, for example, Jack, who in 1769 was sent in order to learn more about medicine in order to assist the company surgeon. High cost and logistical difficulties meant that relatively few castle slaves were sent to the British Isles for training, and the vast majority were trained in situ. In 1695 a carpenter and a bricklayer were recruited by the RAC and sent to the Gold Coast, with each promised bonus payments for every castle slave they trained in their respective crafts. By the early eighteenth century the indentures signed by virtually all British craftsmen employed by the RAC included a requirement to train others on the Gold Coast as a standard part of the terms of employment.[20] Thus in 1721 apothecary John Lyle agreed in his indenture to "make it his business & endeavour to teach qualify and instruct some of the Compa. Servants either Whites or Blacks whose capacity & inclinations he shall find proper & tending thereto in the Art and Mystery of knowing curing and preparing such dying and other Woods Druggs Vegetables Gums Oyls Salts Mineralls & other things wch. may be discovered by him."[21]

In addition to training company slaves in British crafts and skills such as brickmaking and stone masonry, the RAC sought to lessen their dependence on expensive local free labor by training some slaves in skills and crafts particular to the Gold Coast region. The most significant of this group of workers were canoemen, the skilled boatmen who transported people, goods, and messages between ships and shore, as well as between coastal forts. In 1721, for example, RAC officials at Cape Coast Castle reported that they "Have furnished the Dispatch wth 2 Negros to be bred up Sailors," while promising to "breed up Canoemen" from among the male children of company-owned slaves. At that time sixteen canoemen were enslaved and the property of the company at Cape Coast. By 1731 the RAC owned sixty canoemen at Cape Coast, three at Dixcove, three at Succondee, three at Commenda, three at Tantumquerry, two at Winnebah, and one at Accra. However, given that canoemen were required to transfer virtually all of the huge quantities of goods and the large numbers of people between ship and shore, as well as for communication and transport between all forts along the coast, there were never enough qualified company canoemen to eliminate British dependence on local canoemen. Consequently, letters and reports from the Gold Coast forts constantly lamented the insufficient workforce of "Castle working Slaves & Canoemen—the number . . . not sufficient." Supervising the construction of the new slave-trading fort at Anomabu, John Apperley complained that "There is but 13 Cannoe Men, Compy's Slaves at Cape Coast castle that can work in a

Canoe, & but one here." On other occasions the inadequacies of sailors and
canoemen trained by and for the company, rather than the local canoemen
who had been raised in the profession by their fathers, were all too apparent, prompting complaints that the castle slaves made "very bad Sailors."
More significantly, completely replacing free canoemen with slaves was
hardly practical; a 1777 report suggested that the RAC would require at least
one hundred "Slave Canoemen" to guarantee the company's independence,
"and to say nothing of their first cost, which wou'd exceed £2000, their
maintenance alone wou'd nearly amount to the whole charge of Free
Canoemen and Labourers Time, as it now stands."[22]

Male castle slaves were also employed as soldiers, defending British forts
and the people, goods, and slaves within them. The low survival rate among
white British soldiers and laborers left officials little choice but to rely on
slaves. A good many of the soldiers in large West African armed forces were
enslaved, and so Britons on the Gold Coast simply worked within local
traditions when they armed castle slaves, and charged them with protecting
their owners' property against both West African and rival European predation. Under such conditions, it was clearly imperative that RAC officials
and the policies that they enforced treated company slaves well enough to
ensure their loyalty. Proper and adequate payment of maintenance stipends
in trade goods, regular presents and rewards, and a degree of independence
in their personal lives all helped marry castle slaves to the RAC interest.

Unlike slaves in the Americas, the castle slaves on the Gold Coast were
effectively paid so that they could provide for themselves. In fact, they were
paid maintenance stipends that appeared very similar to the wages paid to
indentured white laborers and soldiers; the payments were not in cash but
in tradable commodities such as tobacco, brandy, rum, and cloth. RAC
account books were filled with examples of such payments to the castle
slaves, including numerous entries such as "Castle Slaves, Paid the Sawyers'
four pounds and ten shillings," or "Castle Slaves, Paid the Accra slaves for 1
Month." On those occasions when castle slaves were required to undertake
additional work—for example, during the loading or unloading of a British
ship, or when major works were undertaken or completed at one of the
British forts on the Gold Coast—these men and women received additional
or "over-time" bonus payments. By the middle of the eighteenth century
the average monthly stipend paid to a male slave was about twenty shillings
worth of trade goods. The most highly skilled and consequently the best
paid male slaves received forty shillings per month, unskilled female slaves

generally received between five and fifteen shillings (with those who had children receiving the higher payments), and most boys received about five shillings per month.[23]

A table recording the payment of castle slaves at Cape Coast Castle during 1757 was typical, listing twenty-five different commodities, including many of the goods brought to the coast by Britain in order to trade with West Africans for slaves, gold, ivory, food, and other commodities. Thus these company slaves received payments in the form of tobacco, brandy, rum, clothing, brass pans, iron bars, pewter, cowries, and more than a dozen different styles of fabric. Weapons, including knives, guns, gunpowder, and shot, were all important trading goods, and at times castle slaves received these as part of their stipends paid by company officials. Paying slaves with weapons illustrates the remarkable nature of the institution in the castles and forts of the Gold Coast. Castle slaves were not policed like plantation slaves, and British officials did not regard them as potentially deadly rebels. Rather, they were employees, a bound labor force, and in fact the British would on occasion employ armed castle slaves as a defensive force against local West Africans. The goods paid to castle slaves were regarded by RAC officials as a stipend for maintenance, but these payments in trade goods allowed slaves to treat this allowance as a salary, trading these goods to enhance the quality of their lives. On occasion slaves protested against the form or the amount of their payments. In 1681 slaves at Anomabu complained to RAC agent Richard Thelwall when he proposed to "give them ye: Custom of ye: Country, but they said it was to[o] little." Thelwall increased his offer, and communicated his helplessness in the face of such resistance in a letter to the governor at Cape Coast Castle, dolefully reporting that the company slaves "are gone to consider of it." The power of a group of enslaved workers who could deliberate as to whether or not the amount and form of their payment was sufficient speaks volumes about power relations between castle slaves and their owners in British castles and forts on the Gold Coast during the era of the transatlantic slave trade.[24]

Such examples are common in the records throughout the period during which the British depended upon castle slaves. In August 1778 company slaves rejected a quarterly payment in tobacco, insisting "they wou'd take no Pay, unless a part in Cloth as usual." Especially at Cape Coast, a community filled with a wide range of trade goods, any kind of surplus of particular goods created a glut and depressed prices. Thus, if castle slaves were paid with that particular commodity, their trading and purchasing power was significantly reduced. Moreover, local wars and even occasional periods of famine could raise the price of local foodstuffs, making it even more difficult for castle slaves to translate their trade goods into the necessities of life. In 1766, for example, dire food shortages caused Governor John Hippisley to report to London that "your slaves afford the most piteous examples that can be conceived. Their pay in the most fruitful season is very barely a subsistence." What must be their prospects, he asked, "when this price of corn is raised six times above what it is in ordinary years and can with the greatest difficulty be got at all"? When food was plentiful and trade goods were in demand, castle slaves could live relatively well, and they enjoyed trading and bartering with local people. But when conditions worsened, relations between the people of Cape Coast and the castle slaves could deteriorate, as the British-owned slaves struggled to secure adequate clothing and sufficient food in their dealings with local people. Castle slaves were rarely paid with the best and most desirable trade goods, and so they could not profit from the Atlantic trade as fully as could free West Africans.[25]

On occasion the RAC responded to these difficulties by increasing pay rates, and one such rise occurred in the early 1770s. Hoping to get the most for their money, the RAC spoke not of cost-of-living increases, but rather of incentives for greater effort on the part of the slaves. On this occasion the increase was presented "as an encouragement for them to expedite . . . Buildings" being erected and repaired on the Gold Coast. Castle slaves might sometimes request to be paid in advance, and several who petitioned "to make custom and bury Winnebah Tom," a deceased member of their number, received "17 gallons Rum [and] 1 fathom Long Cloth." Slaves were paid overtime when required to work longer than usual hours, and they regularly received gratuities on special occasions such as this funeral, or when they had worked particularly hard or effectively. In February 1751, for example, a flask of brandy was given "To the Company's Slaves." The arrival of a new governor, Christmas, the accession of a new British monarch, or the completion of a major piece of construction work on the Gold Coast were all examples of occasions when additional gifts and trade goods were distributed to castle slaves.[26]

Slavery in the societies along the Gold Coast was an institution that guaranteed some rights and privileges to slaves, and in general Britain's castle slaves lived and worked in this tradition, enjoying a much greater degree of agency and liberty than did the slaves sold to the British and then shipped for sale to British planters across the Atlantic. The rights and privileges of castle slaves extended to the withholding of their labor, a practice rare enough among eighteenth-century British workers. The best example of this occurred in 1786 after a large supply of shells was discovered on the seashore between Cape Coast Castle and Elmina. Shells could be used in the production of lime, and would thus be of great help in the manufacture of cement and mortar for castle maintenance and construction. The shells were too far from Cape Coast Castle for female castle slaves to make the trip on foot, carrying the shells back along the beach in large basins balanced upon their heads. Consequently, the surveyor had temporary shelters erected on the beach, and he instituted a shift system whereby twelve "laboresses" and their children would spend a week on the beach preparing shells for shipment by boat to Cape Coast Castle, after which they would be relieved by another shift of laboresses and children. However, "This it seems did not suit the Men with whom they cohabited, they therefore on the following Sunday without making the least Complaint, agreed among themselves to abscond, and . . . having done all in their Power to prevail on the whole Body of the Slaves to follow them, they sett off to the Number of 40 Men, accompanied by their Women and Children."[27] The slaves prepared carefully, selling and trading materials in the local community in order to procure gunpowder and arms to protect themselves (against local peoples, rather than against their British masters). Some forty slaves left Cape Coast Castle, leaving behind most of the elderly and infirm. The surveyor, whose plan had prompted the strike and desertion, felt sufficiently threatened that he remained within the castle while negotiations took place.[28]

These slaves had not run away. Their location was not secret, and they welcomed British negotiators from Cape Coast Castle. This action must be understood in terms of labor: it was a tactic designed to challenge a new and undesirable labor practice. For four weeks British officials traveled to and from the encampment of the absconded slaves, who "refused to return to their Duty, unless the Governor stipulated Terms with them, shortened their Hours of Work, and gave them a daily Allowance of Liquor." It was only after exerting significant pressure on local Africans, and particularly the company-paid caboceers, that the runaways were persuaded to return, and only then when "a promise was given that they should not be punished." Not surprisingly, the governor justified his lengthy report to RAC officials in London by stating his missive was intended to demonstrate "how unruly the slaves are grown from too great Lenity, and the necessity of making an Example to convince them of their Dependence, which they now seem to doubt." While the governor was enraged by his inability to enforce discipline among workers that the company owned, his and the company's weakness and the castle slaves' relative strength in determining the conditions of work and daily life were all too apparent, and none of the slaves was punished. The slaves were indeed more independent than dependent.[29]

Company slaves did occasionally run away, as in the case of a gardener named Mortimer at Cape Coast Castle who was caught stealing food in 1778. After hearing reports from local Africans that he was aboard a Portuguese slave ship, complicated negotiations began with the Africans, the Portuguese, and the runaway himself, who swore that he would kill himself unless his British owners guaranteed that they would not punish him or sell him off the coast. However, it soon became apparent that the runaway, the local Africans, and the Portuguese were involved in a complicated ruse, designed to exact payment from the British for the return of the slave, with the profits to be shared. While the con failed and the runaway was returned, he succeeded in escaping serious punishment. The incident reveals that company slaves felt able to work the labor system to their advantage, with little fear of violent repercussions. Britons could and did employ violent punishments against their company slaves, although they did not use violence to spur on work: such were the traditions of West African slavery. The appeals of castle slaves for release from punishment indicates the potential power of the Britons over their enslaved workers, while the success of such appeals and the comparative rarity of serious punishments provides evidence of the relatively strong position of the enslaved.[30]

It appears to have been possible for some slaves to purchase their freedom, as in the case of one man "formerly a slave belonging to the Company, who redeemed himself some Years ago." On occasion others may have sought to escape into the local community when an opportunity presented itself, although this was a relatively rare occurrence: a Gambian slave on the Gold Coast was as ethnically and culturally different as an Italian in early eighteenth-century Scotland. In one instance, on the death of Richard Brew, governor of Anomabu, a number of mulattoes and domestic "House Slaves" (some belonging to Brew, but others to the RAC) "absconded after his Death, and took shelter among the Annamboe People, who received them under pretence that the Deceased had made a Verbal Donation to them of his Mulattoe children" and slaves. These slaves—both company-owned and privately owned—returned to the British "upon a Promise that they should not be sold off the Coast, as most of them are intermarried among the Natives and have Families."[31]

Despite intermarriage and cooperation between castle slaves and local people, relations between the two groups were as likely to be fraught and even violent as they were to be cordial. Over time there was some intermarriage between the two communities, but the regular importation of new castle slaves from Gambia meant that an essentially alien community existed in the space between Gold Coast European forts and local towns and villages, especially Cape Coast. Castle slaves had different languages, dialects, cultures, and rituals, and they occupied a liminal space between the European traders and the Fetu and Fante peoples of the Gold Coast communities. Islamic beliefs and practices had spread widely in Senegambia, and it seems likely that at least some and perhaps many of the castle slaves carried these beliefs with them to British forts on the Gold Coast. The records of the RAC reveal little, although the fact that castle slaves often clashed with local people during Gold Coast religious holidays and festivals may suggest the presence of Islamic faith and an unwillingness to countenance local religious beliefs and practices.

While castle slaves provided vital labor facilitating the British presence and their trade, this work necessarily diminished the opportunities for local African free laborers or the local owners of slaves who sought to sell enslaved labor. The result was tension, and sometimes violence. On one occasion, for example, Birempon Cudjoe, the RAC's principal caboceer in Cape Coast, complained to the Council about a conflict

> betwixt the Town's Soldiers and Company's Slaves, at the time they made their annual Custom, and upon the 16th July last a scuffle ensued betwixt Cudjoe's people and the Company's Slaves, in which, upon a hearing it evidently appeared that the Company's Slaves were the aggressors, they having in particular abused and insulted one of Cudjoe's women, and destroyed a quantity of Fetish Gold and Aggery Beads which she wore.[32]

A decade later Governor John Roberts reported that after learning that "the Towns People and the Company's Slaves were fighting," he had been forced to increase security at Cape Coast Castle and prepare the soldiers (most of them castle slaves) to fire on the local Africans if they attempted to attack the company's property. Again the fighting had occurred during a local religious celebration, and Roberts concluded, "The Company's Men Slaves I keep in the Castle and shall till the Town's People have finished their Custom." Other squabbles were financial in nature. Castle slaves traded with local people, using their payments in trade goods to purchase food, clothing, and other goods. This could result in castle slaves accruing debts, and on occasion RAC officials felt obligated to ensure that such debts were paid, in order to keep trade relations with local communities on a sound footing. For example, in 1681 Richard Thelwall reported that he had advanced one month's pay to slaves before they left Anomabu for Cape Coast Castle, "because they should leave noe debts here."[33]

Although the majority of marriages took place within the castle slave community, some relationships were formed between castle slaves and local Africans, thus eroding at least some of the boundaries between castle slaves and local Africans. In 1769, for example, company officials in London recorded that some of "the castle Slaves are so closely connected with the People in the country by Marriage and other social Ties, that any attempt to remove any of the former would infallibly occasion very great Disturbance and Insurrections among the Natives; and render the Safety of the Forts and Settlements highly precarious, as their Defence depends more on the Attachment of the Slaves, than on their feeble Force and Military Servants."[34] Thus both the ethnic tension and, paradoxically, the familial connections between castle slaves and Gold Coast Africans posed problems for the British. Furthermore, the British were all too aware of their dependence upon castle slaves not just for the maintenance of the forts and their trading operations, but also for the actual defense of these remote outposts.

The governor and Council at Cape Coast found themselves dependent upon castle slaves and thus eager to have as many of these bound workers as possible, but at the same time, they were constantly frustrated by the agency and recalcitrance of these slaves. The clerks at the company's headquarters in Leadenhall Street in London catalogued, copied, and indexed many thousands of letters received from officials at Cape Coast Castle, and a great many of these communications reflected these contradictory impulses. In 1707, for example, Governor Dalby Thomas reported from Cape Coast Castle that "They are in great want of a supply of Castle Working Slaves." Two decades later a letter from the Council in January 1728 echoed this complaint, pointing out that the number of "Castle working slaves" was "not Sufficient," and recommended "putting out Children of Castle working Slaves to Trade." Six months later officials at Cape Coast Castle once again complained about the insufficient "Number of Castle working slaves," but then moved on to a complaint about officials' inability to sell "Castle slaves off the Coast upon their misbehaviour." Castle slaves constituted the largest cadre of workers in British trading forts and castles, yet despite their servile status, these men and women were independent enough to provoke constant complaints by British officials throughout the late seventeenth and the entire eighteenth centuries.[35]

In fact, as generations of new castle slaves and the descendants of former castle slaves became familiar with their position, they became increasingly assertive. Any attempt by company officials on the Gold Coast to change the traditional terms of service of company slaves, and any hint that officials might condemn recalcitrant castle slaves to the Middle Passage and servitude in the Americas, was bitterly denounced and resisted by the castle slaves themselves. Throughout the eighteenth century British officials appealed to London for the authority to sell disobedient and problematic castle slaves for export to the New World, in the hope that the very existence of such a threat would result in greater obedience. The governor and Council sent a particularly strongly worded request in March 1784, in response to "the severe Terms in which you reflect upon the Council for selling off the Coast a Rebellious Company's Slave." Sedition and rebellion were among the very few offenses for which a company slave might be sent to the Americas, yet officials in London nonetheless questioned the wisdom in imposing such a penalty. The slave in question was guilty of "aiding and assisting our Enemies," and the governor and Council observed that if "we have not authority allowed us to act with Severity, we may bid adieu to all Obedience and Decorum amongst your Slaves, who from the Intimations that have been given them that they are not to be sold on any Account, are by no means under that Subjection which the good of your Service requires."[36] The letter concluded with further examples of violence and disobedience on the part of castle slaves, "to convince you that unless a Latitude is allowed the Council in Extra[ordinary] cases how impossible it is to keep that due Subordination among your Slaves, who are not actuated by principle, but can only be awed by the Fear of Punishment."[37]

Two years later the governor reported that much of the brandy transported to the Gold Coast had been lost in large part because "a great deal has been stolen by your own Slaves." Several had been caught red-handed, and they defiantly claimed "that the whole Body of the Slaves were equally concerned and were to share the Booty." In desperation the governor pleaded: "what Punishment can we inflict upon the Delinquents, that will deter the rest?" Among the local African population, theft might result in execution and the enslavement of the culprit's family:

> but notwithstanding our repeated Representations of the necessity of allowing Severity in grave cases, if a Company's slave is found guilty of Treason, or even Murder, an adequate Punishment to his Crime cannot be inflicted, your Injunctions being under the severest penalty on no Account to sell even ONE off the coast: they know this and act accordingly. They are now arrived at that Pitch of Insolence, that unless an example is made of the most notorious Offenders, you will shortly lose them entirely, or at least their services will not be worth the Pay they receive.[38]

However, recognizing that British agents on the Gold Coast were in a relatively weak and vulnerable position, and unable to force the allegiance of the castle slaves, most officials in Africa and London agreed that if castle slaves met with heavy-handed punishment or were threatened with sale to slave ships they would elope, either individually or en masse, or perhaps even rebel. Without them, Britain's highly lucrative trading operation would all but collapse, with significant repercussions for British manufacturers and workers producing goods for West Africa, and for New World planters who were desperate for enslaved West Africans. Company officials in London had proclaimed in 1730 that the "transplanting [of] any of our Black tradesmen or other Slaves (except in case of misdemeanours and as a punishment for great Crimes) from one place to the other . . . might be of Dangerous Consequence and therefore is a practice which ought carefully to be avoided."[39] This policy held good for almost the entire era of the transatlantic slave trade. During the seventeenth and most of the eighteenth centuries, only major theft, violent crime, or rebellion by castle slaves warranted severe punishment or sale. Theft of company property was endemic, especially among the castle slaves who worked as canoemen and helped ship goods from ships to the shore, prompting Governor Dalby Thomas to investigate methods of securing these goods so that "your Slaves could not steal as they do now and ever will do." With free canoemen from the local communities pilfering as much as they could, despite the threat of severe punishment and even enslavement if caught, it is hardly surprising that company slaves sought to line their own pockets in a similar manner.[40]

Yet only on very rare occasions were harsh punishments handed out to castle slaves. It was only a mere two decades before the closure of the transatlantic slave trade that company officials in London finally relented, granting their representatives on the Gold Coast greater powers to punish troublesome castle slaves, including the power to sell serious offenders on to slave ships. In the year that the new Federal Constitution in the United States set a terminal date for the transatlantic slave trade, and the Society for the Abolition of the Slave Trade was established in Britain, it is possible that RAC officials in London saw that the trade might soon be reduced and even end. Perhaps this enabled London officials to consider it less important to guarantee the integrity and rights of the castle slave communities, whose days appeared numbered. Governor Thomas Price responded with evident relief, writing on behalf of the Council at Cape Coast Castle:

> It gives us great Pleasure to find you have empowered us to inflict proper Punishment upon your refractory Slaves; be assured the Power you have been pleased to delegate to us shall not be made improper use of. Our first care was to convene the Company's Slaves and inform them of your Orders respecting them . . . if therefore they now err as before, they know what they have to expect, and must abide by the consequences.[41]

In some ways this new policy reflected an Americanization of British control of castle slaves on the Gold Coast. For the first time, one aspect of the kind of absolute power that New World slave owners enjoyed over enslaved Africans was extended to castle slaves in West Africa: up until this point the British had respected the right of their castle slaves to live and work in a West African tradition of slavery. For almost the entire history of their participation in the transatlantic slave trade, British trade in gold and slaves in West Africa depended upon the labor of castle slaves, over whom they had relatively little of the control enjoyed by slave owners in the Americas. Indeed, planters in mid-seventeenth-century Barbados had enjoyed significantly more power and control over the white servants, many of them vagrants, convicts, and prisoners of war, who had been worked to death in large numbers in the creation of integrated plantations.

Despite all of their relative power and independence during the era of the transatlantic slave trade, castle slaves nonetheless were the property of the Royal African Company, a fact brutally embodied in the death of Yeou, a seven-year-old castle slave at Anomabu in 1716. While cleaning his gun, white soldier Henry Kendrick accidentally discharged the weapon, and the musket ball hit Yeou "in the Left Knee. Which broke the Knee bone all to Pieces. I got a Surgeon to Cutt off his legg as Speedily as I could. But could not Save his Life." Peter Holt's report of this accidental destruction of RAC property ended with the observation that "Neither was the Boy worth so much." For all of their relative freedom, the slaves working in the British forts and castles of the Gold Coast remained property, in a liminal world between British society and labor systems, the slave societies of Africa, and those of New World plantations.[42]

There is virtually no evidence of the nature and extent of interactions between castle slaves and the large number of slaves who were marched to the British forts, incarcerated within them, and then ferried out to the waiting slave ships. It is clear, however, that castle slaves paid a significant role in the daily care and maintenance of the incarcerated slaves, providing them with food and water, cleaning their dungeons, and escorting them to and from the beach to exercise. There would often have been language, ethnic, and cultural barriers between the two groups, and perhaps the castle slaves saw themselves as quite literally a class apart from those who were destined for the slave ships. The great difference between the two groups was best symbolized by the fact that company-owned castle slaves were named individuals, with recognized skills and attributes, families, and so forth, with an almost cast-iron guarantee that they would avoid being consigned to the Middle Passage and slave labor in the Americas. In dramatic contrast were the tens of thousands of nameless, anonymous slaves, regarded more as commodities than as people, who passed through the castles and forts. It is clear that castle slaves bitterly resented any efforts by British authorities to change the terms of their service and grant company officials the right to condemn castle slaves to servitude in the Americas. While this was in part an effort to protect their community, and to ensure that families and relationships were not broken up, it was also based on a deep-seated desire to avoid the horrific conditions faced by those bound for New World plantations, who sailed west in such large numbers, but who never returned.

The vital workforce of company slaves was supplemented by the labor of pawns, once again indicating the ways in which local labor practices were adopted by the British. Pawnship, like slavery, had existed in West African coastal society long before the arrival of the Europeans, but inevitably its function and the experience of this condition changed somewhat as a result of the changes brought about by the trade in gold and slaves. The growth of Atlantic trade, the increasing commercialization of coastal societies, and the expansion of the transatlantic slave trade all encouraged the expansion of pawnship, which institutionalized debt bondage as collateral for loans or debt and thus smoothed debt and credit relations.[43]

The institution of pawnship provided a significant source of labor along the Gold Coast, for both Africans and Europeans. A traditional form of bondage, it grew and developed to match the growth of debts and labor needs occasioned by the rise of the transatlantic slave trade. At its base, pawnship was most often a system wherein individuals were held in debt bondage as collateral for loans or other obligations, with the labor of the individual constituting interest on the debt and covering the subsistence costs of the pawn. On occasion, those owed a debt might seize hostages in order to force repayment or take compensation, but pawnship usually provided a more voluntary and contractual approach to debt and obligation. Pawnship might also be a direct result of poverty, with an individual pawning relatives or even him- or herself, although on other occasions wealthier individuals might pawn dependents in order to raise funds for specific needs, or to provide collateral for nonfinancial forms of debt and obligation. Unlike slaves, who often came from regions far removed from those in which they now lived and worked, many pawns were local and freeborn, for the institution could work only if the pawned individual was valued by a debtor who wanted to redeem the pawn.[44]

Pawnship appears to have been most common in the coastal societies that were closely linked with the Atlantic trade, wherein individuals tended to amass debts as they pursued trade, or as they paid ritual obligations, fines, and other costs. When a family or an individual was unable to pay a debt or meet an obligation, a family member might be pawned to the creditor. Henceforth the labor of the pawn would service the interest on the debt, until such time as the debt could be repaid and the pawn redeemed. In the meantime, the creditor would provide food, clothing, and accommodation for the pawn. While it was often difficult for people to repay debts and thus to redeem pawns, since most were held locally it was possible to observe and regulate the treatment of pawns, and while creditors might be referred to as "owners" or "masters," pawns were not property: the labor of the pawn, but not the pawn him- or herself, belonged to the creditor. Overall, however, pawns and slaves had a distinctly different status within Gold Coast societies, for slaves were generally foreigners, while pawns were members of local families and households.[45]

In contrast to wage laborers and to the castle slaves, pawns were not given a stipend, and they generally received only subsistence in the form of clothing and food. Many pawns were female, and in West African society it was not uncommon for men holding the debt to take on pawns as additional wives, which usually had the effect of canceling the debt and changing the status of the pawned woman. Pawnship as an institution thus functioned to regulate the labor of women, facilitating sexual access to them and allowing men to exercise control over their offspring.[46] Many female pawns experienced the institution as a subservient form of marriage. However, the use of pawns in commercial and political relations with Europeans affected the institution, not least in the way that it was experienced by the pawns themselves. When pawns were transferred to European merchants and officials they were taken outside of the culture in which pawnship functioned, and commodified in a fashion that made it far more likely that they would be treated like slaves. Thus, in 1775 the governor of Cape Coast Castle reported that ten newly received pawns had been "put to different Trades" in the manner of RAC-owned slaves. If white male Britons fathered children by female pawns, local custom regarded the women as no longer bound but rather as wives or at least household members of the men. This quite likely happened, although it is unclear what then happened to these women when, as was often the case, their white partners died. Some would have occupied a liminal space between West African bound service and British freedom, no longer regarded as pawns by West Africans yet condemned to continue serving the British. Only their mulatto children might enjoy real and lasting benefits.[47]

The British and other Europeans trading on the Gold Coast were inevitably drawn into local economic traditions and arrangements, and thus found themselves saddled with pawns when local merchants and others were unable to pay debts. However, the specific labor needs of the British, and the fact that they could not easily move pawns between castles and forts, made this arrangement undesirable, and it is clear that the British took on pawns through necessity rather than choice. Over time the British became more accustomed to pawnship, and learned to recognize when pawns were unlikely to be quickly redeemed. In 1775 Governor David Mill reported from Cape Coast Castle that "the Pawns we have receiv'd in part payment of the Debt have ever since been employed as Labourers, & are of great use to us." Picking out those pawns unlikely to be soon redeemed, Governor Mill had them trained so that their labor would be of most use to the company. The rapidly expanding commercial world around the slave-trading castles and forts along the Gold Coast inevitably changed pawnship. Taken outside of their cultural moorings and held and worked by the Europeans, pawns in the British trading castles probably experienced something closer to slavery than would normally have been the case had they been held as pawns by local people. A typical "Diary of Employment of Labourers at Cape Coast Castle" in 1778 barely differentiated between company-owned slaves and pawns, reporting that "yesterday & this Day has been chiefly taken up in Surveying the Slaves & Pawns; putting out some of the Stoutest to different Trades & the young boys to Canoemen: the small Girls in the Garden." Here and in similar records, pawns were listed alongside or after the company slaves, as in "The Pawns attending the Artisans as Labourers" or "Pawns attending the different workmen." In West African society pawns were regarded as debts, but British records reveal that just as pawns were worked alongside and treated as slaves, so too were they recorded as assets, as property—albeit temporarily—of the company. In James Fort at Accra in 1681, for example, between a long list of trade goods, provisions, and other company possessions and a shorter list of RAC slaves, came a list of "Companyes pawnes."[48]

The English mercantile companies charged with establishing trading posts along the West African coast had initially planned to fully man these with English officials, merchants, soldiers, sailors, and skilled and unskilled workers, who together would facilitate trade and defense. However, the deadly disease environment, together with the poor pay and working conditions, meant that it was increasingly difficult to recruit Britons for service in the "white man's graveyard," and many of those who did venture to Africa did not survive long. British trade in general, and the transatlantic slave trade in particular, depended upon the cooperation and the labor of a combination of a small force of Britons, a large contingent of company-owned African slaves, some locally owned pawns, and both free and enslaved local Africans. Thus British expectations of free and bound labor were necessarily combined with local practices and expectations, and as a consequence all of these forms of labor were moderated. The transatlantic slave trade was serviced and supported by the labor of white-owned African slaves who operated with relative independence and quite significant influence over the terms of their labor and remuneration.

Some historians have concluded that castle slaves and pawns were completely "detached from the local African polities and became tied to the alien interest" of the Europeans for whom they labored. While the castle slaves in particular were ethnically distinct from Gold Coast West Africans, and were not only the property of Europeans but were often trained in peculiarly European skills and crafts, they were geographically, socially, and in terms of their labor positioned between West Africans and Europeans. Castle slavery was—in terms of the relationship between slave and master, and the apparent rights and relative independence of the enslaved—a far more West African form of labor than any form of slavery that developed in British America. To suggest that the RAC "used its slaves in the western manner" oversimplifies the complicated fashion in which company slaves were able to enjoy elements of the free labor experience, as well as African forms of slavery, negotiating and receiving stipends, withdrawing their labor, and even creating at least one militia company within the local community. Local West African *asafo* companies were patrilineal groups with civic and ceremonial roles, including the organization of funeral ceremonies for one of their own. They had a significant military purpose, too, in policing and defending communities against attack, protecting inhabitants against enslavement, and protecting the sovereignty of coastal societies and city-states. The castle slaves' Brofu-Mba company (meaning white men's children or white men's slaves) was one of about seven asafo companies in Cape Coast, and its very existence is telling evidence of the relative independence of this group, on the one hand, and of its distinct place within the local community, on the other hand. There was tremendous variety in the work and even the status of slaves in West African society, and RAC employment of slaves, while unusual by local standards, was able to function effectively in the local setting. However, this was not slavery as any Caribbean or North American planter would have known it.[49]

Castle slaves were the largest and most significant workforce in the British castles and trading posts on the West African coast, and together with free and enslaved mulattoes they composed one of the best examples of what Ira Berlin has described as "Atlantic creoles." Many had been born and raised in far-distant Gambia, and they lived and worked in a liminal setting, physically located between Britons and the peoples of the Gold Coast, and operating between the slavery of Africa and the slavery of the Americas. Fewer and fewer British craftsmen, artisans, laborers, soldiers, and sailors were present in the eighteenth-century castles, and with the dominance of enslaved Africans in the British workforce came a corresponding dominance of African ways of work. The castle slave Atlantic creoles became increasingly important skilled and unskilled workers, a process that was being replicated among the creolized population of enslaved people in Barbados. Yet the process played out very differently in the two locations. The castle slaves on the Gold Coast were enslaved in a hybrid version of West African slavery. In contrast, those enslaved in Barbados would live and work in a new form of slavery, drawing on both British and West African approaches to and utilization of bound labor, and designed by planters to service their labor-hungry integrated sugar plantations.[50]

Chapter 7

"We Have No Power over Them"

People and Work on the Gold Coast

The transatlantic trade that flowed into and out from the Gold Coast depended upon numerous West African workers, a great many of whom were drawn from the burgeoning communities adjacent to forts and trading posts along the Gold Coast. Many of these people continued to work much as they had in the past, as both free and bound laborers in traditional occupations such as salt making, goldsmithing, farming, and fishing. However, as the coast moved from the periphery to the center of West African trade and commerce, population and productivity expanded to meet the demands of ever-growing coastal communities and the hundreds of European ships in need of trade goods and provisions. As the international slave trade increased even more food and materials were needed for the maintenance of the enslaved, both on the West African coast and during the Middle Passage from Africa to the Americas. As Gold Coast communities grew in wealth and size, local rulers and merchants acquired more enslaved wives and workers, and slavery became more common than it had been in small and isolated coastal communities before the arrival of the Europeans.

However, the new opportunities presented by trade with Europeans meant that the work of some West Africans changed in significant ways. New groups emerged, such as the caboceers, linguists, and bomboys: as middlemen, translators, and foremen these individuals would facilitate trade and organize labor for the benefit of the Europeans, local people, and of course for their own profit. Others were like the coastal fishermen, who adapted traditional skills and reconstituted themselves as a group of free workers upon whom the Europeans were completely dependent. As canoemen, the highly skilled boatmen who transported virtually all freight and people between ship and shore, these workers provide the best example of Gold Coast workers adapting to the European presence and trade, yet retaining a great deal of power over the nature and terms of their work. British officials and merchants were required to develop a modus operandi for the day-to-day activities of the West African entrepôts of the transatlantic slave trade, which acknowledged and accommodated the working practices and traditions of the peoples of the Gold Coast. Trade between the Europeans and their African hosts was dependent upon the labor of the people of the Gold Coast, some bound and many free, who adapted traditional working practices in order to facilitate and profit from trade.

Caboceers made up an essential category of brokers, a new managerial class whose members earned a good living by acting as the Europeans' representative in the local community, ironing out any difficulties and ensuring peaceful relations and productive trade for the visitors. Given the relative powerlessness of the British and other European nations on the Gold Coast and the ability of local Africans to cut off trade, withdraw their labor, or in other ways harm the smooth operation of the castles and forts, the services of the caboceers were essential, and such men were well paid, becoming wealthy and influential members of their own communities.

Other Gold Coast residents secured income and prestige by facilitating trade and good relations between West Africans and Europeans in similar fashion. Thus Caboceer Aggerie (nephew of late caboceer Birempon Cudjoe and brother of Cudjoe's successor Botty) was "Captain of the Black Soldiers" in Cape Coast, effectively the local militia commander. The British governor described Aggerie as "a very deserving Sensible Man who has on all occasions proved himself a faithful Servant to the Company and is very useful when disputes happen between the Europeans and the Natives or the Natives with each other on the different parts of the Coast in settling such disputes having great influence with the people, and has often been employed by the Council to settle those matters."[1] Similarly, Birempon Cudjoe's son Frederick Adoy, who may well have been educated by the British, worked as a linguist or translator. Like his cousins Aggerie and Botty, Frederick Ahoy received an annual salary of £60 from the British, a sizable sum. Cudjoe's best-known son was Philip Quaque, who was educated in England and ordained an Anglican minister before returning to Cape Coast as a missionary. In a letter to his benefactors at the Society for the Propagation of the Gospel, Quaque reported that he had "a prospect of doing much good . . . by the countenance & assistance of his Father Cabosheer Cudjo."[2]

Quaque was one of a number of the sons or favored young male relatives of caboceers to be educated by the British, either in the forts or on occasion back in Britain, and it is clear that some on the Gold Coast believed that this was a route to wealth, power, and influence within their own society. In 1750 William Ansah Sessarakoo published an autobiographical account of his life as the son of a wealthy Fante chief on the Gold Coast, and his subsequent enslavement and transportation to Barbados. Sessarakoo recalled that he "had lived for a Time, when a perfect Child, in the Fort with one of the *African* Company's principal Officers, where he had learned to speak *English*." The enslaved African Thomas Osiat, Sessarakoo's contemporary, had been taken to Ireland and educated and baptized in Cork. Eventually Osiat had "obtain'd his Freedom . . . [and] in Time return'd home to Cape Coast," where he eventually became "The grand Caboceroe of this Town . . . where he now lives in very great Grandeur, and is of the utmost Service to the *English*, both for the carrying on of their Trade in the inland Country, and preserving Peace with all the neighbouring Powers, especially the Town of *Elmina*." Education in Britain illustrated the ways that members of this new category of Gold Coast brokers existed between West African and British society, operating within and benefiting from both cultures.[3]

The surviving payroll records demonstrate British dependence on key caboceers and other elite members of Gold Coast communities. In early 1751, for example, the Cape Coast Castle records show Birempon Cudjoe earning an annual salary of £72 as "Caboceer and Linguist," William Anh Sessaroe earning £60 as a writer, James Hinch receiving £50 as "Castle Bomboy" or workers' foreman, George Bunisee earning £48 as "Messenger Extraordinary," and Essinee receiving £27 for his work as the "Warehouse Keeper's Assistant." To the west of Cape Coast, Aleades, Annagee, and Dunboy were all employed by the British as caboceers in Accra, where another Cudjoe worked as a linguist, and men were similarly employed at virtually all of the British forts and castles along the Gold Coast throughout the later seventeenth and the eighteenth centuries.[4]

At times British agents struggled against what they interpreted as the greed and the self-serving agendas of caboceers. In 1756 Governor Charles Bell wrote from Cape Coast Castle acknowledging the safe return of John Agua and George Sackee, who had been educated in England. Bell observed "that neither of 'em is a Person of Consequence & will hardly be of any Service," believing that these servants or lesser relatives of the caboceers and local rulers had been sent abroad for an education so that their masters could gain influence and a share of their salaries upon their return. Bell concluded that adding Agua and Sackee to the company payroll "will only rouse the Greediness of your Caboceers, who will . . . send home their young slaves, who after they have been rarified as Princes in England, will come back to Africa to be made Quills to suck through, according to the Negro Phrase; for whatever we allow to maintain them goes half to their Masters."[5]

Linguists and caboceers were all too aware of British dependence upon them and their skills. In 1715 Peter Holt complained that he had been accosted by Thomas Arvishee, "a negroe who is a Linguister at the castle." Arvishee announced his refusal to repay a debt to Holt, "& gave me very Scornful & Scandalous Language such [as] I should not take from one of my own Colour, upon which I leap't out of ye hammock & gave him a Shove in the face." Arvishee immediately complained about this attack, but the council at Cape Coast Castle, wary of alienating the powerful professional class of caboceers and linguists, reduced Arvishee's debt to Holt by almost one-third, as compensation for the assault.[6]

Caboceers played a vital role in securing free and enslaved laborers from local communities for employment by the British. Such workers were drawn from the ranks of local men and women, often propertyless, whose status ranged from free to servile, including day laborers, soldiers, porters, unskilled workers, pawns, and locally owned enslaved people. These men, women, and children composed a significant proportion of the working population of the towns and villages along the Gold Coast, and they performed a vital role in the exchanges between Europeans and West Africans. The export slave trade required the services of such workers in the coastal communities that were its focal points.[7]

Day laborers worked in a variety of occupations in coastal towns and communities. Composed of impoverished free men and women, and probably including runaway slaves, servants, and pawns, such workers helped to load and unload canoes filled with trading goods or with the daily catch of the fishermen; worked on the construction of buildings in the community and the warehouses and fortifications of European trading companies; aided in the construction and maintenance of canoes and of fishing nets; worked in the fields during peak times of the agricultural cycle; gathered

firewood, lumber, and other materials from the forests; and served as porters for the transportation of goods between the coast and the interior. The
larger European forts and castles provided regular employment for such
laborers, and RAC accounts regularly listed the expense of "Free Canoemen & Labourers Hire," explaining that the expense was "unavoidable, and
cannot be lessened." Replacing such workers with company-owned slaves
would have been prohibitively expensive, for their maintenance stipends
alone "wou'd nearly amount to the whole charge of Free Canomen and
Labourers."[8]

Free black laborers from the local community, or on occasion slaves
rented out by their masters, were employed by the British on an occasional
basis, usually to assist with the construction or maintenance of buildings.
Generally, British officials preferred to rely upon their own white employees, the company-owned castle slaves, members of the mulatto community,
and company-held pawns. Local Africans were very much a last resort, and
they were hired only when there was no alternative. Governor William
Mutter wrote in 1764 that in the absence of a sufficient number of slaves,
"free labourers might be hired, and they would come full as cheap as Company slaves, but then they must not be relied upon entirely, for if they once
saw you could not proceed without their assistance, extravagant wages and
insolent behaviour, would in spite of the greatest indulgences, knock all our
schemes in the head."[9] Even loyal employees of the British did not hesitate
to take advantage of the British when they could. Caboceer Birempon Cudjoe, for example, offered to supply wage laborers to the British at Cape
Coast Castle in 1767 to help with repairs and rebuilding work: it soon
became apparent to the British that rather than being free laborers over
whom they might have some control, these workers were in fact slaves
belonging to Cudjoe and his family, who received all of the slaves' wages.[10]

However, the largest and the most significant group of local workers
were the canoemen, a professional community of fishermen and sea workers. The canoemen provide the best example of West African workers who
were able to enhance traditional working methods and operate in a relatively independent and highly profitable fashion as facilitators of the burgeoning Atlantic trade. As more and more European ships arrived on the
Gold Coast, and the number and size of European forts increased, so too
did the power of the highly skilled canoemen. As the workers responsible
for unloading and loading ships, and for transporting personnel, supplies,
and correspondence between forts and trading posts along the coast, the

canoemen were transformed by European trade from a small community of coastal fishermen into a vital Atlantic labor force, with significant power over the terms of their work. Communities of canoemen were situated by each European fort and alongside most of the towns and communities along the Gold Coast, and as their numbers rose they became one of the most significant sections of the coastal workforce. By the late eighteenth century large forts such as Cape Coast Castle regularly employed almost one hundred canoemen, while smaller forts such as Anomabu depended upon as many as three dozen, with smaller trading posts and lodges employing up to a dozen.[11]

Canoemen were the coastal workers who were most affected by and who most benefited from the trade with Europeans, and they moved from a peripheral role in West African society as subsistence fishermen to a position of vital importance as the skilled workers upon whom trade depended. When European ships' crews approached the Gold Coast, they felt strong Atlantic winds against their backs, and they saw huge rolling waves and a roiling surf on the coastal beaches and rocks, conditions that made it all but impossible for their ships to anchor close to shore. Not a single port or harbor existed along the Gold Coast, nor did the coast offer the haven of river estuaries that could be approached and navigated by oceangoing vessels. William Smith's 1744 description of Cape Coast was typical, and he observed that "The Landing-Place here is so very dangerous that no Boat can venture ashore, but must wait for a Canoe to come off and fetch either Goods or Passengers ashore." Consequently, the unlading and lading of ships, the movement of goods between forts and trading posts, and thus the entirety of European-African trade along the Gold Coast depended upon the highly proficient canoemen, who ferried goods and people between ship and shore. It was a skill that few European sailors mastered. Barbot recorded that in all of his frequent journeys by canoe, "I was never once upset," marveling at how "The rowers know exactly the right moment. . . . Then, Sir, they drive straight at the land with such strength and determination that the canoe appears in sight half-way through the breakers, just as a swell, like a mountain of boiling water, coming from behind, begins to break."[12]

All too aware of how both Europeans and Africans depended upon them, the canoemen and fishermen enjoyed as much power as any single group of coastal African workers in determining the nature of their relationship to Atlantic trade, and the terms of their labor. Often inhabiting

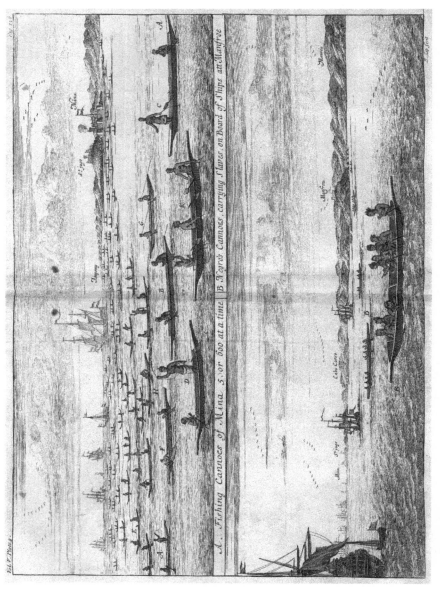

Figure 9. Top: "Fishing Cannoes of Mina 5 or 600 at a time." Bottom: "Negro's Cannoes, carrying Slaves on Board of Ships at Manfroe," in Awnsham and John Churchill (compilers), *Collection of Voyages* (London, 1732), vol. 5, plate 9, p. 156. Courtesy of the Library Company of Philadelphia.

their own communities alongside yet separate from European forts and coastal communities, the canoemen enjoyed an unusual degree of social and professional homogeneity, forming "a class distinct from all others." As craftsmen they objected to undertaking menial labor: one English official complained that a canoeman "would not help me carry the corn to the croome [local town] . . . he told me he came to paddle not to carry corn at all." An RAC report on "Free Canoemen & Labourers Hire" in 1777 explained why the cost of canoemen "is unavoidable, and cannot be lessened." Virtually all goods and people were ferried between ship and shore by canoemen, who were also the means of communication between British posts along the coast. The "Forts are situated along the Sea Coast from West to East about 400 miles. Cape Coast castle the capital is nearly in the Center: from hence all the subordinate forts are supplied by means of canoes." Small wonder that wages of canoemen along the Gold Coast cost the RAC £6,741 between 1770 and 1776.[13]

At a time when many Europeans, including sailors, could not swim, coastal Africans were comfortable with and in the sea. "From the seventh or eighth year of their age they learn to swim, which they do with so much success and perfection, that when they are grown up, if their *Canoe* oversets at any time at Sea, they are not affrighted, but swim back again very quietly from whence they came." The canoes themselves changed little, if at all, during the era of the transatlantic slave trade.[14] John Ogilby provided a detailed description in the late seventeenth century, which would have been just as accurate a century later. The largest canoes were fashioned from a single mighty tree trunk and were as much as forty feet long, five feet wide, and about three feet in depth, and these could carry up to ten tons of goods, but for all their size the skilled canoemen "make such swift-way in still water, that they seem to flye." The canoes were often painted in bright colors, and decorated "with fetishes, behind and before, to keep them safe, as some people do with guardian angels."[15]

Europeans admired the skills involved in making and sailing these canoes, not least because they were unable to emulate them. Occasionally the British bought or made smaller boats for travel up and down the coast, but they rarely enjoyed the services of Britons skilled in constructing and maintaining such craft, let alone sailors who could navigate the treacherous coastal waters. One Cape Coast Castle governor wrote pointedly that he "Wishes you [the RAC] had a Carpenter that understood ye making great Cannoe or small vessels it would be of singular Service." Royal African

Company officials enumerated the goods and people carried between ships and shore by the canoemen, the terms of their employment, their payment, and the regular negotiations between the canoemen and their employers. Long letters back to London, as well as the accounts of visitors to the Gold Coast, make clear European displeasure at the relative power and autonomy of this group of African workers, with constant complaints about theft, refusal to work, and other actions by the canoemen. It is far harder to hear the authentic voices of the canoemen themselves in these records, although the rare occasions on which their sentiments were recorded by British officials, together with the actions they undertook collectively during the later seventeenth and the eighteenth centuries, combine to illuminate their evolving sense of an identity and a power as skilled workers upon whom Europeans and West Africans alike depended.[16]

Whether newly arriving on ships from Europe, or long-term residents of the Gold Coast, Britons constantly marveled at the skill of the canoemen, whose vessels "swim at the top of the foam" in waters that "no European boat can live in."[17] In a novel based on her own experiences on the Gold Coast, Sarah Lee recalled that at Cape Coast, "There was no landing there on boats, on account of the violent lashings of the surf against the low rock and sand. The ship's boats therefore either approached as closely as possible, and their contents were emptied into canoes, which took them ashore, or canoes were hired expressly for the use of each ship." Once each canoe, filled with people and goods from the newly arrived ship, approached "the shore they leap out of the canoe, watch for the incoming wave, and run it up the sand with the water; but even then the passengers are constantly obliged to be carried a short distance, if they would escape a wetting."[18]

Canoemen could work hard, efficiently, and fast. Governor Thomas Melvil wrote from Cape Coast Castle, with evident pride, that "in 3 days the *Basnett* was discharg'd of her Cape Coast Cargo, & in 3 more she fill'd her water & fell down at Annamaboe, wither I sent all yr canoemen, all my own, & a set of free Cape Coast Men." Melvil's satisfaction is understandable: as much as several hundred tons of cargo had been unloaded from a ship lying as far as one mile off the coast, and transported to the shore. The ship had then been prepared for its new cargo of enslaved Africans, and filled with the fresh water and some of the provisions that crew and cargo would require for the Middle Passage. This had been achieved, largely by the canoemen, in less than one week.[19]

Canoemen passed on the skills, the professional and social identities, and the benefits accruing from their labor to their sons. The Gold Coast canoemen often demanded payment in gold (or the debased *kra kra* gold dust used as local currency) rather than in cloth, the commodity most used by the Europeans to buy many other goods and services. The canoemen resisted selling their work for set amounts paid in trade goods, preferring to receive the gold with which they could trade for any commodities. In 1778 John Clemison, an independent trader in the town of Cape Coast, hired canoemen but then tried to pay them in alcohol rather than the gold that they expected and demanded. When they protested, Clemison "took a Cane, & flogg'd one of them." Perhaps not surprisingly the canoemen responded in kind, and they "rais'd a Possy & threw Stones at him, [and] also caught & beat two of his House Slaves." Governor Richard Miles was required to adjudicate, paying the canoemen in gold and giving the injured canoeman some cloth, while demanding compensation from them for their assault on Clemison and his slaves. After the canoemen had departed, Miles, all too aware of the fierce independence of the free workers of the coastal communities, angrily warned Clemison "that shou'd he in future strike any free Man or Woman in the Town, I wou'd give myself no trouble in Life about it, but let him settle it as well as he cou'd himself."[20]

Canoemen regularly objected to being paid in trade goods such as tobacco or alcohol, regarding these as items that should supplement rather than replace their regular payments in gold. Thus John Apperley recorded that he had hired a nine-hand canoe for £1 and employed "9 free Canoe Men at 10/ ea. Currency," but that he had been required to supplement these payments with "1 Galn Brandy & 1 fath. Cloth for ye Canoe Men," as well as providing "To the Canoemen on their return, to drink 1 Gal. Brandy." Similarly, the arrival at Cape Coast Castle of canoemen bearing freight from the outlying forts required the doling out of goods as bonuses, above and beyond their agreed payment. In February 1750, for example, canoemen arriving from Tantumquery received tobacco, canoemen bringing letters from Accra were given rum, canoemen working on the beach received rum and textiles, and more textiles were given to canoemen traveling to work at Succondee. Canoemen who worked in difficult conditions exacted similar bonuses: "sundry Canoemen for venturing off in a bad Sea to save the lives of two white and 13 black men" received textiles, tobacco, and rum, "notwithstanding one white man and one black man were drowned."[21]

Canoemen physically controlled the goods exported from and imported into the Gold Coast, and they regularly supplemented their income by stealing whatever they could, despite (or perhaps with the connivance of) African "bomboy" supervisors and eagle-eyed European ships' captains, merchants, and officials. "Pilferage by the Canoemen" was a common complaint by RAC officials and visiting ships' captains along the Gold Coast. From early on Europeans sought to control the activities of those who handled their trade goods, most especially the canoemen, demanding punishment of those caught cheating or stealing. Peter Gutkind has characterized the first of these regulations, the Portuguese "Manuelinas" of the late fifteenth and early sixteenth centuries, as "labor legislation," which sought to control the agency and power of the canoemen through severe punishment for transgressions, including the selling of offenders into slavery and their transportation to the Portuguese sugar islands. From the beginning, however, the balance of power generally tipped in favor of the canoemen, given the Europeans' dependence upon their labor, and the determination of the canoemen to work and be treated as a community rather than as individuals. Even following the introduction of these new regulations, a Portuguese governor complained that the canoemen "have once again refused to work and all our efforts to punish them have made them more objectionable," and a merchant was attacked by canoemen who objected to his attempt to pay them in cloth rather than gold. The Portuguese, and after them all other Europeans on the Gold Coast, quickly discovered that it was easier to work with the canoemen than against them, as reflected in the admission by a subsequent Portuguese governor that if treated "correctly" the canoemen would faithfully "work long hours and carry out the work with skill and care."[22]

One hundred and fifty years later the British on the Gold Coast faced precisely the same problems: the governor of Cape Coast Castle complained bitterly about the "Imposition of the free Canoemen," observing, "For some Years past we have experienced great Inconvenience and some Losses by employing free Canoemen to assist in discharging the Storeship. Last year they stole a good deal of Brandy, and because some of them were punished, having been caught in the Fact, they have now absolutely refused working for us." Like dockworkers and stevedores across time and culture, canoemen regarded pilferage as an occupational bonus, and they united in protest against the prohibition and punishment of what they regarded as legitimate working activity. British authorities sought greater success in controlling the canoemen and their depredations by employing local men with authority over them. Thomas Price wrote from Cape Coast Castle describing the long-standing "Complaint at this Place, that neither Captains of Ships, your Servants, or others could get canoemen to work when they wanted, and even when they did work, they plundered the Property they were carrying off or on, very considerably." His solution was to employ "four free Waterside Bomboys at four Ackies trade pr Month each, who on their part, bind themselves to furnish what Canoemen may be wanted, as well as to be accountable for any Depredations the Canoemen may commit." With evident satisfaction Price reported the "good Effect of this Measure" as seen in the speedy unloading of the storeship and "the very trifling Depredations they have committed upon the Brandy in particular." But even this measure reflected the agency of the canoemen, for the chief Bomboy was in fact "a Head Man of their own electing." Rather than imposing their own authority, the British officials at Cape Coast Castle were recognizing the authority of, and indeed paying, the canoemen's own leader.[23]

West African law allowed severe punishment and even enslavement of any person caught stealing. The Europeans sometimes enforced similar penalties, but they walked a fine line between attempting to impose European authority while yet recognizing that trade could not occur without these highly skilled men. Free (and sometimes enslaved) canoemen might withdraw their labor for a variety of causes, thus bringing trade to a virtual standstill. Sometimes they protested causes particular to themselves, such as abuse by Europeans or by European-employed bomboys, underpayment or payment in unacceptable trade goods, or the mistreatment or cheating of one of their number. On other occasions canoemen supported the larger African community by refusing to work—for example, when Europeans had failed to pay sufficient rents or provide appropriate gifts to local caboceers and leaders, or had abused or misused local people.[24]

In addition to ferrying people and goods between ship and shore, canoemen moved freight and passengers between forts and along the coast, and were often more dependable in this service than the smaller European boats. Thus Peter Holt wrote from Anomabu to the governor at Cape Coast requesting "a Canoe on Acct. to get Oyster shells" from distant beaches, in order to make lime necessary for the construction of the fort. Similarly, canoes helped transport "great Quantities of Salt from Accra" to Cape Coast.[25]

The canoemen's desire to exploit their skill and exact the maximum profit from their carrying trade affected West African merchants, traders, and producers as much as European fort commanders, factors, and ships' captains. Consequently, the canoemen were as often at odds with local African communities as they were with the Europeans. Moreover, given that each group of canoemen associated themselves and were in turn identified with the Europeans who employed them, these Africans were potential victims in the regular wars between European powers. Thus the canoemen living near Cape Coast Castle were wary of transporting goods past the nearby Dutch fort at Elmina. The accounts for Cape Coast Castle in 1751, for example, recorded that a significant quantity of goods, including various textiles, tobacco and rum, were sent for the maintenance of "Cape Coast Canoemen who were seized on their way to Dixcove by the Dutch Generals Order . . . for Cloths to wear and purchase Necessaries to subsist upon."[26]

The canoemen had originally been fishermen, and during those periods when their services were not required, many continued to work as fishermen in the Gold Coast communities that had begun centuries earlier as small fishing villages. Before, during, and after the era of the slave trade, Gold Coast fishermen provided coastal residents with their major source of protein, and to this day they continue to fish in much the same manner employed by their ancestors. As coastal communities grew in size during the seventeenth and eighteenth centuries, so too did the ranks of the fishermen, who composed the single largest occupational group: while professional canoemen accounted for an estimated 5 to 10 percent of workers, fishermen (and thus occasional canoemen) made up as much as 60 percent of the workforce of coastal communities.[27]

The importance of the work of fishermen was recognized by European visitors. "Their greatest diligence and valour they show in fishing," observed Pieter de Marees in the early seventeenth century, and other European visitors echoed his observation, noting that "their chief Employment is fishing" or that "Fishing [is] their principal imployment." All along the Gold Coast "Their food generally is fish," and Europeans constantly struggled to raise the livestock to produce the meats they favored. The Gold Coast "is not favourable for their pasturage," and European attempts to introduce new or larger animals generally failed. One European lamented that "There are no tame geese, ducks, or turkey hens, and even though they are often brought there by the Christians, they usually die straightaway." While cows, bulls, sheep, goats, pigs, and chickens could all be found, many were often sickly, and they seldom grew as large as they did in Europe. John Atkins acknowledged that food was readily available along the coast but was "neither very cheap nor large," and he reported that a small cow of three hundred pounds "is reckoned a fine Beast."[28]

Fishing in a variety of different ways, working with seasonal fluctuations and extremes of weather, and supplying both local and more distant markets while negotiating with both local African rulers and European trading communities, the fishermen were highly skilled and well organized. As a resident of the Ile de Ré off the west coast of France, Jean Barbot was familiar with and particularly interested in the fishing he witnessed along the late seventeenth-century Gold Coast. He wrote that the residents of the town of Cape Coast "devote themselves more to fishing than to any other occupation," and described the residents of Elmina as "good fishermen": this was, Barbot believed, "a profession more highly esteemed among them than that of merchant." With evident interest he described how "Every morning four to five hundred canoes, with two or three persons in each, go up to two leagues out to sea to fish. It is a pleasure to see these fleets of little vessels."[29] Their canoes were distinctive, and Villault recorded that the small fishing vessels "are very neat and beautiful, painted and adorned with all possible care, [and] they fasten *Fetiches* to them to preserve them from storms & disasters, and when they have done fishing, they draw them up under a place on purpose to keep them dry."[30]

Barbot provided one of the best contemporary descriptions of the work and skill of the Gold Coast fishermen. He described how six mornings each week a large number of fishermen rowed out from each coastal community, so that on "Some days you can see 300–400 at each place." These were relatively small craft compared with the canoes used for transporting people and goods, normally carrying two men, one standing up to fish, the other sitting at the rear to steer the canoe. The fishermen sailed out in the early morning, taking advantage of the breezes from the coast that helped calm the ocean swell, returning in the middle of the day before the ocean breezes picked up, creating "great difficulty and danger in reaching land, on account of the violent breakers."[31]

While some fish was immediately sold and eaten, much was dried for consumption later and for trade with inhabitants of the interior. The fish was dried on and in sand, "and is carried many miles inland, from one hand to another, so that this is a great source of trade." The residents of the European forts and castles on the Gold Coast depended on the fish

caught by local fishermen, both for their own subsistence and as food for
slaves held in the castles and during the Middle Passage. Fishermen traditionally paid a portion of their catch as tribute to local leaders, and over
time Europeans in the largest forts assessed and collected a similar duty.
Barbot recorded, for example, that the fishermen of Elmina "pay one fifth
of their catch, raw, to the Dutch general, not without bitterness." Away
from the larger forts the fishermen continued to pay as much as one-third
of their catch to "the King in whose Dominion that Port is." Cape Coast
boasted one of the best-stocked fisheries along the Gold Coast, yet despite
the existence of a large fishing fleet, local demand was so high "that it is
not without sometimes open Force, that they are brought to Supply and
spare the [Cape Coast Castle] garrison enough for their Subsistence." Fishermen who presented RAC officials with particularly large or magnificent
fish expected—and usually received—an appropriate reward, as when the
Cape Coast fishermen received a half flask of brandy for their gift of "a very
fine Fish."[32]

Like the canoemen, fishermen took collective action against perceived
injustices. When two Anomabu fishermen visited Sekondi and took in a
second catch of the day, they refused to give Gilbert Petrie (the RAC official
in Sekondi) "Fish Custom twice in one Day," at which he had them
"severely flogged & turn'd out of Town." Upon their return to Anomabu
their outraged fellow fishermen "complain'd bitterly" to RAC governor
Richard Brew, telling him "if they had not Satisfaction for the ill Usage they
met with at Succondee, they wod. revenge themselves on ye first Englishmen they met, & went out of the Fort swearing they wod. stop the Works."
Panicked by the threat, Brew arranged for rapid redress of the grievances,
while warning of the "bad Consequences wch. in all Probability wod attend
a Repetition of Mr. Petrie's behaviour to the people of Annamaboo." Just
as with the canoemen, it was easier for the British to work with the fishermen than against them, and it was not uncommon for RAC officials to
employ "the Chief of the Fishermen" as a "Waterside Bomboy."[33]

The villages of these sea workers were often quite separate from both
the coastal towns and the European forts, containing the homes of the
fishermen, the canoemen, and their families, including the "boyes, who are
alwaies waiting in the harbour to help them with their fish, and to make up
their Lines and their Nets for them." These people lived in the "lowest class
of dwelling," consisting of "small conical huts, thatched over with grass,
huddled together like so many hay-cocks upon the sand, and with only a

small aperture, through which the occupant makes his ingress and egress upon his hands and knees." Young boys learned the "way to get a lively-hood" from about "the age of nine or ten," when fishermen took their sons out "to Sea, shews them how to make a *Canoe*, and which way to take fish." Fathers taught "their sons to spin yarn from the bark of trees and to make nets; and once they know how to make Nets, they go with their Fathers to the sea to Fish." Having thus learned "a little how to row or paddle," boys fished together, bringing their catch home, until as young adults "the Sons begin to do their own trade and, taking leave of their Father, go to live with two or three other Boys together in a house." Acquiring a canoe they began fishing in their own right, while some began to "trade with the Merchants and to take them with their Canoes to the ships," thus entering the ranks of the professional fishermen and canoemen.[34]

Having fished in the evenings or early morning, during the afternoons the fishermen "spin the Yarn and knit the Nets, and sit together on the beach knitting the Nets." Meanwhile their "Wives go with their Husbands' Fish to the Market, where everybody comes to buy [it]."[35] Merchants and residents of communities further inland "very often buy fish and carry it to towns in other Countries, in order to make some profit: thus the Fish caught in the Sea is carried well over 100 or 200 miles into the Interior, where it is considered of great value, although it often stinks like Carrion and there are a thousand worms creeping out of it."[36]

As large and discrete professional communities, fishermen and canoe-men occasionally found themselves at odds with local villagers as well as with the Europeans. In 1759, for example, the "very Troublesome" fisher-men of Anomabu "quarelled wth. the rest of the Town." After several days of fighting the fishermen and their families fled, and although RAC official Nathaniel Senior worried that they might settle under a rival "Dutch Fort," thus depriving Anomabu of vitally needed fresh fish, he did not hesitate to purchase "from the Anamaboo People part of the Ground where the Fishermen's Town stood to make a spur to the Fort."[37]

Given their proficiency on the waters off the Gold Coast, it is not sur-prising that some canoemen and fishermen entered the ranks of the Euro-pean merchant marine workforce. European slave ships were often required to spend months on the shores of the Gold Coast, slowly acquiring a full cargo of slaves. Despite the best efforts of ships' captains, many seafarers succumbed to tropical diseases, and the skills of local canoemen and the fishermen made them a logical source for replacement sailors. Some came

to be identified as deep sea sailors: a 1776 report of the labor costs of free
canoemen, for example, pointed out that previous reports had erroneously
included the wages of "some *few* of the free Black Sailors," who were clearly
identified as a different group of maritime workers. West Africans made up
a small but significant proportion of the crews of some of the ships sailing
to and from the Gold Coast. Sarah Lee described the dependence of one
trading ship upon African sailors, focusing upon their "chief, Ben Liverpool, so named because he had once visited that city." Liverpool "presented
what he called his books, and which, in fact, were the testimonials given to
him by various masters under whom he and his men had served." Such
men sailed as far as the Caribbean and Britain, from whence they returned
"by another trader going to the coast."[38]

Recognizing the need for a steady supply of replacement sailors, both
for the vessels that moved up and down the coast, as well as for oceangoing
ships, British officials along the Gold Coast saw the benefit in training both
their own enslaved and local free West Africans as seafarers. In 1707 Dalby
Thomas complained of the lack of "vessells to carry the Goods &c. too &
from ye ffactories & for trade," and he recommended the construction of
two twenty-five-ton and two thirty-five-ton craft, proposing that "a few
White Men would serve they could breed Blacks to be Seamen good
Enough." Over the course of the eighteenth century, free West Africans
were regularly taken aboard coastal and oceangoing vessels "to be bred
Sailors," and British officials on the Gold Coast promised that they would
"do the same by all Ships." Payroll records of Cape Coast Castle in 1751, for
example, identified Tryton, Apponherry, Quashee Adadoe, and Bonetta as
free men who had been trained to be sailors. Similarly, when the governor
of the British fort at Appollonia appointed Richard Dick, "a European
Sailor of a very good Character," as master of "the Company's Boat," he
also "Engaged four free Men Black Sailors to go in the Boat, lusty, stout
young Men." Other documents attested to the existence of a small community of local seafarers, as in the case of "the free Black Sailors" who in 1777
had claims upon the estate of Richard Brew, the late governor of Anomabu
and a wealthy trader. On rare occasions castle slaves were ordered to work
on coastal vessels, but only when there was an insufficient number of white
and free black sailors: in 1777, for example, Governor Richard Miles
reported that in order to facilitate the work of the schooner *Nancy* in bringing shells from Winnebah, he had "mann'd her with such of your Slaves as
have been occasionally employ'd in Boats, and who will answer the purpose

of free Sailors." The capture of other vessels sometimes prompted the recruitment of local sailors, as when two joined with a pair of British soldiers to man a captured Dutch supply ship.[39]

Once on the open seas West African sailors were no longer afforded the protection of Gold Coast working practices, and they faced the same perils as European and American seafarers. In 1799 Royal African Committee officials in London learned that when the Bristol ship *Sally* had departed the Gold Coast, the master, Charles Anderson, needing "more people than he had at that time, to assist him in the navigation of his ship to England, had engaged seven free Blacks, Sailors of Cape Coast, to enter on board." Unfortunately, the *Sally* and her crew had been captured by the French, and subsequent liberation by the Royal Navy had resulted in "the said seven free Men" being "press'd" into service on a naval warship. Company officials immediately wrote to the Lords Commissioners of the Admiralty requesting the "liberation of the seven free black Sailors" and their transfer to the store ship bound for the Gold Coast: at the same time, they wrote to Anderson indicating that he alone was responsible for the £700 bond payable to the Gold Coast relatives of the men should they fail to return. However, while this ship's master would pay the financial penalty, every occasion on which free Gold Coast men failed to return made the recruitment of others more difficult and caused tension between local leaders and communities on the one hand, and the British on the other hand.[40]

"The commercial spirit is very strong in the African," noted one European visitor to the Gold Coast, and he observed that the "whole population are traders to a certain extent." The influx of large quantities of European goods significantly increased both the size of and the social stratification within communities along the Gold Coast. The wealth of local West African leaders and merchants increased dramatically, while the specialization of skills and the division and commoditization of labor transformed local life. British and other European officials on the Gold Coast worked hard to foster relations with local rulers and middlemen. As well as renting land to the Europeans for trading forts, the people of the Gold Coast region furnished mediators, translators, and skilled and unskilled workers. Communities on the Gold Coast moved from the margins of West African society to its commercial center, facilitating trade as workers and mercantile middlemen. In the process these coastal Africans, from the ruling elite down to their slaves, enjoyed privileged access to valuable European trade goods, and to all that these trade goods could buy in West Africa, including commodities ranging from gold to slaves to food. Receiving European trade goods as payment, as rent, as tribute, and as gifts enabled these people to "eat" or consume such goods. As a result the standard of living of what had previously been small and peripheral communities increased dramatically. In contrast to those living in other areas of Africa and elsewhere in the British Atlantic World, the skilled workers, laborers, and slaves of Gold Coastal communities enjoyed payment in luxury goods rather than in the necessities of life, enabling them to enjoy such goods or to trade them on advantageous terms. With Europeans sailing from distant shores and desperate to acquire gold and slaves, Africans were able to demand whatever they wanted, and if one nation could not supply it they might well trade with another. Local tastes and predilections, as well as the demands of those in more distant markets, forced European traders to supply exactly what West Africans wanted, and—to the frequent dismay of European factors—local tastes changed quickly. A surfeit of a previously popular type and color of fabric, for example, would inevitably dampen demand. Thus not just those selling slaves and gold to the Europeans, but all who provided goods, services, and labor, were able to negotiate for payment in trade goods of their choosing, and they were free to decline payment in goods they found unsatisfactory.[41]

By 1700 English, Portuguese, Dutch, Scandinavian, and German companies operated some twenty-five major trading posts and castles as well as a like number of smaller "factories" along the two hundred and fifty miles of the Gold Coast. Yet however large and pervasive Atlantic trade may have been, it appears that most West Africans did not feel their lives were shaped by it any more than did the Europeans who manufactured the items shipped to the Gold Coast. Besides the slaves who were transported across the Atlantic in chains, the West Africans most intimately connected with the Europeans and their trade were those who inhabited the coastal regions, which were transformed from a remote and insignificant backwater to a vibrant region of commercial and cultural exchange. Yet the residents of West African coastal communities who were crucial facilitators of this trade acted in ways that indicated their significant control over and benefit from the interaction, and neither to themselves nor to the Europeans did Gold Coast Africans appear to be weak or victims.[42]

Throughout the seventeenth and eighteenth centuries, Britain's transatlantic slave trade depended upon cordial relations with West Africans who lived and worked according to their own dictates. Participation in international trade certainly affected the lives of many, from the new class of bomboys and caboceers to the fishermen who worked as canoemen. However, Europeans seldom exercised mastery over the Gold Coast residents who worked this trade, and the British, Dutch, and other Europeans were forced to accommodate local people and the terms of their labor. This frequently caused British officials on the Gold Coast enormous frustration, for they had far less control of the workers upon whom they depended than was true either in the British Isles or in the Americas. Given that "the Natives grow daily more insolent," it was perhaps not surprising that white Britons believed that "a Spirit of Liberty (if Mutiny & Riot deserve that Name) has crept into the Breast[s]" of the company-owned slaves who lived and worked in close proximity to local Africans. Writing from Africa against the larger imperial backdrop of the Wilkes controversy in London and the growing popular protests in Britain's mainland American colonies, John Grossle equated such African-held sentiments with those of "the meanest wretch in London Streets, for in all Countries this kind of Liberty is chiefly confined to the lowest class of Men." Thus, at least in the mind of one British imperial and commercial agent, the political radicalism of lower-sort Britons and Americans was associated with the spirited independence of Gold Coast Africans.[43]

With its settled communities along the shoreline, the Gold Coast provided Europeans with opportunities to build a large number of fortified trading posts and castles, and the communities that were adjacent to these structures expanded accordingly. Traditional work, including agricultural production, fishing, canoeing, military service, and salt making, all expanded as Gold Coast residents sought to meet the needs of Europeans on the coast and of European trade and slave ships. Other forms of work changed, as new sources of raw materials and new technologies encouraged people such as metal workers to create or service new products, or familiar articles in far greater quantities. The Atlantic trade also created new groups of workers tied directly to the Europeans, such as the mulatto offspring of white men and African women who were trained for service as oceangoing sailors, clerks, and European craftsmen, but for the vast majority of Africans along the Gold Coast, their work changed in scale and significance rather than in kind. These men and women were now playing a far more significant role in massively expanded trade relations, and they inhabited larger communities more intimately tied to trade with other Africans as well as with Europeans. Yet in their daily work, in how they lived and what they ate, in the clothes they wore and the gods they worshipped, the men and women of the Gold Coast lived lives akin to those of their ancestors, despite the advent of the transatlantic slave trade and its huge impact on Africa as a whole.

Sean Hawkins and Philip D. Morgan have observed that "No people were more uprooted and dislocated; or travelled more within the Empire, by both sea and land; or created more of a trans-imperial culture" than Africans and their descendants. Paradoxically, however, the people of coastal West Africa facilitated this exchange and yet lived and worked in ways that may have been transformed less than those of both white and black people in North America, the Caribbean, and even Britain itself. The Africans transported across the Atlantic transformed life, society, and work on plantations throughout the Americas, and dramatically impacted ideas about free and bound labor. Their lives were forever changed in the process. At the same time, the raw materials they produced were shipped back to Europe, where tobacco, sugar, and the like encouraged dramatic urbanization and industrialization and the emergence of a modern industrial working class. But along the shores of the Gold Coast whence so many New World slaves came, among the men and women who had facilitated the trade that helped trigger this monumental transformations of life and work in the Americas, life and work changed relatively little.[44]

PART IV

Plantation Slavery

Chapter 8

"The Harsh Tyranny of Our Masters"

The Development of Racial Slavery and the Integrated Plantations of Barbados

Throughout the era of the transatlantic slave trade, free and enslaved African laborers on the Gold Coast lived and worked in the context of local customs and expectations, and even British-owned castle slaves enjoyed a significant degree of independence. However, despite the fact that Britons on the Gold Coast became accustomed to West African patterns of labor and servitude, the power relationships that necessitated this accommodation did not extend four thousand miles across the Atlantic. On Barbados the emerging planter elite were freed from the customary restraints of both West African and British society. Historians have argued that it was with the switch to enslaved labor that large integrated plantations developed on Barbados, from where they spread to other regions of British America. However, planter attitudes toward and their brutal deployment of bound labor predated both dependence upon enslaved Africans and the organization of integrated plantations. Throughout the early to mid-seventeenth century, planters had treated bound white workers with a brutality that was largely unknown in either England or West Africa. Planters' behavior toward these bound laborers eased a transition to the exploitation of enslaved Africans in new ways during the later seventeenth century, and the development of a system of slavery that was radically different from the treatment of bound and free African workers on the Gold Coast, whence so many Barbadian slaves had departed.[1]

There were remarkably strong connections between the Gold Coast of West Africa and Barbados: perhaps the majority of British slave ships stopped first at Barbados, and planters on the island rapidly developed a strong preference for enslaved Africans from the Gold Coast. A good many white men traveled to Barbados on trading ships that sailed first to West Africa, and it was along the Guinea Coast that these men would have first encountered European reliance on African labor, watching it operate efficiently and profitably in West African ways and contexts. Officials of the Royal African Company and its successors worked both in West Africa and in Barbados, their success dependent on full and constant communication, and some personnel from the Gold Coast subsequently spent time in Barbados as merchants and even as planters. Yet despite all of these connections, and all of the experience of enslaved and free African labor as it functioned on the Gold Coast, Barbadian planters' prior use of bound white convicts and prisoners completely overrode African precedents. The nature of bound labor on Barbados plantations was intimately connected to the attitudes and practices nurtured by the near absolute power of planters, who came to regard bound laborers not as fellow members of a common society but rather as property, a resource to be controlled and exploited, often with singular brutality. Barbados planters soon perfected a new system of racial slavery, creating a workforce that would power their own plantations and inspire similar systems in Jamaica, the Carolinas, and elsewhere, perhaps the wealthiest colonies in England's New World empire.[2]

By the early 1640s the leading planters in Barbados had begun to develop a plantation society, at first producing cotton, tobacco, and indigo. The plantation system, with its voracious appetite for bound white labor, preceded the rise of sugar and the developing symbiotic relationship between the sweet crop and the savage labor system of slavery. Historians have disagreed about the speed and the nature of the transition from white servitude to African slavery on Barbados. Richard Dunn posits an early and rapid shift, while Hilary Beckles proposes a more gradual transition, and Russell Menard suggests a middle ground, arguing that the pace of change increased after the mid-1640s. It is all but impossible to pinpoint a particular moment when Barbados planters decided to replace white bound laborers with West African slaves, for that moment came for different planters at different times.[3]

The dramatic increase in the number of African slaves appears to have accompanied the development of sugar as the island's main crop, but it was not at first matched by a corresponding decline in the number of white servants. By the end of 1643 fewer than 3,000 enslaved Africans had disembarked in Barbados, where they were massively outnumbered by bound white laborers. Most planters were still growing tobacco, cotton, or indigo, and James Holdip was typical in that he owned no slaves and had twenty-nine bound white laborers working his 200-acre plantation. Within a couple of years sugar had emerged as a commercially significant crop, although not yet a dominant one, and larger planters whose cultivation of sugar realized large and immediate profits quickly amassed substantial numbers of enslaved Africans, at first working these alongside bound white laborers. By the end of 1646 almost 25,000 enslaved Africans had arrived on the island, and bound whites and enslaved Africans labored in almost equal numbers on Barbadian plantations. White bound laborers continued for a while to constitute the workforce of smaller plantations, while enslaved Africans quickly came to dominate larger plantations. The transition was evident on Sir Anthony Ashley Cooper's plantation, which in 1646 was worked by 21 bound whites and 9 enslaved Africans. A year later, 28 white laborers and 102 enslaved Africans worked Sir Thomas Modyford's 500-acre plantation: such a large and profitable landholding had probably helped Modyford invest in new laborers before many of his contemporaries. By the mid-1650s, and despite the continued influx of bound whites from the war-torn British Isles, enslaved Africans formed a majority of the unfree workforce. In 1654 Robert Hooper's 200 acres were worked by 35 white servants and 66 slaves, and by 1656 George Martin had no servants and 60 slaves at work on his 259 acres. By the end of that year close to 46,000 enslaved Africans had come to Barbados.[4]

Throughout the 1640s and 1650s bound servants from the British Isles continued to pour into Barbados, and they only began to substantially decline in numbers during the 1660s, by which time enslaved Africans had dominated the plantation workforce for at least a decade. In 1687 a listing of the "Christian Servants" on the Newton plantation gave the names of five who had died, but then added seven "season'd Servts. bought to supply the places of the Season[ed] dead ones." However, while such bound white labor was clearly still integral to the running of the plantation, the listing of twenty-nine slaves, including a highly skilled refiner and stiller, as well as nine "Negro Pickeneys borne to the Estate," all served to illustrate the transition to enslaved labor that was well under way.[5]

Between 1640 and 1660 Barbados planters spent approximately £1 million purchasing enslaved Africans, perhaps twice the amount they spent on equipment, land, livestock, and everything else required for plantation agriculture. Within a single generation enslaved Africans had become "the principal and most usefull servants of a Plantation," and their status was institutionalized in "An ACT declaring the Negro-slaves of this Island to be Real Estates," a law that began with the observation that "a very considerable part of the wealth of this Island consists in our Negro-slaves, without whose labor we should be utterly unable to manage our Plantations." Codification of the status of the enslaved had begun several years earlier in 1661 with "An Act for the Better Ordering and Governing of Negroes," a slave code that would be reiterated by the Barbados Assembly in 1676, 1682, and 1688. The Barbadian slave code was premised on the belief that the island's plantations "cannot be fully managed and brought into use, without the labor and service of great number[s] of Negroes," and it defined enslaved Africans as being "of barbarous, wilde and savage nature, and such as renders wholly unqualified to be governed by the Laws, Customs and Practices of our Nation." The Assembly thus took the laws governing servants to a new level by defining the enslaved as even further removed from the rights and freedoms of English subjects than were the bound Scots, Irish, and English who had preceded them. As real property they were regarded as being outside of the contractual relationships of service in husbandry and indentured servitude and outside of the common law, and were relegated to bound status more akin to feudal villeinage.[6]

By the 1660s enslaved labor had become essential to the Barbados sugar economy, and African men, women, and children were "adjudged to be Estates Real . . . and [they] shall descend unto the Heirs and Widow of any person dying intestate." Unlike bound white servants before them, enslaved Africans were thus tied by English inheritance law to specific plantations, and they could not easily be removed from the places where they lived, worked, and died; however, the definition of the enslaved as realty was rather more stark than any previous laws related to white servants. As racial slavery took hold of the island, white planters' fear of enslaved Africans led the colonial government to refine their slave code "for the good regulating and ordering" of slaves. Such mild language belied the savage, violent regimen mandated by the laws designed to brutally subject the African labor force who were responsible for an ever-growing proportion of the skilled and unskilled work of England's wealthiest colony. As early as 1654 a visitor to Barbados described enslaved Africans as "miserabell Negors borne to perpetuall slavery thy and thayer seed," whose owners "sele them from one to the other as we doue shepe." These laws articulated planters' developing conception of a racialized bound labor force, liable to commit "heinous and grievous crimes" unless controlled by legally sanctioned violence. Building on their callous treatment of bound white laborers a generation earlier, Barbadian planters began to regard and regulate their increasingly African workforce in explicitly racial terms. The Barbadian slave codes and laws would provide the foundation for strikingly similar formulations in Jamaica, South Carolina, the Leeward Islands, and beyond.[7]

While statistical precision is all but impossible, records from various Barbados plantations, along with the instructions prepared for those who would manage them, together provide a far more full and detailed picture of the transformation of labor on Barbados plantations. It was a relatively small number of large planters, enjoying almost complete control of legislative, executive, and judicial power on the isolated island, who were able to fashion the plantation system for the growing and processing of sugar by a bound workforce. Having used and killed many thousands of bound white servants, and then discarded those who survived, the Barbados plantocracy fashioned the slave plantation "the most distinctive product of European capitalism, colonialism and maritime power in the late seventeenth and early eighteenth centuries." With its intensive application of capital and labor to tropical soil and climate, the plantation "was an absolutely unprecedented social, economic and political institution, and by no means simply an innovation in the organization of agriculture."[8]

It appears likely that by the mid-1650s the population of approximately 20,000 enslaved Africans was rapidly approaching parity with the white population of planters, bound servants, and free men and women, and by 1660 there were almost certainly more enslaved Africans than white people on the island. A generation later, in 1680, the first somewhat reliable statistics were recorded on the island in the most complete and detailed census of any English colony in the Americas before the 1770s. The raw statistics are striking, for they provide a profile of the rapidly changing character of the bound workforce who constituted the foundation of one of the wealthiest colonies in the Americas. The census reveals a dwindling population of only 2,317 white bound laborers, working for 3,044 planters: the almost 90,000 acres under cultivation were worked primarily by 38,782 slaves. The 175 largest planters each owned 60 or more slaves, and an average of at least 265 acres.[9]

In the late seventeenth century and throughout the eighteenth it became less and less common to find white bound laborers at work on larger Barbadian plantations, and plantation accounts came to use the term "servant" in new ways. Thus on the Seawell plantation in 1784, white workers were recorded in the accounts in two categories, under "Workmen's Accounts" and "Servants Wages." The former included skilled artisans such as the mason William Yard, the well-digger William Thomas, the carpenter John Roberts, as well as a glazier and two blacksmiths, all of whom had been hired to render specific services. "Servants" referred not to the bound laborers of a century earlier, but rather to employees of the plantation paid wages for their services. The plantation no longer relied upon the labor of bound white men.[10]

The transition from white to black bound labor, and the related development of the integrated plantations and the ideology on which they rested, can be seen in two of the most valuable surviving documents from mid-seventeenth-century Barbados, Richard Ligon's account of his experiences as a planter between 1647 and 1650, and Henry Drax's instructions for the management of his sugar plantations in 1679. The former describes Barbados a mere two decades after its first settlement, at a time when "the great work of Sugar-making, was but newly practised by the inhabitants there." Published after his return to England, Ligon's account not only described Barbados but also furnished a detailed account of "the whole process of the work of Sugar-making, which is now grown the soul of Trade in this Iland." During Ligon's time on the island, white servants may still have outnumbered enslaved Africans, and both groups of bound laborers were employed in creating and powering the developing sugar economy.[11]

Drax's instructions detail the proper management of a fully fledged integrated sugar plantation thirty years later, and they were written by the son of James Drax, who had been one of Ligon's fellow planters. According to the census of 1680, Colonel Henry Drax owned 705 acres and 327 slaves, and he was one of the island's greatest planters. A member of the Governor's Council, his Drax Hall and Hope plantations were among the largest on the island, and he pioneered the development of integrated plantations powered by an enslaved African workforce. Anxious to return to England, in about 1679 Drax drafted or oversaw the writing of a manual for plantation management, which serves as a guide to new thought and practice on the island as they took form immediately after the transitional period, with enslaved Africans now dominating the plantation workforce. So detailed, precise, and accurate were these instructions that a century later William

Belgrove was able to use them in only a slightly revised form as the basis for his own manual of plantation management and economy.[12]

Bound prisoners, convicts, and servants from the British Isles continued to flow to the island in large numbers during Ligon's time in Barbados, and planters who were occupied with clearing forests, raising different crops, and beginning to work with sugar did not hesitate to exploit their white workers. At the same time, however, larger planters were starting to purchase large numbers of enslaved Africans, but of necessity much of the skilled work continued to be undertaken by free and bound whites. A generation later, however, Drax described a very different system and society. Other commercial crops had all but disappeared, and the sugar that was grown and processed all across the now cleared island was worked almost entirely by slaves, who were increasingly undertaking all aspects of both unskilled and skilled plantation work.

Richard Ligon and his two partners arrived in Barbados in September 1647. After twenty years of settlement, half of the original forests had already been cleared. Ligon found food being grown between the branches of newly felled trees, with cash crops such as indigo on the more open land. However, it was already becoming clear that sugar was "the main Plant, to improve the value of the whole Iland," and after some initial research Ligon and his colleagues decided that rather than clear and plant new land "it was farre better . . . to purchase a plantation that was already furnisht. and stockt with Servants, Slaves, Horses, Cattle, Assinigoes, Camels &c. with a sugar worke, and an Ingenio." Both white servants and slaves were integral to the operation, and Ligon and his associates negotiated with Major William Hilliard, who possessed a plantation of some five hundred acres, a plantation house, a full sugar works and buildings, and housing, "with 96 *Negroes*, and three *Indian* women, with their Children: 28 Christians, 45 Cattle for worke, 8 Milch Cowes, a dozen Horses and Mares, 16 Assinigoes."[13]

Ligon saw Barbados as being "divided into three sorts of men, *viz.* Masters, Servants, and Slaves." Because of their greater cost and their indefinite servitude, enslaved Africans were "preserv'd with greater care than the servants," and Ligon believed that in certain ways enslaved African were—at least initially—better treated by planters than were white servants. Ligon expressed sympathy for white servants, who were "put to very hard labour, ill lodging, and their dyet very sleight," and he contrasted these miserable wretches with enslaved Africans, who were a "happy people" who made

"Very good servants, if they be not spoyled by the English." It is not hard, however, to find evidence in Ligon's account of the brutalization of enslaved Africans. He described how planters examined naked slaves on the ships arriving from West Africa, choosing them "as they do Horses in a Market: the strongest, youthfullest, and most beautifull, yield the greatest prices." Any admission of humanity or spirituality in the Africans was matched by contrary assertions, as when Ligon declared that "most of them are as neer beasts as may be, setting their souls aside." Having described an abortive uprising by bound white servants, Ligon concluded that slaves were less rebellious because "they are held in such awe and slavery, as they are fearful to appear in any daring act." The full violence and terror of racial slavery is implicit in this casual observation, and when he goes on to describe the daily life and work of the plantation, Ligon charts a developing work regimen of appalling character, which had already worked thousands of white servants to death, and which was then being perfected in its equally horrific employment of enslaved Africans.[14]

In the three years that he was in Barbados, between 1647 and 1650, Ligon acknowledged that planters had developed "the skill to know when the Canes were ripe," and had become far more adept at producing sugar that was good enough to transport to and sell in England. He described the planting of canes, the care and maintenance of these plants, and their harvesting and processing fifteen months later. Even during these early days of sugar agriculture and production enslaved Africans were required to undertake a complicated and arduous work regimen. Ligon wrote first about weeding, which might appear a minor detail but was—as he well knew—a vital and backbreaking activity in the cultivation of sugar cane, "for unlesse that be done, all else (and the Planter too) will be undone: and if that be neglected but a little time, it will be a hard matter to recover it again, so fast will the weeds grow there." Enslaved Africans were to be constantly employed tilling, planting, hoeing, and keeping cleared ground and the fast-growing sugar canes free from the weeds that could so easily overcome them.[15]

Ligon described in precise detail the cutting of the cane, its transportation back to the sugar works, the pressing of the cane, and the processing of the sugar, yet his fascination for the intricacies of this new industry and the production of such a valuable resource were expressed in a vision of a plantation machine almost completely devoid of people. Processes, production, and sugar were lovingly described by Ligon, but the incredibly arduous and dangerous work of cane harvesting and sugar production was quite literally dehumanized, with the labor of both white servants and African slaves all but invisible. Ligon more frequently employed pronouns to describe sugar canes rather than the men and women who raised, harvested, and processed them. "The manner of cutting them is with little hand bills about six inches from the ground . . . for if they should be more than two dayes old, the juyce will grow slower. . . . The manner of grinding them, is this. . . ." Only rarely does human agency appear, as when "a *Negre* puts in the Canes of one side, and the rollers draw them through to the other side, where another *Negre* stands, and receives them." Barbados planters were masters of plantations on which they thought of themselves as creating the greatest crop of the age, sugar: labor was simply one component of the manufacturing process, and laborers were objectified as tools. The active agent in these processes was the planter himself: "And when you knock open these pots, you shall find a difference, both in the colour and the goodnesse, of the top and bottom . . . as may be rank'd with Muscavadoes: but in the middle, perfect White, and excellent Lump-Sugar."[16]

Ligon painstakingly enumerated the costs associated with the maintenance of the white bound servants and African slaves who powered his plantation. White male overseers and female house servants were each allowed clothing, as were the male "common servants" and the white women "that weed, and do the common work abroad": at this stage, white men and women continued to work outside, and in the fields, both supervising and working alongside enslaved Africans. However, the clothing allowances for the latter were far more basic and less generous.[17]

Thirty years later, Henry Drax's instructions for the proper management of his plantations described a significantly different system. In the mid-1650s sugar prices had begun to decline, in part because enhanced efficiency increased both production and consumption. As sugar prices dropped, consumption grew, meaning that planters could continue to realize large profits only if they produced more sugar, more cheaply and more efficiently than a generation earlier. However, the drive for increased efficiency in Barbados presented real problems in the later seventeenth and throughout the eighteenth centuries. During the years between Ligon and Drax most of the remaining Barbadian woods and forests had been cleared, leaving relatively little timber for use in construction or as fuel for sugar processing. Moreover, these trees had protected the soil, and their removal and subsequent intensive agriculture combined to loosen the island's thin layer of topsoil, much of which was washed away by the heavy seasonal rains. Excessive planting of sugar cane compounded the problem by exhausting the soil, and as planters sought to maintain and even increase their profits, they colonized less accessible hillside land, which was even more vulnerable to the loss of verdant topsoil. Well into the eighteenth century, visitors to Barbados noted that "The Soil, fertile in the Age past, seems now growing old, and past its teeming-time." And yet, for all that it was drained and depleted, the island nonetheless continued to produce large quantities of high-quality sugar, generating enormous wealth for planters. Drax's manual of plantation economy delineated a finely honed system of sugar agriculture and manufacturing, designed to compensate for the changes in the landscape, and significantly advanced from the nascent forms described by Ligon.[18]

What made continued production possible was a colossal amount of back-breaking labor. In contrast with Ligon's starkly impersonal vision of sugar agriculture and manufacture, Drax placed labor and laborers at the heart of plantation agriculture and sugar production. By the time that Drax wrote his instructions, this labor was being deployed on the integrated plantations that had come to dominate sugar agriculture and production in Barbados. All of the processes and labor involved in sugar-making took place in highly organized and efficiently structured organizations that integrated all aspects of the process along the lines outlined by Drax. This resulted in a smaller number of plantations, which were of an optimum size and were served by large, enslaved workforces. By 1680 just over two hundred planters each owned more than sixty slaves, with another two hundred planters owning between twenty and sixty slaves.[19] Thomas Tryon lamented that a generation earlier,

> the Canes would bear great Crops . . . yet in process of time, the Sugar Canes being of so great a substance, and containing such a quantity of rich Juices in them, and the Planters being limited to so small a proportion of Land, having pressed it so often with one sort, I mean with the Cane, rarely, if ever letting it lye still from the same, is become so Impoverished that they are now forced to Plant and Dung it every year; insomuch that an Hundred Acres of Cane now, require almost double the Labour and Hands, they did formerly.[20]

The result was optimally sized, large, integrated plantations, which in certain ways resembled modern factories rather than early modern farms.

While Ligon had marveled at an elementary, almost impersonal sugar-producing machine, with only passing references to the bound white servants and the enslaved Africans at its heart, Drax described a very different, and far more advanced, system. African labor, arduous and seemingly without end, was central to his narrative, while white labor had become marginal. "I shall Not leave you many white Servants[,] the ffewer the better," Drax informed his prospective plantation manager, although he did promise to try to find some skilled tradesmen in England who could then serve in senior, skilled positions on the plantation. Instead, "I shall Leave with Negros whereof theire will be aboutt [blank space] workers, which will be a Sufficentt Number if they stand welle to Carry on the plantation bussines to a great height."[21]

In 1680 Drax owned 327 enslaved Africans, who massively outnumbered his seven bound white workers. African bound laborers thus powered these integrated plantations, dominating the "welle ordered family" of Drax's plantation, on which planting, harvesting, and processing were "the finall productt of all our Endewors." Plantation labor, both the personnel and the work performed, had been racialized, and from the later seventeenth century until the early nineteenth century Barbadian sugar production depended almost entirely upon the brutally exploited labor of enslaved Africans. The enslaved experienced a harrowing work regimen that broke their bodies, and not until the later eighteenth century and early nineteenth century did changes in land management and crop production begin to slightly relieve these conditions, encouraging the creation of more creolized communities of the enslaved in which births began to outnumber deaths.[22]

Just as planters one and two generations earlier had regarded bound white servants, prisoners, and convicts as a resource to be exploited, even unto death, so too Drax saw enslaved Africans as expendable. With telling indifference he explained that in order to keep sugar production viable it would be necessary "to supply the places of those who shall be deseased or Dy" by annually purchasing ten to fifteen "Choyce Young Negros who will be fitt for plantt serwice." Drax expected his plantation manager to purchase new stock with the advice of experts such as "My Cozn Ltt. Colonel John Codrington," restricting himself to the observation, "I have observed that the Cormante or Gold Cost Negros have always Stood and proved bestt in this plantation[,] theirfor you will doe welle to buy of that Nation than any other."[23]

Barbados planters regularly expressed a preference for slaves from the Gold Coast throughout the seventeenth and eighteenth centuries. It was a preference that may well have been initiated by the practices of Royal African Company agents and merchants in West Africa, who, in accordance with instructions from their London headquarters, employed enslaved men and women from the Gold Coast as "guardians" on slave ships heading to Barbados and the English Americas. Between 1679 and 1705, on at least two dozen voyages for which records survive, and quite likely on many, many more, slave ship guardians helped maintain order among the enslaved cargo. On the *Hannibal*, for example, the captain procured between thirty and forty "gold coast negroes," who then played a role in supervising the cargo of some seven hundred enslaved men, women, and children. Each guardian was furnished with a "cat of nine tails as a badge of his office, which he is not a little proud of, and will exercise with great authority." West Africans, whether they had been free or enslaved before they found themselves on English slave ships, were likely to have had direct and personal experience of West African slavery, and as a result would have been familiar with enslaved people being entrusted with supervisory roles, or even serving as soldiers, and thus the position of guardian or sentinel would have been at least somewhat familiar. Rewarded with extra and quite likely better food, drink, and clothing, as well as a greater degree of freedom aboard ship, Gold Coast guardians supervised slaves from their home region and beyond, activities that they "discharge[d] with great diligence." Enslaved people in West Africa often enjoyed considerable agency and even a degree of liberty, and some exercised authority, carried weapons, and were even soldiers or armed guards. Thus, to use some of the enslaved to guard other slaves did not, at least on the Gold Coast, appear at all unusual. English officials and even ships' captains on the Gold Coast were very familiar with enslavement in a local context, operating in ways very different from those that were developing across the Atlantic, and they drew on this familiarity in creating the slave ship guardians. At the same time, they helped alleviate the problems caused by the deaths of so many white sailors during their time off the West African coast.[24]

The system apparently worked, and there is no evidence of guardians ever assisting in attempted shipboard rebellions. Upon arrival in Barbados, the guardians were likely in better health and condition than the enslaved men and women they had helped guard. Moreover, they had learned how to communicate with English-speaking white men, and they had proved their ability to take on positions of authority even before their arrival in Barbados. As such, when they were sold alongside all of the other slaves, those who had served as guardians quite likely possessed sufficient advantages to ensure that they commanded higher prices, and some may have been promoted more quickly into positions of authority on plantations, as drivers or even as skilled artisans in sugar production. The popularity of Gold Coast slaves among Barbadian planters was surely encouraged by the use of slave guardians, even though the practice faded in the early eighteenth century, as improved weaponry, custom-designed slave ships, and the deployment of larger white crews allowed captains and masters to dispense with guardians. Developing ideas about race, racial difference, and racial slavery as a distinct category may also have encouraged ships' captains and crews to begin treating all of their enslaved cargo as an undifferentiated group of subject people.[25]

By this point, however, Barbadian planters' preferences had become established. In 1681 the Royal African Company's representatives in Barbados wrote to their superiors in London confirming "the dislike People have here to any but Gold Coast Negroes," and Gold Coast Africans and their descendants constituted a significant presence—and probably the largest single group—among both new arrivals and Barbados-born slaves throughout the later seventeenth and eighteenth centuries. Fifteen years later Thomas Phillips confirmed this preference, observing that "The negroes most in demand at *Barbadoes*, are the gold coast, or, as they call them, *Cormantines*." A half-century later, Griffith Hughes recorded in his *Natural History of Barbados* that slaves "from the Kingdom . . . of *Coromantee* . . . are looked upon to be the best for Labour." The names of the enslaved often bore witness to their regional origins, beyond the continued use of African names that were common along the Gold Coast. Robin Cormante, for example, was the highly skilled sugar refiner on the Newton plantation in 1687.[26]

However, the term "Gold Coast" referred to places of departure such as Cape Coast, Anomabu, and Accra, and the enslaved who left these forts and castles were often drawn from a variety of ethnic groups, spread out along the coast and as far as several hundred miles inland. What is very clear is that the appellations applied to the enslaved by white planters said as much about white perceptions of African identity as they did about actual African ethnicity. It appears possible, however, that in their ignorance white planters were informing the creation of *new* African ethnic

identities in Barbados and beyond, fostering cooperation between people
from different societies identified by the planters as members of one group.
Thus, quite distinct Fante, Ashante, Ga, and other West Africans quite possibly developed a sense of common identity as Gold Coast or "Cormantin"
peoples, drawn from disparate peoples inhabiting a large region, yet quite
distinct from other, more distant regions such as Gambia or the Bight of
Biafra. This developing Gold Coast population on Barbados enjoyed a
majority position within the enslaved community, and quite likely an elite
status given that planters thought them more able and hard-working and
thus tended to train them in the most skilled plantation work. Just as the
highland Scotland district, St. Andrew Parish, and a variety of other place
names reflected the enduring presence of Scottish bound laborers on Barbados, so too Accra Beach lay a mile or two southeast of Carlisle Bay, and
from here one could watch the enslaved disembark from the ships that had
carried them from Accra, Anomabu, Cape Coast Castle, and the other Gold
Coast forts.[27]

Enslaved African laborers were described by Drax in terms that echoed
his references to "a good Stock of able working Cattle for Carrying on the
planttations busnes" or the "Assenegros which will be wery usefull in the
plantation on Severall ocations." Even when Drax suggested that his manager treat certain faithful and favored slaves with particular care, his language nonetheless betrayed an attitude to such laborers as useful assets. The
labor undertaken by the enslaved on the integrated plantations of Barbados
was extremely arduous, and descriptions such as an "Exelentt Slawe" or a
"Negro worthy of yr Countenance and Incoradgementt" were somewhat
hollow compliments, reflecting a desire to extract and perhaps reward work
rather than to acknowledge humanity.[28]

The increasing difficulty of replenishing the soil and raising sufficient
quantities of sugar to ensure a profit all contributed to a worsening of
conditions for the now almost entirely enslaved workforce and the development of a new system for the organization of labor. The system of gang
slavery, pioneered by Drax, separated field laborers into separate gangs,
each charged with separate tasks. As the enslaved grew older and stronger
they worked up from the third to the second and eventually the first gang,
before age and infirmity prompted their relegation to the secondary and
then the tertiary gangs. This system soon spread around Barbados and
became the norm by the early to mid-eighteenth century. For the large
majority of enslaved laborers at Drax Hall and Hope plantations, a grueling

work regimen, disease, injury, and insufficient food all contributed to a staggering mortality rate. Drax's expectation that his manager would need to purchase up to fifteen new slaves each year suggested a rather optimistic expectation of an annual mortality rate of 3 to 5 percent. His contemporary Edward Littleton thought an annual mortality rate of 6 percent was more realistic, blithely noting that a Barbados planter who owned one hundred slaves would kill off his entire workforce within nineteen years. Thomas Tryon furnished an equally gloomy prognosis, lamenting the fact that in Barbados "a fourth or fifth part every Year should dye, and be made away with, more than are born." Such predictions were terrifyingly accurate: between 1708 and 1735 Barbadian planters purchased some 85,000 Africans, and yet the island's enslaved population rose by only about 4,000.[29]

Unseasoned slaves fresh from Africa suffered the highest mortality rates, to the evident chagrin of Edward Littleton, who complained, "When a man hath bought a parcel of the best and ablest he can get for money; let him take all the care he can, he shall lose a full third part of them, before they ever come to do him service." And those who were seasoned, and better used to the weather and the disease environment of Barbados, were still vulnerable to the very work they undertook. "If a Stiller slip into a Rum-Cistern, it is sudden death," while a "Mill-feeder" caught in the works would be "squeez'd to pieces"; and if a sugar-boiler were to be scalded, "'tis hard to save either Limb or Life." Others might endeavor to escape, still more might commit suicide, while all who labored in field and sugar works risked "Accidents [by which] they are disabled, and become a burden." According to Littleton, it was the planter who suffered when his enslaved workers were killed or maimed, for "When this happens, the poor Planter is in a hard condition: especially if he is still indebted for them. He must have more Negroes, or his Works must stand, and he must be ruin'd at once."[30]

Thirty years earlier bound white servants and enslaved Africans had labored together on Ligon's and other plantations, clearing the land and learning to grow and process sugar, earning a fortune for planters and making Barbados the richest of England's New World colonies. By 1680, however, sugar profits could be maintained only if production levels were maintained and even increased, while labor and other costs were reduced, all in the face of the problems created by the exhaustion of the soil.

Sugar agriculture in late seventeenth- and eighteenth-century Barbados required a large workforce, and it was vital that this be organized in a way that most effectively drew work from the bound laborers while minimizing evasion and outright resistance. In order to effectively marshal their work-force, Drax and his contemporaries divided the enslaved workforce into gangs, which were set to various tasks according to the month and season. The strongest and ablest men and women were assigned to the first gang; adolescents and a few older men and women no longer capable of first gang work composed the second gang; while children, the elderly, and the least fit were consigned to the third gang. A century later, with the gang system a fundamental part of integrated plantations, another Barbadian planter was convinced that "One of the most important parts of management is a judi-cious division of negroes into gangs." Enslaved drivers would supervise each gang, with the white plantation manager ensuring that overseers and drivers displayed neither undue indulgence nor excessive brutality. A good white or enslaved overseer or driver was a boon to his master, and Drax commended "Monky Nocco who has bene ane Exelentt Slawe and will I hope Continue Soe in the place he is of head owerseer." Drax instructed his plantation man-ager to allow Monky Nocco a food and clothing allowance comparable to that allowed the plantation's few senior white servants and employees.[31]

The primary responsibility of the first gang was the planting, cultiva-tion, and harvesting of sugar cane. This work was undertaken with only the most basic tools, including hand-held hoes and billhooks or bills, which were sharp, hook-shaped knives about nine inches in length. Work began in the early summer, with the plowing of cane fields to a depth of at least six inches. This somewhat eased the next stage, the newly developing method of cane-hole planting. Taking place in the late summer and early autumn, cane-holing was designed to prevent the loss of topsoil during heavy rain and to protect both the soil and the cane itself against wind damage, given the loss of the most of the island's trees and the protection against strong winds that they would have afforded. Cane-holing required the back-breaking labor of the first gang, and Drax describes the earliest incarnations of a process that would soon dominate sugar agriculture throughout the Caribbean. In the earliest years of sugar agriculture, cane had been planted and grown in ways inspired by native planting of maize, in which cane seedlings were planted into holes spaced about three feet apart. However, this system did not allow proper root development, and the crop was insufficiently protected against weeds, wind, and rain. During the 1650s planters drew on English agricultural methods, planting cane seedlings in pairs in parallel trenches that extended the full length of the

FIELD NEGRO.
Sugar Cane in the Background.

Figure 10. Richard Bridgens, "Field Negro," from his *West India Scenery with Illustrations of Negro Character* (London, 1836), lithograph. Courtesy of the Yale Center for British Art, Paul Mellon Collection. This man bears the tools of the plantation field hand: a hoe, a bill hook, a crook to remove dead leaves, and a canteen of water.

Figure 11. William Clark, "Digging, or rather Hoeing, the Cane-Holes,"
from *Ten Views in the Island of Antigua* (London, 1823), hand-colored
aquatint. Courtesy of the Yale Center for British Art, Paul Mellon
Collection. In the foreground slaves are marking out the squares. The
illustrations cannot fully convey the back-breaking labor involved in
moving large quantities of soil and manure.

field. One month after planting, the weaker of each pair of plants was
removed. The digging of trenches exacerbated the problem of soil erosion,
however, providing gullies for rainwater to carry away topsoil. The result
was the development of a new system of cane-holing, which was still under
development when Drax penned his instructions, and he described a hybrid
of the earlier trench method and the emerging new cane-holing with the
zealous enthusiasm of a convert.[32]

Cane-holing almost certainly developed as a means of controlling soil
erosion and of encouraging strong and healthy sugar cane plants. Slaves
from the first gang marked out squares of approximately four to five feet
square, and then dug out each square to a depth of between six and nine
inches. A first-gang slave was expected to dig between sixty and one

hundred holes each day, and a slave who dug an average of eighty holes per day was moving a daily total of between 640 and 1,500 cubic feet of soil. William Dickson believed that a first-gang slave in Barbados would dig about eighty-five holes per day, each at least six inches deep. He acknowledged "that it has always appeared to me a hard task, especially considering the climate, the scanty diet of the Slaves, and the other circumstances under which they perform their Labour." No other agricultural task on the plantations required more physical labor than cane-holing. This strenuous task was compounded by the need for first-gang members to work at the same rapid rate: "The holes are dug, with hoes, by the slaves, in a row, with the driver at one end, to preserve the row. They begin and finish a row of these holes as nearly, at the same instant, as possible." The weaker and those in ill health unable to keep up could expect to feel the driver's lash. Women were often in the majority in the first gang, undertaking some of the most strenuous plantation agricultural labor, and visitors to the island could not help but notice the "almost naked, females working in a cane field . . . labouring with the hoe, to dig, or cut up the ground."[33]

The soil removed from each hole was utilized in a bank around the hole, protecting the cane and the soil against runoff. Various food crops such as yams and peas might then be planted in the spaces between the holes (usually between four holes). Each hole was lined with manure and allowed to collect water, and then one or perhaps two cane cuttings of about two feet in length were planted in the hole, which was regularly cleared of the weeds that could so quickly engulf and destroy the young plants. Drax warned Harewood that if he did not "take Care to keepe the land Clear it will be labour lost," even going so far as to suggest that "you leaue all worke what euer & goe to weeding" rather than risk letting weeds run to seed and multiply around the precious cane plants. Proper cane-holing was vital, and Drax enjoined his plantation manager and overseers to carefully supervise every element of the process, ensuring that the enslaved "Howers . . . Make Large and deepe holes which Most be Constantly observed." Most sugar cane was planted between October and December, when there was sufficient rainfall to encourage the cutting to sprout healthy new plants. All being well, the sugar cane would be fully mature and ready for harvesting some sixteen months later, between January and May.[34]

Cane-holing changed little for successive generations of slaves. A doctor observing first-gang slaves in early nineteenth-century Barbados remarked, "It has often occurred to me, that a gang of Negroes in the act of holing for canes, when hard driven appear to be as formidable as a phalanx of infantry by the rapid movement of their hoes . . . while I have been astonished how such habit could enable beings to persevere, so many hours in such violent effort."[35] It was not unusual for planters to attempt to lighten the load on the first gang by hiring entire gangs of enslaved laborers, often belonging to Barbadians who did not own plantations, and employing these to undertake part of the holing. These transient field laborers were thus regularly employed in the heaviest of field work. Between January and November 1724, for example, the severely undermanned Codrington plantation paid for close to two thousand "days work of . . . Negroes," as well as paying for the "Holeing [of] 23 Acres of Land at 50/ pr. Acre." The total cost for this externally sourced enslaved labor was more than £116, a significant drain on the plantation economy. Half a century later the same practice continued, even on comparatively well-manned plantations. In December 1778 John Newton recorded payments to Jonah Bentham "for 168 days labour of his negroes" as well as another payment "for 54 days ditto." Furthermore, Bentham received a payment of almost £25 in return for having his slaves hole almost eight acres of the Newton plantation.[36]

The manuring of the newly planted cane was a task that might be shared between the first and the second gang, and this normally took place between September and early December. The newly dug holes were lined with manure, and the cane cutting planted therein. Once the buried cane cutting had sprouted new plants, which had then achieved a height of about two feet, the young plants were fertilized with a significant quantity of specially prepared manure. The mixing, transportation, and then the application of sufficient quantities of manure could be almost as arduous as cane-holing, and early in the eighteenth century John Oldmixon observed that manuring was "the greatest Trouble and Expence the Planter is at: for if it were not for this dunging, a third Part of the Negroes would do." Drax believed that "theire is No Producing good Canes withoutt dunging Every holle. [T]here for" he enjoined Harewood, "itt Must be one of your Chiefestt Cares to provid greatt Qwantaty of Dung Every year." Almost a century later, William Belgrove reiterated the point, describing dung as "the Article upon which the success of a Crop almost intirely depends." Consequently, Belgrove wrote at length not only of the need for a large number of livestock to produce manure, but also of the need for "a sufficient Strength of Negroes" employed year-round to gather food for the animals, which would "greatly improve the Dung."[37]

Producing and then distributing and applying sufficient manure was both a gargantuan and an offensive task. The "dung Carriers" were required to carry upon their heads and then "Lay a Large box or baskett well heaped up with dunge" between every two newly dug holes. Each basket could weigh as much as eighty pounds, and the work of carrying and applying the dung was both sickening and exhausting; there is plenty of contemporary evidence to suggest that enslaved workers despised this particularly demeaning task. William Dickson commented on the slave driver behind the men and women carrying the dung atop their heads, "often smacking his whip, and, I wish I could say, I never saw him apply it to the backs of the slaves, to increase their speed." Drax expected a minimum of two hundred acres of his two plantations to be dedicated to sugar cane at any one time, and this meant that a phenomenal amount of dung would be required to supply a sufficient quantity for each and every cane plant. Littleton estimated that a single acre of sugar cane required "thirty load of dung." Assuming that each "load" weighed eighty pounds, then almost one and a quarter tons of dung was required per acre, and so Drax's two hundred acres of sugar cane were nourished by 240 tons of manure, all of it carried and applied by first- and second-gang slaves.[38]

Manuring began with the regular collection of dung from the plantation's animals, including cattle, hogs, and asses, which was sometimes supplemented with human waste. "We take all ways and means for the raising of Dung," claimed Littleton. "Some save the Urine of their People (both Whites and Blacks) to increase and enrich their Dung." Slaves regularly collected this animal dung, and then mixed it with soil, vegetable waste, and lime burned in order to enhance the mineral components of the resulting fertilizer. While the prepared manure might be transported to the sugar fields by cart, it was carried to the carts, and then from the carts through long rows of sugar cane plants, on the backs and the heads of the enslaved. It was foul-smelling and back-breaking work. Justin Roberts has argued that the intensity of the work of holing and dunging resulted in elevated sickness rates among the enslaved workers of the first and second gangs. Throughout much of the seventeenth and eighteenth centuries, enslaved women generally dominated the ranks of the first and second gangs in the fields of Barbados, and they suffered greatly as a result. Contemporaries were aware of this, and in his letter "To a Planter of Sugar" Thomas Tryon complained "that nothing hath more hurt and injur'd the Plantations, than the hard Labour and unkind Usage towards your Black Women."[39]

Even allowing for weakness and ill health occasioned by arduous work during pregnancy, the average number of sick days for women was almost twice the number for men. Enslaved women enjoyed lower mortality rates than men, especially after their childbearing years had ended, but the intensity of first-gang labor in holing and manuring the cane appeared to weaken the health of a higher proportion of women than men. While it was in planters' best interests to protect pregnant and nursing women, the short-handedness of most plantations and the need for labor qualified such considerations. One set of plantation instructions struck a tone of extremely limited generosity by suggesting that "Women who have children at the breast, should not be required to appear in the field till seven o'clock." Furthermore, even women in advanced stages of pregnancy who were excused from the heaviest work "must not be given up to idleness" and were still required to labor. Younger people in the first gang were sick more often than older people, perhaps because they took time to adjust to the brutal work regimen, and to learn strategies to conserve energy and avoid exhaustion, while yet managing to avoid the lash.[40]

Second-gang laborers generally undertook lighter yet still demanding work. They were often responsible for planting, weeding, and harvesting food crops and were constantly employed in weeding the precious sugar cane. Their workload increased when they assisted first-gang slaves in the planting and manuring of cane. At harvest time the second gang would help in the cleaning of newly harvested canes, and they were largely responsible for the collection and drying of the leaves and cane tops, as well as the crushed cane stalks, the trash that would be employed as animal feed and as fuel for the fires so essential for sugar production. During the manufacture of sugar and the distilling of rum the second gang performed a variety of ancillary tasks, which might include the constant application of water to cool equipment and buildings endangered by the fires and intense heat.[41]

Drax provided his most detailed instructions of all for the harvesting and processing of sugar cane, and the manufacture of sugar, molasses, and rum, activities that demanded the work of approximately half of the entire enslaved labor force of a plantation, and which could stretch between January and April. His language reflected the skill and proficiency required to turn sugar cane into marketable commodities, and the very real danger that all of the labor in planting, weeding, and manuring sugar cane might be wasted if the production process was not handled with the very greatest care. This was the area in which his plantation manager's "cheife skille will be required," for "your greatest Care Immaginable must be there used & the moast of your time must be there Spent." What was less clear from Drax's instructions, with their focus on what was necessary to produce good and valuable sugar, was the unrelenting intensity and the very great danger of this work. The cutting of cane and its transportation to the mill occupied the first gang for three months or so, as they cut the thick-stemmed and sharp-leaved cane with razor-sharp bills, removing the leaves and then tying the cane into bundles for transportation to the mill. Once cut, cane had to be pressed within a few hours or else the sugar content—and thus a planter's profits—quickly diminished. Slaves fed the cane into three-roller vertical mills, with one slave feeding cane in through the top gap, and another slave on the other side feeding it back through the bottom gap, with brown cane juice flowing from the rollers into a trough, and thence through pipes into a holding tank in the boiling house. The cane juice had to be boiled within a few hours before it fermented and became useless. Exhausted workers wielding sharp tools and then feeding cut cane into mechanized rollers were prey to injury, and virtually every plantation had workers with scarred or missing limbs. Within the boiling house and the distillery, the work became even more dangerous. Fires and lamps illu-minated the workplace, allowing work to continue around the clock at the peak of the harvest. First- and even second-gang laborers had a variety of other occupations associated with sugar manufacturing, assisting as mill feeders, stokers, firemen, sugar boilers, clarifiers, distillers, and mill boat-swains. The carrying of hogsheads of sugar and large barrels of rum and molasses was work that only first-gang laborers were strong enough to undertake, increasing their workload still further. Thus, preparation of the fields, planting and manuring of the crop, weeding, harvesting, and then processing of the sugar would occupy enslaved laborers year-round.[42]

Drax described the four or five great copper pots in his boiling house, the largest holding between one hundred and two hundred gallons, the smallest perhaps as little as twenty-five gallons. The boiler was responsible for ladling the cane juice into the first and largest pot, skimming off the scum that rose to the top as it boiled, and then estimating when the sugar had been sufficiently purified and reduced to be ladled into the next vat, and the process repeated. With each transfer the cane juice became darker and thicker, and a gallon of juice would eventually be reduced to about one pound of muscovado sugar. Each vat was attended by an enslaved worker, who sweated over the boiling liquid as he skimmed off the impurities. The

Figure 12. Richard Bridgens, "Interior of a Boiling House," from his *West India Scenery with Illustrations of Negro Character* (London, 1836), lithograph. Courtesy of the Yale Center for British Art, Paul Mellon Collection. A white overseer directs the boiling of sugar through a succession of coppers, with the scum being scraped off.

decision on when to transfer the liquid between vats rested with the boiler, and he or she had to make the crucial determination of when the sugar boiling in the final and smallest pot was ready to be tempered with lime juice, which would promote granulation. The boiler then had to decide when the sugar had reached the point of crystallization, making the "strike" by dampening the fire and ladling the sugar into a cooling cistern. The sugar was then transferred to cooling pots, and about twelve hours later it was transferred to clay pots, each with a hole in the base that was temporarily plugged. Several days later the plug was removed, and the molasses

Figure 13. William Clark, "Exterior of the Boiling-House," from *Ten Views in the Island of Antigua* (London, 1823), hand-colored aquatint. Courtesy of the Yale Center for British Art, Paul Mellon Collection. Sugar boiling proceeded in shifts, around the clock, and this shows the boiling house at night, radiating light and heat in an otherwise extremely dark environment.

drained out of the pots was carefully collected and then used in the distilling of rum. A month later the dried sugar was knocked out of the pots: the top and bottom ends were removed and reboiled, while the semi-refined sugar that remained was dried in the sun and then packed into hogsheads for shipment to England. The care of the sugar while it matured in clay pots, and then its sorting and packaging thereafter, attracted as much of Drax's attention as did the work of the "Stillor" in distilling rum from the molasses.[43]

The production of a single hogshead of muscovado sugar could yield as much as one hundred gallons of molasses, and while some might be used for animal feed and yet more exported as a cheap alternative to sugar, most would be distilled by planters in order to make rum. This provided them with an additional and extremely valuable export commodity, as well as a useful product for the reward of the enslaved workforce. So every large plantation had a still house, in which the stillor combined molasses, inferior cane juice, and even the skimmed impurities from the boilers, for it was by combining all of these ingredients "that the greatt qvantaty of Rum is Made." Once combined in a large vat, these ingredients fermented for at least a week, after which the liquid was heated, vaporized in the still, and then condensed into rum. The making, storage, and transportation of the highly inflammable rum was dangerous work. Ligon recorded the death of "an excellent" enslaved African who brought a candle too close to a barrel of rum in the still house. Of first concern was the fact that this unfortunate man had "lost the whole vessell of Spirits"; almost as an afterthought, Ligon acknowledged that the man had lost "his life to boot."[44]

Sugar made fortunes for generations of English and British planters, but the enslaved workforce paid for these profits with their labor, their health, and even their lives. Throughout the seventeenth century and well into the eighteenth, high mortality rates among bound whites and the enslaved African plantation workers meant that a constant influx of new workers was required to maintain the integrated plantations of Barbados and those that copied them elsewhere in the Caribbean and on the mainland of British North America. By 1700 there may have been as many as 50,000 enslaved Africans on Barbados: however, over the preceding seventy-five years almost 212,000 Africans are estimated to have arrived on the island. During that same period only about 110,000 enslaved Africans had landed in Jamaica, the Chesapeake, and the Carolinas combined. High mortality rates and the profits generated by sugar meant that planters imported far more enslaved Africans into Barbados than in all of the rest of British America combined.[45]

During the seventeenth century, Barbados dominated plantation agriculture in the Anglo-American world, and it was on this small island that first tens of thousands of white laborers and then hundreds of thousands of enslaved Africans were worked, many of them to death, in the development of a singularly brutal new system of labor. Initially, planters had depended upon bound white laborers, and when the first enslaved Africans arrived, both white and black plantation workers were employed and treated in similar fashion. As the supply of bound white laborers diminished and as enslaved Africans came to dominate virtually all aspects of plantation work, however, planters—and indeed all whites on Barbados—

came to think of plantation labor as a distinctively and exclusively black occupation. While a handful of white craftsmen, doctors, overseers, and militia men persisted on the island's plantation in supervisory and highly skilled positions, the work of growing, harvesting, and processing sugar cane became the work of enslaved Africans. The plantation labor system was not rooted in a racial ideology, but a century later that labor system was explicitly racialized, not least in the fact that whites could not imagine any other than enslaved Africans doing the work previously done by bound whites.

Chapter 9

"Forced to Labour Beyond Their Natural Strength"

Labor, Discipline, and Community on Eighteenth-Century Barbadian Plantations

Sugar was the gold of the British Caribbean islands, and the precision of the seventeenth-century accounts of sugar cultivation and production by Richard Ligon and Henry Drax reflect the significant value of a commodity produced in a highly skilled and yet remarkably arduous manufacturing process. Barbadian plantation records reveal that by the early eighteenth century white workers, both bound and free, had all but disappeared from the ranks of even the most highly skilled plantation operatives, their places taken by highly qualified and able slaves who became as valuable to planters as their white predecessors. As one early eighteenth-century observer noted, "A Slave that is excellent in any of these Mechanick Employments, is worth 150 or 200 *l.* and I have known 400 *l.* bid for a Boiler, belonging to Sir *John Bowdon's* Plantation in Scotland." By way of comparison, an unskilled healthy adult male slave was "worth from 40 to 50 *l.* a head," underscoring the financial value of enslaved craftsman who were worth three or four times the value of field workers, while a skilled sugar-maker might be worth ten times as much. By the later eighteenth century, the payment by the manager of the Newton plantation to "Quashy, belonging to Wilson & Daniel . . . for learning 2 Negroes the Coopers Trade," provided telling evidence that few white craftsmen and artisans remained on the island's plantations. During the eighteenth century, it was usually enslaved Africans who trained fellow slaves in the craft of sugar and rum production, as well as in such ancillary crafts as carpentry, smithing, and barrel-making.[1]

If enslaved African workers had come to completely dominate Barbadian plantation labor, they labored in an institution that changed significantly over the course of the eighteenth century. Initially, soil exhaustion and declining sugar prices had combined to worsen conditions for enslaved laborers in Barbados, who worked harder and longer to maximize ever-dwindling profits. Yet the tiny island remained profitable, in part because of gradual modernization of the whole system of bound labor, as Barbados once again blazed a new trail forward. With profit in mind, Barbadian planters and managers sought to reduce costs, and they did so by a process of what historians have described as amelioration. By the end of the century planters grew more food for their enslaved workers, and also allowed the enslaved to themselves produce a greater amount of what they ate and to develop their own market for trading commodities. At the same time owners sought to encourage the enslaved workforce to reproduce itself, thus lessening dependence upon expensive replacements from Africa, and this meant improved conditions for family formation, especially for enslaved mothers. Planters began developing rewards and incentives for skilled enslaved craftsmen and domestic servants, whose children often replaced their parents, thus creating a hierarchy within the ranks of the enslaved, a "professional" elite who had a vested interest in the maintenance of a somewhat improved status quo. In the first decade of the eighteenth century nearly 46,000 slaves arrived in Barbados from Africa, but such vast numbers were no longer required a century later. Between 1800 and 1807, with the knowledge that the transatlantic slave trade was drawing to a close and that it would soon become illegal and very difficult to procure African slaves, fewer than 8,000 Africans arrived, even though other regions of British America were eagerly purchasing as many Africans as possible before the supply dried up. Barbados was the only British sugar colony in which the enslaved population was increasing naturally *before* the abolition of the transatlantic slave trade. This meant that plantation slavery had changed in fundamental ways, becoming a more efficient system not just in the deployment of bound labor but also in the encouragement of enslaved families who were treated well enough for parents and children to live long enough to ensure a natural increase in their population. Slavery in Barbados had changed, and this process of amelioration helped explain the fact that the island did not experience any serious slave conspiracies or uprisings during the eighteenth century.[2]

Figure 14. John Augustine Waller, "Plantation Scene and Slave Houses,
Barbados, 1807–1808," from *A Voyage in the West Indies, Containing Various
Observations Made During a Residence in Barbadoes, And Several of the
Leeward Islands* (London, 1820). Courtesy of the Library Company of
Philadelphia. In this somewhat romanticized image, well-dressed and well-
fed slaves are socializing, dancing, and preparing food. A gang going to the
fields armed with hoes, the sugar mill in the background, and the large
planter's mansion atop a hill provide evidence of the labor regime of
plantation slavery, but the illustration stresses the amelioration of slavery
and the improved conditions for slaves in Barbados by the early nineteenth
century.

The owners of the enslaved in Barbados led the way in refashioning
slavery as it would exist throughout nineteenth-century British America.
But this redefinition of enslaved labor developed only slowly over a long
period between the late seventeenth and late eighteenth centuries, and it
was in large part triggered by the increasing difficulty of making money
from sugar, which on many occasions had initially made life worse for the

enslaved, not better. Improved business and management practices, in the face of deteriorating environmental conditions and lower profit margins, help account for the improved conditions of enslaved plantation laborers. The records of the leading Codrington and Newton plantations reveal a great deal about these processes of change and their impact upon enslaved African labor during this difficult period. Deforestation, excessive overplanting, and soil runoff had all rendered "the most Fertil't Spot of all *America*" profoundly "weakened and almost worn out." By 1710 some land was so spent that it was no longer farmed, while the remainder appeared "much worn out and not as fertile as it was . . . one-third of the island now lies waste." Only a remarkable amount of human labor could render the land productive and profitable, and it was enslaved labor on integrated plantations that continued to generate huge wealth on Barbados throughout the eighteenth century. White labor on Barbados all but disappeared, with only a very small number of whites managing and policing the plantations, and with even fewer bound white servants. At Codrington the plantations owned by the Society for the Propagation of the Gospel (SPG) were supervised by a manager and about a dozen white employees (including a keykeeper, the captain of the plantation's sloop, several overseers and apprentices, and two watchmen), while former bound laborers and soldiers composed the impoverished militia tenantry, "Nine or Ten Families . . . extremely neady most of them." This small company of white servants and employees was massively outnumbered by enslaved Africans who undertook virtually all of the actual labor involved in plantation agriculture and sugar manufacturing.[3]

The high attrition rates among the enslaved was made clear by the policy of the plantation mangers at Codrington for restocking their workforce in the early to mid-eighteenth century. Knowing how many newly imported slaves were likely to die in their first few years on the island, managers promoted "the buying of Seasoned ones" whenever possible, and only if these were unavailable or unaffordable would they "buy new Negroes." Hiring slaves from other slave owners was to be avoided if at all possible because of uncertain supply and "the Expence, which is very considerable." Ill health and premature death ravaged the ranks of the enslaved workforce. In one letter the doctor at Codrington described the entire plantation workforce as "very sickly," in large part because "the small pox and the Measles have raged violently thro' the Island." Moreover, "their most fatal Disease is the Dropsy, by which the Society hath lost several negroes, tho' most of them either new Ones or very old Ones." Plantation managers at Codrington faced a steady depletion in the stock of enslaved laborers, creating a vicious circle of increasing work and worsening working conditions for those who survived, and increasing losses for the owners making the purchase of new enslaved laborers all the more difficult.[4] One manager wrote to the SPG, more in hope than expectation, suggesting that expected profits might persuade the SPG to "think of Ading Some Neg.os. to their Plantation we are now Reduced to Two Hundred which is much Short of the Number desired to be kept on ye Estate by General Codrington & of what is sufficient for so Laborious an Estate. . . . Every person here who are Experienced in Plantation Affairs knows that Estates here will Suffer greatly if the Stock of Neg.os. &c. is not kept up."[5] Eventually the plantation's stock of enslaved workers was so depleted that managers suggested "the only Expedient for purchasing a sufficient quantity of Negroes . . . is to buy a Plantation that has as many season'd Negroes upon it as are wanted." While the situation at Codrington was extreme, throughout Barbados "there are but few, if any Plantations that have Hands enough to do their Business without Oppression to them." Perpetually undermanned, yet determined to maximize outputs and profits through the available workforce, planters drove the enslaved to labor that wrecked them, body and soul.[6]

The failure to maintain a sufficient number of enslaved laborers caused major problems at the Codrington plantations. In 1745 the plantation had a severely imbalanced population of enslaved Africans, including 156 men and boys, and 80 women and girls. Fifty-nine of the men and 31 of the women were at least forty years of age, significantly outnumbering the 35 boys and 29 girls aged twenty years or less. This was not a community that could easily replenish itself. The high preponderance of African names may suggest that a majority of the enslaved on the plantation had not been born in Barbados, and that a significant proportion came from Africa: only 85 (36 percent) of the total number bore English, classical, or biblical names, with the remaining 151 (64 percent) having African names. However, although perhaps suggestive of African nativity, the persistence of African names throughout the eighteenth century does not prove this, nor can we be sure that these names retained their traditional meanings and significance. Thus, for example, the male West African "day name" (given according to the day of birth) Cubenah was on occasion given to enslaved females in Barbados. It is possible that West African names were perpetuated by whites, and even by the enslaved themselves, with little awareness of or concern for their original meanings. Eighty Barbados-born men, women, and children on the Seawell plantation had African names in 1796, but it is impossible to know what these names meant to them, to their parents, and to their community. What does appear clear, however, is that over time enslaved parents enjoyed more and more control over the naming of their children. J. Harry Bennett has argued that throughout most of the eighteenth century, African-born slaves formed a significant portion of the Codrington workforce. In 1732 at least 91 of the 241 enslaved were Africans purchased since 1710, while 16 percent of the Codrington slaves in July 1760 were Africans purchased within the preceding four years. In 1740 one observer noted that the enslaved Africans were "of several Countrys," and since they "cannot spake English" many communicated "more by Signes than Speech."[7]

Given Barbadian preferences for Gold Coast slaves, it was no surprise when Codrington manager Abel Alleyne reported that "most of the Negroes are Guinea Negroes and [of] the Caramantine [sic] & Pawpay Country." Between 1712 and 1761 the SPG spent more than £15,000 purchasing approximately 450 enslaved Africans. However, having spent two and one-half times the value of the original stock of slaves buying new slaves, and despite adding one and one-half times the number of original slaves, by 1761 the enslaved population was only two-thirds as large as it had been in 1712. During the first half of the eighteenth century, the enslaved community at Codrington suffered six deaths and enjoyed only one birth for every one hundred of their number. The problem was compounded by high child mortality: between 1743 and 1748 enslaved mothers gave birth to twenty-three children, but during those same years ten of these children perished. The policy of buying two male slaves for every one female slave clearly contributed to the problem. The overall result was clear: the enslaved at Codrington were dying in such numbers that they could not be replaced by natural reproduction, massively increasing the workload of those who survived, and quite likely reducing their life spans as a result. Even plantation managers were well aware that overworked slaves were more vulnerable to diseases such as leprosy, yaws, consumption, and dropsy. It seems likely that other planters on the island would have attributed the problems at Codrington to a failure to regularly replenish the supply of enslaved Africans. During the first half of the eighteenth century, Barbadian planters brought an annual average of approximately 3,000 African slaves, a number equal to about 7 percent of the existing enslaved population. Yet during these years Codrington's managers purchased an average of only nine new slaves each year, approximately 3 percent of its stock in 1712, and thus less than half of the island's average.[8]

The "original Error of not keeping up a constant supply of new negroes as the old ones declined" meant that over the course of the eighteenth century, skilled enslaved craftsmen—many of them directly involved in sugar production, often died without preparing and training their successors. By 1761 communications from the plantation reported to the SPG in London that "We have no Artificers belonging to the Plantation, but two Coopers, and a smith now past Labour." As a result, "The Estate labours under great Disadvantages," having to hire in skilled slave craftsmen at considerable expense. For a while the Codrington estate's still house was not operational, "owing to a total Decline of the Negroes formerly employed in that Branch of Business, and to the not supplying their places with new ones."[9]

In 1775 the situation appeared somewhat improved, with a listing of enslaved "artisans" including one carpenter, three coopers, two blacksmiths, three potters, two basket-makers, one boiler, three clarifiers, one clayer, two millmen, and three distillers. However, the lack of properly qualified enslaved artisans meant that many were given these posts with insufficient training. Thus, when the plantation's sole clayer died in 1780, a field hand with minimal experience was charged with taking the role of making the pots for sugar production. Three years later a watchman was moved to the position of mason, and a decade later the death of the blacksmith led to the promotion of a groom to the role of smith. Often these ill-qualified artisans did not last long in their new posts, and at times the plantation seemed to lack virtually any properly trained enslaved craftsmen. Yet even when desperately short of skilled labor, Codrington's manager did not deign to hire white men, whether bound or free. Plantation work was the work of the enslaved.[10]

An inventory of the plantation and its personnel taken in May 1783 revealed a population of 178 enslaved men, women, and children on the home plantation, referred to as the "upper" plantation. The only skilled artisans listed were Tackey, a smith, and Quow and Yeo, both coopers. No skilled slaves concerned with sugar manufacturing were recorded as being present on the Society's larger upper plantation, perhaps in part because the windmill, the boiling house, the distillery, the curing house, and the rum house were all "in ruins" as a result of the hurricane of 1780. Either their workers had died, or they had been moved to the still operational sugar works of the lower plantation, yet the now combined listing for both plantations included only one boiler, one stiller, and one potter. Sixteen of the enslaved were too old or inform to work, such as Quawcoe Bob, a groom, who was "Old [and] of little value," and the field hand Abraham, who was "Diseased [and] of little value." The large majority of those named in the 1783 inventory were field hands in the first and second gangs. The first and second gangs included twenty-three men such as Africa, William, Caesar General, Pontack Quasha, and Quawcoo, as well as four second-gang boys. The female workforce for the first and second gangs included thirty-four women, including Esley, Mary Coobah, Hagar, and Lubbah, and a further eleven second-gang girls. Led by the enslaved drivers Drummer and John Shary, the first gang undertook the most arduous field work, holing the ground, planting canes, manuring them, harvesting them, and transporting them to the mill. The smaller second gang was directed by two women, Sue and Sarah Bob, and by a boy named Quawcoe Adjoe, and their ranks included those too old, too young, and insufficiently fit for the first gang. However, their work was still considerable, including the planting and tending of food crops among the cane and, in separate fields, carrying dried cane trash to the mill as fuel, turning the mighty mounds of maturing manure, and weeding the cane and food fields. Eighteen boys and twenty girls were listed as belonging to the third gang, the "meatpickers," the "hog meat gang," or the "grass gatherers," who were under the direction of Old Dinah. Their primary task was the collection of fodder for the plantation's livestock, and the plantation managers regularly purchased smaller hoes for their use in this work, but they also assisted in the weeding of the young cane and the application of manure to freshly dug cane holes.[11]

At the time of the 1783 inventory a total of thirty-one children were too young for field work: plantation accounts listed the value of each as £5, until such time as they were deemed old enough to join the third gang (usually about the age of seven or eight), at which point their value increased to £20 or £25, and their days of laboring began. A few might move from the third gang to training for specific work on the plantation, perhaps in the sugar mill, the boiling house, as artisans, or as cooks and servants. Most, however, were destined for a life of field work, and between the ages of about thirteen and fifteen children moved up into the second gang. Some would never become strong and healthy enough to move up to the first gang, but most could expect to rise to this station in their later teens. First-gang labor would wreck their bodies, as they worked in that capacity for perhaps a decade or so before being demoted to the second gang or to other plantation work.[12]

Cain's life cycle was unusual in that he survived in the first gang for longer than most. Purchased as a fifteen-year-old African in 1741, he was strong enough to serve in the first gang until 1771 when he was over fifty years old. At that point, his body worn out, Cain was demoted to the second gang. His value almost halved as a result, from £45 to £25, and after three years in the second gang he moved on to a further three years' work as a cattle keeper. In 1783, no longer capable of full and regular work, Cain was listed as "Old and infirm" until his death, following a fall, in 1786. Like Cain, most of the enslaved worked in the fields, while others on the plantation had specific responsibilities separate from gang work, tending livestock, carrying water, or serving as watchmen and cooks. Awbah had the favored position of cook for the whites on the plantation, having lost all of the fingers from one hand, most likely in the fields or in the sugar cane press. The SPG's ownership of these enslaved men, women, and children in 1783 may be indicated by the comparatively few African names and the higher than usual proportion of biblical or religious names, including Peter, Jacob, Abraham, Providence, Isaac, Samson, Cain, Mary, Mercy, Hannah, Hagar, Daniel, Anthony, Joshua, Thomas, and Margaret. Interestingly, however, the African names appear to have been most prevalent among the young girls of the second and third gangs, although it is unclear whether these were recent purchases or had been born on this or other plantations on the island.[13]

There were a number of reasons why the Codrington plantation was less well organized than others, with the result that conditions were particularly hard for the enslaved. The managers at Codrington faced an unusual situation. The owners, and their employers, were part of the Church of England, charged with using the plantation to earn sufficient revenue to fund a college that would train ministers and religious teachers for the Caribbean, including the enslaved. This meant running an efficient and profitable plantation, which necessarily involved driving an enslaved workforce hard, and accepting relatively high mortality rates among them. However, the church leadership were increasingly uncomfortable with the institution of slavery and were eager to ameliorate the conditions of the slaves that they owned. From the beginning these men pressured plantation managers "to use the slaves belonging to the 2 Plantations late of Gen. Codrington with greater Humanity & Tenderness than is commonly practised by Planters." Moreover, the SPG hoped that the plantation's slaves might serve as a test community for the Christianization of enslaved Africans, but this proposal met enormous local resistance. Reverend William Johnson wrote from Barbados to the SPG, commending this mission but pointing out that "there are several difficulties in this Work, which the Strangers to those parts must be unacquainted with." The first of these was white Barbadians' fear of "the Danger of Instructing the Negroes to read and write, which the Planters say enables them to carry on Plotts against their Common Safety." The few slaves who could read and write had allegedly proved likely to take advantage of this skill by forging their masters' names and "taking up Goods in their Names, giving Tickets to Runaways, and the like." Finally, "few of the Masters would on any Christian Consideration give up so much of their Negroes time, as would be necessary for their Instruction." Baffled by this dilemma, Johnson proposed short, occasional lessons for the Codrington slaves "in the Grounds and Principles of Religion without teaching them to Read or Write."[14]

Beyond these particular problems, the Codrington plantation records and the correspondence between London and the plantation's managers reveals a dark truth about enslaved labor in eighteenth-century Barbados. Even on a plantation whose managers were charged with treating the enslaved more gently, instructing them in Christianity, and—in theory at least—preparing them for freedom, the need for the plantation to cover costs and generate profit, together with local conditions and the firmly held beliefs of fellow planters, all meant that Codrington's enslaved faced the same arduous work regimen as, and died in equal or perhaps even greater numbers than, the enslaved on less-enlightened plantations. The SPG regularly received plantation reports and accounts that differed little from those submitted by other managers to absentee owners, detailing "The Stock of Negroes & Cattle upon the Society's Plantations," equating the enslaved with livestock and reporting on the mortality rates among them. Even the mortality of the enslaved and of livestock were equated, as when John Smallridge complained that he had been unable to purchase "either Beast or Negro this year, the distemper among Cattle continuing still on this Island, and amongst Negros in Severall Estates." Most horrifying of all, in 1724 the plantation manager had commissioned and begun using a brand to burn "SOCIETY" on the bodies of the enslaved at Codrington, marking them as the property of the missionary arm of the Church of England. Only when the Reverend Arthur Holt wrote to the SPG in London complaining of this practice was it discontinued.[15]

For all of the reforming zeal of the SPG, it was labor that defined the enslaved on their Barbados plantations. Those who did not work sufficiently hard, or who were judged to be surly or disobedient, were threatened with sale off the island. One manager wrote to the SPG of his "hope [that] the rumor of Shipping will make some of them mind there Manners."[16] However, there are some indications in the surviving records of the SPG that the enslaved on their Barbados plantation were aware that the white men who managed the plantation and supervised their lives and labor were answerable to distant owners who were more inclined to ameliorate the condition of the enslaved than were other plantation owners. This is evident in one remarkable and unprecedented incident in the summer of 1738, in which a group of slaves withdrew their labor and marched to Bridgetown "to complain of hard labour, hard usage: whant [sic] of Cloaths, Victuals &c." According to John Vaughton, the plantation manager, the island's "Attorney general took a deal of pains & was very Strickt in his Enquiry of the Occasion & could gett no just Reason of complaints from them, but on ye Contrary told them that he thought that they had been too tenderly used which might be the Occasion of their breaking into those Disorders."[17]

The protesting slaves were persuaded to return to Codrington, and to Vaughton's evident horror they "came through the Country Singing and Dancing with Drawn knives as great as if they had gain'd a conquest." Their celebrations continued at the plantation, but Vaughton and his managers did not hesitate to use the whip and the threat of further violence to ensure that the protestors "Submitted and agreed to go to their work the next Morning which they did do." Vaughton went on to defend, somewhat contradictorily, both his previous gentle treatment of the enslaved and what he defined as the need to use violence to ensure good discipline. For "their Slavish Tempers they will Always Retain: & will putt Masters or Overseers under Necessities to use them as they may not be Inclinable to doe." Thus the enslaved were themselves held responsible for the need to use violent coercion in order to extract work and ensure obedience. Furthermore, Vaughton agreed with the attorney general that preferential treatment and an easing of the burden of physical labor in fact encouraged unrest. One of the leaders of this protest had been "for many years past kept in Easy Offices & [was] one that never workt but little in ye field Excepting this Crop." This man had been charged with keeping the sheep, but because the sheep had not increased in number— which Vaughton attributed to the slave's dishonesty—he had been removed to much harder field labor. While Vaughton interpreted this man's protest as evidence of his own faults, it is likely that the slave— whether or not he had participated in sheep stealing—was bitterly resentful of a change in working conditions that brought him back to the unrelenting labor of the first gang. Vaughton ended his letter by praising the island's authorities for not executing the ringleaders of this peaceful protest, "which our Laws will doe on such Occasions," instead ordering "them Publickly whipt several times in Town then to Return them to the Plantation & there to receive Punishment likewise." This, and similar punishments for others involved, were essential, according to Vaughton, for "we are under Necessity to humble them." Were there to be "the least Encouragement of such Complaints" by enslaved laborers, he continued, "it will be impossible for any person to do Business."[18]

What is clear from the plantation accounts and from the lists of enslaved personnel is that at this time the Codrington plantations were operating with only about two-thirds of the necessary enslaved workers. Significant overwork, with physical punishment to spur on those who did not perform adequately, all would have given the enslaved very real motives for protest. The constant and desperate need for labor was reflected in the plantation accounts, with frequent and significant expenses for the hire of enslaved labor from other owners. In November 1722 alone, the managers of Codrington paid three Barbadians for over three hundred days' worth of labor performed by the slaves that they owned. However, even on what was likely the most enlightened large plantation in eighteenth-century Barbados, violent control of the enslaved workforce remained constant. And back in Lambeth Palace in London, the records of the clerics of the SPG's discussion of the protest by overworked enslaved Africans in 1738 reveals their unquestioning agreement that the enslaved had behaved with "Wickedness" and that "all Negroes are ready to . . . [conspire] against their Masters." While castle slaves could withdraw their labor and negotiate with their British masters on the eighteenth-century Gold Coast, with a reasonable hope of avoiding punishment, their enslaved brethren on the most enlightened plantation in Barbados faced a radically different situation.[19]

Planters in Barbados led the way in English America, pioneering the development of integrated plantations worked by bound laborers, the transition to almost total dependence upon an enslaved workforce, and agricultural and manufacturing innovations to improve the growing and the production of sugar and the replenishment and continued productivity of exhausted soil. Even at the close of the eighteenth century, Barbados planters continued to lead, finding new ways to increase revenue on plantations that had produced sugar for one and one-half centuries. In stark contrast with the Codrington plantation was the Newton plantation, which was run with far greater efficiency, and which serves as an example of the Barbadian improvements. With 459 acres and over 250 slaves, Newton was one of the largest and the oldest plantations in late eighteenth-century Barbados. By changing land use and refocusing sugar processing, plantation manager Samson Wood was able to maintain high profit margins. He oversaw a plantation in which food production was larger than ever before, decreasing costs and increasing the health and longevity of an increasingly creolized population of enslaved workers, born and raised in Barbados. At the same time, the proportion of the sugar crop turned into clayed sugar and rum was increased, bringing greater efficiency and profits. The result was that in 1796–97, even the first gang at Newton spent only 33.7 percent of their time working in sugar agriculture and processing, likely the lowest percentage in the history of sugar production on the island. In contrast, labor associated with food crops had increased, to account for 27.8 percent of the time of first gang slaves at Newton, while livestock work accounted for a further 14.6 percent of their time. Soil management, trash work, plantation maintenance, guard duty, transportation, and other activities accounted for the remaining 33.9 percent of the time of first-gang slaves. Much the same was true for the second gang, who devoted 36 percent of their time to provision crops alone. Several years later Wood wrote confidently to one of the plantation owners of the store of food for the enslaved: "I should not fear, we have plenty of corn for *them* in our Granary, even, I should think, if we failed in our Indian corn Crop."[20]

The Newton plantation displayed an agricultural diversity that had not existed on Barbadian plantations a century or even a half-century earlier, and this innovation was replicated across the island, profoundly affecting the labor and the lives of the enslaved. The change is made clear in an accounting of all of Newton's fields in 1797. Six fields were listed as "Holed & prepared for a Crop of Canes," with maize planted in the

"Banks" of each field. Seven fields were filled with "Young Canes, growing for the ensuing crop," while only two fields were being used for a second, less productive crop of sugar from plants already cut and harvested. Four fields were planted with "Guinea Corn," two with Guinea corn and peas, one with potatoes and Indian corn, and one more with a variety of "Provisions." While a century earlier planters and managers had grown sugar to the exclusion of all else, working malnourished bound whites and enslaved Africans to death, by the end of the eighteenth century money was made by means of a far more balanced and diversified plantation agriculture, with far more efficient production of more high-quality sugar from smaller amounts of land. However, the enslaved still undertook the most physical and the most demanding or labor. Thus, for example, on 5 May 1796, fifty-four of the first gang at Newton were holing, while on 19 October 1796, sixty-seven first-gang workers were "throwing out dung." Several months later, on 14 February 1797, sixty-three of the first gang were working all hours "Cutting Canes," while nine were working in the boiling house and two were working on the carts transporting the harvested cane.[21]

On the one hand, these changes indicated the ability of planters and managers to ensure the continued profitability of sugar production, and this relied on the work undertaken by the enslaved labor force. On the other hand, the decrease in the proportion of the plantation devoted to sugar production and the increase in the amount of land and time allocated to provision crops meant an improved work schedule and diet for the enslaved. A year later, Wood reported to Thomas Lane that at Newton plantation, "Your Land [is] in High Cultivation[,] your buildings in excellent order, your Stock and Negroes in perfect health, well disciplined, & . . . well behaved and good laborers." There was more than a little self-congratulation within this letter, yet it spoke to the "unremitting attention" of planters and managers interested in developing a more balanced agricultural and manufacturing system, with a drive to achieve various kinds of at least partial self-sufficiency, both in foodstuffs and in enslaved African laborers. A generation or two earlier, planters had used all suitable land for the cultivation of sugar, which left only a small amount of inferior land for food cultivation. Planters had hoped that the enormous profitability of sugar would enable them to import cheap foodstuffs such as fish from New England and grains and root crops from the Middle Atlantic colonies, but inevitably there were times when food was in short supply. Wood recalled a time when the enslaved had been "half starved," which "had broke their

Constitutions . . . & was the Cause of our losing very many." Wood wrote
with conviction that it was in the best interests of planters to ensure that
the enslaved were well fed and cared for, and he concluded, "there is no
spot whatever even an apparent heap of stones where I have not something
growing over the rock from some happy fissure of earth," including pump-
kins, other squash, peas, potatoes, and a variety of vegetables. With more
food production and a somewhat less strenuous work regimen because less
land was devoted to sugar, mortality rates decreased among the enslaved.
In a typical year, the deaths of two slaves from dysentery and of three slaves
who were "superannuated" were compensated for by the birth and survival
of six girls and three boys. Wood proudly recorded "Increase 4" in his
account, tabulating corresponding increases or decreases in the stock of
cattle and horses on the same page. While the health of the enslaved was
improving, and the quality of their lives may have been enhanced, they
nonetheless remained stock, to be worked hard and treated with cruelty
whenever deemed necessary by planters and overseers. Only when it had
become financially imperative had their treatment been improved to the
extent that the number of births exceeded the number of deaths.[22]

The first generations of enslaved Africans in Barbados had faced a labor
system that dominated their waking hours, and with deaths outnumbering
births it proved remarkably difficult to develop any familial and social stability. Their material conditions were basic at best, and their earliest habitations were barely sufficient. A former prisoner of war who had begun his
bound labor in Barbados in 1652 recalled the small houses of the enslaved
as being "almost like dog houses, and are covered with the leaves of trees."
Archaeological evidence suggests that many of these homes were constructed from four posts, joined by a latticed wall of vines and twigs that
were then covered with wattle and daub, with a thatched roof of palm
branches, cane trash, and plantain leaves. It seems likely that these houses
were constructed by the enslaved themselves in a fashion reminiscent of the
"Guinea forest house" common on the Gold Coast, adapted to make use
of the materials available in Barbados. Even by the later eighteenth century,
many of the homes of the enslaved had improved little. One observer noted
the "inattention in the Gentlemen of Barbados to the houses of their
negroes," and for many of the enslaved, the shortage of timber and proper
building materials meant that their homes remained "of a mean order . . .
of very coarse construction, and . . . dark, close and smoky." This particular
visitor to the island was surprised, upon attempting to inspect some of

these habitations, to find that "the negroes were tenacious of their homes and disliked to have their huts exposed to the prying eyes of strangers." However poor these buildings may have been, they could still be important to enslaved Africans, perhaps in part because of West African traditions that involved the burial of family members beneath or close to family homes. As a result, the proposed relocation of one large group of enslaved families from their homes caused great discontent: their overseer wrote to the plantation owner that "the Negroes seem very unhappy & dissatisfied to have their houses removed . . . they are not unhappy nor unwilling to work at the lower Estate but very much so to remove their houses."[23]

To European eyes, the clustering of the homes of the enslaved in close proximity and in irregular patterns appeared confused and untidy. In reality, such arrangements were the result both of a limited amount of space and of West African precedents. These homes were sparsely furnished, with only benches and stools, and perhaps a rudimentary table and chairs, along with earthen pots and bowls, and grinding stones for corn. Bedding was often made up of dried leaves and other vegetable matter. Enslaved drivers, craftsmen, boilers, and other men of rank enjoyed marginally better homes and more furnishings. The houses of the enslaved were clustered together into small villages, commonly referred to as the "Negro yard," and provision gardens, burial plots, and water supplies were all close by.[24]

Planters were responsible for providing the basic dietary requirements of their enslaved workforce, and even in the later seventeenth century the innovative Henry Drax was prescient in his injunction to plant a wide variety of crops, including potatoes, Guinea corn, plantains, maize and cassava, palm (for oil), and ginger. In addition to grain, Drax enjoined his plantation manager to provide "Weekly one pound of ffish or two Mackrell[,] if Large, otherwise three" to each enslaved field worker, as well as "two quarts of Molases." Overseers, head boilers, and other trusted and skilled workers could expect to receive as much as double this allowance.[25]These provisions were often insufficient, however, and the enslaved would go to great lengths to steal or otherwise procure food. One plantation manager reported that three enslaved laborers had died due to "the Effects of their Eating putrid Flesh," having dug up and then consumed the bodies of dead animals.[26]

The garden plots worked by enslaved plantation laborers provided opportunities not just to enhance their food supply but also to produce commodities that could be exchanged or sold beyond the plantation. West Africans had been part of a society in which markets played a vital social and cultural function, in addition to providing a means of exchanging goods and foodstuffs, and they sought to continue these activities in their New World situation. Their underground economy became so extensive as to attract the attention of the planters and the island's legislative assembly. In 1708 (and again in 1733) the Assembly acted to prohibit planters' employment of their enslaved laborers in the island's markets, which gave the enslaved the opportunity to "traffick among themselves," not only buying and selling their own produce but also acting to "buy, receive and dispose of all sorts of stolen Goods." The act mandated a punishment of twenty lashes for any slave who breached its terms, yet the underground economy proved all but impossible to eradicate. Enslaved producers and hawkers generated a wide variety of cheap foodstuffs that were essential for the urban populations of Barbados, although in the process they severely undercut the descendants of white bound servants, many of whom were struggling to survive as subsistence farmers on scraps of inaccessible and marginal land.[27]

However essential garden plots were to the health of the enslaved, they were nonetheless dependent upon the whims of planters and managers. Moreover, the enslaved were required to work on them to produce their own food, making them part of regulated labor rather than an independent enterprise. In the later eighteenth century, as the island became more self-sufficient in food, thus cutting costs and preserving profit margins, a prominent group of planters explained that

> On the afternoon which shall be given to them they shall be regularly attended by the overseer, and made to work in their respective gardens, as if they were employed in plantation-business. They should be made not only to prepare and plant the ground with provisions, but they should be required to keep their fences and hedge-rows in neat order, so that the whole may be made not only productive but agreeable to the view.[28]

At the Grove House plantation the homes and gardens of the enslaved were removed from the vicinity of the planter's mansion for aesthetic reasons, and "the ground from which they were removed was now disposed into regular walks, along which were planted Mahogany trees, Cabbage and Cocoanut trees, and along two other of the walks Bamboos." Beautiful surroundings for the planter were seen as being of greater import than the homes and provision plots of the enslaved. For all that these provision plots provided food and perhaps even the opportunity to participate in the island's unofficial economy, they remained part and parcel of plantation labor.[29]

Increasing creolization and, over the course of the eighteenth century, a steadily declining proportion of African-born slaves may have helped to enhance family and community life among the enslaved in Barbados. While slaves were regularly sold on to other planters, and some shipped to other colonies, over the course of the eighteenth century stability in family life increased among the many slaves laboring in large numbers on the bigger plantations. While West African polygamy had initially been tolerated on the island, over time this appears to have lessened, and over the course of the eighteenth century monogamous nuclear families become more common.[30]

Even with the general preference for Africans who had sailed from the Gold Coast, there was a diversity of ethnicity, language, and culture among the enslaved that even whites could recognize: Griffith Hughes observed that "Our Slaves, in their Mirth and Diversions, differ according to the several Customs of so many Nations intermixed." He found it remarkable that even second-generation Africans remained "tenaciously addicted to the Rites, Ceremonies, and Superstitions of their own Countries, particularly in their Plays, Dances, Music, Marriages, and Burials." Hughes's observation that such slaves "cannot be intirely weaned from these Customs" illustrated white planters' suspicion of all elements of African culture. However, between the late seventeenth century and the closing of the transatlantic slave trade, a striking creolization of enslaved society occurred. By the late eighteenth century the island had an overall population density of almost six hundred inhabitants per square mile (compared with approximately seventy-five in Jamaica), and with roughly equal numbers of men and women and a rising birth rate, slave families and a nascent slave culture were becoming more settled in Barbados. A diminishing number of Africans within the enslaved population meant that African language and culture inevitably weakened, although surviving pottery, jewelry and other items unearthed by archaeologists suggest that in Barbados as elsewhere in the Caribbean, the enslaved struggled to preserve certain elements of their heritage that continued to bring meaning and fulfillment to their lives.[31]

Planters' greatest fear was violent resistance and rebellion by the enslaved. Their fears that the enslaved might "beat Drums, blow Horns, or use any other loud Instruments" in order to communicate, or to gather together large and illicit gatherings of the enslaved, were so great that planters mandated punishments of overseers and plantation managers who did not prevent such gatherings or who failed to regularly search for and destroy drums and horns. Yet despite these injunctions and strict prohibition of slave gatherings off plantations at night or on rest days, the enslaved gathered together regularly. Music and dance were integral to such assemblies, and weekend and holiday dances may have been tolerated by planters as a safety valve: better a dance than a rebellion. Musical instruments appear to have included drums constructed from hollow logs with skins stretched over one end, pottery vessels perhaps beaten with palms, and either rocks or jagged-edged sticks clapped or rubbed together—and there was also clapping, foot stomping, and the rhythmic slapping of parts of one's own body. It was possible to make music from almost nothing, making it all but impossible for planters to prevent or fully control such expressions. Ritual activity may have had deeper social and cultural significance for the enslaved, and on occasion white observers took note of this.[32] In 1729, for example, an Anglican minister wrote to his bishop in London, seeking a stronger attempt "to restrain the Negroes of this island . . . from what they call their plays (frequently performed on the Lord's Days), in which with their various instruments of horrid music, howling, and dancing about the graves of the dead, they offer victuals and strong liquor to the souls of the deceased . . . in which sacrifices to the enemies of souls, the Oby Negroes or conjurors are the leaders."[33] Despite this clergyman's condemnation, the persistence of African culture and rituals and the evolution of new Afro-Caribbean forms clearly occurred among the enslaved. Europeans unfamiliar with rhythmic polyphony heard only a discordant cacophony, and the call-and-response and the spontaneous vocalizing of the enslaved, to say nothing of the frenetic and explosive motions of dancers, all appeared to the plantocracy as evidence of the savagery of their human property.[34]

Violence remained an essential and ever-present part of this agricultural system, and planters did not hesitate to rationalize their use of brute force. "In all governments," wrote one, "a distribution of rewards and punishments must be admitted. The idle, the refractory, and the vitious must be corrected and punished." According to this planter, "The stroke of the whip does not materially injure a negro by laceration of his body. It operates by the effect it has on his mind." Henry Drax had provided a manual for punishment of those who labored on his plantation, and he favored the speedy meting out of violent correction, given what he interpreted as enslaved Africans' tendency toward "awoyding punishmentts . . . [by] hang[ing] themselves." He believed the most common offense to be theft, although he acknowledged that if "itt be for there body its the more excusable." Such action would still merit punishment, but hunger mitigated the crime. However, the theft of "Sugr Molases or Rum which is our Money and the finall productt of all our Endewors" was an entirely different matter, and Drax believed "No punishment tooe terrible onn Such an octation as doeth Not deprive the party of Either life or Limbs." A century later Thomas Lane reported without surprise that a slave who stole "keys & took some coarse bad sugar" had been hanged. The enslaved might steal from neighboring plantations, as well as from their own, increasing the risk. A slave named McKeith was caught "asteeling Indian Corn" and badly beaten, but as soon as he recovered he went out again "& got so much beaten that all I could do [could] not save his life; nor neither would he tell me where it was done." Some slaves were willing to risk their lives, so great was the desire for food, either for the enslaved or for his or her family, or to provide access to other goods.[35]

The small size and increasing population density of Barbados made running away and marronage difficult, yet this did not prevent the most desperate among the enslaved from seeking an escape. While small patches of woods and forests still existed, and isolated highland areas and caves remained little known and unpopulated, it had been possible for both bound whites and blacks to escape detection, but by the later seventeenth century this had become all but impossible. For those who ran away and were then captured, few options remained. Early in the nineteenth century a visiting army office watched as a "runaway Negro was bought in [to Bridgetown] with his hands tied behind him; yet such was the strength and activity of this fellow that he leaped over the railing of the bridge and was smothered in the mud." For this man, suicide was preferable to punishment and reintroduction to the enslaved workforce. Far more common was the occasional absence from work, recorded in numerous plantation accounts and lists of the enslaved and their activities, often without comment. Clearly a safety valve of sorts, occasional absences from work might be tolerated by drivers and overseers. On 20 May 1796, for example, fifty-eight enslaved laborers were recorded as working "in the field Gang" at the Newton plantation, with twenty-four occupied with other plantation activities. One more took care of a particularly sick woman, one of five recorded as being too unwell to work. One, Cudjoe, was simply listed as "Absent." Three months later, twenty members of the second gang were weeding the sugar canes, but this time Dublin was absent.[36]

Rebellions, both real and imagined, changed over time. A planned island-wide insurrection in 1675, supposedly three years in the planning, was believed to have been "hatched by the *Cormantee* or *Gold-Co[a]st Negro[e]s*" with the intention of establishing "a King, one *Coffee* an Ancient Gold-Cost *Negro*." The African identification of the rebels is perhaps not surprising, given that at this time the large majority of the enslaved had been born in Africa, and Gold Coast guardians appear to have held privileged positions within the enslaved community. The plot was discovered when a young female domestic slave overheard and then reported to her master a debate between two young "Cormantee Negro[es]" as to whether or not all whites should be killed. The published account of the proposed rebellion castigated the "ungrateful wretches (who I have often heard confess to live better in Servitude there, than at Libertey in their own Native Country." Punishment was sure and swift, and in the first instance six were burned alive and eleven beheaded, and after further investigation twenty-five more were executed, and five committed suicide before they could be executed. While some betrayed or simply invented accomplices under the duress of interrogation and torture, others defied their punishment in ways that impressed onlookers.[37] When one, chained to the stake before being burned alive, appeared ready to name accomplices, his companion "was Heard to Chide him in these words, *Thou Fool, are there not enough of our Country-men killed already? Art thou minded to kill them all?* Then the aforesaid *Negro* that was going to make Confession, would not speak one word more."[38] Observing this, the white crowd taunted the condemned, "*we shall see you fry bravely by and by*," to which he "answered undauntedly, *If you Roast me to day, you cannot Roast me tomorrow*." Considering that the reported language of the enslaved likely bore little resemblance to the creolized dialect of African-born or even second-generation slaves, it seems likely that such sentiments were invented by an English author who clearly admired the spirit of the condemned.[39]

While the planned uprising in 1675 was dominated by African-born rebels, an abortive rebellion in 1692 was led by four enslaved artisans, some or all of whom may well have been born on the island. Taking advantage of European wars and the absence of a strong military force, they planned to use black and perhaps even disaffected bound Irish servants to burn ships and boats, thus preventing communication with the outside world until the rebellion was complete. The savage retributive force of the planto-cracy was felt, and after being tortured, Ben and Sambo were sentenced to be starved to death on gibbets, then, when almost dead, decapitated and their bodies quartered. They endured the first stage of this punishment for four days, apparently hoping for the planned rebellion that would lead to their release, but after Sambo's death Ben accepted the offer of his life in return for a full confession. This involved his implication of dozens of slaves, including a shockingly high number of supposedly privileged men such as drivers, carpenters, bricklayers, blacksmiths, "and such others that have more favour showne them by their Masters." In all some ninety slaves were executed.[40]

There is no evidence of a major rebellion planned or attempted in eighteenth-century Barbados, however, although these years witnessed a great degree of such activity elsewhere in British America. It is possible, of course, that the enslaved considered and even planned such uprisings, although the island's legally mandated armed tenant militia likely played a role in discouraging rebellion, as did the absence of the places of refuge available to Jamaican, South Carolinian, and other slaves. To the planter elite, this lengthy period of calm and the increasingly creolized and appar-ently settled nature of the enslaved population may have encouraged a cer-tain loosening of their rule. The domestic food supply increased, and conditions were somewhat ameliorated as planters sought to lessen their dependence upon imported Africans and maintain high levels of profit. While this is not to underestimate the constant, brutal exercise of power, felt most often and most completely in the plantation work regimen, improved diet, and conditions of life and work; the loosening of controls over music, dance, trade, and other social and cultural activities; the grant-ing of a fair degree of control in family formation; and the acceptance of a certain degree of absenteeism may well have helped to discourage at least some of the enslaved from attempting violent rebellion.[41]

The remarkable degree of creolization helped to foster conditions that initially made rebellion somewhat less likely. By the end of the eighteenth century at least 90 percent of the Barbadian population had been born on the island, making it—by a significant margin—the New World's most "demographically creolised" sugar plantation society. While in the later seventeenth and early eighteenth centuries Barbadian planters had preferred to buy and work enslaved Africans from the Gold Coast, by the later eighteenth century they were happy with a native-born enslaved population, and they regarded African-born slaves as more unruly and disruptive: the lack of large-scale violent resistance by the slaves was, according to their masters, the result of a declining proportion of troublesome Africans. A survey of 3,112 slaves on twenty-two of the island's plantations in 1788 revealed that only 429 had been born in Africa. By the turn of the nineteenth century, the population of enslaved Africans was about 46 percent male and 54 percent female, and family organization had been relatively stable for generations.[42]

Hilary Beckles has convincingly argued that this high degree of creolization led to significant changes in the lives and work of the enslaved. Occupational specialization, sometimes within enslaved families, had led to the consolidation of privileges for enslaved artisans, and account books reveal the use of the term "salary" to describe regular payments in money to enslaved overseers, watchmen, craftsmen, and others. Thus, for example, the chief driver at the Newton plantation received an annual salary of £10 "as an encouragement for his good behaviour and attention to the negroes," and similar salaries were paid to drivers on the Codrington plantation. For many of the enslaved, better food, housing, clothing, more stable families, and the steady accumulation of small but significant rights and privileges had significantly improved their quality of life. Such advances, however, had come at a heavy price. Sugar remained immensely profitable in Barbados, and it is possible that between 1750 and 1830 production per acre almost tripled. Yet such success had been exhaustingly wrenched from worn-out soil, with generations of slaves rejuvenating the landscape by manuring and cane-holing. Earlier generations had paid a heavy price for the somewhat improved lives of their descendants. Without doubt planters and plantation managers encouraged the perception that life was better and that the enslaved were benefiting materially from the successes of the island's sugar economy. While violence, sexual exploitation, and many other elements of racial slavery continued to taint the lives of the Barbadian bound workforce, there were significant advances, not least the passage of a law by the Barbados Assembly in 1804 making it a criminal offense, punishable by death, for a white man to murder a slave.[43]

In fact, so profound were these advances, and so tangible were the improvements in the lives of the enslaved, that it appears possible that planters faced increasing difficulty justifying and enforcing racial slavery. Slaves were no doubt aware of the increasing calls to end the transatlantic slave trade, not least from Barbadian planters who were happy with their creolized and self-reproducing enslaved population. With abolition less than a year away, one Barbadian planter went so far as to "sincerely wish that the trade had been totally abolished twenty years ago." The enslaved were aware, too, of the revolution by the enslaved in San Domingue, culminating in Haitian independence in 1804 and the creation of the first black republic in the western hemisphere. Hilary Beckles has argued that late eighteenth- and early nineteenth-century creolized Barbadian slaves were well aware of the larger situation and came to believe that the improvements in their own situation would soon result in their being freed by order of the British government. Believing that Barbadian planters were preventing this from happening, the island suffered its first slave insurrection in over a century, and its only major slave rebellion. Bussa's Rebellion in 1816 was led by the slave elite, by drivers, masons, sugar-boilers, coopers, carpenters, and the like, the highly creolized slaves who had—in their own eyes and those of their masters—enjoyed better lives and conditions than their grandparents and great-grandparents. But they were not free, their bodies and labor the property of others, and Bussa's Rebellion bore witness to an enduring struggle against the men and women who owned them. The rebels were crushed in a matter of days, by British troops and the impoverished whites who composed the Barbadian militia. To this day, however, a large statue of an enslaved man breaking his chains, the Bussa Emancipation Statue, stands proudly in the center of one of the island's major intersections. After independence the island's government named the rebellious leader the first national hero of Barbados.[44]

Throughout the seventeenth and eighteenth centuries, Barbadian planters had proved remarkably innovative in transforming the Barbadian landscape, applying human labor and new technologies in the growing and production of sugar. At first, sugar agriculture and production had been relatively simple, drawing the bounty of a rich environment and utilizing the labor of both bound whites and enslaved Africans. However, soil exhaustion and environmental degradation, together with declining sugar prices, combined to force planters to cut costs and increase efficiency through "the expensive operations of agriculture" on their plantations. They succeeded, but it was enslaved Africans who paid the price, and from the mid-seventeenth century onward, generations of enslaved men, women, and children were required to work longer and harder than ever. Thomas Tryon's antislavery sentiments encouraged him to exaggerate, but he highlighted a very real problem in his assertion that planters had been forced to "treble the Labour and Hands" in order to realize a profit. In fact, most plantations were short-handed and dependent upon externally sourced enslaved labor at peak times. While agricultural techniques and the technology of sugar manufacturing continued to advance, creating a productive process without parallel in the early modern world, the entire system remained dependent upon the efficient deployment of skilled and semiskilled enslaved labor. Real and threatened violence were deployed by planters, managers, overseers, and drivers to enforce discipline and a work regimen that destroyed both body and soul. The early groups of white and black bound laborers had been replaced by the regimented gang system, designed to deploy each enslaved laborer most efficiently, maximizing the work that he or she performed.[45]

If Barbadian plantation labor had originated in service and apprenticeship in husbandry in England, and in traditional slavery in West Africa, it had developed in Barbados in ways entirely distinct from those earlier systems. Barbados planters had the economic incentive to transform labor and production. Moreover, they enjoyed the political, judicial, and military power that enabled them to render their labor force all but unrecognizable to those who worked bound men and women in the fields of West Africa and Great Britain. On Barbados the enslaved were dehumanized in ways that were scarcely possible on the eastern side of the Atlantic: "the great body of the slaves, the field-people, on sugar plantations, are generally treated more like beasts of burden, than like human creatures." Visitors to Barbados encountered a labor system without precedent, and they struggled to comprehend and describe what they saw. Capital and power had transformed unfree labor, and on the integrated plantations of Barbados, a new and frightful system of racial slavery came into existence.[46]

The gang system on integrated plantations, with its focus on caneholing, manuring, and then the harvesting and processing of sugar, defined race and labor in late seventeenth-, eighteenth-, and early nineteenth-century Barbados. Violent discipline, punishment, rape, and all of the accompanying horrors of racial slavery were part of daily life for the enslaved, but it was an evolving system of sugar agriculture and production that made racial slavery desirable and profitable to slave owners, and it defined the daily lives and labor of tens of thousands of enslaved Africans in Barbados and beyond.[47]

Thomas Tryon took the unusual step of writing about plantation slavery and sugar production from the point of view of these enslaved laborers. Tryon acknowledged that "man is born to Labour, and had not hands only given to him to put Victuals into his Mouth, but first to use them Tilling the Earth, and getting Food and all other things requisite for humane Life, yet certainly the merciful God never intended that any of his Creatures should be forced to Labour beyond their natural strength, nor have burthens imposed on their weary Shoulders, greater than they are able to bear."[48]

Tryon had seen the enslaved at work in the fields, at the sugar mills, in the boiling houses, and in the distilleries, and he wrote with passion about this labor and its effects. In the cane fields the enslaved were forced "to work all day in the scorching heat . . . wherein no Mortal can endure so many hours severe Labour." Denied adequate time to rest, the field workers were subjected to "unreasonable Beating, made to Labour beyond our strength and abilities of Nature, but many of our Masters will not allow us Food that's sufficient, either in quantity or quality, to support and maintain Health, Strength and Vigour: so that being pined with want as well as worn out with excessive Drudgery, we oft times perish, or at least become poor, lean, feeble, and hardly able to go [on]."[49] Often, his imagined enslaved spokesman complained, "we are forc'd to work so long at the *Wind-Mills*, until we become so *Weary, Dull, Faint, Heavy* and *Sleepy*, that we are as it were deprived of our natural Senses, or like men in a maze, that we fall into danger, and oft times our Hands and Arms are crusht to pieces, and some times most part of our Bodies."[50] Work in the boiling houses was no better, for:

we are forced to stand and work at the Coppers, in the hot sulpherous Fumes, till Nature being overcome with weariness and want of proper Rest we fall into the fierce boyling Syrups, and in these disastors little or no pitty is taken of us, for though some indeed profess . . . sorrow for our mischances, it is cheifly for their own sakes, not

ours, because thereby they have lost the worth of so much Money
as we were reckon'd at.[51]

Enslaved Africans were the engine that had powered the great sugar economy, "the most necessary, and the most valuable" tool of the Barbados
planters. However, as Edward Littleton noted, "Our Negroes, which cost us
so dear, are also extremely casual," by which he meant that the labor force
that drove the machine was fragile.[52] The enslaved worked "in continual
drudgery, till our Heart-strings crack and our Nerves are enfeebled, and
our Marrow is exhausted, and our Bones fall under their Burthens, and our
Spirits are consumed, and our Souls in Weariness and Anguish; wish Death
rather than Life."[53] From the early seventeenth century on, enslaved Africans in Barbados struggled to create homes and families, to nurture culture
and faith. In a variety of ways they resisted elements of slavery, and on
occasion tried to escape it. Yet by and large, for generations of the enslaved
on Barbados, it was the island's remarkable and omnipresent system of
labor that defined and dominated their lives.

Conclusion

Overseers were labor enforcers of the circum-Atlantic world of work described in this book, men empowered by their employers to exercise power over the laboring poor, using legal power and violence to enforce labor discipline. In England the word "overseer" had long been applied to those with authority and governing power over others, and in the early modern era the increasing ranks of vagrants and of under- and unemployed people were subject to parish overseers of the poor, an office that would be re-created in the American colonies, on the Gold Coast, and on Barbados, as well as elsewhere in England's far-flung colonies. The word developed a new meaning when it was applied to the white men who governed groups of enslaved African laborers in strikingly different fashion in the New World, and eventually it would be applied to those who supervised British convicts sent to Australia.[1]

The word "overseer" epitomizes the fluid connections between the people and cultures of the British Isles and West Africa, and their transport and transformation on the island of Barbados. Under intense demographic pressure, and facing significant economic, political, and religious changes, English society in the sixteenth and early seventeenth centuries had been forced to confront a significantly increased population, which traditional forms of rural labor could not accommodate. New institutions, several involving involuntary, bound labor, were developed in response. Although legal and cultural restraints on employers' activities remained, bound labor increased and English authorities believed that their nation was overpopulated by the idle poor, many of them vagrants and criminals who could and should be forced to work.

The colonization of Barbados occurred in this context. But with English authorities overwhelmed by the political and economic strife of the mid-seventeenth century, the planter elite who rapidly assumed power on the island were able to fashion labor and agriculture as they saw fit. The Barbadian planter elite enjoyed a degree of political, administrative, and judicial power over the island's inhabitants that would have been the envy of Stuart monarchs. Living beyond the pale of English law and custom, planters were able to take certain ideas and beliefs from England, and work unfree Britons—vagrants, convicts, and prisoners of war—far more harshly than would have been possible in Britain. Plantations growing tobacco, cotton, and indigo and worked by bound British laborers generated sufficient income for their owners to begin to buy enslaved African laborers.[2]

English trade with West Africa grew rapidly from the mid-sixteenth century onward. Concentrated on the Gold Coast, the company that organized trade was intended to be manned and operated by Britons, from the governor and senior officers down to laboring artisans, manual workers, soldiers, and sailors. This soon proved impractical, and West African laborers came to dominate the "British" workforce. Britons on the Gold Coast proved adept at utilizing free and enslaved African labor on local terms, accommodating radically different forms and practices of labor. This continued throughout the eighteenth century, as a creolized labor force became dominant at Cape Coast Castle, Anomabu, and the other British trading posts.

The adaptability of Britons, as seen in their employment of local labor on the West Coast of Africa, took a very different form on Barbados. Free of customary restraints on the actions of employers and those who owned or controlled labor, whether British or West African, a small and cohesive group of elite Barbadian planters held all of the cards. These planters dominated the Governor's Council and the Assembly, as well as the magistracy, giving them control of the executive, legislative, and judicial functions of government on the island. Unified and remarkably potent, the planter elite were freed from the shackles of British and African custom and convention when it came to procuring, organizing, and disciplining their workforce, and they transformed English agricultural labor and enslaved African labor into an entirely new entity, creating a new gang labor system to service remarkably innovative integrated plantations. At first this new power was expressed in the use of white servants in ways that violated the norms of service and apprenticeship in husbandry, and which horrified many who saw or experienced it. Some of the terminology of English labor and service survived in Barbados, yet bound labor very quickly came to mean something very different on the island's plantations.

Bound labor defined Barbadian agriculture from the start. Whereas in England servants in husbandry, or on occasion pauper apprentices, composed only a small proportion of a household workforce that might also include a farmer's own family as well as irregularly employed wage laborers, on Barbados bound laborers dominated the planter's workforce. In England, a highly skilled and experienced older servant could command high wages and privileges, and such men hoped to soon create their own households. In the plantation fields of Barbados such distinctions did not apply. While a few white servants with useful artisanal skills, or those who became adept at sugar manufacturing, might enjoy better food, provisions, and clothes, most were part of a largely undifferentiated bound rural workforce.

By the later seventeenth century, Africans dominated the Barbadian workforce, and bound whites quickly disappeared from the ranks of laborers involved in sugar agriculture and manufacturing. It proved ever more difficult to make profits from the depleted Barbadian soil, and enslaved workers toiled endlessly to grow cane, to make good sugar and rum, and to increase the wealth of their masters. Although not facing the horrors of enslavement, the white servants who survived and who remained on the island found that they and their descendants enjoyed little improvement in their lives. A precious few found work as overseers, or lived in shabby homes on marginal ground as militia men, charged with protecting the island against foreign attack and slave rebellions. Others lived in abject poverty in the island's highlands. At the same time, the lot of African slaves worsened, with increasing numbers suffering the Middle Passage and forced labor on the small Caribbean island and throughout British North America. In some ways the enslaved Gold Coast guardians on seventeenth-century Royal African Company ships bound for Barbados embodied the transition between African and Barbadian slavery experienced by so many of their brethren. The enslaved guardians began the voyage as privileged individuals, who worked with and alongside the representatives of the men who owned them. Echoing the complicated nature of slavery as a social and cultural institution in West Africa, guardians straddled the divide between Old and New World enslavement. Upon arrival in Barbados, the last remaining trappings of African slavery fell away, and they were sold alongside the men and women they had supervised and condemned to a lifetime of New World slavery.

The brutal white servant regime helped make possible the development of the violent system of racialized black slavery in Barbados, as planters hardened attitudes toward and legal control over the men, women, and children who labored on their plantations. Historians continue to speculate as to whether or not a transition from white bound or free labor to African slavery was inevitable in Britain's New World colonies. David Eltis has controversially argued that slavery contradicted economic motives, and that the continued employment of white European labor on New World plantations would have been more profitable: for Eltis, ideology rather than economics explains the switch to enslaved African labor. Robin Blackburn echoes Eltis by suggesting that building plantations on white labor would have required little more innovation than was required in the utilization of enslaved African labor. Yet, Blackburn contends, despite their often brutal treatment, white laborers were able to call on the traditional rights of Englishmen, Christians, and so forth, while African allusions to their heritage and culture had no resonance among white planters. While this was perhaps true, the heavy deployment of vagrants, convicts, and prisoners—people judged to have forfeited many of their rights, including the right to life in the British Isles—meant that in seventeenth-century Barbados white laborers could be, and were, worked as virtual "white slaves."[3]

Eltis is surely right in concluding that the extremely arduous and often deadly nature of work on sugar plantations demanded coerced labor. From the mid-seventeenth century on, an increasing and ever cheaper flow of African slaves coincided with both a decline in the numbers of white bound laborers and a rise in their cost. However, had more vagrants, convicts, and prisoners been cheaply available from the British Isles, Barbadian planters would have been more than willing to work them hard, alongside African slaves, and even to death. An uncertain supply of bound Britons who were largely devoid of rights and privileges, to say nothing of increased imperial oversight of British colonies, no doubt had an effect on the decisions made by planters. Moreover, the advantages of having an enslaved African population that could reproduce itself, as opposed to the predominantly male population of vagrants, convicts, and prisoners of war, became all the more apparent.[4]

The sugar economy encouraged the consolidation of land holdings into optimally sized large plantations on Barbados, with the result that many smaller planters lost their land while former indentured servants faced declining opportunities for land ownership or productive employment. Plantations and thus power were concentrated in fewer hands, and after decades of rapid growth the white population declined dramatically during the later seventeenth century. In stark contrast, the number of enslaved Africans increased exponentially. Having once dominated the workforce, by about 1650 bound whites labored alongside African slaves in roughly equal numbers, and thereafter the number of slaves grew rapidly as the number of bound whites decreased. In 1655 approximately 23,000 white residents still outnumbered the roughly 20,000 blacks on the island, but by 1684 there were over 46,600 blacks, compared with under 20,000 whites, and by 1712 almost 42,000 blacks massively outnumbered just over 12,500 whites. Before about 1660 bound white servant labor had been cheaper than enslaved African labor, but thereafter the supply of white servants declined and their cost increased, not least because the Navigation Acts restricted the supply of Scottish prisoners favored by planters. Furthermore, the survival of an increasing number of former servants with few options posed a social and economic problem for the planter elite. At the same time the growing efficiency of the transatlantic slave trade increased the flow of ever-cheaper African slaves. The Barbados census of 1680 provides a detailed picture of the resulting changes in the character of the plantation workforce, recording the inhabitants of all eleven of the island's parishes, totaling 37,315 slaves but only 2,193 white servants.[5]

At first the transition from white servants to African slaves may not have been obvious to contemporaries. During the later 1640s, the 1650s, and well into the 1660s, the supply of both white and black bound labor had increased to meet the demands of the rapidly developing sugar plantations. As sugar came to dominate the agriculture and exports of Barbados in the later 1640s, the ratio of white laborers to plantations increased, from 4.3 to 5.0 per estate. Even as the number and proportion of slaves increased, planters remained committed to the deployment of white bound labor, and Barbadian plantations continued to rely on their labor. Throughout the 1640s and 1650s, the average size of plantations and their bound workforces continued to increase, and white servants remained integral to the labor of the plantation economy. Moreover, planters continued to work hard to retain control over white servants, not least in the "Act for the Good Governing of Servants" (1661), which defined running away or the harboring of runaways as theft of property, to be punished by drastic extensions of the terms of service of offending servants.[6]

Over the course of the eighteenth century a racial ideology came to form an increasingly solid foundation for plantation slavery in Barbados and throughout British America. Although the island's plantation labor force had originally been composed of bound men, women, and children from the British Isles, their servile status had been defined in terms of class and lost status. The "Act for the Good Governing of Servants" had complained about the "Unruliness, Obstinacy, and Refractoriness" of bound white laborers who, as vagrants, criminals, and prisoners of war, had been legally bound into servile status. But from the time of the first slave codes, attitudes toward plantation workers and justifications for their servile status were increasingly racialized, defining the enslaved in bestial terms as "Barbarous, Wild, and Savage" and thus essentially different from the white servants who preceded them.[7]

The centrality of class and labor in explaining the development of plantation slavery in Barbados raises questions about historians' ideas regarding the development of ideas and practices of race and racism. David Eltis has argued that ideological rather than economic factors explain the advent of racial slavery, and he, David Barry Gaspar, and others see evidence for this in the rapid development of draconian slave codes defining enslaved Africans as property and without rights. Other scholars have suggested that such fixed ideas and practices of race were unusual in the seventeenth and even the eighteenth centuries. Utilizing detailed readings of contemporary drama, poetry, and religious writings, Roxann Wheeler, Mary Floyd Wilson, Kim Hall, Colin Kidd, and others have all demonstrated that multiple understandings of race existed in Britain and its Atlantic World, with a binary understanding of black and white emerging only in the eighteenth century, and not achieving primacy until the nineteenth century.[8]

The attitudes toward and treatment of bound white laborers in early Barbados informed the development of ideas and practices of plantation slavery, and the evolution of a belief that only enslaved Africans were fit for such work. Thus it was a class-based system of labor rather than abstract ideas of racial difference that provided the foundation for slavery in Barbados, and for a system that spread to Jamaica, the Carolinas, and beyond. A time of particularly intense social and political dislocation in the British Isles provided the preconditions that encouraged large landowners in Barbados to treat English, Scottish, and Irish convicts, vagrants, rebels, and prisoners of war as persons whose lives were forfeit, and who could be treated as a disposable labor force. English authorities were preoccupied with domestic strife and a conflict over authority in the home islands throughout the second and third quarters of the seventeenth century.

During the pivotal mid-seventeenth century, as the Barbadian colony exploded and drew in more laborers than all other English colonies combined, English oversight of the actual organization of the Barbadian plantations and their labor forces was minimal. Radically different groups were thrown together on the small island, and planters who controlled law-making, the judiciary, and military power refigured their control of men and women whose lives were forfeit, and in the process they ascribed new identities to bound laborers. With minimal restraint, Barbadian planters employed bound labor to clear the island, to create plantations, and to raise and process the crops that made it England's greatest wealth-producing center of the mid-seventeenth century. Control of bound white laborers and then enslaved Africans was based upon selective application of English principles and precedents in the treatment of bound laborers and of property, drawing upon martial law, the law of treason, and the various statutes designed to control the lower orders of English society. The legal codes developed in Barbados spread to Jamaica, the Leeward Islands, South Carolina, and beyond.[9]

The integrated plantations and bound labor that developed on Barbados and then spread elsewhere had been shaped by the unique conditions on the island. A small planter elite had quickly taken control of the island, taking advantage of minimal English oversight and the ready availability of tens of thousands of bound whites with few rights and little hope. The transition to sugar brought huge profits but quickly exhausted and damaged the soil, thus encouraging the extraction of the maximum labor from the plantation workforce in order to maintain profits. Bound British workers also became more expensive and increasingly troublesome, for there was no place in Barbadian society for those who survived their terms of bondage, while the declining cost of enslaved Africans furnished planters with an attractive alternative. The switch to an enslaved plantation workforce resulted in little improvement in the conditions for white bound laborers and their descendants, and those who were unable to leave the island were mired in poverty and regarded with disgust by planters and with pity by the enslaved, who dismissively referred to impoverished whites as "poor backras" and "ecky-beckies."[10]

Such attitudes toward and treatment of the plantation bound labor force fundamentally shaped Barbadian plantation slavery and spread to Jamaica, the Carolinas, and elsewhere: this was a system founded on the unfree labor of both whites and blacks, even though the finished product of plantation slavery and the codes that supported it offered poorer whites greater opportunities and status. Plantation slavery would come to be defined by race, but it originated in the development of new ways of utilizing bound white laborers, drawing on English precedents in the unfamiliar terrain of Barbados. Enslaved Africans were then integrated into this system, which was perfected around them. Yet thousands of miles to the east, Britons proved perfectly capable of continuing to employ enslaved Africans as bound workers who lived and worked at very different points on the continuum of free and unfree labor. Seventeenth- and eighteenth-century company slaves on the Gold Coast were very different bound laborers from white bound servants in early to mid-seventeenth century Barbados, and the enslaved Africans who replaced them. Over the course of the eighteenth century Britons on the Gold Coast proved adept at accommodating West African labor forms, including a form of slavery that granted a remarkably high degree of independence to the enslaved.

At precisely the same time, in Barbados, a newly developed racialized slavery hardened and became institutionalized, born of a class-based labor system first applied to bound white men and women. Over the course of the eighteenth century Barbados developed the most creolized enslaved workforce of any British colony. By the end of that century the island no longer depended upon Africa for its workforce, for with as many births as deaths the Barbadian slave population had become self-sustaining, growing more of its own food, with more settled and stable enslaved families and communities, who were better fed and who enjoyed a somewhat more balanced work regimen. A new modus operandi developed in which the enslaved enjoyed some benefits and carved out a limited degree of autonomy in certain areas of their lives. Context was everything in this world of Atlantic creoles, with different labor systems—and consequently different attitudes toward and practices of race—coexisting in different parts of the British Atlantic.[11]

For too long historians of British North America have focused upon Virginia in an attempt to explain the development of race and slavery in what would become the United States. Although recent work has demonstrated that Chesapeake planters began preferring slaves to white laborers well before the 1670s, the fact is that Virginia and Maryland planters were unable to purchase many Africans until later in the century. In numerical terms the Chesapeake was a sideshow, and during the seventeenth century a great many more white bound laborers and enslaved Africans went to Barbados: for every enslaved African who stepped ashore in the Chesapeake before 1701, nearly fifteen had disembarked in Barbados. The island functioned as a laboratory of labor, and elements of the Barbadian plantation and slavery systems spread out and took root throughout much of British America. A good many planters left Barbados in the later seventeenth century, taking slaves and the ideas and practices of the Barbadian slave system with them. They traveled to Jamaica, to the Leeward Islands, to the Carolinas, and to the Chesapeake: of those recorded as leaving the island in 1679, more than twice as many went to the Chesapeake as to the Carolinas.[12]

It was in the Carolinas and Jamaica, however, that Barbadian ideas and practices took root and spread on the largest scale. Sir Thomas Modyford provides an illustrative example of the process. The wealthy son of a businessman who had become mayor of Exeter, Modyford arrived in Barbados as an associate of Richard Ligon. After cooperating in running one large plantation, Ligon returned to England, but Modyford remained to become one of the largest planters on Barbados: with his brother-in-law Thomas Kendall, for example, he owned a five-hundred-acre plantation. As a large planter Modyford enjoyed power and influence on Barbados, and he eventually rose to become speaker of the House of Assembly. Well connected in England, he was appointed as a factor of the Company of Royal Adventurers, the predecessor of the Royal African Company, and he led the way in the transition to an enslaved African plantation workforce. In 1664 Modyford was appointed governor of the newly captured island of Jamaica, and he arrived on the island with a great many of his own slaves. Continuing to work as a factor for the Royal Adventurers, he encouraged a mighty influx of enslaved Africans. Just over two hundred enslaved Africans are estimated to have arrived in Jamaica during the 1650s, but during the following decade more than 15,500 arrived, and as governor and a factor for the Royal Adventurers between 1664 and 1700, but most especially as an experienced Barbadian planter, Modyford helped to lead this expansion. Perhaps of greatest significance was his introduction of Jamaica's first comprehensive slave act, a direct copy of the Barbadian slave code.[13]

On the North American mainland Barbadian ideas and practices had enormous influence in the Carolinas. Modyford's friend John Colleton and his family provide an equally useful example. Like Modyford, Colleton had been born into a wealthy mercantile family in Exeter, and for generations his family had been prominent in the city's Society of Adventurers Trading Beyond the Seas. Colleton arrived in Barbados with his son Peter just as sugar was taking hold, and he quickly became a large planter. A decade later Sir John returned to England, but he left his sons on Barbados, to run plantations there and to provide leadership for the Barbados Adventurers, a group of Barbadian planters seeking to remove their slaves to the fresh soil of the Carolinas. The Colletons began with a small ninety-acre plantation in St. Peter Parish, but by the time John was appointed to the Governor's Council in 1659 the family had spent more than £30,000 and owned over seven hundred acres, with their largest holding being the Cliff Plantation, halfway down the island's east coast.[14]

Following his return to England in 1660, Colleton assumed several significant offices. He was appointed a commissioner for trade and a member of the Select Committee for Foreign Plantations, and he was a founding member of the Company of Royal Adventurers. Knighted in 1661, Sir John Colleton was powerful and influential, and his experiences in Barbados had convinced him of the profitability of the Barbadian plantation system and of the opportunities for its expansion. The Colletons were given huge land grants in the new Carolina colony, and Peter Colleton—governor of Barbados in the mid-1670s—led the Barbados Adventurers' efforts on the new mainland colony. These entrepreneurs knew that Barbados could provide Carolina with seasoned planters and laborers at low cost, and Modyford and Peter Colleton wrote to the Carolina Proprietors that many in Barbados were "willing and ready to remove spedily theither to begin a setlement." They eagerly extolled "the aptnes of the people heare . . . as well for their experienced planters as for the number of there Negroes" fit for plantation labor on the American mainland. By the early eighteenth century the Colleton family would own well over 18,000 acres of South Carolina land. Following Sir John Colleton's death in 1667, Peter returned to England, but several younger brothers remained in Barbados and later went to South Carolina. Peter Colleton understood the great need for a cheap and reliable flow of enslaved Africans if the new Carolina colony and the developing Jamaican colony were to succeed, and with three other Carolina Proprietors he took a leading role in the creation of the Royal African Company in place of the now defunct Royal Adventurers. At the same time, his younger brother James rose to become governor of South Carolina. In short, this one family provides a perfect example of the interconnectedness of the Royal African Company, the plantation labor system that had developed on Barbados, and the spread of that system to South Carolina.[15]

The unwillingness of smaller planters and poor whites to accept the large land claims of the colony's proprietors was enhanced by the large size of South Carolina, which combined to create better options for white bound laborers and their descendants than had been true on Barbados. However, the plantation slavery developed in Barbados on the backs of both bound whites and then enslaved Africans was exported wholesale to South Carolina, and the more slaves a planter brought to the new colony, the more land he received and the greater his power in the new colony. When Simon Merringer arrived from Barbados in the early 1670s, for example, he received three thousand acres on the basis of the number of enslaved Africans and bound whites who accompanied him. By the second summer of settlement, almost half of all whites and well over half of all enslaved Africans in South Carolina had come from Barbados, and in London John Locke noted, "The Barbadians endeavour to rule all."[16]

This book has adopted a circum-Atlantic perspective, examining the ways in which Britons employed bound and free labor in related Atlantic World settings, and their relation to the development of plantation slavery on Barbados. It has examined labor practices in the early modern British Isles, white and black labor in the forts and coastal communities of the Gold Coast in West Africa, and the degree to which these British and West African labor practices created the British Atlantic World's first integrated plantations in Barbados. Categories and forms of labor and race were tremendously complicated in all of these locations, and often there were no clear lines of demarcation between white and black workers: the category and indeed the experience of bound labor was often blurred. It was only in Barbados, from the later seventeenth century onward, that more rigid definitions of labor and subsequently of race usurped the more fluid ideas and practices of the larger British Atlantic World. Britons on the Gold Coast continued to prove willing and able to own and employ slaves in a thoroughly West African fashion, while across the Atlantic on Barbados the treatment of bound white laborers provided the foundation for Britons to treat the enslaved in a completely different way. Racial slavery was perhaps the most important new form of labor created in and by the early modern British Atlantic World.

As planters' ideas about Africans and their race coalesced into an ideology of difference and inferiority on New World plantations, an altogether different set of attitudes toward Africans—both enslaved and free—persisted among Britons on the Gold Coast of West Africa. This is not to say that Britons in Africa were any less confident of their racial superiority.

They certainly regarded the tens of thousands of Africans who were loaded onto ships bound for the Americas as commodities. However, Britons in West Africa were required to deal with a wide range of Africans, from the local leaders who sanctioned trading operations; to the merchants and translators who facilitated trade and the purchase of slaves; to the free, enslaved, and pawned Africans upon whose labor the British trading operations depended. These Britons lived and operated in a society in which enslavement was not racialized and could not carry the deeply negative connotations that were developing in Barbados and elsewhere in the New World. Generation after generation of British officials, merchants, and laborers in West Africa worked within a system that depended upon enslaved labor in a system that accorded rights and respect to these bound laborers. On Barbados, very different ideas and practices of bound labor encouraged planters to think about and treat enslaved Africans in markedly different ways than was true in West Africa, stripping Barbados slaves of the rights, privileges, and humanity enjoyed by their enslaved brethren on the Gold Coast. British resentment of the trading acumen, the alien customs and traditions, and the wealth and authority of Africans who enjoyed power over the sojourning Europeans was often expressed in derogatory and even racist language. Thus, at the turn of the eighteenth century William Bosman described West Africans as "all without exception, [being] Crafty, Villanous and Fraudulent, and very seldom to be trusted." Seventy years later John Roberts wrote of the "barbarous manners of the natives" who he believed to exist "in a state of anarchy" with not the least understanding of "liberty, and property." Perhaps it was inevitable that Britons would think of themselves as racially superior to Africans, but African power and European weakness and indeed dependence upon local people made it necessary for Britons on the Gold Coast to accommodate and respect Africans and their society, including its labor system. Plantation slavery, and the particular forms of racism that emanated from it, were developed not in West Africa but rather in Barbados, where they were based upon attitudes toward bound labor that had originated in the maltreatment of many thousands of white vagrants, criminals, and prisoners.[17]

Racial slavery on the integrated plantations of Barbados bore little resemblance and appeared relatively disconnected from the myriad forms of bound and free labor of whites and blacks that continued to support the British transatlantic slave trade in West Africa throughout the later seventeenth and the eighteenth centuries. Barbadian plantation slavery, in short, marked a radical and dramatic shift in labor practice and ideology, particular to its New World environment. This new development was of signal importance because of the "Barbadian Diaspora" that spread out from mid-seventeenth-century England's wealthiest colony to Jamaica, the Leeward Islands, the Carolinas, and beyond. It is hard to exaggerate the influence of wealthy and successful Barbadian planters and the new agricultural and labor system that they had fashioned. The Barbadian system thrived and spread, informing the development of plantation slavery in South Carolina, which in turn helped export refined versions of that system throughout the "Deep South" of what became the United States, forming the heart and soul of the "Slave Belt." Perhaps the influence of Barbadian slavery can be seen most clearly in the ways in which its slave code was copied, often almost verbatim, in Jamaica, Antigua, South Carolina, and elsewhere. The Barbadian slave code was "the premier slave law code in the English colonies."[18]

Ideas about the nature and usage of bound labor, to say nothing of a developing racial ideology, that had all germinated in Barbados took root all around the Caribbean and then throughout the Deep South of mainland British America. Barbadian-inspired systems of slavery differed dramatically from that found in the Chesapeake colonies, and the latter began to fade in the later eighteenth century. The ideology of the American Revolution, together with a shift by an increasing number of planters to less labor-intensive crops such as wheat, meant that the slavery of the Upper South was, at least in comparison with the more intensive slavery further South, in relative decline from the late eighteenth century onward. In short, the slavery that dominated antebellum America had its roots not in the Chesapeake but on Barbados.[19]

Eventually, at the end of the eighteenth century, the ideas and practices of racial slavery developed in Barbados and adopted throughout much of British America proved so powerful as to influence British treatment of castle slaves on the Gold Coast. Since the mid-seventeenth century, Britons on the Gold Coast had accommodated themselves to West African labor practices, using enslaved labor in Africa on African terms. In 1787 this changed, when RAC officials in London finally granted the governor and Council at Cape Coast the authority to send recalcitrant or obdurate castle slaves in chains to the New World. For generations, castle slaves had enjoyed a relatively high degree of self-determination, especially when compared with slaves in British America, but with this decision Barbadian slavery symbolically trumped West African slavery in the lives of castle slaves.

A PRIVATE of the 5ᵗʰ WEST INDIA REGIMENT.

Figure 15. J. C. Stadler after Charles Hamilton Smith, "A Private of the 5th West India Regiment," (1812), aquatint. Courtesy of the Council of the National Army Museum, London. This soldier, quite possibly a slave purchased in West Africa within the preceding decade, wore a regular British infantry uniform.

All the way to the end of the transatlantic slave trade, and even beyond, Britons nonetheless proved capable of using enslaved Africans in very African ways, not just on the coast of West Africa but even in Barbados and elsewhere in the British Americas. Between 1756 and 1815 Britain mobilized larger armies than ever before, deploying them all around the world. These commitments, as well as a Caribbean climate that killed or rendered unfit a large proportion of freshly arrived soldiers, encouraged British military leaders to employ enslaved laborers, first in support roles, and later as fully armed and equipped soldiers. During the 1790s Earl Effingham purchased slaves to strengthen Jamaican defenses, and as the French Revolutionary Wars and then the Napoleonic Wars intensified, the need for large defensive forces to protect valuable Caribbean colonies and to free up British regulars for service elsewhere encouraged an expansion of this black military force. At first, slaves and free blacks and mulattoes were purchased and recruited in the Caribbean itself, but later increasingly large numbers of African slaves were purchased by the British army. Between 1795 and 1808 the British government spent about £925,000 on approximately 13,400 enslaved Africans for the West India regiments. During the late eighteenth and the first third of the nineteenth centuries, it was often not poor whites from the Caribbean or the British Isles who defended the British Caribbean against foreign attack or protected planters against slave rebellions. In Barbados, Jamaica, and elsewhere, enslaved Africans populated the West Indian regiments. African traditions of employing enslaved Africans in military service transferred to India, where enslaved East Africans served in Britain's Ceylon Regiments, and to the Caribbean, where a professional standing slave army testified to the continued ability of Britons to countenance African forms of slavery. For all that Barbados had nurtured a new form of racial slavery, separate and different from forms of bound labor in early modern England and West Africa, Britons were nonetheless able to continue to see and deploy enslaved Africans along a continuum of bound labor. The man stationed in Barbados, wearing a British army uniform, carrying a rifle, and receiving a minimal stipend, was closer to the armed company slaves of Cape Coast Castle than he was to the enslaved sugar plantation workers who labored a few hundred yards from the garrison outside Bridgetown. Slavery existed on a continuum of bound labor, and despite the fact that on Barbados this labor form developed in new ways that were then replicated throughout British merica, it nonetheless remained a fundamentally flexible system.[20]

Notes

Introduction

1. Statistics from Voyages: The Transatlantic Slave Trade Database, http://www .slavevoyages.org/tast/assessment/estimates.faces, accessed 2 August 2011. The creators of the Trans-Atlantic Slave Trade Database have created a series of estimates that employ "algorithms based on data in the main database and on patterns of the slave trade over time to fill in gaps in the historical record and construct an estimate of the total slave trade." See "Voyages: The Transatlantic Slave Trade Database. Guide. Understanding and Using the Online Database and Website" (May 2008), 20, available at http://www.slavevoyages.org/tast/database/guide/VoyagesGuide.pdf , accessed on 2 August 2011.

2. This concept of "circum-Atlantic" history has been advanced by a number of scholars. See, in particular, David Armitage, "Three Concepts of Atlantic History," in *The British Atlantic World, 1500–1800,* ed. David Armitage and Michael J. Braddick (New York: Palgrave Macmillan, 2002), 16–29; Joseph Roach, *Cities of the Dead: Circum-Atlantic Performance* (New York: Columbia University Press, 1996); Paul Gilroy, *The Black Atlantic: Modernity and Double Consciousness* (London: Verso, 1993), 41–71. The British state came into existence with the Act of Union between England and Scotland in 1707. However, although England dominated imperial activity before the Union, the peoples of Scotland, Ireland, and Wales all participated in the creation and population of English colonies, and in the trade with the Gold Coast. Thus, for all that it is politically anachronistic, in this book I shall use the term British, as well as English, to refer to this shared social and economic participation in trade and colonization.

3. Only a small proportion of the large body of work on the Atlantic World focuses on labor, comparing and linking labor practices in different regions. See Alexander X. Byrd, *Captives and Voyagers: Black Migrants Across the Eighteenth-Century British Atlantic World* (Baton Rouge: Louisiana State University Press, 2008); Frederick C. Knight, *Working the Diaspora: The Impact of African Labor on the Anglo-American World, 1650–1850* (New York: New York University Press, 2010); David Eltis, "Labor and Coercion in the English Atlantic World from the Seventeenth Century to the Early Twentieth Century," *Slavery and Abolition,* 14 (1993), 207–226; John Donoghue,

"Unfree Labor, Imperialism, and Radical Republicanism in the Atlantic World, 1630–1661," *Labor: Studies in Working Class History of the Americas*, 1 (2004), 47–68.

4. Pawns were—at least in theory—temporary rather than permanent slaves. Pawns were not owned, and thus could not be sold like slaves: one owned the labor of a pawn, but not the person. British authorities on the Gold Coast held pawns as well as enslaved Africans, and were well attuned to the differences between the two. See Toyin Falola and Paul E. Lovejoy, eds., *Pawnship in Africa: Debt Bondage in Historical Perspective* (Boulder: Westview Press, 1994).

5. Ira Berlin has effectively critiqued historians' tendency to treat labor forms as unchanging. See Berlin, *Many Thousands Gone: The First Two Centuries of Slavery in North America* (Cambridge, Mass.: Belknap Press of Harvard University Press, 1998), 4.

6. *A New Map of the Island of Barbadoes, wherein every Parish, Plantation, Watermill, Windmill & Cattlemill, is described with the name of the Present Possessor, and all things els Remarkable according to a Late Exact Survey thereof* (London: Philip Lea and John Sellers, 1675). For an excellent discussion of this map, see Jeanette D. Black, "Map 32: A New Map of the Island of Barbadoes," *The Blathwayt Atlas*, Vol. 2: *Commentary* (Providence: Brown University Press, 1975), 180–185. This estimate of the Barbadian population in 1675 is drawn from Richard S. Dunn, "The Barbados Census of 1680: Profile of the Richest Colony in English America," *William and Mary Quarterly*, 3rd ser., 26 (1969), 7–8.

7. Anonymous letter, Barbados, 20 March 1676, reprinted in P. Hume Brown, ed., *The Register of the Privy Council of Scotland*, 3rd ser. (Glasgow: James Hedderwick and Sons, 1911), IV, 671–675.

8. Anonymous letter, Barbados, 1676, 671–675.

9. Christopher Tomlins, *Freedom Bound: Law, Labor, and Civic Identity in Colonizing English America, 1580–1865* (Cambridge: Cambridge University Press, 2010), 428–431, 450–451.

10. Richard O'Shea, Will, 15 April 1653, Will Record Books, Barbados Department of Archives, RB6, XI, 561.

11. Sir Dalby Thomas, *An Historical Account of the Rise and Growth of the West-India Collonies, And of the Great Advantages they are to England, in respect to Trade* (London: for John Hindmarsh, 1690), 14, 4, 5, 16, 40. For Thomas's detailed descriptions of sugar agriculture and production, see 14–19. For an account of his life, see *Oxford Dictionary of National Biography*, online edition, http://www.oxforddnb.com/view/article/49984, accessed 4 August 2011.

12. Elizabeth I issued the first charter to the Senegal Adventurers in 1588, and in 1618 James I granted a monopoly to the Company of Adventurers of London Trading to Gynney and Bynney, better known as the Guinea Company. Interested primarily in gold, the company moved its focus from Gambia and Sierra Leone to the Gold Coast during the 1620s, establishing the first English trading post at Kormantin in 1631. From the 1640s on, English participation in the transatlantic slave trade grew rapidly, but much of this trade was carried by independent merchant adventurers and by other

nations. Following the Restoration, the Duke of York and a group of gold-hungry courtiers formed the Company of Royal Adventurers into Africa, which was re-chartered in 1663 as the Company of Royal Adventurers of England trading into Africa, which assumed control of the English forts along the Gold Coast. This was the first charter to explicitly encompass the slave trade, and increased competition with the Dutch helped precipitate a war during which the English captured Cape Coast Castle, which became the British headquarters in West Africa. The company was replaced by the Royal African Company (RAC) in 1672, which was dominated by merchants, and the slave trade quickly became the central focus of the company's activities. Increasing challenges to the company's monopoly led to a compromise in 1689 that ended the RAC monopoly and opened African trade to all English merchants. By 1730 the RAC no longer functioned as a trading company, instead subsisting on an annual parlia-mentary subsidy granted to preserve the forts and trading posts for the benefit of British trade. In 1750 the African Trade Act opened the entire western coast of Africa to all Britons, and the forts of the Gold Coast and adjacent coastal areas were reorga-nized under a new Company of Merchants Trading to Africa, to be maintained by an annual parliamentary subsidy. See K. G. Davies, *The Royal African Company* (1957; London: Routledge, 1999), 6, 16–17, 39–40; P. E. H. Hair and Robin Law, "The English in West Africa to 1700," in *The Oxford History of the British Empire,* Vol. 1: *The Origins of Empire: British Overseas Enterprise to the Close of the Seventeenth Century,* ed. Nicho-las Canny (Oxford: Oxford University Press, 1998), 251–259; Ty M. Reese, "Toiling in the Empire: Labor in Three Anglo-American Ports, London, Philadelphia and Cape Coast Castle, 1750–1783" (Ph.D. diss., University of Toledo, 1999), 64–66. "Royal Afri-can Company" and "RAC" will be used throughout this book to refer to the various companies responsible for British trade on the Gold Coast.

13. Dalby Thomas to RAC, Cape Coast Castle, 22 October 1708, Abstracts of Let-ters Received by the Royal African Company of England from the Coast of Africa No. 1. From March the 20th 1705 To August the 15th 1715, National Archives, T70/5, 50; Thomas to RAC, Cape Coast Castle, 28 April 1704, Abstracts of Letters Received by the Royal African Company of England so far as relate to the Committee of Correspon-dence No. 5. From May the 31st 1704 To October the 3d 1706, National Archives, T70/ 14, 90. "Castle Slaves" were owned by the Royal African Company and worked in West African trading posts and forts.

14. Seth Grosvenor and James Phipps to African Committee, Cape Coast Castle, 11 July 1712, Extracts of Letters Received by the Royal African Company so far as relate to the Committee of Shipping From October the 22d 1705 To February the 3d 1719, RAC, T70/26, 33.

15. An Act of Council made at Cape Coast Castle November 5 1737, Extracts, 1720–1742, RAC, T70/4, 105; Copy of the List of the Living and Dead at the Royal African Company's Forts . . . List of Such Factors Artificers and Soldiers . . . Living on the Castle & out ffactoreys, Cape Coast Castle 8 August 1674, RAC, T70/1440, 1–2; Philip Quaque to Rev. Dr. Daniel Burton, Cape Coast Castle, 27 September 1770, and Quaque

to Burton, Cape Coast Castle, 28 September 1766, in Vincent Carretta and Ty M. Reese, eds., *The Life and Letters of Philip Quaque: The First African Anglican Missionary* (Athens: University of Georgia Press, 2010), 92, 43.

16. Extract of Letters Received by the Royal African Company of England so far as relate to the Committee of Shipping From October the 22d to February the 3d 1719, RAC, T70/26, 22; John Apperley to the African Committee, Anomabu, 22 April 1753, Inward Letter Books, Second, 1753–1762, RAC, T70/30, 27; John Apperley to the African Committee, Anomabu, 19 March 1756, Inward Letter Books, Second, 1753–1762, RAC, T70/30, 144.

17. Thomas, *An Historical Account*, 30; Thomas to RAC, Cape Coast Castle, 28 March 1706, Extracts of Letters Received by the Royal African Company of England so far as relate to the Committee of Shipping From October the 22d 1705 To February the 3d 1719, National Archives, T70/26, 8. These statistics were drawn from the Voyages database, http://www.slavevoyages.org/tast/assessment/estimates.faces, accessed 2 August 2011.

18. William Ansah Sessarakoo, *The Royal African: or, memoirs of the young prince of Annamaboe. Comprehending a distinct account of his country and family; his elder brother's voyage to France, and Reception there; the Manner in which himself was confided by his Father to the Captain who sold him; his Condition while a Slave in Barbadoes; the true Cause of his being redeemed; his Voyage from thence; and Reception here in England. Interspers'd throughout With several Historical Remarks on the Commerce of the European Nations, whose Subjects frequent the Coast of Guinea. To which is prefixed A Letter from the Author to a Person of Distinction, in Reference to some natural Curiosities in Africa; as well as explaining the Motives which induced him to compose these Memoirs* (London: For W. Reeve, 1749), 16, 15, 16, 42.

19. Venture Smith, *A Narrative of the Life and Adventures of Venture, A Native of Africa: But resident above sixty years in the United States of America. Related by Himself* (New London: C. Holt, 1798), 13.

20. These two brief memoirs are held in the Bodleian Library, Oxford University. They have been transcribed in Jerome S. Handler, "Life Histories of Enslaved Africans in Barbados," *Slavery & Abolition*, 19 (1998), 129–140, 133–134, 133; *The Case of the Royal African-Company And of the Plantations* (London, 1714), 2.

21. Seth Rockman, *Scraping By: Wage Labor, Slavery, and Survival in Early Baltimore* (Baltimore: Johns Hopkins University Press, 2009), 2. See also Peter Linebaugh and Marcus Rediker, *The Many-Headed Hydra: Sailors, Slaves, Commoners and the Hidden History of the Revolutionary Atlantic* (Boston: Beacon Press, 2000), 40–70, and Justin Roberts, *Sunup to Sundown: Slavery and the Enlightenment in the British Atlantic, 1750–1807* (Cambridge: Cambridge University Press, forthcoming).

22. Roach, *Cities of the Dead*, 4.

Chapter 1. England

1. Jane Whittle, *The Development of Agrarian Capitalism: Land and Labour in Norfolk, 1440–1580* (Oxford: Clarendon Press, 2000), 286–287, 299, 275–276.

2. Samuel Cohn, "After the Black Death: Labour Legislation and Attitudes Towards Labour in Late-Medieval Western Europe," *Economic History Review*, 60 (2007), 457–485; Ann Kussmaul, *Servants in Husbandry in Early Modern England* (Cambridge: Cambridge University Press, 1981).

3. Christopher Tomlins, *Freedom Bound: Law, Labor, and Civic Identity in Colonizing English America, 1580–1865* (Cambridge: Cambridge University Press, 2010), 234–235; Robert J. Steinfeld, *The Invention of Free Labor: The Employment Relation in English and American Law and Culture, 1350–1870* (Chapel Hill: University of North Carolina Press, 1991), 22–23.

4. Whittle, *Development of Agrarian Capitalism*, 255.

5. Samuel Johnson, "Family," in *A Dictionary of the English Language*, Vol. 1 (London: W. Strahan, 1755); Keith Wrightson, *Earthly Necessities: Economic Lives in Early Modern Britain* (New Haven: Yale University Press, 2000), 30–33; Naomi Tadmor, "The Concept of the Household-Family in Eighteenth-Century England," *Past & Present*, 151 (1996), 111–140. Steinfeld has argued that early modern labor was far from free, and was more bound and unfree than has been assumed, and thus more intimately related to the forms of indentured servitude and bound labor employed in colonies. See Steinfeld, *The Invention of Free Labor*.

6. Jane Whittle, "Servants in Rural England c. 1450–1650: Hired Work as a Means of Accumulating Wealth and Skills Before Marriage," in *The Marital Economy in Scandinavia and Britain, 1400–1900*, ed. Maria Ågren and Amy Louise Erickson (Aldershot: Ashgate, 2005), 91–92; Wrightson, *Earthly Necessities*, 32–33; Kussmaul, *Servants in Husbandry*, 3, 34. See also Donald Woodward, "Early Modern Servants in Husbandry Revisited," *Agricultural History Review*, 48 (2000), 141–150; Ilana Krausman Ben-Amos, "Service and the Coming of Age of Young Men in Seventeenth Century England," *Continuity and Change*, 3 (1988), 41–64; Carolyn Steedman, "Service and Servitude in the World of Labour: Service in England, 1750–1820," in *The Age of Culture Revolutions: Britain and France, 1750–1820*, ed. Colin Jones and Dror Wahrman (Berkeley: University of California Press, 2002), 124–136; E. A. Wrigley, R. S. Davies, J. E. Oppen, and R. S. Schofield, *English Population History from Family Reconstitution, 1580–1837* (Cambridge: Cambridge University Press, 1997), 130.

7. Steinfeld, *The Invention of Free Labor*, 19; K. D. M. Snell, *Annals of the Labouring Poor: Social Change and Agrarian England, 1660–1900* (1985; Cambridge: Cambridge University Press, 1987), 73.

8. Susan Dwyer Amussen, *An Ordered Society: Gender and Class in Early Modern England* (New York: Columbia University Press, 1988), 160–161.

9. Kussmaul, *Servants in Husbandry*, 9, 34–49, 32–33, 44–47, 70–75; Wrightson, *Earthly Necessities*, 35; Amussen, *An Ordered Society*, 40.

10. Sir William Wentworth, "Advice to his Son" (1604), quoted in Woodward, "Early Modern Servants," 143.

11. Henry Best (1642), quoted in Woodward, "Early Modern Servants," 142.

12. Alexandra Shepard, "Poverty, Labour and the Language of Social Description in Early Modern England," *Past & Present*, 201 (2008), 63, 51–95; Craig Muldrew, *Food, Energy and the Creation of Industriousness: Work and Material Culture in Agrarian England, 1550–1780* (Cambridge: Cambridge University Press, 2011), 219, 319.

13. For a classic analysis of this Puritan position, see Christopher Hill, *Society and Puritanism in Pre-Revolutionary England* (1958; New York: St. Martin's Press, 1997), 99–117, 219–253. See also David Underdown, *Revel, Riot and Rebellion: Popular Politics and Culture in England, 1603–1660* (Oxford: Oxford University Press, 1985), 9–43; David Underdown, *Fire from Heaven: Life in an English Town in the Seventeenth Century* (New Haven: Yale University Press, 1992), 61–89; and Keith Wrightson and David Levine, *Poverty and Piety in an English Village: Terling, 1525–1700* (1979; Oxford: Clarendon Press, 2001), 110–141, 173–185.

14. Robert A. Dodgshon, *Land and Society in Early Scotland* (Oxford: Clarendon Press, 1981), 101–114, 118–124; Wrightson, *Earthly Necessities*, 36, 121, 136–145; Wrigley et al., *English Population History*, 614–615; E. A. Wrigley and R. S. Schofield, *The Population History of England, 1541–1871: A Reconstruction* (Cambridge, Mass.: Harvard University Press, 1981), 528; J. R. Wordie, "The Chronology of English Enclosure, 1500–1914," *Economic History Review*, 36 (1983).

15. Margaret Spuffod, *Contrasting Communities: English Villagers in the Sixteenth and Seventeenth Centuries* (Cambridge: Cambridge University Press, 1974), 76, 80–82, 165–166; *The Agrarian History of England and Wales*, Vol. 4: *1500–1640*, ed. Joan Thirsk (Cambridge: Cambridge University Press, 1967), 406–409.

16. Thomas More, *Utopia, translated by Ralph Robynson, 1556*, ed. David Harris Sacks (Boston: Bedford/St. Martin's, 1999), 101. See also Joan Thirsk, "Tudor Enclosures," in Thirsk, *The Rural Economy of England: Collected Essays* (London: Hambledon Press, 1984), 65–83.

17. More, *Utopia*, 101, 102.

18. More, *Utopia*, 103. See also Thirsk, "Tudor Enclosures"; *The Agrarian History of England and Wales*, Vol. 3: *1348–1500*, ed. Edward Miller (Cambridge: Cambridge University Press, 1991), 810; and Robert C. Allen, *Enclosure and the Yeoman* (Oxford: Clarendon Press, 1992).

19. Spuffod, *Contrasting Communities*, 13; E. A. Wrigley, "A Simple Model of London's Importance in Changing English Society and Economy, 1650–1750," *Past & Present*, 37 (1967), 49.

20. Wrightson, *Earthly Necessities*, 148–150, 159–160, 197–198; Susan Dyer Amussen, *Caribbean Exchanges: Slavery and the Transformation of English Society, 1640–1700* (Chapel Hill: University of North Carolina Press, 2007), 16; Dodgshon, *Land and Society*, 251.

21. "An Homyly against Idlenesse," in *The seconde tome of homilies of such matters as were promised and intituled in the former part of Homylyes, set out by the aucthoritie of the Queenes Maiestie. And to be read in euery paryshe churche agreablye* (London: Richarde Iugge, 1563), 264, 265.

22. A. L. Beier, *Masterless Men: The Vagrancy Problem in England, 1560–1640* (New York: Methuen, 1985).

23. Smith, cited in Tomlins, *Freedom Bound*, 228–231; William Gouge, *Of Domesticall Duties: Eight Treatises* (London: John Haviland for William Bladen, 1622), 18. See also Amussen, *An Ordered Society*, 31–38; John Donoghue, "Unfree Labor, Imperialism, and Radical Republicanism in the Atlantic World, 1630–1661," *Labor: Studies in Working Class History of the Americas*, 1 (2004), 47–68; Tomlins, *Freedom Bound*, 236–245; Steinfeld, *The Invention of Free Labor*, 23–24; Kussmaul, *Servants in Husbandry*, 33–34.

24. Whittle, *Development of Agrarian Capitalism*, 298, 279, 275–276, 287, 290, 296. See also L. R. Poos, "The Social Context of Statute of Laborers Enforcement," *Law and History Review*, 1 (1983), 31–33; R. Keith Kelsall, "Wage Regulation Under the Statute of Artificers," in *Wage Regulation in Pre-Industrial England*, ed. Walter E. Minchinton (Newton Abbot: David and Charles, 1972), 124–127.

25. Paul Slack, *The English Poor Law, 1531–1782* (Cambridge: Cambridge University Press, 1990), 17–36; Steve Hindle, *On the Parish? The Micro-Politics of Poor Relief in Rural England, c. 1550–1750* (Oxford: Clarendon Press, 2004), 2–3.

26. Sir Thomas Smith, *De republica Anglorum The maner of gouernement or policie of the realme of England, compiled by the honorable man Thomas Smyth, Doctor of the ciuil lawes, knight, and principall secretarie vnto the two most worthie princes, King Edwarde the sixt, and Queene Elizabeth. Seene and allowe* (London: Henrie Midleton for Gregorie Seton, 1583), 113; Hindle, *On the Parish*, 205–207.

27. "An Act Touching Divers Orders for Artificers, Labourers, Servants of Husbandry and Apprentices" (1563), *Select Statutes and Other Constitutional Documents Illustrative of the Reigns of Elizabeth and James I*, ed. George Prothero (Oxford: Clarendon Press, 1894), 50; Hindle, *On the Parish*, 213.

28. C. S. L. Davies, "Slavery and Protector Somerset: The Vagrancy Act of 1547," *Economic History Review*, 2nd ser., 19 (1966), 534, 533–549. See also Slack, *The English Poor Law*, 10.

29. Davies, "Slavery and Protector Somerset," 541, 545; Christopher A. Whatley, "Scottish 'Collier Serfs,' British Coal Workers? Aspects of Scottish Collier Society in the Eighteenth Century," *Labour History Review*, 60 (1995), 66–79; Whatley, "'The Fettering Bonds of Brotherhood': Combination and Labour Relations in the Scottish Coal-Mining Industry," *Social History*, 12 (1987), 139–154.

30. A. L. Beier, "'A New Serfdom: Labor Laws, Vagrancy Statutes, and Labor Discipline in England, 1350–1800," in *Cast Out: Vagrancy and Homelessness in Global and Historical Perspective*, ed. A. L. Beier and Paul Ocobock (Athens: Ohio University Press, 2008), 35–38.

31. Steinfeld, *The Invention of Free Labor*, 3–6.

32. Simon P. Newman, "Theorizing Class in an Atlantic World: A Case Study of Glasgow," in *Class Matters: Early North America and the Atlantic World*, ed. Simon

Middleton and Billy G. Smith (Philadelphia: University of Pennsylvania Press, 2008), 16–34; Wrightson, *Earthly Necessities*, 240, 316–317.

33. Tomlins, *Freedom Bound*, 31–66. See also David W. Galenson, *White Servitude in Colonial America: An Economic Analysis* (Cambridge: Cambridge University Press, 1981), 15–19, and Richard S. Dunn, "Servants and Slaves: The Recruitment and Employment of Labor," in *Colonial British America: Essays in the New History of the Early Modern Era*, ed. Jack P. Greene and J. R. Pole (Baltimore: Johns Hopkins University Press, 1984), 157–194.

34. Galenson, *White Servitude*, 125.

35. John Donoghue, "Child Slavery and the Global Economy: Historical Perspectives on a Contemporary Problem," in *A Child's Right to a Healthy Environment*, ed. James Garbarino and Garry Sigman (New York: Springer, 2000), 205–207.

Chapter 2. The Gold Coast

1. Paul E. Lovejoy, *Transformations in Slavery: A History of Slavery in Africa*, African studies series, 2nd ed. (Cambridge: Cambridge University Press, 2000), xxi.

2. *The Golden Coast, Or a Description of Guinney* (London: printed for S. Speed, 1665), 14; Herbert S. Klein, *The Atlantic Slave Trade* (Cambridge: Cambridge University Press, 1999), 56; Thornton, *Africa and Africans in the Making of the Atlantic World, 1400–1800* (Cambridge: Cambridge University Press, 1992), 74; J. D. Fage, "Slavery and the Slave Trade in the Context of West African History," in *Forced Migration: The Impact of the Export Slave Trade on African Societies*, ed. J. E. Inikori (London: Hutchinson University Library for Africa, 1982), 159; Lovejoy, *Transformations in Slavery*, 120–123.

3. J. D. Fage, "Slaves and Society in Western Africa, c. 1445–c. 1700," *The Worlds of Unfree Labour: From Indentured Servitude to Slavery*, ed. Colin A. Palmer (Aldershot: Ashgate, 1998), 259–264; James Kwesi Anquandah, "Researching the Historic Slave Trade in Ghana: An Overview," in *The Transatlantic Slave Trade: Landmarks, Legacies, Expectations*, ed. James Kwesi Anquandah (Accra: Sub-Saharan Publishers, 2007), 23–56; Akosua Adoma Perbi, *A History of Indigenous Slavery in Ghana from the Fifteenth to the Nineteenth Century* (Accra: Sub-Saharan Publishers, 2004), 13–68.

4. Anquandah, "Researching the Historic Slave Trade in Ghana"; Kwabena Adu-Boahen, "Bondage Under the Guns of the Forts: European Presence and Slavery in Coastal West Africa, Seventeenth Century," unpublished working paper presented at symposium on "Africa, Europe, and the Americas, 1500–1700," Ghana, 2009.

5. Fage, "Slaves and Society in Western Africa," 269–276.

6. Thomas Phillips, *A Journal of a Voyage Made in the Hannibal of London, Ann. 1693, 1694, from England, to Cape Monseradoe, in Africa: And Thence along the Coast of Guiney to Whidaw, the island of St. Thomas. And so forward to Barbadoes*, in Awnsham Churchill and John Churchill, eds., *A Collection of Voyages and Travels, Some Now First Printed from Original Manuscripts, Others Now Published in English. In Six Volumes* (London, 1732), VI, 206.

7. Nathaniel Senior to the Committee, Cape Coast Castle, 23 May 1759, Inward Letter Books, Second, 1753–1762, RAC, T70/30, 292. "8 ounces" refers to any trade goods valued at eight ounces of gold dust, the standard for exchange of goods, commodities, and even services and labor.

8. William Hickes, "Remarks on the Scheme of Trade," appended to Cape Coast "Warehouse Keepers Accot. for Feb. 1797," "Scheme of Goods wanted And Abstract of Letters from the Coast of Africa so far as relate to the Committee of Goods, No. 2, From August the 26th 1705 to February the 3d 1719," RAC, T70/22, 36.

9. William Hickes, "Remarks on the Scheme of Trade"; Dalby Thomas to RAC, Cape Coast Castle, 26 March 1706, "Schemes of Goods Wanted and Abstracts of Letters from the Coast of Africa so far as relate to the Committee of Goods, No. 2, From August the 26th 1705 to February the 3d 1719," T70/22, 9; "Recd. 10 January 1706," "Schemes of Goods wanted And Abstract of Letters from the Coast of Africa so far as relate to the Committee of Goods. No. 2. From August the 26th 1705 to February the 3d 1719," RAC, T70/22, 2.

10. Kwame Yeboa Daaku, *Trade and Politics on the Gold Coast, 1600 to 1720* (Oxford: Clarendon Press, 1970), 15; Klein, *Atlantic Slave Trade*, 7–8, 18; Lovejoy, *Transformations in Slavery*, 47–58, 80, 68.

11. Klein, *Atlantic Slave Trade*, 52; Ira Berlin, *Many Thousands Gone: The First Two Centuries of Slavery in North America* (Cambridge, Mass.: Harvard University Press, 1998), 21–22; Christopher R. DeCorse, *An Archaeology of Elmina: Africans and Europeans on the Gold Coast, 1400–1900* (Washington, D.C.: Smithsonian Institution Press, 2001), 32–36; P. E. H. Hair and Robin Law, "The English in West Africa to 1700," in *The Oxford History of the British Empire*, Vol. 1: *The Origins of Empire: British Overseas Enterprise to the Close of the Seventeenth Century*, ed. Nicholas Canny (Oxford: Oxford University Press, 1998), 241; Daaku, *Trade and Politics on the Gold Coast*; Ray A. Kea, *Settlements, Trade, and Polities in the Seventeenth-Century Gold Coast* (Baltimore: Johns Hopkins University Press, 1982); J. D. Fage, "Upper and Lower Guinea," in *The Cambridge History of Africa*, Vol. 3: *From c. 1050 to c. 1600*, ed. Ronald Oliver (Cambridge: Cambridge University Press, 1977), 463–518; Walter Rodney, "The Gold Coast," in *The Cambridge History of Africa*, Vol. 4: *From c. 1600 to c. 1790*, ed. Richard Gray (Cambridge: Cambridge University Press, 1975), 296–324; Hair and Law, "English in West Africa," 246–259. The gold trade initially attracted Europeans to the area and triggered the growth of African trading communities along the coast. By the early sixteenth century Portuguese traders were purchasing over four hundred kilograms of gold per annum; this constituted approximately one-quarter of West African gold production at that time, and may have accounted for as much as 10 percent of the total world supply. See Daaku, *Trade and Politics*, 8.

12. Rodney, "The Gold Coast," 296–317; Rebecca Shumway, *The Fante and the Transatlantic Slave Trade* (Rochester: University of Rochester Press, 2011), 8–17; Fage, "Upper and Lower Guinea," 494–495.

13. The Portuguese castle at Elmina was conquered by the Dutch in 1637, and it remained in Dutch hands for the remainder of the transatlantic slave trading era. See Albert van Dantzig, *Forts and Castles of Ghana* (Accra: Sedco, 1980); Kwesi J. Anquandah, *Castles and Forts of Ghana* (Atalante: Ghana Museums and Monuments Board, 1999); Rosemary M. Cave, *Gold Coast Forts* (London: Thomas Nelson and Sons, 1957); W. J. Varley, "The Castles and Forts of the Gold Coast," *Transactions of the Gold Coast and Togoland Historical Society*, 1 (1952), 1–17; Rodney, "The Guinea Coast," 307–309; David Northrup, "West Africans and the Atlantic, 1550–1800," in *Black Experience and the Empire*, ed. Philip D. Morgan and Sean Hawkins (Oxford: Oxford University Press, 2004), 41.

14. Kea, *Settlements, Trade, and Polities*, 38; Berlin, *Many Thousands Gone*, 21–22; DeCorse, *An Archaeology of Elmina*, 32–36.

15. Rodney, "The Gold Coast," 307–321.

16. Lovejoy, *Transformations in Slavery*, 47, 49, 58; Klein, *Atlantic Slave Trade*, 33–34.

17. Erick Tilleman, *En Kort Og Enfoldig Beretning Om Det Landskab Guinea Og Dets Beskaffenhed (1697): A Short and Simple Account of the Country Guinea and Its Nature*, trans. and ed. Selena Axelrod Winsnes (Madison: University of Wisconsin Press, 1994), 19; Nicolas Villault, *A Relation of the Coasts of Africk Called Guinee: With a Description of the Countrys, Manners and Customs of the Inhabitants; of the Productions of the Earth, and the Merchandise and Commodities it affords; with some Historical Observations upon the Coasts. Being Collected in a Voyage by the Sieur Villault, Escuyer, Sieur de Bellefond, in the years 1666 and 1667* (London: printed for John Starkey, 1670), 135; John Atkins, *A Voyage to Guinea, Brazil and the West Indies, In His Majesty's Ships, The Swallow and Weymouth* (London: printed for Caesar Ward and Raymond Chandler, 1735), 105; P. E. H. Hair, Adam Jones, and Robin Law, eds., *Barbot on Guinea: The Writings of Jean Barbot on West Africa, 1678–1712* (London: The Hakluyt Society, 1992), II, 334; Samuel Eyles to RAC, "Cabo Corso Castle," 14 January 1707/ 1708, "Abstracts of letters Received by the Royal African Company of England from the Coast of Africa From March the 20th 1705 to August the 15th 1715," RAC, T70/5, 46; John Roberts to RAC, Cape Coast Castle, 11 July 178, "Inward Letter Books, B, 1773–1781," RAC, T70/32, 122; Albert van Dantzig, "Effects of the Atlantic Slave Trade on Some West African Societies," in Inikori, ed., *Forced Migration*, 188.

18. Rodney, "The Guinea Coast," 307; Klein, *Atlantic Slave Trade*, 105, 91–92.

19. Van Dantzig, "Effects of the Atlantic Slave Trade on Some West African Societies," 188, 198–199; Lovejoy, *Transformations in Slavery*, 5, 19–20.

20. "List of the Principal Kings, Caboceers, and others in the Pay of the Committee as they stood ultimo December 1776," Table Number 10, Report on the Public Accounts of Cape Coast Castle and the Out Forts depending thereon from the first day of January 1770 to the 31st day of December 1776, RAC, T70/155, 14–16; David Mills to RAC, Cape Coast Castle, 30 December 1775, Inward Letter Books, B, 1773–1781, RAC, T70/32, 30–31.

21. "Presents and Dashees," Report on the Public Accounts of Cape Coast Castle and the Out Forts depending thereon from the first day of January 1770 to the 31st day of December 1776, RAC, T70/155, 14–16.

22. "Charges and Palavers," Report on the Public Accounts of Cape Coast Castle and the Out Forts depending thereon from the first day of January 1770 to the 31st day of December 1776, RAC, T70/155, 26–27.

23. Willem Bosman, *A New and Accurate Description of the Coast of Guinea, Divided into the Gold, the Slave, and the Ivory Coasts* (London: for James Knapton, 1705), 56; Thomas Melvil to the Committee, Cape Coast Castle, 20 June 1754, Inward Letter Books, Second, 1753–1762, RAC, T70/30, 62, 61; John Apperley to the Committee, Cape Coast Castle, 13 June 1754, Inward Letter Books, Second, 1753–1762, RAC, T70/30, 58.

24. "Presents and Dashees," Report on the Public Accounts of Cape Coast Castle and the Out Forts depending thereon from the first day of January 1770 to the 31st day of December 1776, RAC, T70/155, 14–16.

25. "Free Canoemen & Labourers Hire" and "Presents and Dashees," Report on the Public Accounts of Cape Coast Castle and the Out Forts depending thereon from the first day of January 1770 to the 31st day of December 1776, RAC, T70/155, 11–12, 13.

26. "List of the Principal Kings, Caboceers and others in the Pay of the Committee as they stood ultimo December 1776," Report on the Public Accounts of Cape Coast Castle and the Out Forts depending thereon from the first day of January 1770 to the 31st day of December 1776, RAC, T70/155, Table 10.

27. Robert J. Steinfeld, *The Invention of Free Labor: The Employment Relation in English and American Law and Culture, 1350–1870* (Chapel Hill: University of North Carolina Press, 1991), 55–73.

Chapter 3. Barbados

1. Hilary McD. Beckles, *A History of Barbados: From Amerindian Settlement to Nation-State*, (Cambridge: Cambridge University Press, 1990), 2–6; John Scott, "The Description of Barbados," in P. F. Campbell, *Some Early Barbadian History, As Well As The Text of a Book Published Anonymously in 1741 Entitled Memoirs of the First Settlement of the Island of Barbados . . . And A transcription of a Manuscript Entitled The Description of Barbados Written About the Year 1741 by Major John Scott* (Wildey, St. Michael, Barbados: Caribbean Graphics & Letchworth, 1993), 4–11, 27. The best single study of labor in early Barbados is Hilary McD. Beckles, *White Servitude and Black Slavery in Barbados, 1627–1715* (Knoxville: University of Tennessee Press, 1989). Beckles adopts a Marxist perspective, describing "a market system of brutal servitude" (xiv) for white bound laborers.

2. Lois Carr and Lorena S. Walsh, "Economic Diversification and Labor Organization in the Chesapeake, 1650–1820," in *Work and Labor in Early America*, ed. Stephen Innes (Chapel Hill: University of North Carolina Press, 1988), 155. See also the argument made by Richard Dunn in the first chapter of his magisterial work on Caribbean

slavery, entitled "Beyond the Line." See Richard S. Dunn, *Sugar and Slaves: The Rise of the Planter Class in the English West Indies, 1624–1713* (Chapel Hill: University of North Carolina Press, 1972), 3–45.

3. P. F. Campbell, *Some Early Barbadian History*, 26–57; Beckles, *A History of Barbados*, 7–13; Dunn, *Sugar and Slaves*, 46–47.

4. Sir Henry Colt, "The Voyage of Sr Henrye Colt Knight to Ye Ilands of Ye Antilleas In Ye Shipp Called Ye *Alexander*" (1631), from Cambridge University Library MSS., Mm. 3, 9, in *Colonising Expeditions to the West Indies and Guiana, 1623–1667*, ed. Vincent T. Harlow, Publications of the Hakluyt Society, 2nd ser., 56 (London: for the Hakluyt Society, 1925), 66–67, 75; John Oldmixon, *The British Empire in America, Containing the History of the Discovery, Settlement, Progress and Present State of all the British Colonies, on the Continent and Islands of America* (London: for John Nicholson, Benjamin Tooke, Richard Parker, Ralph Smith, 1708), II, 7.

5. Richard Ligon, *A True & Exact History of the Island of Barbados. Illustrated with a Mapp of the Island, as also the Principall Trees and Plants there, set forth in their due Proportions and Shapes, drawne out by their severall and respective Scales. Together with the Ingenio that makes the Sugar, with the Plots of the severall Houses, and other places, that are used in the whole process of Sugar-making, viz. the Boyling-room, the Filling-room, the Curing-house, Still-house, and Furnaces; All cut in Copper* (London: for Humphrey Moseley, 1657), 21, 23, 24.

6. Ligon, *A True & Exact History*, 22, 24.

7. For a discussion of the traditional view of the "sugar revolution," see B. W. Higman, "The Making of the Sugar Revolution," in *In the Shadow of the Plantation: Caribbean History and Legacy*, ed. Alvin O. Thompson (Kingston, Jamaica: Ian Randle, 2002), 40–71. The recent revisions of this view are developed in Russell Menard, *Sweet Negotiations: Sugar, Slavery, and Plantation Agriculture in Early Barbados* (Charlottesville: University of Virginia Press, 2006), xii–xiii, 4–5, 34–35.

8. Dunn, *Sugar and Slaves*, 58, 91, 96–98; Richard S. Dunn, "The Barbados Census of 1680: Profile of the Richest Colony in English America," *William and Mary Quarterly*, 3rd ser., 26 (1969), 7–8.

9. Historians have traditionally accepted that Dutch merchants financed the transfer of sugar from the mainland to Barbados, which involved learning to grow the crop and to harvest and then produce sugar, as well as furnishing an increasingly large supply of slaves. See, for example, Dunn, *Sugar and Slaves*, 66–67. More recently, however, Russell Menard has argued that there is little direct evidence of extensive Dutch activity, while there is abundant evidence that Martin Noell and other London merchants supplied the planters with capital and slaves. See Menard, *Sweet Negotiations*; Stuart B. Schwartz, *Sugar Plantations in the Formation of Brazilian Society: Bahia, 1550–1835* (Cambridge: Cambridge University Press, 1985), 6–19, 139–146.

10. Dunn, *Sugar and Slaves*, 65, 188–189, 199–200. Russell Menard has argued that "Sugar did not transform Barbados on its own; rather, it sped up and intensified a process already under way in response to the activities of planters who grew what

are usually considered minor crops." However, in the scale of sugar agriculture and production, the size of the workforce it required, and the kinds of work undertaken, and in the production of wealth for the planter elite, sugar changed Barbados in the most dramatic of fashions. Menard, *Sweet Negotiations*, 4.

11. William Hay to Archibald Hay, Barbados, 10 September 1645, Hay of Haystoun Family Papers, National Archives of Scotland, GD/34/945.

12. Beckles, *White Servitude*, 5; Menard, *Sweet Negotiations*, 36. See also Ann Kussmaul, *Servants in Husbandry in Early Modern England* (Cambridge: Cambridge University Press, 1981); David W. Galenson, *Traders, Planters, and Slaves: Market Behaviour in Early English America* (Cambridge: Cambridge University Press, 1986), 8. Galenson has argued that indentured servants in British colonies closely resembled English servants in husbandry, but his study does not take into account the unique conditions and the extremes of Barbados. See Galenson, *White Servitude in Colonial America: An Economic Analysis* (Cambridge: Cambridge University Press, 1981), 5–8.

13. "List of Christi[a]n Servants, Slaves and livestock on the Estate of Barbara Newton, 11 April 1687," MS. Collection 523, ms. 1105/1, Newton Papers, Special Collections, University of London Library. A collection including twenty-six indentures of servants bound to travel to and labor in Barbados in 1683 included three different preprinted forms, each including language of this sort. See Indentured servant contracts for the colonies of Maryland, Virginia, Pennsylvania, and Barbados, January to December 1683, Folger Shakespeare Library, Manuscripts Collection, V.b.16.

14. "An Act establishing the Court of Common-Pleas in this Island" (29 August 1661), *Acts of Assembly, Passed in the Island of Barbadoes, From 1648, to 1718* (London: John Baskett, 1721), 14; "An Act that the bringing Writs of Errors, and other Equitable Matters, before the Governor and Council, to be by them determined" (15 January 1655), *Acts of Assembly*, 10; "An Act for the good Governing of Servants, and Ordaining of Rights between Masters and Servants" (27 September 1661), *Acts of Assembly*, 24, 27.

15. Campbell, *Some Early Barbadian History*, 92; Indentured servant contracts, Folger Library; Beckles, *White Servitude*, 44.

16. "An ACT to prevent the prejudice that may happen to this Island, by loose and vagrant Persons, in and about the same," *Acts, Passed in the Island of Barbados. From 1643 to 1762, inclusive; Carefully revised, innumerable Errors corrected; and the Whole compared and examined, with the original Acts, In the Secretary's Office, By the Late Richard Hall . . .* (London: printed for Richard Hall, 1764), 18.

17. Beckles, *White Servitude*, 18; Menard, *Sweet Negotiations*, 34–35.

18. Ligon, *A True & Exact History*, 24.

19. Ligon, *A True & Exact History*, 85, 22.

20. Ligon, *A True & Exact History*, 85–86; Galenson, *Traders, Planters, and Slaves*, 2; Beckles, *A History of Barbados*, 22.

21. "Some Observations of the Island of Barbados," *Calendar of State Papers, Colonial Series, America and West Indies, 1661–1668*, ed. W. Noel Sainsbury (London: H.M. Stationery Office, 1880), V, 529; Oldmixon, *British Empire in America*, 79; Scott, "The

Description of Barbados," 259; Dunn, *Sugar and Slaves*, 46, 48, 85. See also Beckles, *A History of Barbados*, 13–15, 20–24; Campbell, *Some Early Barbadian History*, 57–59; Menard, *Sweet Negotiations*, 34.

22. Beckles, *White Servitude*, 39.

23. "Act for the good Governing of Servants," *Acts of Assembly*, 22, 23.

Chapter 4. "White Slaves"

1. An intercepted letter from William George to anonymous, May 1655, in *A Collection of the State Papers of John Thurloe, Esq; Secretary, First, to the Council of State, And afterwards to The Two Protectors, Oliver and Richard Cromwell* (London: Thomas Birch, 1742), III, 495. This is an early use of the term "Barbadosed," referring to the transportation of white Britons—usually without their consent—to labor on Barbados plantations. See also Mark S. Quintanilla, "Late Seventeenth-Century Indentured Servants in Barbados," *Journal of Caribbean History*, 27 (1993), 114–128; John Donoghue, " 'Out of the Land of Bondage': The English Revolution and the Atlantic Origins of Abolition," *American Historical Review*, 115 (2010), 960; Hilary McD. Beckles, *White Servitude and Black Slavery in Barbados, 1627–1715* (Knoxville: University of Tennessee Press, 1989), 68.

2. Trevor Burnard, "Thomas Thistlewood Becomes a Creole," in Bruce Clayton and John A. Salmond, eds., *Varieties of Southern History: New Essays on a Region and Its People* (Westport, Conn.: Greenwood Press, 1996), 100; "Certaine Propositions for the better accommodating ye Foreigne Plantations with Servants reported from the Committee to the Councell of Foreign Plantations" (1664), Papers Relating to English Colonies in America and the West Indies, 1627–1699, Egerton 2395, British Library Manuscripts Collection, 277; Hilary McD. Beckles, "Land Distribution and Class Formation in Barbados, 1630–1700: The Rise of a Wage Proletariat," *Journal of the Barbados Museum and Historical Society*, 36 (1980), 137, 139–140; Hilary McD. Beckles, *A History of Barbados: From Amerindian Settlement to Nation-State* (Cambridge: Cambridge University Press, 1989), 15.

3. Aubrey Gwynn, "Indentured Servants and Negro Slaves in Barbados (1642–1650)," *Studies: An Irish Quarterly Review*, 19 (1930), 292.

4. Sir Henry Colt, "The Voyage of Sr Henry Colt Knight to Ye Ilands of Ye Antilleas In Ye Shipp Called Ye *Alexander*" (1631), in *Colonising Expeditions to the West Indies and Guiana, 1623–1667*, ed. Vincent T. Harlow (London: for the Hakluyt Society, 1925), 66, 74; Beckles, *White Servitude*, 2.

5. "Certaine Propositions," 277. The Council existed between 1660 and 1672, at which point it was supplanted by the Council of Trade and Foreign Plantations, allowing us to date this document. See G. E. Aylmer, *The Crown's Servants: Government and the Civil Service Under Charles II, 1660–1685* (Oxford: Oxford University Press, 2002), 50–55.

6. "Certaine Propositions," 277–278; Beckles, *White Servitude*, 48; John Oldmixon, *The British Empire in America, Containing the History of the Discovery, Settlement,*

Progress and present State of all the British Colonies, on the Continent and Islands of America (London: for John Nicholson, Benjamin Tooke, Richard Parker, Ralph Smith, 1708), II, 113.

7. Henry Whistler, "A Journall of a voyadg from Stokes Bay and Intended by Gods assistance for the West Inga: and performed by the Right Honorable Generall Penn: Admirall: As folowes. Taken by Mr. Henry Whistler, 1654," Sloane Ms. 3926, Manuscripts Collection, British Library, 9.

8. Richard Ligon, *A True & Exact History of the Island of Barbados. Illustrated with a Mapp of the Island, as also the Principall Trees and Plants there, set forth in their due Proportions and Shapes, drawne out by their severall and respective Scales. Together with the Ingenio that makes the Sugar, with the Plots of the seveall Houses, and other places, that are used in the whole process of Sugar-making, viz. the Boyling-room, the Filling-room, the Curing-house, Still-house, and Furnaces; All cut in Copper* (London: for Humphrey Moseley, 1657), 40. This argument has been developed by Hilary Beckles, who disagrees with previous historians by concluding that relatively few former servants were able to join the ranks of the planters. Beckles, "Land Distribution and Class Formation," 136–137.

9. Beckles, *White Servitude*, 5; Beckles, *A History of Barbados*, 17, 24–25.

10. Beckles, *A History of Barbados*, 29; Russell R. Menard, *Sweet Negotiations: Sugar, Slavery, and Plantation Agriculture in Early Barbados* (Charlottesville: University of Virginia Press, 2006), 44; Richard S. Dunn, "The Barbados Census of 1680: Profile of the Richest Colony in English America," *William and Mary Quarterly*, 3rd ser., 26 (1969), 26–27; "Some Observations on the Island Barbadoes," American and West Indies, Colonial Papers, National Archives, CO 1/21, no. 170, 529.

11. Beckles, *White Servitude*, 80–90, 119; Ligon, *A True & Exact History*, 43.

12. "Certaine Propositions," 277–278. For a dated but still useful study of this group, see Abbot Emerson Smith, *Colonists in Bondage: White Servitude and Convict Labor in America, 1607–1776* (Chapel Hill: University of North Carolina Press, 1947).

13. Beckles, *White Servitude*, 48–49; P. Hume Brown, ed., *The Register of the Privy Council of Scotland* (Glasgow: James Hedderwick and Sons, 1908), 3rd ser., I, 181; II, 101, 195.

14. Brown, *Register of the Privy Council of Scotland*, 3rd ser., III, 259.

15. Christopher Jeaffreson to Colonel Hill, 19 February 1685, in Peter Cordy Jeaffreson, ed., *A Young Squire of the Seventeenth Century. From the Papers (A.D. 1676–1686) of Christopher Jeaffreson of Dullingham House, Cambridgeshire* (London: Hurst and Blackett, 1878), II, 166; Beckles, *White Servitude*, 59.

16. Beckles, *White Servitude*, 49; Untitled document (1667) in Brown, *Register of the Privy Council of Scotland*, 3rd ser., II, 307. See also Ian B. Cowan, *The Scottish Covenanters, 1660–1688* (London: Gollancz, 1976).

17. William Fulbecke, *The Pandectes of the Law of Nations, Contayning Severall Discourses of the questions, points, and matters of law, wherein the nations of the world doe consent and accord* (London: Adam Islip for Thomas Wight, 1602), 46v. See also

Geoffrey Parker, "Early Modern Europe," in *The Laws of War: Constraints on Warfare in the Western World*, ed. Michael Howard, George J. Andreopoulos, and Mark R. Shuman (New Haven: Yale University Press, 40–58.

18. "A German Indentured Servant in Barbados in 1652: The Account of Heinrich Von Uchteritz," ed. and trans. Alexander Gunkel and Jerome S. Handler, *Journal of the Barbados Museum and Historical Society*, 33 (1970), 92, 93.

19. "A German Indentured Servant in Barbados," 92; Brown, *Register of the Privy Council of Scotland*, 3rd ser., I, 266.

20. Marcellus Rivers and Oxenbridge Foyle, *England's slavery, or Barbados merchandize; represented in a petition to the high court of Parliament, by Marcellus Rivers and Oxenbridge Foyle gentlemen, on behalf of themselves and three-score and ten more free-born Englishmen sold (uncondemned) into slavery: together with letters written to some honourable members of Parliament* (London, 1659), 5.

21. Rivers and Foyle, *England's Slavery*, 5, 6, 8.

22. Nicholas Canny, *Kingdom and Colony: Ireland in the Atlantic World, 1560–1800* (Baltimore: Johns Hopkins University Press, 1988); Oliver Cromwell to William Lenthall, Dublin, 17 September 1649, quoted in O'Callaghan, *To Hell or Barbados*, 25; Sir William Petty's estimate is cited in Peter Linebaugh and Marcus Rediker, *The Many-Headed Hydra: Sailors, Slaves, Commoners and the Hidden History of the Revolutionary Atlantic* (Boston: Beacon Press, 2000), 123 ; "The Clonmacnoise Decrees," 4 December 1649, reprinted in Denis Murphy, *Cromwell in Ireland: A History of Cromwell's Irish Campaign* (Dublin: M. H. Gill & Son, 1897), 406–408; Petition quoted in O'Callaghan, *To Hell or Barbados*, 80.

23. Gwynn, "Indentured Servants and Negro Slaves," 279–294; O'Callaghan, *To Hell or Barbados*, 85–86; Hilary McD. Beckles, "A 'Riotous and Unruly Lot': Irish Indentured Servants and Freemen in the English West Indies, 1644–1713," in *Caribbean Slavery in the Atlantic World*, ed. Verene A. Shepherd and Hilary McD. Beckles (Kingston, Jamaica: Ian Randle, 2000), 231.

24. Hilary McD. Beckles, "Rebels and Reactionaries: The Political Response of White Labourers to Planter-Class Hegemony in Seventeenth Century Barbados," *Journal of Caribbean History*, 15 (1981), 8, 9–10; Beckles, "A 'Riotous and Unruly Lot,'" 226–238.

25. Ligon, *A True & Exact History*, 45, 46; Beckles, "Rebels and Reactionaries," 8, 10; Barbados Council, quoted in Shona Johnston, "'Being None of Any Account': Religion and Economic Status in Seventeenth Century Barbados," unpublished paper presented at the annual conference of the Omohundro Institute of Early American History and Culture, 2009, 4; Board of Trade, Barbados, 20 January 1692, CO 28/1, National Archives. I am grateful to Dr. Johnston for sharing her paper.

26. Jenny Shaw, "Island Purgatory: Irish Catholics and the Reconfiguring of the English Caribbean, 1650–1700" (Ph.D. diss., New York University, 2009), 131–228; "Instructions for the Lord Willoughby of Parham, 4 February 1667," CO1/21, 15, National Archives.

27. John Camden Hotten, ed., *The Original Lists of Persons of Quality: Emigrants; Religious Exiles; Political Rebels; Serving Men Sold for a Term of Years; Apprentices, Children Stolen; Maidens Pressed, and Others Who Went from Great Britain to the American Plantations, 1600–1700* . . . (New York: G. A. Barker and Co., 1931), 317–319; Quintanilla, "Late Seventeenth-Century Indentured Servants in Barbados," 114, 115, 116, 117, 120, 119, 121–122.

28. Henry Pitman, *A Relation of the great sufferings and strange adventures of Henry Pitman, Chirurgeon to the late Duke of Monmouth* . . . (London: Andrew Sowle, 1689), 435–436, 444.

29. Pitman, *A Relation of the great sufferings,* 444, 448; Quintanilla, "Late Seventeenth-Century Indentured Servants," 121–122.

30. Quintanilla, "Late Seventeenth-Century Indentured Servants," 114–117.

31. The list of prisoners is in Treasury: Entry Books of Warrants relating to the Payment of Money, National Archives, T53/42. See also "Prisoners of the '45 Rising," *Journal of the Barbados Museum and Historical Society,* 30 (1963), 73–90. The names, homes, and occupations of 103 of the men sent to Barbados are recorded, and of these 96 have their ages; P. F. Campbell, *Some Early Barbadian History, As Well As The Text of a Book Published Anonymously in 1741 Entitled Memoirs of the First Settlement of the Island of Barbados* . . . *And A transcription of a Manuscript Entitled The Description of Barbados Written About the Year 1741 by Major John Scott* (Wildey, St. Michael, Barbados: Caribbean Graphics & Letchworth Ltd., 1993), 92.

32. Beckles, *White Servitude,* 10; William Dickson, *Letters on Slavery. By William Dickson, Formerly Private Secretary to the Late Hon. Edward Hay, Governor of Barbados* (London: J. Phillips, 1789), 44–45.

33. "Some Observations of the Island Barbadoes," 529; Lord William Willoughby to Williamson, Barbados, 7 May 1667, reprinted in *Analecta Hibernica,* 4 (1932), 265.

34. "The Humble Address and Petition of the Representatives of the Island of Barbados: In behalfe of themselves and the Inhabitants thereof," n.d., reprinted in *Analecta Hibernica,* 4 (1932), 266.

35. Lord William Willoughby to Privy Council, Barbados, 16 December 1667, reprinted in *Analecta Hibernica,* 4 (1932), 266–267.

36. "Grievances of the Inhabitants of Barbados," 24 November 1675, in *Analecta Hibernica,* 4 (1932), 268–269.

37. Oldmixon, *The British Empire in America,* II, 116; James Hooper, Indenture No. 12, March 1683, and Humphrey Golding, Indenture No. 24, 17 May 1683, Indentured servant contracts for the colonies of Maryland, Virginia, Pennsylvania, and Barbados, January to December 1683, Folger Shakespeare Library, Manuscripts Collection, V.B.16. Only two of the twenty-six servants bound for Barbados whose indentures survive in this collection were recorded as having marketable skills.

38. "Proposal of Leonard Wilson, Journeyman carpenter, rejected" (1716), Codrington Plantation Records, Archives of the United Society for the Propagation of

the Gospel, Rhodes House Library, Bodleian Library Oxford, Folder 19; Neville Conville, "Furniture and Furnishings in Barbados During the Seventeenth Century," *Journal of the Barbados Museum and Historical Society*, 24 (1957), 110.

39. Connell, "Furniture and Furnishing," 112; Jerome S. Handler, "A Historical Sketch of Pottery Manufacture in Barbados," *Journal of the Barbados Museum and Historical Society*, 30 (1963), 133, 135–136.

40. Dale W. Tomich, *Slavery in the Circuit of Sugar: Martinique and the World Economy, 1830–1848* (Baltimore: Johns Hopkins University Press, 1990), 126–129; Menard, *Sweet Negotiations*, 17.

41. Drax in Peter Thompson, "Henry Drax's Instructions on the Management of a Seventeenth-Century Barbadian Sugar Plantation," *William and Mary Quarterly*, 3rd ser., 66 (2009), 592. The best contemporary descriptions of these processes can be found in Ligon and in Drax. See Ligon, *A True and Exact History*, 55–56, 89–93, and Thompson, "Drax's Instructions," 591–598. An excellent description and analysis by a historian can be found in Dunn, *Sugar and Slaves*, 191–200.

42. Beckles, *A History of Barbados*, 29; David Watts, "Origins of Barbadian Cane Hole Agriculture," *Journal of the Barbados Museum and Historical Society*, 32 (1968), 143–151.

43. Beckles, "Class Formation in Slave Society: The Rise of a Black Labour Elite and the Development of a White Lumpen Proletariat in Seventeenth Century Barbados," *Journal of the Barbados Museum and Historical Society*, 37 (1983), 20–34; Susan Dwyer Amussen, *Caribbean Exchanges: Slavery and the Transformation of English Society, 1640–1700* (Chapel Hill: University of North Carolina Press, 2007), 64.

44. Ligon, *A True & Exact History*, 44. See also Beckles, *White Servitude*, 120.

45. Ligon, *A True & Exact History*, 44; Beckles, *White Servitude*, 91.

46. Oldmixon, *British Empire in America*, II, 116.

47. Sir Thomas Montgomery to the Lords of Trade and Plantations, Barbados, 1688, quoted in Beckles, *White Servitude*, 92.

48. "Some Observations on the Island Barbadoes," 120.

49. "An ACT for the encouragement of White Servants, and to ascertain their allowance of Provisions and Clothes," *Acts, Passed in the Island of Barbados. From 1643 to 1762, inclusive; Carefully revised, innumerable Errors corrected; and the Whole compared and examined, with the original Acts, In the Secretary's Office, By the Late Richard Hall . . .* (London: printed for Richard Hall, 1764), 157, 158.

50. Oldmixon, *British Empire in America*, II, 116.

51. John Eston to John Newton, London, 1 March 1684, The Newton Papers, Special Collections, University of London Library, MS. Collection 523, Ms. 1055/1, 1.

52. "An Act for the good Governing of Servants, and ordaining the Rights between Masters and Servants," *Acts, Passed in the Island of Barbados. From 1643 to 1762, inclusive; Carefully revised, innumerable Errors corrected; and the Whole compared and examined, with the original Acts, In the Secretary's Office, By the Late Richard Hall . . .* (London: printed for Richard Hall, 1764), 35, 40, 41, 42, 36, 37, 39.

53. Ligon, *A True & Exact History*, 44; Beckles, "Rebels and Reactionaries," 11 ; "An ACT for the encouragement of White Servants," 158, 159.

54. Beckles, "Rebels and Reactionaries."

55. Ligon, *A True & Exact History*, 45.

56. Ligon, *A True & Exact History*, 46; Beckles, "Rebels and Reactionaries," 13.

57. William Dickson, *Mitigation of Slavery, In Two Parts* (London: R. and A. Taylor, 1814), 26; Beckles, "Rebels and Reactionaries," 4–5; Hilary McD. Beckles, "Black Men in White Skins: The Formation of a White Proletariat in West Indian Slave Society," *Journal of Imperial and Commonwealth History*, 15 (1986), 12.

58. Beckles, *A History of Barbados*, 29–30; Menard, *Sweet Negotiations*, 5; John J. McCusker and Russell R. Menard, *The Economy of British America, 1607–1789* (Chapel Hill: University of North Carolina Press, 1985), 165; "An ACT for the encouragement of White Servants" (1703), *Acts, Passed in the Island of Barbados. From 1643 to 1672* (London: printed for Richard Hall, 1764), 158.

59. Beckles, "Black Men in White Skins," 14.

60. Governor Francis Russell to Lords of Trade and Plantations, Barbados, 23 March 1695, "America and West Indies: March 1695," *Calendar of State Papers Colonial, America and West Indies*, Vol. 14: *1693–1696*, ed. J. W. Fortescue (London: Mackie and Company for H.M. Stationery Office, 1903), 446.

61. Russell to Lords of Trade, 23 March 1695, *Calendar of State Papers . . .* , Vol. 14, 446, 447.

62. Beckles, "Rebels and Reactionaries," 18; Beckles; *White Servitude*, 114.

63. Beckles, *White Servitude*, 123–124; Thompson, "Drax's Instructions," 587; Dunn, "Barbados Census of 1680," 8.

64. "List of Christi[a]n Servants," 1–2; Conrade Adams, "Inventory of the Negroes, horses, Cattle and All other Appurtenances belonging to the Rendezvous Plantation. Taken the 17th day of February 1704.5," Codrington Plantation records, Archives of the United Society for the Propagation of the Gospel, Rhodes House Library, Bodleian Library, Oxford, folder 4.

65. Dunn, "The Barbados Census of 1680," 8; Beckles, "Land Distribution," 136–143; Beckles, "Class Formation in Slave Society," 20–34; Christopher Tomlins, *Freedom Bound: Law, Labor, and Civic Identity in Colonizing English America, 1550–1865* (Cambridge: Cambridge University Press, 2010), 8, 13, 17, 2–27.

66. Thompson, "Drax's Instructions," 570; Will of Edmund Burke, 7 March 1661, Will Record Books, Barbados Department of Archives, RB6, XV, 9–10; Will of Desmond Dehollerine, 24 June 1670, in Will Record Books, Barbados Department of Archives, RB6, VIII, 100–101.

67. John Williamson, *Medical and Miscellaneous Observations Relative to the West India Islands*, (Edinburgh: A. Smellie, 1817), I, 27. See also Jill Sheppard, *The "Redlegs" of Barbados: Their Origins and History* (Millwood, N.Y.: KTO Press, 1977); H. N. Coleridge (1834) and Sir Andrew Halliday (1834), quoted in Edward T. Price, "The Redlegs of Barbados," *Journal of the Barbados Museum and Historical Society*, 29 (1962), 48;

John Poyer, *The History of Barbados, From the First Discovery of the Island, In the Year 1605, Till the Accession of Lord Seaforth*, 1801 (London: for J. Mawman, 1808), 60. The *Oxford English Dictionary* suggests that the term "redlegs" was based on "redshanks," a term applied to impoverished Scots and Irishmen from the mid-sixteenth century on. See online *Oxford English Dictionary*, http://www.oed.com/view/Entry/160476# eid26402666, accessed 15 February 2012.

68. Ld. Millington and John Alleyne Holder, "An Inventory taken this Day of the Plantations belonging to the Honrble. & Reverend Society, 1783, May 2," Codrington Plantation Records, Archives of the United Society for the Propagation of the Gospel, Rhodes House Library, Bodleian Library Oxford, Folder 44.

69. "Some Observations on the Island Barbadoes," American and West Indies, Colonial Papers, National Archives, CO 1/21, no. 170, 120; Beckles, "Land Distribution," 140–141; *The Diaries of George Washington*, ed. Donald Jackson and Dorothy Twohig (Charlottesville: University Press of Virginia, 1976), I, 91–92. For discussion of indentured servitude in Virginia, see David W. Galenson, *White Servitude in Colonial America: An Economic Analysis* (New York: Cambridge University Press, 1981); Edmund S. Morgan, *American Slavery, American Freedom: The Ordeal of Colonial Virginia* (New York: W. W. Norton, 1975).

70. "John Poyer's Letter to Lord Seaforth," *Journal of the Barbados Museum and Historical Society*, 8 (1941), 161, 162; David Lambert, *White Creole Culture, Politics and Identity During the Age of Abolition* (Cambridge: Cambridge University Press, 2005), 73–101.

71. George Pinkard, *Notes on the West Indies, Including Observations Relative to the Creoles and Slaves of the Western Colonies, and the Indians of South America: Interspersed with Remarks Upon the Seasoning or Yellow Fever of Hot Climates*, 2nd ed. (London: Baldwin, Cradock and Joy, 1816), I, 309.

72. Pinckard, *Notes on the West Indies*, I, 310–311; Quintanilla, "Late Seventeenth-Century Indentured Servants," 122–123; Edward Eliot, *Christianity and Slavery; In A Course of Lectures Preached at the Cathedral and Parish Church of St. Michael, Barbados* (London: J. Hatchard and Son, 1833), 225–226.

73. Patricia A. Molen, "Population and Social Patterns in Barbados in the Early Eighteenth Century," *William and Mary Quarterly*, 3rd ser., 28 (1971), 287–300.

74. Eliot, *Christianity and Slavery*, 226.

75. Frederic William Naylor Bayley, *Four Years' Residence in the West Indies, During the Years 1826, 7, 8, and 9. By the Son of a Military Officer* (London: William Kidd, 1833), 62.

76. Sir Andrew Halliday, quoted in Price, "The Redlegs of Barbados," 48. See also Hilary McD. Beckles, "Black over White: The 'Poor-White' Problem in Barbados Slave Society," *Immigrants & Minorities*, 7 (1988), 1–15, and Beckles, "Black Men in White Skins," 7–21.

77. Henry Nelson Coleridge, *Six Months in the West Indies in 1825* (New York: G. & C. Carol, and E. Bliss & E. White, 1826), 261.

78. Coleridge, *Six Months in the West Indies*, 262.

79. Lambert, *White Creole Culture*, 19–20, 77–78.

80. Natalie A. Zacek, *Settler Society in the English Leeward Islands, 1670–1776* (Cambridge: Cambridge University Press, 2010), 5–9, 68–69; Christer Petley, *Slaveholders in Jamaica: Colonial Society and Culture During the Era of Abolition* (London: Pickering and Chatto, 2009), 24–27; Verene A. Shepherd, "Land, Labour and Social Status: Non-Sugar Producers in Jamaica in Slavery and Freedom," in *Working Slavery, Pricing Freedom: Perspectives from the Caribbean, Africa and the African Diaspora*, ed. Verene A. Shepherd (Kingston, Jamaica: Ian Randle, 2002), 153–178.

81. Tomlins, *Freedom Bound*, 2–27, 9–10, 78–81, 231, 411, 429.

Chapter 5. "A Company of White Negroes"

1. See K. G. Davies, *The Royal African Company* (1957; London: Routledge, 1999), 6, 16–17, 39–40; P. E. H. Hair and Robin Law, "The English in West Africa to 1700," in *The Oxford History of the British Empire*, Vol. 1: *The Origins of Empire: British Overseas Enterprise to the Close of the Seventeenth Century*, ed. Nicholas Canny (Oxford: Oxford University Press, 1998), 251–259; Ty M. Reese, "Toiling in the Empire: Labor in Three Anglo-American Ports, London, Philadelphia and Cape Coast Castle, 1750–1783" (Ph.D. diss., University of Toledo, 1999), 64–66; "A Description of the Castles Forts and Settlements Belonging to the Royal African Company of England on the Gold Coast of Africa," RAC, T70/1470, 33–53. For the best account of the history of Cape Coast Castle, see William St. Clair, *The Grand Slave Emporium: Cape Coast Castle and the British Slave Trade* (London: Profile Books Ltd., 2006).

2. P. D. Curtin, "'The White Man's Grave:' Image and Reality, 1780–1850," *Journal of British Studies*, 1 (1961), 94–110; Davies, *Royal African Company*, 241–242, 256; St. Clair, *Grand Slave Emporium*, 101.

3. Kenneth Morgan, ed., *The British Transatlantic Slave Trade*, Vol. 2: *The Royal African Company* (London: Pickering and Chatto, 2003), xv, xvii.

4. St. Clair, *The Grand Slave Emporium*, 32. See also Albert van Dantzig, *Forts and Castles of Ghana* (Accra: Sedco, 1980); Kwesi J. Anquandah, *Castles and Forts of Ghana* (Atalante: Ghana Museums and Monuments Board, 1999); Rosemary M. Cave, *Gold Coast Forts* (London: Thomas Nelson and Sons, 1957); W. J. Varley, "Castles and Forts of the Gold Coast," *Transactions of the Gold Coast and Togoland Historical Society*, 1 (1952), 1–17.

5. Erick Tilleman, *En Kort Og Enfoldig Beretning Om Det Landskab Guinea Og Dets Beskaffenhed (1697). A Short and Simple Account of the Country Guines and Its Nature*, trans. and ed. Selena Axelrod Winsnes (Madison: African Studies Program, University of Wisconsin, 1994), 2; Jean Barbot, *Barbot on Guinea: The Writings of Jean Barbot on West Africa, 1678–1712*, ed. P. E. H. Hair, Adam Jones, and Robin Law (London: The Hakluyt Society, 1992), II, 391, 547.

6. Tilleman, *A Short and Simple Account*, 22.

7. St. Clair, *The Grand Slave Emporium*, 82–83.

8. Philip D. Curtin, "Introduction," in *Africa Remembered: Narratives by West Africans from the Era of the Slave Trade*, ed. Curtin (Madison: University of Wisconsin Press, 1967), 13; Davies, *Royal African Company*, 241.

9. Thomas Phillips, *A Journal of a Voyage Made in the Hannibal of London, Ann. 1693, 1694, from England to Cape Monseradoe, in Africa; and thence along the Coast of Guiney to Whidaw, the Island of St. Thomas, And so forward to Barbadoes. With a Cursory Account of the Country, the People, their Manners, Forts, Trade &c., in A Collection of Voyages and Travels, Some Now First Printed from Original Manuscripts, Others Now First Published in English*, ed. A. Churchill and J. Churchill (London: for John Walthoe, 1732), VI, 205; Henry Greebil, Henry Spurway, and Daniel Bridge to RAC, Cape Coast Castle, 8 November 1680, "From Africa and the West Indies, 1678–1681," RAC, T70/1, 111–112; Copy of a Letter from David Mill Esqr. Governor of Cape Coast Castle Dated 15th April 1775 Received 22d July 1775, Inward Letter Books, B, 1773–1781, T70/32, 24; Reese, "Toiling in the Empire," 58.

10. Andrew Thompson to RAC, Annamboe, 4 March 1708, Abstract of Letters Received by the Royal African Company of England from the Coast of Africa No. 1. From March the 20th 1705 to August the 15th 1715, RAC, T70/5, 42; Messrs. James and Phipps to RAC, Cape Coast Castle, 5 December 1719, 12 January 1720, Extracts of Letters of the Committee of Shipping, 1719 to 1724, RAC, T70/27, 1, 2.

11. John Adams, *Sketches Taken During Ten Voyages to Africa, Between the Years 1786 and 1800 . . .* (1822), in *The British Transatlantic Slave Trade*, Vol. 1: *The Operation of the Slave Trade in Africa*, ed. Robin Law (London: Pickering and Chatto, 2003), 339; Phillips, *Journal of a Voyage Made in the Hannibal*, VI, 205.

12. "List of such Factors Artificers and Soldiers . . . Living in the Castle and out ffactoreys. Cape Coast 8 August 1674," Copy of the List of Living and Dead at the Royal African Company's Forts No. 1 From December the 15th 1673 to April the 31st 1675," RAC, T70/1440, 1–2. See also Curtin, "'The White Man's Grave': Image and Reality, 1780–1850," *Journal of British Studies*, 1 (1961), 95; Mary J. Dobson, "Mortality Gradients and Disease Exchanges: Comparisons from Old England and Colonial America," *Social History of Medicine*, 2 (1989), 264, 271. See also Daniel Blake Smith, "Mortality and Family in the Colonial Chesapeake," *Journal of Interdisciplinary History*, 8 (1978), 403–427, and Lorena S. Walsh and Russell R. Menard, "Death in the Chesapeake: Two Life Tables for Men in Early Colonial Maryland," *Maryland Historical Magazine*, 69 (1974), 211–227.

13. Curtin, "The White Man's Grave," 97–98, 102; St. Clair, *Grand Slave Emporium*, 101, 112.

14. Dalby Thomas to RAC, Cape Coast Castle, 14 July 1705, Extract of Letters Received by the Royal African Company of England so far as relate to the Committee of Shipping From October the 22d 1705 to February the 3d 1719, RAC, T70/26, 4.

15. Henry Greenbill, Henry Spurway, Theo Eysing, and Daniell Bridge to RAC, Cape Coast Castle, 8 November 1680, From Africa and the West Indies, 1678–1681, RAC, T70/1, 97; Dalby Thomas to RAC, Cape Coast Castle, 22 October 1708, Abstracts

of Letters Received by the Royal African Company of England from the Coast of Africa, No. 1, From March the 20th 1705 to August the 15th 1715, RAC, T70/5, 50; James Phipps and Walter Charles to RAC, Cape Coast Castle, 16 December 1718, Extracts of Letters Received by the Royal African Company of England so far as relate to the Committee of Shipping From October the 22d 1705 to February the 3d 1719, RAC, T70/26, 64; Servants of the Companies. Register of all Servants (A) 1750–1769, RAC, T70/1454, 3–4.

16. Messrs. Phipps, Dodson, and Stevenson to RAC, Cape Coast Castle, 6 April 1720, Abstracts of Letters Received by the Royal African Company from the Coast of Africa No. 3. From January the 12th 1719 to August the 26th 1732, T70/7, 4–5.

17. Messrs. James, Phipps &c. to RAC, Cape Coast Castle, 8 February 1720, Extracts of Letters of the Committee of Shipping, 1719 to 1724, RAC, T70/27, 2–3.

18. Sick, Wounded and Dead, Report on the Public Accounts of Cape Coast Castle and the Out Forts depending thereon from the first day of January 1770 to the 31st day of December 1776, RAC, T70/155, 25.

19. John Apperley to the Committee &c., Annamaboe, 10 March 1755, Inward Letter Books, Second, 1753–1762, RAC, T70/30, 6; To the Committee &c., Cape Coast Castle, 24 April 1753, Inward Letter Books, 1753–1762, RAC, T70/30, 29, 30; Apperley's death was noted in Inward Letter Books, Second, 1753–1762, RAC, T70/30, 164.

20. Nathaniel Bradley, Mathias Halstead, and Maccabbees Hollis to RAC, Cape Coast Castle, 3 October 1678, Abstract of Letters Received by the Royal African Company of England so far as relate to the Committee of Goods, No. 1, From March the 27th 1678 to February the 6th 1681, RAC, T70/20, 6; Nathaniel Bradley, Maccabees Hollis, and Arthur Habin to RAC, Cape Coast Castle, 23 August 1679, From Africa and the West Indies, 1678–1681, RAC, T70/1, 42; Davies, *Royal African Company*, 241–243.

21. "White Men's Salaries," "Black Men's Pay," "Free Canoemen & Labourers Hire," and "Castle Slaves," all for 1770, in Report on the Public Accounts of Cape Coast Castle and the Out Forts depending thereon from the first day of January 1770 to the 31st day of December 1776, RAC, T70/155, 3, 6, 11, 9, 13.

22. John Atkins, *A Voyage to Guinea, Brazil, & the West Indies, In His Majesty's Ships, The Swallow and Weymouth* (1735; London: Frank Cass, 1970), 89–90.

23. Atkins, *A Voyage to Guinea*, 90–91.

24. See, for example, the detailed list of materials purchased for shipment to West Africa in 1742: Minute Book of the Court of Assistants of the Royal African Company of England. No. 21. From May the 8th 1735 to August the 25th 1743, RAC, T70/94, 273–275.

25. Reese, "Toiling in the Empire," 133–135.

26. Draft of an indenture form, 11 October 1752, Minutes of the African Committee meetings, 1750–1755, RAC, T70/143, 91; Cape Coast Castle, 6th Octor. 1731. Messrs. Braithwaite & Peake write, Abstract of Letters Received by the Royal African Company of England from the Coast of Africa No. 3. From January the 12th 1719 to August the 26th 1732, RAC, T70/7, 187.

27. Messrs. Seth Grosvenor and James Phipps to RAC, Cape Coast Castle, 4 May 1712, Extracts of Letters Received by the Royal African Company of England so far as relate to the Committee of Shipping From October the 22d 1705 to February the 3d 1719, RAC, T70/26, 33.

28. Edward Colston to Samuel Humfreys et al., London, 12 December 1689, Copies of Letters sent by the Royal African Company of England to the Coast of Africa. From December the 10th 1685 to April the 5th 1698, RAC, T70/50, 102. John Apperley to African Committee, 8 September 1753, RAC, T70/30, 34, as quoted in Reese, "Toiling in the Empire," 137.

29. Reese, "Toiling in the Empire," 139.

30. Officers of this Castle their Pay Bill for the Month of February 1750, Cape Coast Journal C. Commencing February the 1st 1751 ending June the 16th 1751, RAC, T70/425, 7; St. Clair, The Grand Slave Emporium, 130; Reese, "Toiling in the Empire," 133–134.

31. Thomas Phipps to James Phipps, 23 December 1703, quoted in David Henige, "'Companies Are Always Ungrateful': James Phipps of Cape Coast, a Victim of the African Trade," African Economic History, 9 (1980), 31.

32. Henige, "Companies Are Always Ungrateful," 29–31.

33. Indenture of John Lyle, 1 September 1721, Copies of Indentures Covenants and Deeds entered into by Sundrys with the Royal African Company of England, No. 2 From November the 25th 1719 to January the 25th 1732, RAC, T70/1423, 77. St. Clair, The Grand Slave Emporium, 82–83; Sarah Lee, The African Wanderers: Or, The Adventures of Carlos and Antonio, Embracing Interesting Descriptions of the Manners and Customs of the Western Tribes, and the Natural Productions of the Country, 2nd ed. (London: Grant and Griffith, 1850), 68.

34. Dalby Thomas to RAC, Cape Coast Castle, 23 March 1704, Abstract of Letters Received by the Royal African Company of England so far as relate to the Committee of Correspondence No. 5. From May the 31st 1704 to October the 3d 1706, RAC, T70/14, 45; Messrs. James, Phipps &c. to RAC, Cape Coast Castle, 8 February 1720, Extract of Letters of the Committee of Shipping 1719 to 1724, RAC, T70/27, 2; Mr. Chas. Bell to the Committee, Cape Coast Castle, 20 March 1756, Inward Letter Books, Second, 1753–1762, RAC, T70/30, 146.

35. Atkins, A Voyage to Guinea, 92.

36. John Morice to William Ronan et al., London, 19 November 1695, Copies of Letters sent by the Royal African Company of England to the Coast of Africa. From December the 19th 1685 to April the 5th 1698, RAC, T70/50, 167; Henry Greenhill et al to RAC, Cape Coast Castle, 28 September 1681, Abstracts of Letters From May 28 1681 to Apr. 8 1684, RAC, T70/16, 23.

37. Seth Grosvenor and James Phipps to RAC, Cape Coast Castle, 4 May 1712, Extracts of Letters Received by the Royal African Company of England so far as relate to the Committee of Shipping From October the 22d 1705 to February the 3d 1719, RAC, T70/26, 33; John Apperley to RAC, Anomabu, 10 March 1755, Inward Letter

Books, Second, 1753–1762, RAC, T70/30, 5; John Roberts to RAC, Cape Coast Castle, 26 October 1780, Inward Letter Books, B, 1773–1781, RAC, T70/32, 125; Reese, "Toiling in the Empire," 136.

38. Thomas Melvil to RAC, Cape Coast Castle, 11 March 1753, Inward Letter Books, Second, 1753–1762, RAC, T70/30, 9.

39. James Phipps and Walter Charles to RAC, Cape Coast Castle, 5 December 1719, Extracts of Letters of the Committee of Shipping, 1719 to 1724, RAC, T70/27, 1.

40. James Phipps and Walter Charles to RAC, Cape Coast Castle, 16 December 1718, Extracts of Letters Received by the Royal African Company of England so far as relate to the Committee of Shipping From October the 22d 1705 to February the 3d 1719, RAC, T70/26, 64–65.

41. James Phipps et al. to RAC, Cape Coast Castle, 3 February 1720, Extracts of Letters of the Committee of Shipping, 1719 to 1724, RAC, T70/27, 2.

42. African Committee to Erasmus Carver, 2 February 1764, RAC, T70/69, 1–2. See Ty M. Reese, "The Drudgery of the Slave Trade: Labor at Cape Coast Castle, 1750–1790," in *The Atlantic Economy During the Seventeenth and Eighteenth Centuries: Organization, Operation, Practice and Personnel,* ed. Peter A. Coclanis (Columbia: University of South Carolina Press, 2005), 285.

43. Servants of the Companies. Register of all Servants (A) 1750–1769, RAC, T70/1454, 1v, 2v.

44. St. Clair, *The Grand Slave Emporium,* 128–129.

45. Barbot, *Barbot on Guinea,* II, 397.

46. Artificers and Soldiers their Pay Bill for the Month of February 1751, Cape Coast Journal C. Commencing February the 1st 1751 ending June the 16th 1751, T70/425, 7; St. Clair, *The Grand Slave Emporium,* 130.

47. Seth Grosvenor and James Phipps to RAC, Cape Coast Castle, 11 July 1712, Extracts of Letters Received by the Royal African Company of England so far as relate to the Committee of Shipping From October the 22d 1705 to February the 3d 1719, RAC, T70/26, 33v.

48. An Act of Council made at Cape Coast Castle November 5 1737, Extracts, 1720–1742, RAC, T70/4, 105; St. Clair, *The Grand Slave Emporium,* 101.

49. Wednesday 12th April 1780, Cape Coast Castle, Journal at Appollonia, 1780, RAC, T70/1470, 5; Seth Grosvenor, James Phipps, et al. to RAC, Cape Coast Castle, 6 October 1713, Abstracts of Letters from Sept. 12, 1712, to Dec. 19, 1715, RAC, T70/3, 13. See also Davies, *The Royal African Company,* 251.

50. David Miller to RAC, Cape Coast Castle, 29 July 1774, Inward Letter Books, B, 1773–1781, RAC, T70/32, 15.

51. David Miller to RAC, Cape Coast Castle, 29 July 1774, Inward Letter Books, B, 1773–1781, RAC, T70/32, 16.

52. John Morice to Mr. William Ronan et al., London, 22 October 1795, Copies of Letters sent by the Royal African Company of England to the Coast of Africa. From

December the 10th 1685 to April the 5th 1698, RAC, T70/50, 166. See also Davies, *The Royal African Company*, 242–243.

53. Dalby Thomas to RAC, Cape Coast Castle, May 1706, Extracts of Letters Received by the Royal African Company of England so far as relate to the Committee of Shipping From October the 22d 1705 to February the 3d 1719, RAC, T70/26, 10.

54. St. Clair, *The Grand Slave Emporium*, 144.

55. John Apperley to RAC, Anomabu, 22 April 1753, Inward Letter Books, Second, 1753–1762, RAC, T70/30, 27–28.

56. Thomas Melvil to RAC, Cape Coast Castle, 24 April 1753, Inward Letter Books, Second, 1753–1762, RAC, T70/30, 29.

57. List of Persons shipped on Board the Tankerville Capt. David Adam for Cape Coast Castle on the Coast of Africa. Dec. the 13th 1758, Detached Papers, 1757, 1758, RAC, T70/1528.

58. 11 August 1777, Diary of Employment of Labourers at Cape Coast Castle, 1777–1778, RAC, T70/1469, 3.

59. 2 April 1778, Diary of Employment of Labourers at Cape Coast Castle, 1777–1778, RAC, T70/1469, 15.

60. Bernard Weuves to RAC, Cape Coast Castle, 29 April 1782, Inward Letter Books, C, 1781–1799, T70/33, 35; James Morgue et al. to RAC, Cape Coast Castle, 9 July 1785, Inward Letter Books, C, 1781–1799, RAC, T70/33, 110–111. See also Emma Christopher, *A Merciless Place: The Lost Story of Britain's Convict Disaster in Africa* (Oxford: Oxford University Press, 2010), and St. Clair, *The Grand Slave Emporium*, 131–132.

61. *Barbot on Guinea*, II, 381; St. Clair, *The Grand Slave Emporium*, 147–148, 154.

62. Servants of the Companies. Register of all Servants (A) 1750–1769, RAC, T70/1454, 2v, 15v; Ty M. Reese, "Class at an African Commercial Enclave," in *Class Matters: Early North America and the Atlantic World*, ed. Simon Middleton and Billy G. Smith (Philadelphia: University of Pennsylvania Press, 2008), 84.

63. Copy of a Letter from the Governor and Council at Cape Coast Castle, Dated Cape Coast Castle 15th September 1788, Received 20th March 1789, Inward Letter Books, C, 1781–1799, RAC, T70/33, 191; "On March 25, 1789, At a Meeting of the Committee of the Company of Merchants, held in London," reprinted in Crooks, *Records Relating to the Gold Coast Settlements*, 77. See also *The Life and Letters of Philip Quaque, The First African Anglican Minister*, ed. Vincent Carretta and Ty M. Reese (Athens: University of Georgia Press, 2010), and F. L. Bartels, "Philip Quaque, 1741–1816," *Transactions of the Gold Coast & Togoland Historical Society*, 1 (1955), 153–177.

64. Theresa S. Singleton, "The Slave Trade Remembered on the Former Gold and Slave Coasts," in *From Slavery to Emancipation in the Atlantic World*, ed. Sylvia Frey and Betty Wood (London: Frank Cass, 1999), 153–154.

65. David Mills to RAC, Cape Coast Castle, 29 July 1774, Inward Letter Books, B, 1773–1781, RAC, T70/32, 16.

66. Cape Coast Journal C for February 1751, Cape Coast Journal C, 1 February to 16 June 1751, RAC, T70/425, 7; Servants of the Companies: Register of all Servants 1750–1769, RAC, T70/1454, 7.

67. Dalby Thomas to RAC, Cape Coast Castle, 14 July 1705, Extracts of Letters Received by the Royal African Company of England so far as relate to the Committee of Shipping from October the 22d 1705 to February the 3d 1719, RAC, T70/26, 4 Wm. Feilde, T. Miles, Edgar Hickman, J. Gordon to RAC, Cape Coast Castle, 30 June 1790, Inward Letter Books, C, 1781–1799, T70/33, 25.Copy of a Letter from the Governor and Council at Cape Coast Castle dated 30th June 179, Received 19th October 1790, Inward Letter Books, C, 1781–1799, RAC, T70/33, 245. Walter Rodney, "The Gold Coast," in *The Cambridge History of Africa,* Vol. 4: *From c. 1600 to c. 1790,* ed. Richard Gray (Cambridge: Cambridge University Press, 1975), 308.

Chapter 6. "A Spirit of Liberty"

1. James Phipps et al. to RAC, Cape Coast Castle, n.d., Extracts of Letters of the Committee of Shipping, 1719 to 1724, RAC, T70/27, 3v, National Archives. Pawnship was a West African tradition, and it represented the condition of being held as a pledge, or as security for the repayment of a loan. Individuals or groups of people were given as pawns, sometimes for quite lengthy periods, and the British found themselves forced to accept pawns from local leaders, merchants, and others. Pawns were bound but not necessarily slaves, and their labor belonged to the person holding the pawns. See Toyin Falola and Paul E. Lovejoy, "Pawnship in Historical Perspective," in *Pawnship in Africa: Debt Bondage in Historical Perspective,* ed. Falola and Lovejoy (Boulder: Westview Press, 1994), 1–26.

2. Christopher Tomlins has made a compelling argument that for the large majority of indentured servants in seventeenth- and eighteenth-century British North America, service provided a means to improve their condition. See Christopher Tomlins, *Freedom Bound: Law, Labor, and Civic Identity in Colonizing English America, 1580–1865* (Cambridge: Cambridge University Press, 2010).

3. Copy of a Letter from the Governor and Council at Cape Coast Castle, 25 June 1778, Inward Letter Books, B, 1773–1781, T70/32, 76.

4. Court of Assistants of the Royal African Company of England to Messrs. John Brathwaite, Robert Cruikshank, and Benjamin Peake, Africa House, London, 9 July 1730, Copies of Letters sent by the Royal African Company of London to Cape Coast Castle, No. 1, From July the 18th 1728 to April the 15th 1740, RAC, T70/54, 79; Cabo Corse Castle, 29th, 30th July & 3d August 1708, Abstracts of Letters Received by the Royal African Company of England from the Coast of Africa No. 1. From March the 20th 1705 to August the 15th 1715, RAC T70/5, 47v. See also Walter Rodney, "African Slavery and Other Forms of Social Oppression on the Upper Guinea Coast in the Context of the Atlantic Slave Trade," in J. E. Inikori, ed., *Forced Migration: The Impact of the Export Slave Trade on African Societies* (London: Hutchinson University Library

for Africa, 1982), 67; Ty M. Reese, "Facilitating the Slave Trade: Company Slaves at Cape Coast Castle, 1750–1807," *Slavery & Abolition*, 31 (2010), 364.

5. Illegible to RAC, Cape Coast Castle, 24 April 1753, Inward Letter Books, Second, 1753–1762, RAC, T70/30, 28–29; John Apperley to the Committee, Anomabu, 19 March 1756, Inward letter Books, Second, 1753–1762, RAC, T70/30, 144.

6. Report of Cape Coast Castle for 1770–76, RAC, T70/155, quoted in Ty M. Reese, " 'Toiling in the Empire': Labor in Three Anglo-American Ports, London, Philadelphia and Cape Coast Castle, 1750–1783" (Ph.D. diss., University of Toledo, 1999), 152; Castle Slaves, Report on the Public Accounts of Cape Coast Castle and the Out Forts depending thereon from the first day of January 1770 to the 31st day of December 1776, RAC, T70/155, 9, 10; Monday 8 May 1780, Cape Coast Castle, Journal at Appollonia, 1780, T70/1470, 16; John Roberts to African Committee, Cape Coast Castle, 17 July 1780, RAC, T70/32.

7. Castle Slaves, Report on the Public Accounts of Cape Coast Castle and the Out Forts depending thereon from the first day of January 1770 to the 31st day of December 1776, RAC, T70/155, 10; William St. Clair, *The Grand Slave Emporium: Cape Coast Castle and the British Slave Trade* (London: Profile Books, 2006), 136–137.

8. Minutes of Council at Cape Coast Castle, 18 August 1789, in J. J. Crooks, ed., *Records Relating to the Gold Coast Settlements, from 1750 to 1874* (1923; London: Frank Cass, 1973), 79–80.

9. Schedule of slaves at Cape Coast Castle in 1752, reprinted in Crooks, *Records Relating to the Gold Coast Settlements*, 4; A Description of the Castle Forts and Settlements Belonging to the Royal African Company of England On The Gold Coast of Africa and at Whydah [1737], RAC, T70/1470, 33; List of Slaves, Artificers, at the several Forts, upon the Gold Coast & Whydah, in 1751, & 1756, September 1751, Detached Papers, 1757, 1758, RAC, T70/1528.

10. Diary of Employment of Labourers at Cape Coast Castle, 1777–1778, RAC, T70/1469, 1, 3. See also St. Clair, *The Grand Slave Emporium*, 144.

11. Monday 8 May 1780, Cape Coast Castle, Journal at Appollonia, 1780, T70/1470, 16.

12. John Apperley to African Committee, Anomabu, 22 April 1753, Inward Letter Books, Second, 1753–1762, 27–28. See also St. Clair, *The Grand Slave Emporium*, 133.

13. James Nightingale to Governor, 3 March 1682, Copies of Letters sent by the out-factors at the Royal African Company of England to the Chief Factors at Cape Coast Castle, reprinted in *The English in West Africa, 1681–1683: The Local Correspondence of the Royal African Company of England, 1681–1699*, Part 1 (Oxford: Oxford University Press, 1997), 38.

14. Nightingale to Governor [?], 15 March 1682, in the *English in West Africa*, 39.

15. Messrs. Franklin et al. to RAC, Cape Coast Castle, 27 January 1728, Abstract of Letters Received by the Royal African Company of England from the Coast of Africa, No. 3. From January the 12th 1719 to August the 26th 1732, RAC, T70/7, 140; Dalby Thomas to RAC, Cape Coast Castle, 25 February 1707, Extracts of Letters Received by

the Royal African Company of England so far as relate to the Committee of Shipping From October the 22d 1705 to February the 3d 1719, RAC, T70/26, 21; William Mutter to the Committee, Cape Coast Castle, 10 May 1764, Inward Letter Books, A, 1762–1773, RAC, T70/31, 83; Illegible to RAC, Cape Coast Castle, 24 April 1753, Inward Letter Books, Second, 1753–1762, RAC, T70/30, 28–29.

16. John Apperley to the Committee, Anomabu, 19 March 1756, Inward letter Books, Second, 1753–1762, RAC, T70/30, 143–144; William Cross to RAC, Commenda, 2 November 1686, from RAC Letter Books in the Bodleian Library, University of Oxford, reprinted in *The English in West Africa, 1685–1688: The Local Correspondence of the Royal African Company of England, 1681–1699*, Part 2, ed. Robin Law (Oxford: Oxford University Press, 2001), 92.

17. For an excellent analysis of this double burden, see Jennifer L. Morgan, *Laboring Women: Reproduction and Gender in New World Slavery* (Philadelphia: University of Pennsylvania Press, 2004). For a discussion of female castle slaves, see Rebecca Shumway, "Gender and Creolization on the Gold Coast: Castle Slaves in the Era of the Slave Trade," unpublished paper. Shumway argues that there was more general abuse of female castle slaves by white men, but does not consider the slaves owned by white merchants and officials in their own right, and the advantages (similar to those enjoyed by fur traders among Native Americans) that accrued to white men in taking a local African "wench."

18. William Mutter to the Committee, Cape Coast Castle, 10 May 1764, Inward Letter Books, A, 1762–1773, RAC, T70/31, 83.

19. Nathaniel Senior to RAC, Cape Coast Castle, 3 February 1759, Inward Letter Books, Second, 1753–1762, RAC, T70/30, 271.

20. John Grosle to African Committee, Cape Coast Castle, 20 April 1769, RAC, T70/1028; K. G. Davies, *The Royal African Company* (1957; London: Routledge, 1999), 242.

21. Copies of Indentures Covenants and Deeds entered into by Sundrys with the Royal African Company of England, No. 2, from November the 25th 1719 to January the 25th 1732, RAC, T70/1423, 77.

22. Messrs. Phipps, Dodson, and Boyl to RAC, Cape Coast Castle, 28 June 1721, Abstract of Letters Received by the Royal African Company of England from the Coast of Africa No. 3, From January the 12th 1719 to August the 26th 1732, RAC, 70/7, 22; A Description of the Castles Forts and Settlements Belonging to the Royal African Company of England On the Gold Coast of AFRICA and at Whydah [1737], in "Journal at Appollonia," RAC, T70/1470, 42, 33, 35, 38, 46, 48, 51; Messrs. Franklin, Reed, Prake to RAC, Cape Coast Castle, 27 January 1728, Abstract of Letters Received by the Royal African Company of England from the Coast of Africa No. 3, From January the 12th 1719 to August the 26th 1732, RAC, 70/7, 140; John Apperley to RAC, Annamaboe, 19 March 1756, Inward Letter Books, Second, 1753–1762, RAC, T70/30, 138; Messrs. Braithwayt & Cruikshank, Cape Coast Castle, 28 June 1729, Abstract of Letters Received by the Royal African Company of England from the Coast of Africa No. 3,

From January the 12th 1719 to August the 26th 1732, RAC, 70/7,145; Free Canoemen & Labourers Hire, Report on the Public Accounts of Cape Coast Castle and the Out Forts depending thereon from the first day of January 1770 to the 31st day of December 1776, RAC, T70/155, 12; Peter C. W. Gutkind, "Trade and Labor in Early Precolonial African History," in *The Workers of African Trade*, ed. Catherine Coquery-Vidrovitch and Paul Lovejoy (Beverly Hills, Calif.: Sage Publications, 1985), 29–30.

23. Cape Coast Journal C, Commencing February the 1st 1751 ending June the 16th 1751, RAC, T70/425, 16, 21; Reese, "Facilitating the Slave Trade," 370.

24. 1757. Goods issued for the Pay of Castle Slaves, Detached Papers, 1757, 1758, RAC, T70/1528, T70/1528; Richard Thelwall to Governor, Anamaboe, 22 October 1681, Copies of Letters sent by the Outfactors of the Royal African Company of England to the Chief Agents at Cape Coast castle, From January the 27th 1680 to 1681, Ms. Rawlinson C.745, Bodleian Library.

25. Sunday 9th [August 1778], Diary at Cape Coast Castle, RAC, T70/1468, 31; John Hippisley to African Committee, Cape Coast Castle, 14 June 1766, RAC, &70/31. See also Ty M. Reese, "Class at an African Commercial Enclave," in *Class Matters: Early North America and the Atlantic World*, ed. Simon Middleton and Billy G. Smith (Philadelphia: University of Pennsylvania Press, 2008), 76.

26. Castle Slaves, Report on the Public Accounts of Cape Coast Castle and the Out Forts depending thereon from the first day of January 1770 to the 31st day of December 1776, RAC, T70/155, 10; Castle Slaves, Cape Coast Journal C. Commencing February the 1st 1751 ending June the 16th 1751, RAC, T70/425, 13; "Presents and Dashees," 27 February 1751, Cape Coast Journal C. Commencing February the 1st 1751, ending June the 16th 1751, RAC, T70/425, 8.

27. James Morgue et al. to RAC, Cape Coast Council, 19 February 1786, Inward Letter Books, C, 1781–1799, RAC, T70/33, 124.

28. St. Clair, *The Grand Slave Emporium*, 144–145.

29. James Morgue et al. to RAC, Cape Coast Council, 19 February 1786, Inward Letter Books, C, 1781–1799, RAC, T70/33, 124–125. See also St. Clair, *The Grand Slave Emporium*, 144–145.

30. St. Clair, *The Grand Slave Emporium*, 142.

31. James Morgue et al. to RAC, Cape Coast Castle, 31 March 1784, Inward Letter Books, C, 1781–1799, RAC, T70/33, 96; James Morgue et al. to RAC, Cape Coast Castle, 9 July 1785, Inward Letter Books, C, 1781–1799, RAC, T70/33, 109.

32. August 16, 1772. At a Council held at Cape Coast Castle, reprinted in Crooks, ed., *Records Relating to the Gold Coast Settlements*, 38.

33. John Roberts to RAC, Cape Coast Castle, 20 July 1780, Inward Letter Books, B, 1773–1781, RAC, T70/32, 145–146; Richard Thelwall to Governor, Anamaboe, 22 October 1681, Copies of Letters sent by the Outfactors of the Royal African Company of England to the Chief Agents at Cape Coast Castle, From January the 27th 1680 to 1681, Ms. Rawlinson C.745, Bodleian Library.

34. Quoted in St. Clair, *The Grand Slave Emporium*, 138–139.

35. Dalby Thomas to African Committee, Cape Coast Castle, 7 March 1707, Extracts of Letters Received by the Royal African Company of England so far as relate to the Committee of Shipping from October the 22d to February the 3d 1719, RAC, T70/26, 22; Abstract of Letters Received by the Royal African Company of England from the Coast of Africa, No. 3, From January the 12th 1719 to August the 26th 1732, RAC, T70/7, 140, 145.

36. James Morgue et al. to RAC, Cape Coast Castle, 31 March 1784, Inward Letter Books, C, 1781–1799, RAC, T70/33, 96.

37. James Morgue et al. to RAC, Cape Coast Castle, 31 March 1784, Inward Letter Books, C, 1781–1799, RAC, T70/33, 96.

38. James Morgue et al. to RAC, Cape Coast Council, 19 February 1786, Inward Letter Books, C, 1781–1799, RAC, T70/33, 123–125.

39. From the Court of Assistants of the Royal African Company of England to Messrs. John Braithwaite, Robert Cruikshank, and Benjamin Peake, London, 9 July 1730, Copies of Letters sent by the Royal African Company of England. No. 1. From July the 18th 1728 to April the 15th 1740, RAC, T70/54, 79.

40. Dalby Thomas to RAC, Cape Coast Castle, 26 March 1706, Extracts of Letters Received by the Royal African Committee of England so far as relate to the Committee of Shipping From October the 22d 1705 to February the 3d 1719, RAC, T70/26, 8.

41. Thomas Price et al. to RAC, Cape Coast Castle, 16 March 1787, Inward Letter Books, C, 1781–1799, RAC, T70/33, 146.

42. Peter Holt to RAC, Anomabu, 30 May 1716, Abstracts of Letters Received by the Royal African Company of England so far as relate to the Committee of Accounts No. 2. From November the 3d 1714 to August the 4th 1719, RAC, T70/19, 41v.

43. Falola and Lovejoy, "Pawnship in Historical Perspective," 1.

44. Falola and Lovejoy, "Pawnship in Historical Perspective," 1–26.

45. Falola and Lovejoy, "Pawnship in Historical Perspective," 2–4; Reese, "Toiling in the Empire," 154.

46. Falola and Lovejoy, "Pawnship in Historical Perspective," 11.

47. David Mills to RAC, Cape Coast Castle, 5 January 1775, Inward Letter Books, B, 1773–1781, RAC, T70/32, 21.

48. Copy of a Letter from David Mill Esqr. Governor of Cape Coast Castle dated January 5 1775 Recd 2 June 1775, Inward Letter Books, B, 1773–1781, RAC, T70/32, 21; Monday 9 February 1778, Diary of Employment of Labourers at Cape Coast Castle, 1777–1778, RAC, T70/1469, 11v; Tuesday 10 February 1778, Diary of Employment of Labourers at Cape Coast Castle, 1777–1778, RAC, T70/1469, 11v; Monday 23 February 1778, Diary of Employment of Labourers at Cape Coast Castle, 1777–1778, RAC, T70/1469, 12v; Ralph Hassell to RAC, James Fort Accra, 11 October 1681, reprinted in *The English in West Africa*, 175. See also Falola and Lovejoy, "Pawnship in Historical Perspective," 14.

49. J. D. Fage, "Upper and Lower Guinea," in *The Cambridge History of Africa*, Vol. 3: *From c. 1050 to c. 1600*, ed. Ronald Oliver (Cambridge: Cambridge University

Press, 1977), 513; Rebecca Shumway, *The Fante and the Transatlantic Slave Trade* (Rochester: University of Rochester Press, 2011), 144–152; Reese, "Toiling in the Empire," 145. See also Suzanne Miers and Igor Kopytoff, "African 'Slavery' as an Institution of Marginality," in *Slavery in Africa: Historical and Anthropological Perspectives*, ed. Suzanne Miers and Igor Kopytoff (Madison: University of Wisconsin Press, 1977), 30–81; Theresa A. Singleton, "The Slave Trade Remembered on the Former Gold and Slave Coasts," in *From Slavery to Emancipation in the Atlantic World*, ed. Sylvia Frey and Betty Wood (London: Frank Cass, 1999), 153–154; Reese, "Class at an African Commercial Enclave," 79.

50. Ira Berlin, "From Creole to African: Atlantic Creoles and the Origins of African-American Society in Mainland North America," *William and Mary Quarterly*, 3rd ser., 53 (1996), 251–288; Shumway, *The Fante*, 35–36.

Chapter 7. "We Have No Power over Them"

1. Copy of a Letter from the Governor and Council at Cape Coast Castle Dated Cape Coast Castle 11th July 1778 Received 26th October 1780, Inward Letter Books, B, 1773–1781, RAC, T70/32, 111.

2. Copy of a Letter from the Governor and Council at Cape Coast Castle Dated Cape Coast Castle 11th July 1778 Received 26th October 1780, Inward Letter Books, B, 1773–1781, RAC, T70/32, 111; Servants of the Companies. Register of all Servants (A) 1750–1769, RAC, T70/1454, 2v; A Letter from the Revd. Mr. Philip Quaque, Missy. Schoolmaster & Catechist to the Negroes on the Gold Coast of Africa, dated Cape Coast Castle, Feb. 28, 1766, Extracted from the Registry of the Prerogative Court of Canterbury, Papers of the Society for the Propagation of the Gospel in Foreign Parts, Lambeth Palace Library, Ms. 1124, III, 230. See also F. L. Bartels, "Philip Quaque, 1741–1816," *Transactions of the Gold Coast and Togoland Historical Society*, 1 (1955), 153.

3. William Ansah Sessarakoo, *The Royal African, or, Memoirs of the Young Prince of Annamaboe: Comprehending a distinct account of his country and family, his elder brother's voyage to France . . . his condition while a slave in Barbadoes . . . his voyage from thence and reception here in England* (London: for E. Reeve, 1749), 35; William Smith, *A New Voyage to Guinea: Describing the Customs, Manners, Soil, Climate, Habits, Buildings, Education, Manual Arts, Agriculture, Trade, Employments, Languages, Ranks of Distinction, Habitations, Diversions, Marriages, and whatever else is Memorable among the Inhabitants* (London: John Nourse, 1744), 124.

4. Caboceers Black Servants and Soldiers their Pay Bill for the Month of February 1750, Cape Coast Journal C, Commencing February the 1st 1751 ending June the 16th 1751, RAC, T70/425, 7, 28; Sundry Accounts Dr. to Goods for Sale at James Fort Accra . . . for the Month of February 1751, Cape Coast Journal C, Commencing February the 1st 1751 ending June the 16th 1751, RAC, T70/425, 7, 20.

5. Charles Bell to the Committee, Cape Coast Castle, 20 March 1756, Inward Letter Books, Second, 1753–1762, RAC, T70/30, 146.

6. Peter Holt to RAC, December 1715, Abstracts of Letters from Sept. 12, 1712 to Dec. 19, 1715, RAC, T70/3, 146.

7. In the seventeenth century, for example, day laborers may have made up as much as 15 percent of the working population, with soldiers composing a further 25 percent. See Raymond A. Kea, *Settlements, Trade, and Politics in the Seventeenth Century Gold Coast* (Baltimore: Johns Hopkins University Press, 1982), 41; J. E. Inikori, "Introduction," in *Forced Migration: The Impact of the Export Slave Trade on African Societies*, ed. J. E. Inikori (London: Hutchinson University Library for Africa, 1982), 44.

8. Free Canoemen & Labourers Hire, Report on the Public Accounts of Cape Coast castle and the Out Forts depending thereon from the first day of January 1770 to the 31st day of December 1776, RAC, T70/155, 11, 12. For other examples of the cost of free labourers, see Cape Coast Journal C. Commencing February the 1st 1751 ending June the 16th 1751, RAC, T70/425, 9, 16. See Kea, *Settlements, Trade, and Politics*, 297–298.

9. Governor William Mutter to RAC, Cape Coast Castle, 10 January 1764, quoted in Ty M. Reese, "Toiling in the Empire: Labor in Three Anglo-American Ports, London, Philadelphia and Cape Coast Castle, 1750–1783" (Ph.D. diss., University of Toledo, 1999), 128.

10. Gilbert Petrie to RAC, Cape Coast Castle, 31 June 1767, Inward Letter Book, Africa to England, 162–1773, RAC, quoted in Reese, "Toiling in the Empire," 118.

11. Peter C. W. Gutkind, "Trade and Labor in Early Precolonial African History," in *The Workers of African Trade*, ed. Catherine Coquery-Vidrovitch and Paul Lovejoy (London: Sage, 1985), 28–30. The term "indirect participation" is used by Ty M. Reese in "Toiling in the Empire," 2.

12. Smith, *A New Voyage to Guinea*, 129; Jean Barbot, *Barbot on Guinea: The Writings of Jean Barbot on West Africa, 1678–1712*, ed. P. E. H. Hair, Adam Jones, and Robin Law (London: The Hakluyt Society, 1992), II, 530–531.

13. Sarah Lee, *Stories of Strange Lands; And fragments from the Notes of a traveller* (London: Edward Moxon, 1835), 126; Edward Barter, writing in 1695, quoted in Gutkind, "Trade and Labor," 36; Free Canoemen & Labourers Hire, Report on the Public Accounts of Cape Coast Castle and the Out Forts depending thereon from the first day of January 1770 to the 31st day of December 1776, RAC, T70/155, 11–12.

14. Nicolas Villault, *A Relation of the Coasts of Africk Called Guinee; With A Description of the Countrys, Manners and Customs of the Inhabitants; of the productions of the Earth, and the Merchandise and Commodities it affords; with some Historical Observations upon the Coasts. Being Collected in a Voyage By the Sieur Villault, Escuyer, Sieur de Bellefond, in the years 1666 and 1667. Written in French, and faithfully Englished* (London: Printed for John Starkey, 1670), 152; Gutkind, "Trade and Labor," 25.

15. John Ogilby, *Africa. Being an Accurate Decription of the Regions of Aegypt, Barbary, Lybia, and Billedulgerid, The Land of Negroes, Guinee, AEthiopia, and the Abyssines, With all the Adjacent Islands, either in the Mediterranean, Atlantick, Southerm or Oriental Sea, belonging thereunto . . . Collected and Translated from the most Authentick*

Authors, and Augmented with later Observations . . . (London: Printed by Thomas Johnson, 1670), II, 454–455; Barbot, *On Guinea*, II, 531.

16. Dalby Thomas to RAC, Cape Coast Castle, 25 October 1708, Abstract of Letters Received by the Royal African Company of England from the Coast of Africa No. 1, From March the 20th to August the 15th 1715, T70/5, 50.

17. Lee, *Stories of Strange Lands*, 126.

18. Sarah Lee, *The African Wanderers: Or, The Adventures of Carlos and Antonio. Embracing Interesting Descriptions of the Manners and Customs of the Western tribes, and the Natural Productions of the Country*, 2nd ed. (London: Grant and Griffith, 1850), 68.

19. Thomas Melvil to RAC, Cape Coast Castle, 9 January 1755, Inward Letter Books, Second, 1753–1762, RAC, T70/30, 82.

20. Richard Miles, Diary at Cape Coast Castle, 1777–1778, RAC, T70/1468, 41–42; Catherine Coquery-Vidrovitch and Paul Lovejoy, "The Workers of Trade in Precolonial Africa," in *The Workers of African Trade*, 20, 18–19.

21. John Apperley to RAC, Annamaboe, 19 March 1756, Inward Letter Books, Second, 1753–1762, RAC, T70/30, 139; Cape Coast Journal C, Commencing February the 1st 1751 ending June the 16th 1751, RAC, T70/425, 9; Cape Coast Journal C, Commencing February the 1st 1751 ending June the 16th 1751, RAC, T70/425, 67. See also Gutkind, "Trade and Labor," 37.

22. Peter Holt to RAC, Annamaboe, 20 June 1715, Abstract of Letters from Sept. 12, 1712, to Dec. 19, 1715, RAC, T70/3, 144; Portuguese Governor quoted in Gutkind, "Trade and Labor," 27–28.

23. James Morgue to RAC, Cape Coast Castle, 9 July 1785, Inward Letter Books, 1781–1799, RAC, T70/33, 113; Thomas Price to RAC, Cape Coast Castle, 16 March 1787, Inward Letter Books, 1781–1799, RAC, T70/33, 147.

24. Gutkind, "Trade and Labor," 30.

25. Peter Holt to Cape Coast Castle, Annamaboe, 20 June 1715, "Abstracts of Letters Received by the Royal African Company of England as far as relate to the Committee of Accounts, No. 2, From November the 3d 1714 to August the 4th 1719," T70/19, 17; Robert Bowyer to RAC, Cape Coast Castle, 28 February 1716, "Abstracts of Letters Received by the Royal African Company of England as far as relate to the Committee of Accounts, No. 2, From November the 3d 1714 to August the 4th 1719, T70/19, 53.

26. Cape Coast Journal C, Commencing February the 1st 1751 ending June the 16th 1751, RAC, T70/425, 71.

27. J. F. Ade Ajayi and B. O. Oloruntimehin, "West Africa in the Anti-Slave Trade Era," in *The Cambridge History of Africa*, Vol. 5: *From c. 1790 to c. 1870*, ed. John E. Flint (Cambridge: Cambridge University Press, 1976), 209; Kea, *Settlements, Trade, and Politics*, 41.

28. Pieter de Marees, *Description and Historical Account of the Gold Kingdom of Guinea (1602)*, trans. and ed. Albert van Dantzig and Adam Jones (Oxford: Published for the British Academy by the Oxford University Press, 1987), 121; Smith, *New Voyage*

to Guinea, 123; Villault, *Relation of the Coasts of Africk*, 219, 160; Brodie Cruickshank, *Eighteen Years on the Gold Coast of Africa Including an Account of the Native Tribes and their Intercourse with the Europeans*, 2 vols. (London: Hurst and Blackett, 1853; repr. London: Frank Cass and Co. Ltd., 1966), 275; Erick Tilleman, *En Kort Og Enfoldig Beretning Om Det Landskab Guinea Og Dets Beskaffenhed (1697). A Short and Simple Account of the Country Guines and Its Nature*, trans. and ed. Selena Axelrod Winsnes (Madison: African Studies Program, University of Wisconsin, 1994), 39; Atkins, *A Voyage to Guinea*, 112.

29. Barbot, *On Guinea*, II, 407, 381.

30. Villault, *Relation of the Coasts of Africk*, 220.

31. Barbot, *On Guinea*, II, 519.

32. Tilleman, *A Short and Simple Account*, 29; Barbot, *On Guinea*, II, 546–548, 381; Villault, *Relation of the Coasts of Africk*, 221; A Description of the Castles Forts and Settlements Belonging to the Royal African Company of England On the Gold Coast of AFRICA and at Whydah [1737], in Journal at Appollonia, RAC, T70/1470, 43–44; "Presents and Dashees," February 1751, Cape Coast Journal C, Commencing February the 1st 1751 ending June the 16th 1751, RAC, T70/425, 8. See also J. D. Fage, "Upper and Lower Guinea," in *The Cambridge History of Africa: Vol. 3: From c. 1050 to c. 1600*, ed. Ronald Oliver (Cambridge: Cambridge University Press, 1977), 501; Paul E. Lovejoy, *Transformations in Slavery: A History of Slavery in Africa* (1983; Cambridge: Cambridge University Press, 2000), 19; Herbert S. Klein, *The Atlantic Slave Trade* (Cambridge: Cambridge University Press, 1999), 105, 121–122.

33. Thomas Westgate and Richard Bew to RAC, Cape Coast Castle, 12 January 1759, Inward Letter Books, Second, 1753–1762, RAC, T70/30, 276; List of the Principal Kings, Caboceers and others in the Pay of the Committee as they stood ultimo December 1776, Report on the Public Accounts of Cape Coast Castle and the Out Forts depending thereon from the first day of January 1770 to the 31st day of December 1776, RAC, T70/155, table 11.

34. Villault, *Relation of the Coasts of Africk*, 220–221; Cruickshank, *Eighteen Years on the Gold Coast*, I, 284; Villault, *Relation of the Coasts of Africk*, 152; Barbot, *On Guinea*, II, 519; Villault, *Relation of the Coasts of Africk*, 153; Marees, *Description and Historical Account*, 26–27.

35. Marees, *Description and Historical Account*, 125, 41.

36. Marees, *Description and Historical Account*, 63–64.

37. Nathaniel Senior to RAC, Cape Coast Castle, 31 July 1759, Inward Letter Books, Second, 1753–1762, RAC, T70/30, 307.

38. Free Canoemen & Labourers Hire, Report on the Public Accounts of Cape Coast Castle and the Out Forts depending thereon from the first day of January 1770 to the 31st day of December 1776, RAC, T70/155, 12; Lee, *The African Wanderers*, 56, 55.

39. Dalby Thomas to RAC, Cape Coast Castle, 25 February 1707, Extract of Letters Received by the Royal African Company of England so far as relate to the Committee of Shipping from October the 22d 1705 To February the 3d 1719, RAC, T70/26, 21;

Messrs. Phipps, Dodson & Boyle to RAC, Cape Coast Castle, 28 June 1721, Abstract of Letters Received by the Royal African Company of England from the Coast of Africa No. 3, From January the 12th 1719 to August the 26th 1732, RAC, T70/7, 22; Cape Coast Journal C for February 1751, RAC, T70/425, 28; Wednesday 12th April, Journal at Appollonia, 1780, RAC, T70/1470, 5; Richard Miles and J. B. Weures to RAC, Cape Coast Castle, 5 January 1777, Inward Letter Books, B, 1773–1781, RAC, T70/32, 44; Richard Miles to RAC, Cape Coast Castle, 10 October 1777, Inward Letter Books, B, 1773–1781, RAC, T70/32, 69; Governor Bernard Weuves to RAC, Cape Coast, 27 July 1781, Inward Letter Book: Africa to England, 1781–1799, RAC, T70/33, 12–13.

40. J. J. Crooks, *Records Relating to the Gold Coast Settlements, From 1750 to 1874* (1923), (London: Frank Cass, 1973), 97.

41. Cruickshank, *Eighteen Years on the Gold Coast*, 280–281. See, in particular, Ty M. Reese, " 'Eating' Luxury: Fante Middlemen, British Goods, and Changing Dependencies on the Gold Coast, 1750–1821," *William and Mary Quarterly*, 3rd ser., 66 (2009), 853–872.

42. P. E. H. Hair, *The Atlantic Slave Trade and Black Africa* (London: Historical Association, 1978), 32. See also David Northrup, "West Africans and the Atlantic, 1550–1800," in *Black Experience and the Empire*, ed. Philip D. Morgan and Sean Hawkins (Oxford: Oxford University Press, 2004), 41.

43. Copy of a Letter from John Grossle Esqr. to the Committee dated Cape Coast Castle 26th October 1769 reced 19th February 1770 by the Merlin Sloop of War, Inward Letter Books, A, 1762–1773, RAC, T70/31, 367.

44. Sean Hawkins and Philip D. Morgan, "Blacks and the British Empire: An Introduction," in *Black Experience and the Empire*, 1.

Chapter 8. "The Harsh Tyranny of Our Masters"

1. The connection between enslaved labor and the development of large integrated plantations has been made most effectively by Russell R. Menard in *Sweet Negotiations: Sugar, Slavery, and Plantation Agriculture in Early Barbados* (Charlottesville: University of Virginia Press, 2006).

2. For discussion of planter unity and power in early Barbados, and the rise of the integrated plantation system, see Richard S. Dunn, *Sugar and Slaves: The Rise of the Planter Class in the English West Indies, 1624–1713* (Chapel Hill: University of North Carolina Press, 1972), 46–47; Hilary McD. Beckles, "Rebels and Reactionaries: The Political Response of White Labourers to Planter-Class Hegemony in Seventeenth Century Barbados," *Journal of Caribbean History*, 15 (1981), 1–19; Hilary McD. Beckles, *White Servitude and Black Slavery in Barbados, 1627–1715* (Knoxville: University of Tennessee Press, 1989), xiv, 38, 71–79; Hilary McD. Beckles, *A History of Barbados: From Early Settlement to Nation-State* (Cambridge: Cambridge University Press, 1990), 22–23; Menard, *Sweet Negotiations*. Menard has made a strong argument that Barbados was "well on its way to becoming a plantation colony and a slave society in response

to the activities of men raising cotton, tobacco, and indigo before sugar came to dominate the island's economy. Sugar did not bring plantation agriculture and African slavery to Barbados: rather, it quickened, deepened, and drove to a conclusion a transformation already under way when sugar emerged as the island's major crop." Menard, *Sweet Negotiations*, xii–xiii.

3. Dunn, *Sugar and Slaves*, 64, 67–74, 87; Beckles, *A History of Barbados*, 18–23, 28–31; Beckles, *White Servitude and Black Slavery*, 3, 68–74, 115, 132–135; Menard, *Sweet Negotiations*, xii–xiii, 44–47, 70–76, 431–435. Quintanilla has demonstrated that even as larger planters began replacing white servants with African slaves, smaller planters continued to prefer white servants, demonstrating the uneven process of change; see Mark S. Quintanilla, "Late Seventeenth-Century Indentured Servants in Barbados," *Journal of Caribbean History*, 27 (1993), 114–128.

4. Dunn, *Sugar and Slaves*, 68. By the end of 1643 an estimated 2,671 enslaved Africans had arrived in Barbados, a number that rose rapidly to 24,965 by the end of 1646, and then 45,711 by the end of 1656. Estimates drawn from David Eltis et al., *Voyages: The Trans-Atlantic Slave Trade Database*, http://www.slavevoyages.org/tast/assessment/estimates.faces, consulted 27 May 2012.

5. List of Christian Servants, Slaves and Livestock on the Estate of Barbara Newton, 11 April 1687. Newton Papers, Special Collections, University of London Library, Ms. Collection 523, ms. 1105/1.

6. "Certaine Propisitions for the better accommodating ye Foreigne Plantations with Servants reported from the Committee to the Councell of Foreigne Plantations" (1664), Papers Relating to English Colonies in America and the West Indies, 1627–1699, British Library Manuscripts Collection, Egerton 2395, 277. "An Act for the Better Ordering and Governing of Negroes," 27 September 1661, Records of the Colonial Office and Predecessors, Barbados Acts, National Archives, CO 30/2, 16–26. The quotation is taken from the fourth iteration of this slave code, "An ACT for the Governing of Negroes," 6 August 1688, *Acts, Passed in the Island of Barbados. From 1643, to 1762, inclusive; Carefully revised, innumerable Errors corrected . . .* (London: for Richard Hall, 1764), 112–113. See also Menard, *Sweet Negotiations*, 34–35, 49.

7. "An ACT declaring the Negro-slaves of this Island to be Real Estates," 29 April 1668, in *Acts, Passed in the Island of Barbados*, 64; "An ACT for the governing of Negroes," 8 August 1688, in *Acts, Passed in the Island of Barbados*, 112, 113; Henry Whistler, "Journal of the West India Expedition," in *The Narrative of General Venables: With an Appendix of Papers Relating to the Expedition to the West Indies and the Conquest of Jamaica, 1654–1655* (London: Longman's Green and Co., 1900), 146; "An Act for the governing on Negroes," 112, 116.

8. Robin Blackburn, *The Making of New World Slavery: From the Baroque to the Modern, 1492–1800* (London: Verso, 1997), 350; Sidney W. Mintz, foreword to Ramiro Guerra y Sánchez, *Sugar and Society in the Caribbean: An Economic History of Cuban Agriculture* (New Haven: Yale University Press, 1964), xiv.

9. The inaccuracies of contemporary sources are highlighted in Dunn, *Sugar and Slaves*, 75–76, and David Eltis, "The Total Product of Barbados, 1664–1701," *Journal of Economic History*, 55 (1995), 324, n. 10; Barbados Census of 1680, American and West Indies, Colonial Papers, January–May 1680, National Archives, CO 1/44, 142–379. See also Dunn, *Sugar and Slaves*, 84–116. Dunn acknowledges the potential inaccuracies and undercounting within the census, yet it remains a useful guide. Perhaps the most useful estimates are contained in table 7.1 in John J. McCusker and Russell R. Menard, *The Economy of British America, 1607–1789* (Chapel Hill: University of North Carolina Press, 1985), 153.

10. Abstract of Accounts for Lower Plantation, 20 November 1783–31 December 1784, Newton Papers, Special Collections, University of London Library, Ms. Collection 523, vol. 56, 16–17.

11. Richard Ligon, *A True & Exact History of the Island of Barbados. Illustrated with a Mapp of the Island, as Also the Principall Trees and Plants there, set forth in Their due Proportion and Shapes, drawne out by their severall and respective Scales . . .* (London: for Humphrey Mosley, 1657), 85, 86.

12. "Instruction whch I would have observed Mr Richard Harwood in the Management of My plantation according to the Articles of Agreement between us which are here unto Annexed," Rawlinson Mss. A348, Bodleian Library, University of Oxford. This manuscript has been expertly edited in Peter Thompson, "Henry Drax's Instructions on the Management of a Seventeenth-Century Barbadian Sugar Plantation," *William and Mary Quarterly*, 3rd ser., 66 (2009), 565–604; William Belgrove, *A Treatise Upon Husbandry or Planting: A Regular Bred and Long Experienc'd planter, of the island of Barbados. And may be of great use to the planters of the West India Islands* (Boston: D. Fowle, 1755).

13. Ligon, *True & Exact History*, 24, 22; David Watts, "The Origins of Barbadian Cane Hole Agriculture," *Journal of the Barbados Museum and Historical Society*, 32 (1968), 146.

14. Ligon, *True & Exact History*, 43, 44, 46, 47.

15. Ligon, *True & Exact History*, 85–86, 55.

16. Ligon, *True & Exact History*, 89, 90, 92.

17. Ligon, *True & Exact History*, 115.

18. John Atkins, *A Voyage to Guinea, Brazil, & the West Indies, In His Majesty's Ships, The Swallow and Weymouth* (London: for Caesar Ward and Richard Chandler, 1735), 210. See also Menard, *Sweet Negotiations*, 5; Watts, "Origins of Barbadian Cane Hole Agriculture," 146–148.

19. Menard, *Sweet Negotiations*, 94–95.

20. Thomas Tryon, *The merchant, citizen and country-man's instructor: or, a necessary companion for all people. Containing, I. Directions to planters of sugar, and to make it. II. To a Planter touching Cotton, and the Advantage thereof. III. The Art of Distillation, and the great Advantage thereof to England . . .* (London: for E. Harris and G. Conyers,

1701), 202. See also Philippe Rosenberg, "Thomas Tryon and the Seventeenth-Century Dimensions of Antislavery," *William and Mary Quarterly*, 3rd ser., 61 (2004), 609–642.

21. Thompson, "Henry Drax's Instructions," 587, 584–585. See also Dale W. Tomich, *Slavery in the Circuit of Sugar: Martinique and the World Economy, 1830–1848* (Baltimore: Johns Hopkins University Press, 1990), 126.

22. Thompson, "Henry Drax's Instructions," 569, 587, 588.

23. Thompson, "Henry Drax's Instructions," 585.

24. Thomas Phillips, *A Journal of a Voyage Made in the Hannibal of London, Ann. 1693, 1694, From England, to Cape Monseradoe, in Africa: And thence along the Coast of Guiney to Whidaw, the Island of St. Thomas, And so forward to Barbadoes*, in Awnsham Churchill and John Churchill, eds., *A Collection of Voyages and Travels, some Now First Printed from Original Manuscripts, Others Now First Published in English. In Six Volumes. With a General preface, giving an Account of the Progress of Navigation, from its first Beginning* (London, 1732), VI, 229–230. For a discussion of this source, and of guardians and "sentinels" in general, see Stephanie E. Smallwood, "African Guardians, European Slave Ships, and the Changing Dynamics of Power in the Early Modern Atlantic," *William and Mary Quarterly*, 3rd ser., 64 (2007), 679–716.

25. Smallwood, "African Guardians," 684–696, 707–708.

26. Edwyn Stede and Stephen Gascoigne to RAC, Barbados, 30 May 1681, Abstract of Letters from 22 October 1678 to 30 May 1681, Company of Royal Adventurers of England Trading with Africa and Successors, National Archives, T70/15, 63; Phillips, *Journal of a Voyage Made*, VI, 214; Griffith Hughes, *The Natural History of Barbados* (London: printed for the author, 1750), 14; List of Christian Servants, Slaves and Livestock on the Estate of Barbara Newton, 11 April 1687. Newton Papers, Special Collections, University of London Library, Ms. Collection 523, ms. 1105/1.

27. Jerome S. Handler and Frederick W. Lange, *Plantation Slavery in Barbados: An Archaeological and Historical Investigation* (Cambridge, Mass.: Harvard University Press, 1978), 26–28.

28. Thompson, "Henry Drax's Instructions," 583, 584, 600.

29. Thompson, "Henry Drax's Instructions," 585, 576–577; Edward Littleton, *The Groans of the Plantations: Or, A True Account of their Grievous and Extreme Sufferings By the Heavy Impositions upon Sugar, And Other Hardships Relating more particularly to the Island of Barbados* (London: M. Clark, 1698), 18. Thomas Tryon, *Friendly advice to the gentlemen-planters of the East and West Indies In three parts. I. A brief treatise of the most principal fruits and herbs that grow in the East & West Indies; giving an account of their respective vertues both for food and physick, and what planet and sign they are under. Together with some directions for the preservation of health and life in those hot climates. II. The complaints of the negro-slaves against the hard usages and barbarous cruelties inflicted upon them. III. A discourse in way of dialogue, between an Ethiopean or negro-slave, and a Christian that was his master in America. By Philotheos Physiologus* (London: Printed by Andrew Sowle, 1684), 144–145. See also Dunn, *Sugar and Slaves*, 323, 314; Menard, *Sweet Negotiations*, 96.

30. Littleton, *Groans of the Plantations*, 19–20.

31. In his later reworking of Drax's instructions, Belgrove provided a detailed calendar of work on a Barbadian sugar plantation. See Belgrove, *A Treatise Upon Husbandry*, 10–20; Philip Gibbes, *Instructions for the Treatment of Negroes* (London: for Shepperson and Reynolds, 1797), 69; Thompson, "Henry Drax's Instructions," 600.

32. Watts, "Origins of Barbadian Cane Hole Agriculture," 143–151.

33. William Dickson, *Mitigation of Slavery, In Two Parts* . . . (London: R. and A. Taylor, 1814), 275; William Dickson, *Letters on Slavery* (London: J. Phillips, 1789), 23; George Pinckard, *Notes on the West Indies, Including Observations Relative to the Creoles and Slaves of the Western Colonies, and the Indians of South America* . . . (London: Baldwin, Craddock and Joy, 1816), I, 140. See also Justin Roberts, "Working Between the Lines: Labor and Agriculture on Two Barbadian Sugar Plantations, 1796–1797," *William and Mary Quarterly*, 3rd ser., 63 (2006), 562.

34. Thompson, "Henry Drax's Instructions," 591, 591. See also Barry Higman, *Slave Populations of the British Caribbean, 1807–1834* (Baltimore: Johns Hopkins University Press, 1984), 162; Watts, "Barbadian Cane Hole Agriculture," 149–150; Thompson, "Henry Drax's Instructions," 585. This explication of sugar manufacture rests in large part on one of the best descriptions of sugar cane agriculture and manufacturing, which can be found in Dunn, *Sugar and Slaves*, 190–201.

35. Dr. Jones, 1812, quoted in Higman, *Slave Populations*, 163.

36. John Vaughton, Copy of the Plantation Accounts taken from their plantation books, Barbados, 20 July 1725, Codrington Plantation Records, Archives of the SPG, Rhodes House Library, Bodleian Library, C/WIN/BAR/8, folder 159; John Newton, Journal, December 1778, The Newton Papers, Special Collections, University of London Library, Ms. Collection 523, vol. 47, 21. See also Heather Cateau, "The New 'Negro' Business: Hiring in the British West Indies, 1750–1810," in Alvin O. Thompson, ed., *In the Shadow of the Plantation: Caribbean History and Legacy* (Kingston, Jamaica: Ian Randle, 2002), 100–120.

37. John Oldmixon, *The British Empire in America, Containing the History of the Discovery, Settlement, progress and Present State of all the British Colonies, on the Continent and Islands of America* (London: for John Nicholson, 1708), II, 139; Thompson, "Henry Drax's Instructions," 589; Belgrove, *A Treatise Upon Husbandry*, 5, 10.

38. Dickson, *Letters on Slavery*, 23; Thompson, "Henry Drax's Instructions," 590; Littleton, *Groans of the Plantations*, 18.

39. Littleton, *Groans of the Plantations*, 18; Thompson, "Henry Drax's Instructions," 589–590; Tryon, *The merchant, citizen*, 185.

40. Edwin Lascelles et al., *Instructions for the Management of a Plantation in Barbados. And for the Treatment of Negroes &c.* (London, 1786), 24–25. See also Justin Roberts, "Negotiating Sickness: Health and Work on Barbadian, Jamaican and Virginian Plantations, 1750–1810," unpublished paper presented at the McNeil Center for Early American Studies, November 2007, 7, 11–14.

41. Higman, *Slave Populations*, 166–167.

42. Higman, *Slave Populations*, 165, 164, 166.

43. Thompson, "Henry Drax's Instructions," 592, 593, 594.

44. Thompson, "Henry Drax's Instructions," 595; Ligon, *True & Exact History*, 93.

45. McCusker and Menard, *The Economy of British America*, 151; estimates drawn from Eltis et al., Voyages: The Trans-Atlantic Slave Trade Database, http://www.slavev-oyages.org/tast/assessment/estimates.faces, consulted 17 February 2012.

Chapter 9. "Forced to Labour Beyond Their Natural Strength"

1. John Oldmixon, *The British Empire in America, Containing the History of the Discovery, Settlement, Progress and Present State of all the British Colonies, on the Continent and Islands of America*, II, 117; John Newton, Journal, 13 December 1775, Newton Papers, Special Collections, University of London Library, Ms. Collection 523, XXXI, 19.

2. For discussion of this process of amelioration, see J. R. Ward, *British West Indian Slavery, 1750–1834: The Process of Amelioration* (Oxford: Oxford University Press, 1988); Richard B. Sheridan, "Why the Condition of Slaves Was 'Less Intolerable in Barbadoes' Than in the Other Sugar Colonies," in Hilard McD. Beckles, ed., *Inside Slavery: Process and Legacy in the Caribbean Experience* (Kingston, Jamaica: Canoe Press, 1996), 31–50; David Lambert, *White Creole Culture, Politics and Identity During the Age of Abolition* (Cambridge: Cambridge University Press, 2005), 43–45. Estimates drawn from David Eltis et al., Voyages: The Trans-Atlantic Slave Trade Database, http://www.slavevoyages.org/tast/index.faces, consulted 17 February 2012.

3. Thomas Tryon, *England's Grandeur, And Way to get Wealth: Or, Promotion of Trade Made Easy, and Lands advanced . . .* (London: J. Harris and G. Conyers, 1699), 11; *A State of the Present Conditions of the island of Barbados, by a Merchant Trading to the West Indies* (London, 1710), quoted in David Watts, "Origins of Barbadian Cane Hole Agriculture," *Journal of the Barbados Museum and Historical Society*, 32 (1968), 148; quotation regarding white families cited in J. Harry Bennett, Jr., *Bondsmen and Bishops: Slavery and Apprenticeship on the Codrington Plantation of Barbados* (Berkeley: University of California Press, 1958), 3.

At his death in 1710, Christopher Codrington III bequeathed his three Barbadian sugar plantations to the Society for the Propagation of the Gospel in Foreign Parts (SPG). Thereafter the plantations were administered by employees of the SPG, with the intention that profits be used to build and run a college, which would help with the training of a ministry who would bring Christianity to the enslaved population of the British Caribbean islands. The SPG kept particularly detailed records, which are located in the library at Lambeth Palace, and in the Rhodes House Library of the Bodleian Library at Oxford University. See *Bondsmen and Bishops*. The Newton and Seawell plantations belonged to the Newton family, and the surviving papers related to these two plantations are housed in Special Collections, Senate House Library, University of London. See also Justin Roberts, "Working Between the Lines: Labor and

Agriculture on Two Barbadian Sugar Plantations, 1796–1797," *William and Mary Quarterly*, 3rd ser., 63 (2006), 551–586.

4. Abel Alleyne to SPG Secretary, Barbados, 22 October 1740, Minutes of the SPG, Vol. 4, Lambeth Palace Library, 75; William Cattell to SPG, Barbados, 20 July 1747, Minutes of SPG, V, 166. Dropsy refers to edema.

5. John Vaughton to the Revd. Dr. David Humphreys, Barbados, 10 August 1738, Codrington Plantation Records, Archives of the United Society for the Propagation of the Gospel, Rhodes House Library, Bodleian Library, Oxford, C/WIN/Bar/3, folder 34.

6. Codrington Plantation Attorneys to SPG, 11 July 1761, Codrington Plantation Records, Bodleian, C/WIN/BAR/3, folder 39; Thomas Tryon, *The merchant, citizen and country-man's instructor: or, a necessary companion for all people. Containing, I. Directions to planters of sugar, and to make it. II. To a Planter touching Cotton, and the Advantage thereof. III. The Art of Distillation, and the great Advantage thereof to England* (London: for E. Harris and G. Conyers, 1701), 192. Historians have agreed that most Barbados plantations were perpetually understaffed. See, for example, Russell R. Menard, *Sweet Negotiations: Sugar, Slavery, and Plantation Agriculture in Early Barbados* (Charlottesville: University of Virginia Press, 2006), 92–93.

7. "A List of the Negroes, Cattle, Horses and Asses Living the 31st of Decemr. 1745," Codrington Plantation Records, Bodleian, C/WIN/BAR/8, folder 126. See also Jerome S. Handler and JoAnn Jacoby, "Slave Names and Naming in Barbados, 1650–1830," *William and Mary Quarterly*, 3rd ser., 53 (1996), 694–701, 724–725. See also David DeCamp, "African Day Names in Jamaica," *Language*, 43 (1967), 139–149; Bennett, *Bondsmen and Bishops*, 33.

8. Alleyne quoted in Bennett, *Bondsmen and Bishops*, 33. See also Bennett, *Bondsmen and Bishops*, 52–56, 61.

9. Codrington Plantation Attorneys to SPG, 11 July 1761, Codrington Plantation Records, Bodleian, C/WIN/BAR/3, folder 39.

10. Table showing average value of enslaved men by occupational groups in 1775, Bennett, *Bondsmen and Bishops*, 16, 20.

11. An Inventory Taken this Day of the Plantations belonging to the Honrble. & Reverend Society, 1783 May 2, Codrington Plantation Records, Bodleian, C/WIN/BAR/3, folder 44. For a description of the activities of the three gangs, see Bennett, *Bondsmen and Bishops*, 39.

12. An Inventory Taken this Day of the Plantations belonging to the Honrble. & Reverend Society, 1783 May 2, Codrington Plantation Records, Bodleian, C/WIN/BAR/3, folder 44.

13. Cain is taken from Bennett, *Bondsmen and Bishops*, 17; An Inventory Taken this Day of the Plantations belonging to the Honrble. & Reverend Society, 1783 May 2, Codrington Plantation Records, Bodleian, C/WIN/BAR/3, folder 44.

14. John Philips, 16 February 1710, Minutes of SPG, II, 223; William Johnson to SPG, Barbados, 15 April 1737, Minutes of the SPG, III, 127.

15. "The Stock of negroes & Cattle upon the Society's Plantation as by Inventory taken in Augst. 1765," SPG, Ms. 1124, vol. 3, 160–161; John Smallridge to SPG, Barbados, 13 June 1715, Codrington Plantation Records, Bodleian, C/WIN/Bar/2, folder 18; Bennett, *Bondsmen and Bishops*, 27.

16. Smallridge to SPG, Barbados, 23 July 1722, Codrington Plantation Records, Bodleian, C/WIN/Bar/2, folder 27.

17. John Vaughton to the Reverend David Humphreys, Barbados, 15 July 1738, Codrington Plantation Records, Bodleian, C/WIN/BAR/3, folder 34. See also Minutes of SPG, 14 December 1738, Papers of the SPG, Lambeth Palace, III, 209–214.

18. Vaughton, quoted in Bennett, *Bondsmen and Bishops*, 28; Vaughton to Humphreys, 15 July 1738, Codrington Plantation Records, C/WIN/BAR/3, folder 34.

19. John Smallridge, The Plantation Accts. to ye 1st January 1722, Codrington Plantation Records, Archives of the SPG, Rhodes House Library, Bodleian Library, C/WIN/BAR/8, folder 157; Minutes of SPG, 14 December 1738, Papers of the SPG, Lambeth Palace, III, 214. See also Bennett, *Bondsmen and Bishops*, 28.

20. Samson Wood to Thomas Lane, 7 June 1800, Newton Papers, Special Collections, University of London Library, Ms. Collection 523, ms. 409; Justin Roberts, "Working Between the Lines: Labor and Agriculture on Two Barbadian Sugar Plantations, 1796–1797," *William and Mary Quarterly*, 3rd ser., 63 (2006), 555, 557, 562–570.

21. Samson Wood, "An Account of the several Fields, according to the Plot of Newton Plantation, how disposed of & under cultivation for the Year 1797," Newton Papers, Special Collections, University of London Library, Ms. Collection 523, ms. 315 ; "Numbers and occupations of slaves, Newton Plantation, 1796–1797," Newton Papers, Special Collections, University of London Library, Ms. Collection 523, ms. 110, pp. 1, 66, 118.

22. Samson Wood to Thomas Lane, 18 November 1801, Newton Papers, Special Collections, University of London Library, Ms. Collection 523, ms. 458; Samson Wood, "Increase of Negroes on the Newton Plantation from August 1st 1796 to August 1st 1797," Special Collections, University of London Library, Ms. Collection 523, ms. 315.

23. Alexander Gunkel and Jerome S. Handler, eds., "A German Indentured Servant in Barbados in 1652: The Account of Heinrich Von Uchteritz," *Journal of the Barbados Museum and Historical Society*, 33 (1970), 92; Philip Gibbes to Sir William Fitzherbert, London, 9 June 1780, Fitzherbert Collection, Microfilm Collections, Barbados National Archives, MF D239, E20555; Pinckard, *Notes on the West Indies*, I, 143, 197; Seale Yearwood to Applewhaite Frere, 26 April 1797, Manuscripts Collection, Barbados Museum and Historical Collection, Cabinet 26, Box 109B. See also Handler, "An Archaeological Investigation," 70. See also Jerome S. Handler, "An Archaeological Investigation of the Domestic Life of Plantation Slaves in Barbados," *Journal of the Barbados Museum and Historical Society*, 34 (1972), 68, and Handler, "Plantation Slave Settlements in Barbados, 1650s to 1834," in Alvin O. Thompson, ed., *In the Shadow of*

the Plantation: Caribbean History and Legacy (Kingston, Jamaica: Ian Randle, 2002), 131–132.

24. Handler, "Plantation Slave Settlements in Barbados," 128–129; Handler, "An Archaeological Investigation," 68–69.

25. Thompson, "Henry Drax's Instructions," 585–586, 601.

26. Sir John Gay Alleyne to Lady Sarah Fitzherbert, Barbados, 3 March 1795, Fitzherbert Collection, Microfilm Collections, Barbados National Archives, MF D239, E20570.

27. "An Act to prohibit the Inhabitants of this Island from employing, their Negroes or other Slaves, in selling or bartering," 6 January 1708, *Acts, Passed in the Island of Barbados*, 185. See also Hilary McD. Beckles, "An Economic Life of Their Own: Slaves as Commodity Producers and Distributors in Barbados," *Slavery & Abolition*, 12 (1991), 31–47, and Beckles, *White Servitude and Black Slavery in Barbados, 1627–1715* (Knoxville: University of Tennessee Press, 1989), 148.

28. Edwin Lascelles et al., *Instructions for the Management of a Plantation in Barbadoes. And for the Treatment of Negroes &c.* (London, 1786), 25.

29. William Senhouse, "The Autobiographical Manuscript of William Senhouse," *Journal of the Barbados Museum and Historical Society*, 3 (1935), 14.

30. Hilary McD. Beckles, *A History of Barbados: From Amerindian Settlement to Nation-State* (Cambridge: Cambridge University Press, 1989), 61–63.

31. Griffith Hughes, *The Natural History of Barbados* (London: printed for the author, 1750), 16, 15. See also Beckles, *History of Barbados*, 41–42, 51.

32. "An ACT for the governing of Negroes," 8 August 1688, *Acts, Passed in the Island of Barbados. From 1643, to 1762, inclusive; Carefully revised, innumerable Errors corrected; and the Whole compared and examined, with the original Acts, In the Secretary's Office, by the Late Richard Hall* (London: printed for Richard Hall, 1764), 114. From the first articulation of the slave code, "An Act for the Better Ordering and Governing of Negroes," 27 September 1661, the enslaved had been forbidden from leaving plantations without the written permission of their master. See, for example, "An ACT for the governing of Negroes" (1688), *Acts, Passed in the Island of Barbados*, 114. See also Jerome S. Handler and Charlotte J. Frisbie, "Aspects of Slave Life in Barbados: Music and Its Cultural Context," *Caribbean Studies*, 11 (1972), 5–46.

33. Arthur Holt to Bishop of London, Barbados, 7 March 1729, Fulham Papers, Lambeth Palace Library, XV, folios 266–267, ms. 119. See also John A. Schutz and Maud O'Neil, "Arthur Holt: Anglican Clergyman, Reports on Barbados, 1725–1733," *Journal of Negro History*, 31 (1946), 444–469.

34. Handler and Frisbie, "Aspects of Slave Life in Barbados," 19–25.

35. Philip Gibbes, *Instructions for the Treatment of Negroes* (London: for Shepperson and Reynolds, 1797), 71; Thompson, "Henry Drax's Instructions," 587, 588; Marginal comments on report by Thomas Lane, 1794–1797, Newton Papers, Special Collections, University of London Library, Ms. Collection 523, ms. 973, 1; Applewhaite

Yearwood to Applewhaite Frere, 1796, Manuscripts Collection, Barbados Museum and Historical Collection, Cabinet 26, Box 109B.

36. Numbers and Occupations of Slaves, Newton Plantation, 1796/97, Newton Papers, Special Collections, University of London Library, Ms. Collection 523, ms. 110, 14, 48. Jerome Handler, "Escaping Slavery in a Caribbean Plantation Society: Marrionage in Barbados, 1650s–1830s," reprinted from *New West Indian Guide/Nieuwe West-Indische Gids*, 71 (1997), Pamphlets Collection of Barbados National Archives, Pam A2091, 183–225; Jerome S. Handler, ed., "Memoirs of an Old Army Officer: Richard A. Wyvill's Visits to Barbados in 1796 and 1805–6," *Journal of the Barbados Museum and Historical Society*, 35 (1975), 25.

37. *Great Newes from the Barbadoes. A True and Faithfull Account of the Grand Conspiracy of the Negroes against the English, and the Happy Discovery of the Same. With the Number of those that were burned alive, beheaded, and otherwise executed for their horrible crimes* (London: for L. Curtis, 1676), 9, 10–11, 12. See also Beckles, *A History of Barbados*, 37–38.

38. *Great Newes from the Barbadoes*, 12.

39. *Great Newes from the Barbadoes*, 12.

40. Quoted in Michael Craton, *Testing the Chains: Resistance to Slavery in the British West Indies* (Ithaca, N.Y.: Cornell University Press, 1982), 111–112; Beckles, *A History of Barbados*, 40.

41. Sheridan, "Why the Condition of Slaves Was 'Less Intolerable in Barbadoes,'" 31–50; Beckles, *A History of Barbados*, 55–57.

42. Hilary McD. Beckles, "Creolisation in Action: The Slave Labour Elite and Anti-Slavery in Barbados," *Caribbean Quarterly*, 44 (1998), 110–111; Barry Higman, *Slave Populations of the British Caribbean, 1807–1834* (Baltimore: Johns Hopkins University Press, 1984), 116; William Dickson, *Mitigation of Slavery, In Two Parts* (London: R. and A. Taylor, 1814), 205.

43. Beckles, "Creolisation in Action," 116–122.

44. Robert Haynes to Thomas Lane, Barbados, 16 September 1806, Newton Papers, Special Collections, University of London Library, Ms. Collection 523, ms. 620; Beckles, "Creolisation in Action," 116–123; Craton, *Testing the Chains*, 254–266, and Hilary McD. Beckles, "The Slave-Drivers' War: Bussa and the 1816 Barbados Slave Rebellion," *Boletin de Estudios Latinoamericanos y del Caribe*, 39 (1985), 85–110.

45. Daniel McKinnon, *A Tour Through the British West Indies in the Years 1802 and 1803*, (London: J. White, 1804), 28; Tryon, *England's Grandeur*, 12.

46. William Dickson, *Letters on Slavery, By William Dickson, Formerly Private Secretary to the Late Hon. Edward Hay, Governor of Barbados* (London: J. Phillips, 1789), 6.

47. Thompson, "Henry Drax's Instructions," 574.

48. Thomas Tryon, *Friendly Advice to the Gentlemen-Planters of the East and West Indies In three parts. I. A brief treatise of the most principal fruits and herbs that grow in the East & West Indies; giving an account of their respective vertues both for food and*

physick, and what planet and sign they are under. Together with some directions for the preservation of health and life in those hot climates. II. The complaints of the negro-slaves against the hard usages and barbarous cruelties inflicted upon them. III. A discourse in way of dialogue, between an Ethiopean or negro-slave, and a Christian that was his master in America. By Philotheos Physiologus (London: Andrew Sowle, 1684), 87.

49. Tryon, *Friendly Advice*, 90, 106.

50. Tryon, *Friendly Advice*, 89.

51. Tryon, *Friendly Advice*, 89–90.

52. Edward B. Littleton, *The Groans of the Plantations: or a True Account of their Grievous and Extreme Sufferings by the heavy Impositions upon Sugar, and other hardships, Relating More Particularly to the Island of Barbados* (London: M. Clark, 1689), 7, 19.

53. Tryon, *Friendly Advice*, 88.

Conclusion

1. All of these usages are recorded in the *Oxford English Dictionary*, online edition, http://www.oed.com/view/Entry/135039?rskey = iDvIy1&result = 1& isAdvanced = false#eid, accessed 21 September 2011.

2. Richard S. Dunn, *Sugar and Slaves: The Rise of the Planter Class in the English West Indies, 1624–1713* (Chapel Hill: University of North Carolina Press, 1972), 3–45.

3. For an excellent discussion of scholarship on the transition from white to African labor, see Seymour Drescher, "White Atlantic? The Choice for African Slave Labor in the Plantation Americas," in *Slavery in the Development of the Americas*, ed. David Eltis, Frank D. Lewis, and Kenneth L. Sokoloff (Cambridge: Cambridge University Press, 2004), 31–69; David Eltis, *The Rise of African Slavery in the Americas* (Cambridge: Cambridge University Press, 2000), 5–7, 11–12, 14–17, 46–50; Robin Blackburn, *The Making of New World Slavery: From the Baroque to the Modern, 1492–1800* (London: Verso, 1997), 352–353, 355–358.

4. Eltis, *The Rise of African Slavery*, 52, 55–66.

5. Barbados Census, 1680, America and West Indies, Colonial Papers, January–May 1680, National Archives, CO1/44, 244. See also Richard S. Dunn, "The Barbados Census of 1680: Profile of the Richest Colony in English America," *William and Mary Quarterly*, 3rd ser., 26 (1969), 3–30. Beckles estimates that in 1652 approximately 13,000 white bound laborers and 15,000 enslaved Africans worked in sugar fields and works on Barbados. See Hilary McD. Beckles, "'Black Men in White Skins': The Formation of a White Proletariat in West Indian Slave Society," *Journal of Imperial and Commonwealth History*, 15 (1986), 9; Beckles, *A History of Barbados*, 27–31; Dunn, *Sugar and Slaves*, 87.

6. "An Act for the Good Governing of Servants. and Ordaining of Rights Between Masters and Servants," 27 September 1661, *Acts of Assembly. Passed in the Island of Barbadoes. From 1648, to 1718* (London: John Baskett, 1721), 22–29; Menard, *Sweet Negotiations*, 35, 45.

7. "ACT for the good Governing of Servants," 35, and "An Act for the Governing of Negroes," 8 August 1688, *Acts, Passed in the Island of Barbados. From 1643, to 1762, inclusive; Carefully revised, innumerable Errors corrected . . .* (London: for Richard Hall, 1764), 112.

8. Eltis, *The Rise of African Slavery in the Americas*; David Barry Gaspar, "'Rigid and Inclement': Origins of the Jamaica Slave Laws of the Seventeenth Century," in *The Many Legalities of Early America*, ed. Christopher L. Tomlins and Bruce H. Mann (Chapel Hill: University of North Carolina Press, 1996), 78–96; Roxann Wilson, *The Complexion of Race: Categories of Difference in Eighteenth-Century British Culture* (Philadelphia: University of Pennsylvania Press, 2000); Mary Floyd-Wilson, *English Ethnicity and Race in Early Modern Drama* (Cambridge: Cambridge University Press, 2003); Kim F. Hall, *Things of Darkness: Economies of Race and Gender in Early Modern England* (Ithaca, N.Y.: Cornell University Press, 1995); Colin Kidd, *British Identities Before Nationalism: Ethnicity and Nationhood in the Atlantic World, 1600–1800* (Cambridge: Cambridge University Press, 1999), and *The Forging of Races: Race and Scripture in the Protestant Atlantic World, 1600–2000* (Cambridge: Cambridge University Press, 2006).

9. Blackburn, *The Making of New World Slavery*, 13; Gaspar, "Rigid and Inclement," 78–96.

10. David Lambert, *White Creole Culture, Politics and Identity During the Age of Abolition* (Cambridge: Cambridge University Press, 2005), 101.

11. The best articulation of this idea of Atlantic creoles is Ira Berlin, "From Creole to African: Atlantic Creoles and the Origins of African-American Society in Mainland North America," *William and Mary Quarterly*, 3rd ser., 53 (1996), 251–88.

12. For a review of the debates over the development of racism and slavery in Virginia, see Alden T. Vaughan, "The Origins Debates: Slavery and Racism in Seventeenth-Century Virginia," in *The Worlds of Unfree Labour: From Indentured Servitude to Slavery*, ed. Colin A. Palmer (Aldershot: Ashgate, 1998), 25–68. The newest interpretation of an earlier beginning to the shift to slavery has been proposed by John C. Coombs, "The Phases of Conversion: A New Chronology for the Rise of Slavery in Early Virginia," *William and Mary Quarterly*, 3rd ser., 68 (2011), 332–360. See also Douglas M. Bradburn and John C. Coombs, "Smoke and Mirrors: Reinterpreting the Society and Economy of the Seventeenth-Century Chesapeake," *Atlantic Studies*, 3 (2006), 131–157. Coombs's work poses a direct challenge to Edmund Morgan's longstanding argument that Bacon's Rebellion played a critical role in the transition from servitude to slavery, as well as Russell Menard's argument that a diminishing supply of servants played a critical role. See Edmund S. Morgan, *American Slavery, American Freedom: The Ordeal of Colonial Virginia* (New York: W. W. Norton, 1975); Russell Menard, "From Servants to Slaves: The Transformation of the Chesapeake Labor System," *Southern Studies*, 16 (1977), 355–390. According to the Estimates function of the Transatlantic Slave Trade database, in the years up to and including 1700 about 16,150 enslaved Africans arrived in the Chesapeake, compared with over 236,700 who arrived

in Barbados. Far fewer data survive to allow us to estimate the numbers of white servants with similar precision. See Voyages: The Transatlantic Slave Trade Database, http://www.slavevoyages.org/tast/assessment/estimates.faces, accessed 28 February 2012. The nature and significance of the Barbadian diaspora is effectively summarized in Daniel C. Littlefield, "Colonial and Revolutionary United States," in *The Oxford Handbook of Slavery in the Americas*, ed. Robert L. Paquette and Mark M. Smith (Oxford: Oxford University Press, 2010), 202–207.

13. Modyford's role in the transmission of Barbadian labor practices, and most especially the Barbadian slave code, is detailed in Gaspar, "'Rigid and Inclement,'" 78–96. See also Alfred D. Chandler, "The Expansion of Barbados," *Journal of the Barbados Museum and Historical Society*, 13 (1946), 109.

14. Colleton Deed, 16 March 1647, entered 17 July 1647, in Re-Copies of Deeds, Barbados Department of Archives, RB 3/2.116; Colleton Deed, 21 May 1651, Re-Copies of Deeds, RB 3/3.879. See also J. E. Buchanan, "The Colleton Family and the Early History of South Carolina and Barbados" (Ph.D. diss., University of Edinburgh, 1989), 16–40.

15. Sir Thomas Modyford and Peter Colleton, "Proposalls of Severall Gentlemen of Barbados," 12 August 1663, *Collections of the South Carolina Historical Society* (Richmond: W. E. Jones, 1897), V, p. 11; Buchanan, "The Colleton Family," 43–158. See also S. Max Edelson, *Plantation Enterprise in Colonial South Carolina* (Cambridge, Mass.: Harvard University Press, 2006), 3–4, 13–52.

16. A. S. Salley, ed., *Warrants for Lands in South Carolina*, Vol. 1: *1672–1679* (Columbia: for the Historical Commission of South Carolina, 1910), 84. See also Peter H. Wood, *Black Majority: Negroes in Colonial South Carolina from 1670 Through the Stono Rebellion* (New York: W. W. Norton, 1974), 16–24; Wood, *Black Majority*, 24; "Warrants, 1671," marginalia in John Locke's handwriting, reprinted in *Collections of the South Carolina Historical Society* (Richmond: W. E. Jones, 1897), V, 347. Indigenous people also provided a source of bound labor; see Alan Gallay, *The Indian Slave Trade: The Rise of the English Empire in the American South, 1670–1717* (New Haven: Yale University Press, 2002).

17. William Bosman, *A New and Accurate Description of the Coast of Guinea, Divided into the Gold, the Slave, and the Ivory Coasts* (London: for James Knapton, 1705), 117; John Roberts in Rowland Cotton, *Extracts From An Account of the State of the British Forts, on the Gold Coast of Africa, Taken by Captain Cotton, of His Majesty's Ship, Pallas, in May, and June, 1777. To Which are Added, Observations by John Roberts, Governor of Cape Coast Castle* (London: for J. Brew, 1778), 16, 17. For a discussion of the development of ideas about race in the British Atlantic World, with particular reference to the late eighteenth-century Guinea coast, see Emma Christopher, *A Merciless Place: The Lost Story of Britain's Convict Disaster in Africa* (Oxford: Oxford University Press, 2010), 167–185.

18. The most recent analysis of this aspect of the Barbadian diaspora is Justin Roberts and Ian Beamish, "Venturing Out: The Barbadian Diaspora and the Carolina

Colony, 1650–1685," in *Crisis and Conflict in the Early Carolinas*, ed. Bradford Wood and Michelle LeMaster (Columbia: University of South Carolina Press, forthcoming). Roberts and Beamish provide a welcome corrective that places the exodus of Barbadian planters and slaves to the Carolinas in the context of migration to a variety of locations. See also Wood, *Black Majority*, 13–34; Richard S. Dunn, "The English Sugar Islands and the Founding of South Carolina," *South Carolina Historical Magazine*, 72 (1971), 81–93; Richard Waterhouse, "England, the Caribbean, and the Settlement of Carolina," *Journal of American Studies*, 9 (1975), 259–281; Edelson, *Plantation Enterprise*, 4, 43–44; Bradley J. Nicholson, "Legal Borrowing and the Origins of Slave Law in the British Colonies," *American Journal of Legal History*, 38 (1994), 38–54; Dunn, *Sugar and Slaves*, 238–241.

19. For a discussion of the development of the task system from the earlier gang system, see Philip D. Morgan, "Task and Gang Systems: The Organization of Labor on New World Plantations," in *Work and Labor in Early America*, ed. Stephen Innes (Chapel Hill: University of North Carolina Press, 1988), 189–220.

20. Roger N. Buckley, *Slaves in Red Coats: The British West India Regiments, 1795–1815* (New Haven: Yale University Press, 1979), and Buckley, "The British Army's African Recruitment Policy, 1790–1807," *Contributions in Black Studies*, 5 (2008), 5–16. See also A. B. Ellis, *The History of the First West India Regiment* (London: Chapman and Hall, 1885).

Bibliography

Manuscript Primary Sources

BARBADOS DEPARTMENT OF ARCHIVES

Hughes/Queree Plantation Notes, Queree Notebooks A-BIS; BLA-COD; FARMER'S-G; H-LAK; LAM-Mt. PLEASANT; MT. POWER-P; SHO-U; V-Y.

Deeds 1775–1778, vol. 146.

Re-Copied Deed Record Books, RB3, 4, 5.

Re-Copied Will Record Books, RB6.

Turners Hall, Barbados: Fitzherbert Collection. Microfilm D239, Microfilm E20751, Microfilm E20752.

BARBADOS MUSEUM AND HISTORICAL SOCIETY, ST. ANN'S GARRISON

Old Seale Yearwood to Applewhaite Frere, 26 April 1797. In Box 109B, Cabinet 26. Manuscript.

Applewhaite Yearwood to Applewhaite Frere, 1796. In Box 109B, Cabinet 26. Manuscript.

St. John Parish vestry book, 1649–1699.

BRITISH LIBRARY

"Certaine Propositions for the better accommodating ye Foreigne Plantations with Servants reported from the Committee to the Councell of Forreigne Plantions," n.d. Papers Relating to English Colonies in America and the West Indies, 1627–1699. Egerton 2395, 277–278.

"An Estimate of the Barbadoes and the now Inhabitants there," n.d. Papers Relating to English Colonies in America and the West Indies, 1627–1699. Egerton 2395, 625–627.

Whistler, Henry, "'A Journall of a voyadg from Stokes Bay and Intended by Gods assistance for the West Inga: and performed by the Right Honorable Generall penn: Admirall: As folowes. Taken by Mr. Henry Whistler, 1654.'" Sloane Ms. 3926.

FOLGER SHAKESPEARE LIBRARY, WASHINGTON, D.C.

Indentured servant contracts for the colonies of Maryland, Virginia, Pennsylvania, and Barbados, January to December 1683. Manuscripts Collection, V.B.16.

FURLEY COLLECTION, BALME LIBRARY, UNIVERSITY OF GHANA, LEGON

Dutch Records, Diaries and Correspondence, N1–78.
English Records, E1–35.

LAMBETH PALACE LIBRARY

Papers of the Society for the Propagation of the Gospel in Foreign Parts.

NATIONAL ARCHIVES, PUBLIC RECORD OFFICE, KEW

Privy Council and related bodies: America and West Indies, Colonial Papers (General
    Series). 1574–1757. CO1 to CO140.
Company of Royal Adventurers of England Trading with Africa and Successors:
    Records, 1660–1833. T70.

PUBLIC RECORDS AND ARCHIVES ADMINISTRATION DEPARTMENT,
ACCRA, GHANA

British Castle Letter Books, ADM 1/2/418–9
Copies of Wills of Officers, 1792–1805, ADM 1/2/421

RHODES HOUSE LIBRARY, BODLEIAN LIBRARY, OXFORD UNIVERSITY

Codrington Plantation Records, Archives of the United Society for the Propagation of
    the Gospel, Rhodes House Library, Bodleian Library, Oxford. C/WIN/BAR/1–8.

SPECIAL COLLECTIONS, UNIVERSITY OF LONDON

The Newton Papers, Special Collections, University of London Library. Ms. Collection
    523: vols. 41, 47, 56, 270, 271, and mss. 110, 111, 315, 409, 441, 458, 523, 973, 1055/1,
    1105/1.

Published Primary Sources

*An Account of the Number of Forts and Castles, Necessary to be Kept up and Maintained
    on the Coast of Africa, For Preserving and Securing to Great Britain The Trade to
    Those Parts* . . . Pamphlet. Folger Shakespeare Library. London?, 1730?
*Acts, Passed in the Island of Barbados. From 1643, to 1762, inclusive; Carefully revised,
    innumerable Errors corrected; and the Whole compared and examined, with the origi-
    nal Acts, In the Secretary's Office, by the Late Richard Hall.* . .. London: Printed for
    Richard Hall, 1764.
Adams, John. *Sketches Taken During Ten Voyages to Africa, Between the Years 1786 and
    1800; Including Observations on the Country Between Cape Palmas and the River
    Congo; And Cursory Remarks on the Physical and Moral Character of the Inhabi-
    tants: With an Appendix Containing an Account of the European trade with the West
    Coast of Africa.* London: Hurst, Robinson, and Co., 1822.

Astley, Thomas. *A New General Collection of Voyages and Travels: consisting of the most esteemed relations which have been hitherto published in any language, comprehending everything remarkable in its kind in Europe, Asia, Africa, and America, collected by Thomas Astley.* Vol. 3, *1745–1747.* New York: Barnes and Noble, 1968.

Atkins, John. *The Navy Surgeon, or A Practical System of Surgery.* London: C. Ward, 1734.

————. *A Voyage to Guinea, Brazil, & the West Indies, In His Majesty's Ships, The Swallow and Weymouth* . . . London: Printed for Caesar Ward and Richard Chandler, 1735. Reprinted London: Frank Cass, 1970.

Baker, Robert. *Travails in Guinea: Robert Baker's "Brefe Dyscourse,"* ed. P. E. H. Hair. Liverpool historical essays. Liverpool: Liverpool University Press, 1990.

Barbot, Jean. *Barbot on Guinea: The Writings of Jean Barbot on West Africa, 1678–1712.* Ed. P. E. H. Hair, Adam Jones, and Robin Law. 2 vols. 2nd ser., nos. 175 and 176, General Editor P. E. H. Hair. London: The Hakluyt Society, 1992.

Barker, Robert. *The Unfortunate Shipwright, or Cruel Captain . . . A Narrative of Robert Barker, Late Carpenter Aboard the Thetis . . . In a Voyage to the Coast of Guinea and Antigua.* London: L. How, 1762.

Barlow, Edward. *Barlow's Journal of His Life at Sea in King's Ships, East and West Indiamen and Other Merchantmen from 1659 to 1703,* ed. Basil Lubbock. London, 1934.

Bellgrove, William. *A Treatise Upon Husbandry or Planting: A Regular Bred and Long Experienc'd planter, of the island of Barbados. And may be of great use to the planters of the West India Islands.* Boston: D. Fowle, 1755.

Benezet, Anthony. *Some Historical Account of Guinea, Its Situation, Produce, and the General Disposition of its Inhabitants, With an Inquiry into the Rise and Progress of the Slave Trade, Its Nature and Lamentable Effects* (1771). London: J. Phillips, 1788; London: Franck Cass, 1968.

Blake, John William. *Europeans in West Africa, 1450–1560.* London: Printed for the Hakluyt Society, 1942.

Bleau, Robert. *A Letter From One of the Royal African-Company's Chief Agents on the African Coasts.* Broadside. London, 1713.

Bohun, Edmund. *A Brief but most True Relation of the late Barbarous and Bloody Plot of the Negro's in the Island of Barbado's on Friday the 21. of October 1692. To kill the governour and all the planters, and to destroy the government there established.* London, 1693.

Bosman, Willem. *A New and Accurate Description of the Coast of Guinea, Divided into the Gold, the Slave, and the Ivory Coasts.* London: for James Knapton, 1705.

Bowdich, Thomas Edward. *Mission from Cape Coast Castle to Ashantee, with a Statistical Account of that Kingdom and Geographical Notices of Other Parts of the Interior of Africa.* London: John Murray, 1819.

Brown, P. Hume, ed. *The Register of the Privy Council of Scotland.* 3rd ser., Vols. 1–4. Glasgow: James Hedderwick and Sons, 1908–1911.

Burton, Thomas. *Diary of Thomas Burton, esq. Member in the Parliament of Oliver and Richard Cromwell, From 1656 to 1659*. 4 vols. London: Henry Colburn, 1828.

Campbell, P. F. *Some Early Barbadian History, As Well As The Text of a Book Published Anonymously in 1741 Entitled Memoirs of the First Settlement of the Island of Barbados . . . And A transcription of a Manuscript Entitled The Description of Barbados Written About the Year 1741 by Major John Scott*. Wildey, St. Michael, Barbados: Caribbean Graphics & Letchworth, 1993.

The Case of the Royal African-Company And of the Plantations. Pamphlet. London: Royal African Company,1714.

Churchill, Awnsham, and John Churchill. *A Collection of Voyages and Travels, Some Now first printed from Original Manuscripts, Others Now first Published in ENGLISH. In Six VOLUMES. With a General PREFACE, giving an Account of the Progress of navigation, from its first Beginning*. 6 vols. London: for John Walthoe, 1732.

Colt, Henry. "The Voyage of Sr Henrye Colt Knight to Ye Ilands of Ye Antilleas In Ye Shipp Called Ye *Alexander*" (1631). Cambridge University Library MSS., Mm. 3, 9. In *Colonising Expeditions to the West Indies and Guiana, 1623–1667*, ed. Vincent T. Harlow. Publications of the Hakluyt Society, 2nd ser., 56. London: for the Hakluyt Society, 1925, 54–102.

Cotton, Rowland. *Extracts From An Account of the State of the British Forts, on the Gold Coast of Africa, Taken by Captain Cotton, of His Majesty's Ship, Pallas, in May, and June, 1777. To Which Are Added, Observations by John Roberts, Governor of Cape Coast Castle . . .* London: for J. Bew, 1778.

Crooks, J. J. *Records Relating to the Gold Coast Settlements: From 1750 to 1874*. 1923; London: Frank Cass, 1973.

Crow, Hugh. *Memoirs of the Late Captain Hugh Crow of Liverpool, Comprising a Narrative of his Life Together with Descriptive Sketches of the Western Coast of Africa, Particularly of Bonny, the Manners and Customs of the Inhabitants, the Production of the Soil and the Trade of the Country to Which are Added Anecdotes and Observations Illustrative of the Negro Character*. Cass Library of African Studies. Travels and Narratives, no. 60. London: Frank Cass, 1970.

Cruickshank, Brodie. *Eighteen Years on the Gold Coast of Africa Including an Account of the Native Tribes and their Intercourse with the Europeans*. 2 vols. London: Hurst and Blackett, 1853; London: Frank Cass, 1966.

Cugoano, Ottobah. *Thoughts and Sentiments on the Evil and Wicked Traffic of the Slavery and Commerce of the Human Species Humbly Submitted to the Inhabitants of Great-Britain*. London, 1787.

Curtin, Philip D., ed. *Africa Remembered: Narratives by West Africans from the Era of the Slave Trade*. Madison: University of Wisconsin Press, 1967.

Dantzig, Albert van. *The Dutch and the Guinea Coast, 1674–1742: A Collection of Documents from the General State Archive at the Hague*. Accra, 1978.

A Detection of the State and Situation Of The Present Sugar Planters of Barbadoes And The Leeward Islands; With an Answer to the Query, Why does not England, or Her Sugar Islands, or both, make and settle more Sugar Colonies in the West-Indies. London: J. Wilford, 1732.

Dickson, William. *Letters on Slavery, By William Dickson, Formerly Private Secretary to the Late Hon. Edward Hay, Governor of Barbados . . .* London: J. Phillips, 1789.

———. *Mitigation of Slavery, In Two Parts.* Part I: *Letters and Papers of the Late Hon. Joshua Steele, Vice President of the London Society of Arts, Etc. And Member of His Majesty's Council in BARBADOES, Describing the Steps by Which, to his own great Profit, he raised the oppressed Slaves on his Sugar Plantations, nearly to the Condition of hired Servants; his Observations on the Slave-Laws, &c.* Part II, *Letters to Thomas Clarkson, Esq. M.A. Proving that bought Slaves, who keep not up their Numbers by the Births, do not nearly refund their Purchase-Money, and that the Planter's true Resource is to rear his Slaves; the great Success of the Plough, in raising the Sugar-cane, &c.* London: R. and A. Taylor, 1814.

Drax, Henry. "Henry Drax's Instructionson for the Management of a Seventeenth-Century Barbadian Sugar Plantation," ed. Peter Thompson. *William and Mary Quarterly*, 3rd ser., 66 (2009), 565–604.

Dupuis, Joseph. *Journal of a Residence in Ashantee. By Joseph Dupuis, Esq. Late His Britannic Majesty's Envoy and Consul for that Kingdom. Comprising Notes and Researches Relative to the Gold Coast, and the Interior of Western Africa; Chiefly Collected from Arabic Mss. and Information Communicated by the Moslems of Guinea: To Which is Prefixed An Account of the Origin and Causes of the Present War.* London: Henry Colburn, 1824.

An ease for overseers of the poore abstracted from the statutes, allowed by practise, and now reduced into forme, as a necessarie directorie for imploying, releeuing, and ordering of the poore. With an easie and readie table for recording the number, names, ages, exercises and defects of the poore, fit to be obserued of the ouerseers in euery parish. Also hereunto is annexed a prospect for rich men to induce them to giue, and a patterne for poore men to prouoke them to labour, very pertinent to the matter. The principall heads hereof appeare in the next page. London: John Legat, 1601.

Edwards, Bryan. *The History, Civil and Commercial, of the British Colonies in the West Indies.* 3 vols. London: John Stockdale, 1801.

Eliot, Edward. *Christianity and Slavery; In A Course of lectures Preached at the Cathedral and Parish Church of St. Michael, Barbados.* London: Hatchard and Son, 1833.

Eltis, David, Martin Halbert et al. *Voyages: The Trans-Atlantic Slave Trade Database.* http://www.slavevoyages.org/tast/index.faces.

Equiano, Olaudah. *The Interesting Narrative of the Life of Olaudah Equiano, or Gustavus Vassa, the African. Written by Himself.* 2 vols. London: T. Wilkins, 1789.

Extracts from a collection of voyages and travels. 1745.

Falconbridge, Alexander. *An Account of the Slave Trade on the Coast of Africa.* London: Printed by J. Phillips, 1788.

Falconbridge, A. M., Christopher Fyfe, Isaac DuBois, and Alexander Falconbridge. *Narrative of Two Voyages to the River Sierra Leone During the Years 1791–1792–1793.* Liverpool: Liverpool University Press, 2000.

Firth, C. H., ed., *The Narrative of General Venables: With an Appendix of Papers Relating to the Expedition to the West Indies and the Conquest of Jamaica, 1654–1655.* London: Longmans, Green and Co., 1900.

A General Description of all Trades. London, 1747.

Gibbes, Philip. *Instructions for the Treatment of Negroes.* London: for Shepperson and Reynolds, 1797.

The Golden Coast, or a Description of Guinney . . . Together With a Relation of Such Persons as Got Wonderful Estates by their Trade Thither. London: for S. Speed, 1665.

Grace, Edward. *Letters of a West African Trader,* ed. T. S. Ashton. London, 1950.

Great Newes from the Barbadoes. Or a true and Faithful Account of the Grand Conspiracy of the Negroes against the English and the Happy Discovery of the same. With the Number of those that were burned alive, beheaded, and otherwise executed for their horrible crimes. London: for L. Curtis, 1676.

Gronniosaw, James Albert Ukawsaw. *A Narrative of the Most Remarkable Particulars in the Life of James Albert Ukawsaw Gronniosaw, an African Prince, as Related by Himself.* Bath: W. Gye, 1775.

Hakluyt, Richard. *The Principal Navigations, Voyages, Traffiques and Discoveries of the English Nation, made by Sea or overland, to the Remote and Farthest Distant Quarters of the Earth, at any time within the compasse of these 1600 yeres . . . London: George Bishop, Ralph Newberie, and Robert Barker, 1599–1600. Vol. 2, The Second Comprehendeth the Voyages, Trafficks, &c. of the English Nation, made without the Streight of Gibraltar, to the Islands of the Acores, of Porto Santo, Madera, and the Canaries, to the kingdomes of Barbary, to the Isles of Capo Verde, to the Rivers of Senega, Gambia, Madrabumba, and Sierra Leona, to the Coast of Guinea and Benin . . . 3 vols.* London: George Bishop, Ralph Newberie, and Robert Barker, 1598–1600.

Handler, Jerome S., and Lon Shelby, ed. and trans., "A Seventeenth Century Commentary on Labor and Military Problems in Barbados." *Journal of the Barbados Museum and Historical Society,* 34 (1973), 117–121.

Harris, John. *Navigantium atque itinerantium bibliotheca, Or, A Complete Collection of Voyages and Travels.* 2 vols. London: T. Woodward, 1744–1748.

Hippisley, John. *Essays I. on the Populousness of Africa. II. On the Trade at the Forts on the Gold Coast. III. On the Necessity of Erecting a Fort at Cape Appolonia.* London: T. Lownds, 1764.

Hollingsworth, S. *A Dissertation on the Manners, Governments and Spirit of Africa, to which is Added Observations on the Present Application to Parliament for Abolishing Negro Slavery in the British West Indies.* Edinburgh: for William Creech, 1788.

Hotten, John Camden, ed. *The Original Lists of Persons of Quality; Emigrants; Religious Exiles; Political Rebels; Serving Men Sold for a Term of Years; Apprentices, Children Stolen; Maidens Pressed, And Others Who Went from Great Britain to the American*

Plantations, 1600–1700. With Their Ages, the Localities Where They Formerly Lived in the Mother Country, the Names of the Ships in which they Embarked, And Other Interesting Particulars. New York: G. A. Baker and Co., 1931.

Houstoun, James. *The Works of James Houston, M.D., Containing Memoirs of his Life and Travels in Asia, Africa, America and Most Parts of Europe.* London: S. Bladon, 1753.

Hughes, Griffith. *The Natural History of Barbados.* London: printed for the author, 1750.

Hutton, William. *A Voyage to Africa, Including a Narrative of an Embassy to One of the Interior Kingdoms.* London: for Longman, Hurst, Rees, Orme, and Brown, 1821.

Isert, Paul Erdmann, and Selena Axelrod Winsnes. *Letters on West Africa and the Slave Trade : Paul Erdmann Isert's Journey to Guinea and the Caribbean Islands in Columbia, 1788. 7.* Oxford: Published for the British Academy by Oxford University Press, 1992.

Jeaffreson, Christoper. *A Young Squire of the Seventeenth Century. From The Papers (A.D. 1676–1686) of Christopher Jeaffreson, of Dullingham House, Cambridgeshire,* ed. John Cordy Jeaffreson. 2 vols. London: Hurst and Blackett, 1878.

Lascelles, Edwin, James Colleton, Edward Drax, Francis Ford, John Brathwaite, John Walter, William Thorpe Holder, James Holder, and Philp Gibbes, *Instructions for the Management of a Plantation in Barbadoes. And for the Treatment of Negroes & c.* London, 1786.

Lee, Sarah [nee Sarah Bowdich]. *The African Wanderers: Or, The Adventures of Carlos and Antonio. Embracing Interesting Descriptions of the Manners and Customs of the Western Tribes, and the Natural Productions of the Country,* 2nd ed. London: Grant and Griffith, 1850.

————. *Stories of Strange Lands; And fragments from the Notes of a Traveller.* London: Edward Moxon, 1835.

Ligon, Richard. *A True & Exact History of the Island of Barbados. Illustrated with a Mapp of the Island, as also the Principall Trees and Plants there, set forth in their due Proportions and Shapes, drawne out by their severall and respective Scales. Together with the Ingenio that makes the Sugar, with the Plots of the severall Houses, and other places, that are used in the whole process of Sugar-making, viz. the Boyling-room, the Filling-room, the Curing-house, Still-house, and Furnaces; All cut in Copper.* London: for Humphrey Moseley, 1657.

Littleton, Edward B. *The Groans of the Plantations: or a True Account of their Grievous and Extreme Sufferings by the heavy Impositions upon Sugar, and other hardships, Relating More Particularly to the Island of Barbados.* London: M. Clark, 1689.

Marees, Pieter de. *Description and Historical Account of the Gold Kingdom of Guinea* (1602). Translated from the Dutch and edited by Albert van Dantzig and Adam Jones. Oxford: Published for the British Academy by the Oxford University Press, 1987.

McKinnen, Daniel. *A Tour Through the British West Indies in the Years 1802 and 1803, Giving a Particular Account of the Bahama Islands*. London: J. White, 1804.

Memoirs of the First Settlement of the Island of Barbados, And Other The Carribbee Islands, With the Governors and Commanders in Chief of Barbados to the Year 1642. Extracted from Ancient Records, Papers and Accounts. . .. London: Printed for E. Owen, 1743. Reprinted in P. F. Campbell, *Some Early Barbadian History, As Well As The Text of a Book Published Anonymously in 1741 Entitled Memoirs of the First Settlement of the Island of Barbados . . . And A transcription of a Manuscript Entitled The Description of Barbados Written About the Year 1741 by Major John Scott*. Wildey, St. Michael, Barbados: Caribbean Graphics & Letchworth, 1993, 197–231.

Meredith, Henry. *An Account of the Gold Coast of Africa*. London: Longman, Hurst, Rees, Orme, and Brown, 1812.

Modyford, Thomas, and Peter Colleton. "Proposalls of Severall Gentlemen of Barbados," 12 August 1663, *Collections of the South Carolina Historical Society*. Vol. 5. Richmond: W. E. Jones, 1897, 11.

Montagu, Edward. "Edward Montagu's Notes On the Debates in the Protector's Council Concerning the Last Indian Expedition: The Grounds of the Undertaking the Designe of Attemptinge the Kinge of Spaine in the West Indies." In C. H. Firth, ed., *The Clarke Papers: Selections from the Papers of William Clarke, Secretary to the Council of the Army 1647–1649, and to General Monck and the Commanders of the Army in Scotland, 1651–1660*. Vol. 3. London: Camden Society, 1899, 203–206.

Moore, Francis. *Travels into the Inland Parts of Africa*. London: by Edward Cave, 1738.

More, Thomas. *Utopia, translated by Ralph Robynson, 1556*. Ed. David Harris Sacks. Boston: Bedford/St. Martin's, 1999.

Ogilby, John. *Africa. Being an Accurate Decription of the Regions of Aegypt, Barbary, Lybia, and Billedulgerid, The Land of Negroes, Guinee, AEthiopia, and the Abyssines, With all the Adjacent Islands, either in the Mediterranean, Atlantick, Southerm or Oriental Sea, belonging thereunto . . . Collected and Translated from the most Authentick Authors, and Augmented with later Observations . . . .* 2 vols. London: Printed by Thomas Johnson, 1670.

Oldmixon, John. *The British Empire in America, Containing the History of the Discovery, Settlement, Progress and present State of all the British Colonies, on the Continent and Islands of America*. 2 vols. London: for John Nicholson, Benjamin Tooke, Richard Parker, Ralph Smith, 1708.

Owen, Nicholas. *Journal of a Slave Dealer . . . On the Coast of Africa and America, From . . . 1746 . . . to . . . 1757*, ed. Eveline C. Martin. London: Routledge, 1930.

Phillips, Thomas. *A Journal of a Voyage Made in the Hannibal of London, Ann. 1693, 1694, from England, to Cape Monseradoe, in Africa: And Thence along the Coast of Guiney to Whidaw, the island of St. Thomas. And so forward to Barbadoes*. In Awnsham Churchill and John Churchill, eds., *A Collection of Voyages and Travels, Some Now First Printed from Original Manuscripts, Others Now Published in English*. 6 vols. London: for John Walthoe et al., 1732.

Pinckard, George. *Notes on the West Indies: including observations relative to the Creoles and slaves of the western colonies and the Indian of South America: interspersed with remarks upon the seasoning or yellow fever of hot climates*, 2nd ed. 2 vols. London: Baldwin, Cradock, and Joy, 1816.

Pitman, Henry. *A Relation of the great sufferings and strange adventures of Henry Pitman, Chirurgeon to the late Duke of Monmouth, containing an account 1. Of the Occasion of his being engaged in the Duke's service. 2. Of his trial, condemnation and transportation to Barbadoes; with the most severe and unchristian Act made against him and his fellow sufferers, by the Governor and General Assembly of that Island* . . . London: Andrew Sowle, 1689.

Potkay, Adam, and Sandra Burr. *Black Atlantic Writers of the Eighteenth Century: Living the New Exodus in England and the Americas*. Houndmills, Basingstoke: Macmillan, 1995.

Poyer, John. *The History of Barbados, From the First Discovery of the Island, In the Year 1605, Till the Accession of Lord Seaforth, 1801*. London: for J. Mawman, 1808.

———. "John Poyer's Letter to Lord Seaforth." *Journal of the Barbados Museum and Historical Society*, 8 (1941), 150–165.

"Prisoners of the '45 Rising." *Journal of the Barbados Museum and Historical Society*, 30 (1963), 73–90.

Quaque, Philip. *The Life and Letters of Philip Quaque, The First African Anglican Minister*, ed. Vincent Carretta and Ty M. Reese. Athens: University of Georgia Press, 2010.

Remarks on the Supplement to the African Company's Case. Pamphlet. Folger Shakespeare Library. London, 1730.

Rivers, Marcellus, and Oxenbridge Foyle. *England's Slavery: or Barbados Merchandize: Represented in a Petition to the High and Honorable Court of Parliament by Marcellus Rivers and Oxenbridge Foyle, Gentlemen, on behalf of themselves and three score and ten more Free-born Englishment sold (uncondemned) into slavery*. London, 1659.

Roemer, Ludewig Ferdinand. *A Reliable Account of the Coast of Guinea (1760)*. Trans. from the Dutch and ed. Selena Axelrod Winsnes. Oxford: Oxford University Press, 2000.

Romer, Ludvig Ferdinand, and Selena Axelrod Winsnes. *A Reliable Account of the Coast of Guinea (1760)*. Fontes historiae africanae; new ser. 3. Oxford: Published for the British Academy by Oxford University Press, 2000.

Sanders, Joanne McRee. *Barbados Records: Wills and Administrations*. Vol. 1, *1639–1680*. Marceline, Mo.: Sanders Historical Publications, 1979.

———. *Barbados Records: Wills and Administrations*. Vol. 2, *1681–1700*. Marceline, Mo.: Sanders Historical Publications, 1980.

———. *Barbados Records: Wills and Administrations*. Vol. 3, *1701–1725*. Houston, Tex.: Sanders Historical Publications, 1981.

The seconde tome of homilies of such matters as were promised and intituled in the former part of Homylyes, set out by the aucthoritie of the Queenes Maiestie. And to be read in euery paryshe churche agreablye. London: Richarde Iugge, 1563.

Senhouse, William. "The Autobiographical Manuscript of William Senhouse." *Journal of the Barbados Museum and Historical Society*, 3 (1935), 3–19.

Sessarakoo, William Ansah. *The Royal African, or, Memoirs of the young Prince of Annamaboe: Comprehending a distinct account of his country and family, his elder brother's voyage to France . . . his condition while a slave in Barbadoes . . . his voyage from thence and reception here in England. . . .* London: for W. Reeve, 1749.

Sloane, Hans. *A Voyage to the Islands Madera, Barbados, Nieves, S. Christophers and Jamaica.* 2 vols. London: by B. M., 1707.

Smith, Sir Thomas. *De republica Anglorum The maner of gouernement or policie of the realme of England, compiled by the honorable man Thomas Smyth, Doctor of the ciuil lawes, knight, and principall secretarie vnto the two most worthie princes, King Edwarde the sixt, and Queene Elizabeth. Seene and allowe.* London: Henrie Midleton for Gregorie Seton, 1583.

Smith, Venture. *A Narrative of the Life and Adventures of Venture, A Native of Africa: But resident above sixty years in the United States of America. Related by Himself.* New London: C. Holt, 1798.

Smith, William. *A New Voyage to Guinea: Describing the Customs, Manners, Soil, Climate, Habits, Buildings, Education . . . Habitations, Diversions, Marriages, and Whatever Else is Memorable Among the Inhabitants. Likewise, an Account of Their Animals, Minerals, &c. with Great Variety of Entertaining Incidents, Worthy of Observation, that Happen'd During the Author's Travels in that Large Country. Illus. with Cuts, Engrav'd from Drawings Taken from the Life.* London: John Nourse, 1744.

Snelgrave, William. *A New Account of Guinea, and the Slave-Trade, Containing, I. the History of the Late Conquest of the Kingdom of Whidaw by the King of Dahome . . . II. the Manner How the Negroes Become Slaves . . . III. A Relation of the Author's Being Taken by Pirates, and the Many Dangers he Underwent.* London: J. Wren, 1754.

Stanfield, James Field. *Observations on a Guinea Voyage. in a Series of Letters Addressed to the Rev. Thomas Clarkson.* London: Printed by J. Phillips, 1788.

The State of the British Trade to the Coast of Africa Considered. Pamphlet. Folger Shakespeare Library. London, 1730.

A State of the Present Condition of the Island of Barbadoes by a Merchant Trading to the West Indies. London, 1710.

Tattersfield, Nigel. *The Forgotten Trade: Comprising the Log of the Daniel and Henry of 1700 and Accounts of the Slave Trade from the Minor Ports of England, 1698–1725.* London: Jonathan Cape, 1991.

Thomas, Dalby. *Extract of a Letter Received the 16th of this Instant March 1710/11, by the Royal-African Company, from Sir Dalby Thomas their Chief Agent on the Coast of Africa, dated the 3d of August last.* Folger Shakespeare Library. Broadside. London, 1711.

————. *An Historical Account of the Rise and Growth of the West-India Collonies, And of the Great Advantages they are to England, in respect to Trade.* London: for John Hindmarsh, 1690.

Tilleman, Erick. *En Kort Og Enfoldig Beretning Om Det Landskab Guinea Og Dets Beskaffenhed (1697). A Short and Simple Account of the Country Guines and its Nature,* translated and edited Selena Axelrod Winsnes. Madison: African Studies Program, University of Wisconsin, 1994.

A True Account of the Forts and Castles belonging to the Royal African Company, upon the Gold Coast in Africa, with the Number of Men, and Guns, the Nature of the said Forts and Castles, and the Guns placed on them, as taken from sundry Persons very lately come from thence. Broadside. Folger Shakespeare Library. London, 1698.

Tryon, Thomas. *England's Grandeur, And Way to get Wealth: Or, Promotion of Trade Made Easy, and Lands advanced.* . . . London: J. Harris and G. Conyers, 1699.

————. *Friendly Advice to the Gentlemen-Planters of the East and West Indies In three parts. I. A brief treatise of the most principal fruits and herbs that grow in the East & West Indies; giving an account of their respective vertues both for food and physick, and what planet and sign they are under. Together with some directions for the preservation of health and life in those hot climates. II. The complaints of the negro-slaves against the hard usages and barbarous cruelties inflicted upon them. III. A discourse in way of dialogue, between an Ethiopean or negro-slave, and a Christian that was his master in America. By Philotheos Physiologus.* London: Andrew Sowle, 1684.

————. *The merchant, citizen and country-man's instructor: or, a necessary companion for all people. Containing, I. Directions to planters of sugar, and to make it. II. To a Planter touching Cotton, and the Advantage thereof. III. The Art of Distillation, and the great Advantage thereof to England.* . . . London: for E. Harris and G. Conyers, 1701.

Uchteritz, Heinrich Von. "A German Indentured Servant in Barbados in 1652: The Account of Heinrich Von Uchteritz." Ed. and trans. Alexander Gunkel and Jerome S. Handler, *Journal of the Barbados Museum and Historical Society,* 33 (1970), 91–100.

Villault, Nicolas. *A Relation of the Coasts of Africk Called Guinee; With A Description of the Countrys, Manners and Customs of the Inhabitants; of the productions of the Earth, and the Merchandise and Commodities it affords; with some Historical Observations upon the Coasts. Being Collected in a Voyage By the Sieur Villault, Escuyer, Sieur de Bellefond, in the years 1666 and 1667. Written in French, and faithfully Englished.* 2nd ed. London: Printed for John Starkey, 1670.

Windham, Thomas. "The Voyage of M. Thomas Windham to Guinea and the Kingdom of Benin" (1589). In *Europeans in West Africa,* ed. J. W. Blake. 2nd ser. London: Printed for the Hakluyt Society, 1942, 1:86–87, 2:314–320.

Wyvill, Richard A. "Memoirs of an Old Army Officer: Richard A. Wyvill's Visits to Barbados in 1796 and 1806–6." *Journal of the Barbados Museum and Historical Society,* 35 (1975), 21–30.

Index

Acknowledgments

This book has taken the best part of a decade to research and write, and I am glad to be able to acknowledge the help and encouragement of family, friends, and colleagues. I began this work after receiving a Research Readership from the British Academy, and I set out to explore how participation in an Atlantic World exchange of goods and people changed labor around the British Atlantic. It was a wonderful opportunity, and in the National Archives and the British Library I became a student again, diving into primary and secondary sources to learn as much as I could about Caribbean and West African history. At times, however, it did feel like a somewhat ill-fated fellowship. During these two years both my wife and I were unwell, and first my father and then my mother fell ill and died. I am extremely grateful to Ken Emond and his colleagues at the British Academy for allowing me the time and the space to cope with life's challenges. Thanks to research grants from the Leverhulme Trust, the Carnegie Trust, the Nuffield Foundation, the Eccles Centre at the British Library, and the Library Company of Philadelphia, I was able to pursue further research in Barbados, Ghana, London, and the United States, and slowly the largest and most challenging research project of my career began to take shape. A Leverhulme Trust Major Research Fellowship has afforded me the time to complete this project, and I drafted the manuscript while in residence at the Robert H. Smith International Center for Jefferson Studies, and at the Folger Shakespeare Library, two particularly congenial research institutions.

I am grateful for the expert support, assistance, and advice of numerous librarians and archivists, including those at the Balme Library of the University of Ghana in Legon; the Barbados Department of Archives; the Barbados Museum and Historical Society; the British Library; the Department of Public Records and Archives, Accra, Ghana; the Department of Special Collections of the University of London Library; the Eccles Centre for American Studies at the British Library; the Folger Shakespeare Library; Lambeth Palace Library; the Library Company of Philadelphia; the National

Archives in Kew; and the Rhodes House Library, Bodleian Library, Oxford. Thanks to the support of the History Department at the University of Glasgow, and of the University of Pennsylvania Press, I was able to secure the illustrations that appear in this book.

I have presented earlier versions of this project in a variety of locations, and I appreciate the criticisms and the suggestions that I received from colleagues at two of the annual conferences of the British Group of Early American Historians; two of the Biennial Conferences of the European Association of Early American Historians; the Georgetown seminar in Atlantic World History; Mike Zuckerman's wonderful "salon" in Philadelphia; the community of early Americanists in Paris and their Réseau pour le développement européen de l'histoire de la jeune Amérique; the Department of History at the University of the West Indies, Cave Hill, Barbados; and the Early Modern History group at the University of Glasgow.

Friends and colleagues have provided vital support and encouragement, by discussing, reading, criticizing, and supporting my research, and by writing letters of recommendation to support numerous grant applications. I am particularly grateful to Tony Badger, Hilary Beckles, Holly Brewer, Trevor Burnard, Richard Carwardine, Frank Cogliano, Max Edelson, Alison Games, Paul Halliday, Brendan McConville, Simon Middleton, Joe Miller, Kenneth Morgan, Phil Morgan, Marina Moskowitz, Peter Onuf, Andrew O'Shaughnessy, Ty Reese, Liam Riordan, Justin Roberts, Alex Shepard, Don Spaeth, Peter Thompson, and Betty Wood. Frank Cogliano is one of my closest friends in this profession, and our joint graduate reading group and video seminar has invigorated my thinking about early America and the Atlantic World over far too many cakes, cookies, and scones. While walking on the hills at the southern tip of the Isle of Bute, Peter Onuf "conceptualized" this project, and reinvigorated me, as only he can. Peter Thompson has always believed in this book, and it has been strengthened by his remarkable work on Henry Drax's plantation instructions and by enthusiastic discussions over the occasional pint of bitter. Trevor Burnard and Roderick MacDonald, old and true friends, have finally won me over to Caribbean history, and Joe Miller provided timely advice and suggestions about African history over messy but delicious barbecue beef sandwiches. I have found the scholarship of Hilary Beckles invaluable, and we have presented our work together and discussed it in Venice, Glasgow, and Barbados, a process that has come to involve the exchange of single malt whisky for good Barbadian "sugar cane brandy." I am fortunate that so many of my discussions with colleagues and friends involve the camaraderie that comes with the consumption and exchange of good food and drink.

I am particularly grateful to Ron Hoffman and his colleagues at the Omohundro Institute for organizing a remarkable gathering of scholars in Ghana in 2007, which broadened my horizons and introduced me to so many new people and new ideas. Justin Roberts, Ty Reese, Jenny Shaw, Shona Johnston, and Rebecca Shumway all shared unpublished work with me, and Justin has become a good friend and collaborator. John Thornton and Trevor Burnard improved this book with the most constructive and encouraging of reader's reports, and Bob Lockhart has shared his wide knowledge of the field and his great editing skills. Fellow early Americanist and friend for more years than either of us care to remember, he has brought his enthusiasm and great skill that helped make this a better book. At Glasgow my friends and colleagues Alex Shepard, Don Spaeth, and Thomas Munck have kept me grounded in the history of early modern Europe, and over cocktails at Rogano's, Marina's and my very good friend Bronagh Ní Chonaill encouraged, joked, and commiserated. My oldest friends, Anthony King, Dominic Christian, and Matthew Reissenberger, have known me since our schooldays. They will never let me take myself or my work too seriously, yet as we celebrated our fiftieth birthdays in Barcelona they each wanted to learn about this project, to discuss my work, and to encourage, cajole, and distract in equal measure. Dominic and his wife, Kate, provided great encouragement when I was at my lowest ebb, and I am very grateful to them both.

My deepest debts are to my family. Giles, Jem, Fiz, Tim, Alison, Clare, Christopher, Lucy, and Joseph have helped me more than they will ever know. My parents in law, Dan and Else Moskowitz, have supported and encouraged me, and provided a tremendously welcoming research HQ in Washington. My late parents encouraged me as I began this book, and I miss, more than I can begin to express, my father's eagerness to talk about my work and my mother's interest in the ordinary working people who are the subject of this book.

My darling wife, Marina, deserves the greatest thanks of all. Were it not for her I could not have got through the past decade, let alone completed this book. She has thought and talked about this project from the beginning, helping me with the grant applications with which I started, and then with making sense of what I was finding. I cannot find the words to express the depth of my love for her, and I cannot begin to explain the joy I find with her. All that I can say is that this book is for Marina.

Lightning Source UK Ltd.
Milton Keynes UK
UKHW010037100820
367846UK00013B/39